Interpretation, Relativism, and the Metaphysics of Culture

Interpretation, Relativism, and the Metaphysics of Culture

Themes in the Philosophy of Joseph Margolis

Edited by
Michael Krausz
and Richard Shusterman

Humanity
Books

an imprint of Prometheus Books
59 John Glenn Drive, Amherst, New York 14228-2197

Published 1999 by Humanity Books, an imprint of Prometheus Books

Inquiries should be addressed to Humanity Books, 59 John Glenn Drive, Amherst, New York 14228–2197. VOICE: 716–691–0133, ext. 207. FAX: 716–564–2711.

03 02 01 00 99   6 5 4 3 2

Library of Congress Cataloging-in-Publication Data

Interpretation, relativism, and the metaphysics of culture / edited by Michael
    Krausz and Richard Shusterman.
        p.   cm.
    Includes bibliographical references and index.
    ISBN 1–57392–656–6 (cloth)
    1. Interpretation (Philosophy). 2. Relativity—Congresses. 3. Culture—
Philosophy—Congresses. 4. Margolis, Joseph, 1924–   —Congresses.
I. Krausz, Michael. II. Shusterman, Richard.
B824.17.I48   1999
110—dc21   97–27672
                                                                   CIP

Printed in the United States of America on acid-free paper

Contents

6 Contents

Part II: Relativism

Part III: The Metaphysics of Culture

Part IV: Reply

Introduction

Richard Shusterman and Michael Krausz

I

This volume is an outgrowth of a conference on the work of Joseph Margolis, sponsored by Temple University's Institute for Aesthetics and Cultural Studies and by the Greater Philadelphia Philosophy Consortium in the spring of 1992. Papers presented at the conference included those of Michael Krausz, Peter McCormick, Tom Rockmore, and Gail Soffer. The conference was organized by Richard Shusterman.

The tripartite title of this volume should not mislead readers into thinking that they are here presented with a mere miscellany of papers relating to three very different topics in epistemology and ontology. Instead, this book seeks to show how these issues are intimately related on the conceptual level and are best treated together. Moreover, in showing this, it also aims to give witness and thanks to the contemporary philosopher who has perhaps done the most to unite these topics in a single though very complex and nuanced argument—Joseph Margolis.

This introduction will not attempt to capture the richness and detail of Margolis's treatment of interpretation, relativism, and the metaphysics of culture; nor will it try to trace all the many ways that

these issues are interwoven in his intricate and ever expanding
philosophical web; nor will it seek to propose alternative positions
that challenge or critique his views. Those tasks are discharged by
the fourteen papers which follow, and by Margolis's concluding
response. Here, simply to prime the reader's perspective and
interest, we provide a very brief, incomplete introduction to the
close conceptual linkage between interpretation, relativism, and the
metaphysics of culture, while suggesting the distinction of Margolis's treatment of these issues. Moreover, to guide the reader, we
offer the following menu of key issues to be discussed by contribu-
tors: on the idea of interpretation, the aims of interpretation, convergence and nonconvergence to the best interpretation, understanding and interpreting, interpretation and the fixity of meaning—
L. Stern, N. Carroll, G. Soffer, P. McCormick, M. Krausz, P. J.
Waugh; on intentionality—L. Stern, M. Wartofsky, P. Caws, J.
Waugh, and E. Zemach; on relativism, rationality, and objectivity—
L. Stern, N. Carroll, G. Soffer, P. McCormick, N. Rescher, M.
Krausz, and T. Rockmore; on realism and universalism—L. Stern,
T. Rockmore, M. Wartofsky, and J. Waugh; on pragmatism—L.
Stern and R. Shusterman; on emergence, embodiment, and the
self—M. Wartofsky, D. Jacquette, and J. Waugh; on metaphysics,
history, and the flux—L. Stern, N. Carroll, M. Wartofsky, D.
Jacquette, J. Mohanty, P. Caws, and R. Shusterman.

II

Our uncertain age is deeply hermeneutic; and philosophy, both analytic and continental, has taken a distinctive interpretive turn. As
Davidson insists that "all understanding of the speech of another
involves radical interpretation," so Gadamer asserts still more glob-
ally "all understanding is interpretation."[1] Philosophy's new devo-
tion to interpretation derives in large part from its loss of faith in
foundationalism and its idea of a pure, uninterpreted factual reality
that could be grasped by some direct, apodictic perception or uncovered by scientific discovery. In the foundationalist picture, facts form
the realm of absolute, objective truth and scientific explanation,
while interpretation is but the realm of variant and vague opinion.

Nietzsche, one of the most influential critics of foundationalism's notion of a God's-eye view of the naked facts of reality, specifically makes his critique through the ubiquity of interpretation: "Facts are precisely what there is not, only interpretations."[2]

As interpretation displaces the foundational notion of fact, so, with Nietzsche, perspectivism comes to displace the God's-eye point of view. Interpretation is an intrinsically perspectival notion, recognizing the possibility of conflicting interpretations from variant perspectives and contexts, or from differing purposes. In this epistemological context, the Nietzschean death of God signals the replacement of a fixed unitary vision of an absolute truth by a dynamic, open struggle between competing interpretations of the world. Moreover, as there are no independent facts of the world, interpretations do not merely describe the world, but they shape or create it. The world itself seems caught in the flux of its varying perspectival interpretations, and this is nowhere more evident than in the variant, changing, and often conflictual world of human culture.

As fundamentally perspectivist and contextual, interpretation seems to suggest some sort of relativism, at the very least that interpretations are in some way relative to context or perspective. Yet despite philosophy's recent celebration of interpretation, we find no comparable support of relativism. Indeed, the very advocates of interpretation seem extremely quick and vehemently keen to distance themselves from relativism.

If Gadamer resists relativism by offering in its stead the notion of an essential unifying horizon of tradition that can fuse and embrace all horizons, analytic hermeneuts such as Rorty, Putnam, and Davidson usually deploy a more negative antirelativist strategy. Relativism is easily discredited by identifying it with the idea that "anything goes," that any view is as good or as true as any other. Despite its apparent congeniality to interpretation, no attempt is made to develop a serious notion of relativism that would avoid the obvious contradictions and inadequacies of such crude accounts of relativism.

Margolis is the notable exception. Through a compelling combination of historical exegesis and systematic elaboration, Margolis develops and defends a relativistic logic (labeled "robust relativism") that avoids the standard critiques by introducing truth values that are weaker than the standard ones and not governed by *tertium non datur.* This logic allows him to recognize the pluralities and contradictions of interpretive practice without either reconciling them in an essentialist unifying synthesis (like Gadamer) or consigning them as Nelson Goodman does to a plurality of worlds. Is Margolis's relativist logic fully consistent and adequate to the needs of interpretive practice in the natural and human sciences? Several of the papers here explore and sometimes challenge aspects of this logic and its related theory of interpretation.

If our epistemology is hermeneutic and relativistic, what sort of reality underlies this epistemological approach, at once justifying it and being determined by it? We come, then, to metaphysics. What sort of entities are those cultural entities that defy foundationalist absolutism and logical binarism, admitting variant, conflicting interpretations that are simultaneously apt?

In foundationalism's world of absolute fact, entities are firmly fixed through essences that give them their unchanging identities. In a relativistic antifoundationalism, there seems no place for fixed essences, which determine once and for all times and contexts the properties and limits of an entity. An antiessentialistic metaphysic that is sensitive to variant contexts and temporal change is therefore needed. But the metaphysics for hermeneutic relativism must allow for the persistence and reidentification of entities through changing times and contexts. Otherwise, it could not account for the viability of discourse, the enduring, fruitful communication through which the interpretive practices of a culture are sustained.

Moreover, a metaphysics adequate to cultural practices must not only reconcile variance and flux with stable persistence; it also must accommodate the fact that cultural entities are rooted in the material world though not strictly reducible or identical to the physical things in which they are embodied. Margolis develops a complex metaphysics of flux and physically embodied cultural emergence that aims to address these needs.

In Margolis's immense and wide-ranging opus, this metaphysics is applied throughout the varied realms of culture, from artworks of all genres to historical texts and events, and even to the human person as such—who is revealed as a physically embodied, changeable, ongoing, self-interpreting text, continuously interpreting and refashioning the cultural practices by which this human person is and will be reshaped. Several papers of this volume critically explore Margolis's metaphysics of culture, their criticisms ranging from subtle issues of detail within his system to very general questions of the need, viability, and value of a hermeneutic, relativistic metaphysics of flux.

That Margolis's work inspires such careful study and criticism testifies to its originality and importance. It also bears witness to his admirable ethos of philosophical critique. Joseph Margolis is a philosopher as ready to take and meet objections as he is keen to direct them at others. He does both with zest, good-natured fairness, and an endurance worthy of the label Socratic.

NOTES

1. See Donald Davidson, "Radical Interpretation," in *Inquiries into Truth and Interpretation* (Oxford: Oxford University Press, 1984), p. 125; and H-G Gadamer, *Truth and Method* (New York: Crossroad, 1982), p. 350. This is not to deny that such hermeneutic universalism is sometimes contested. See Richard Shusterman, "Beneath Interpretation," in *Pragmatist Aesthetics* (Oxford: Blackwell, 1992).

2. F. Nietzsche, *The Will to Power* (New York: Vintage, 1968), para. 481.

PART I

Interpretation

Some Aspects of Interpreting

Laurent Stern

If we wish to gain a clear understanding of interpreting, we cannot restrict our attention to just one field in the physical or social sciences, the humanities, or the arts. The interpretation of texts and artifacts, of words and deeds, of intentions and motives cannot be understood independently of each other. Interpreting has a historical dimension, whereas interpretation is constitutive of history. Self-understanding and the understanding of others are interdependent. These are just some of Margolis's intuitions that I share—the list of our agreements is long; its recital would be tedious. We also share a fundamental assumption: one and the same concept of interpretation is used in all fields of inquiry.

Margolis is a philosophical polyglot—he speaks more philosophical languages than are spoken in our better and larger philosophy departments. But even philosophical polyglots must recommend their views by arguments. I have not been convinced by his arguments in support of his views or by his reasons for rejecting opposite views. Although this volume is not formally a *Festschrift,* a discussion of our disagreements must give way to the appreciation of his accomplishments and the celebration of our agreements. But it would be disingenuous if I failed to mention my reservations.

Even the casual reader of his books must have been struck by a

tension between two deeply held convictions: There is no convergence to the best interpretation, yet there are decisive arguments
against all interpretations that are irreconcilable with the author's
views. Irritation with opposing views provides the leaven animating
his books; friend and foe, philosophers major and minor are targets
of his devastating criticism. The failings castigated are seldom
minor and they are couched in universal negative terms: His opponents nowhere demonstrated, never proved, utterly failed to show
whatever happens to be a fundamental precondition for their most
important thesis. He often adds that all this is marvelously simple
and quite easy to see.

To be sure, it is easy to distill a howler from an unsympathetic
reading of a philosopher—but such exercises must be left as homework for our graduate students. Let them discover that Davidson
committed the fallacy of division (*if* he did), and let them reveal
that—in criticizing Davidson—Margolis misread him (*if* he did).
The homework is complete only if the students provide a reformulation of a given argument that excludes the unsympathetic reading.
This is not Margolis's aim—he wishes to show that his opponents
are irremediably mistaken. After clearing the field, he expects that
his all-embracing and in many ways admirable view will remain as
the only viable option.

I will submit an incomplete homework: I will not provide a
reformulation of Margolis's or Davidson's arguments that would
make them impervious to logic chopping. For my topic is precisely
the abovementioned tension between those two deeply held convictions. This tension may account for his providing us with—in Jer-
rold Levinson's words—"a one-man intellectual tradition." The
philosophical aspect of that tension is of considerable importance.
Two examples will introduce my topic.

The two readings of the controversy between Davidson and
Margolis will provide the first example. Davidson writes (as quoted
by Margolis):[1]

> ... a correct understanding of the speech, beliefs, desires, inten-
> tions and other propositional attitudes of a person leads us to the
> conclusion that most of a person's beliefs must be true, and so
> there is a legitimate presumption that any of them, if it coheres
> with most of the rest, is true.

Margolis adds the following gloss:

> Given the unguarded generosity of Davidson's remark, it may seem churlish to complain that it suffers from the fallacy of division. It is true "in a sense" that, relative to our survival, "most of a person's beliefs must be true." Taken in a strictly "holist" sense (Davidson's preference)—that is, taken in a sense that yields no particular truths, a sense that cannot function criterially—it is a breach of elementary philosophical logic to conclude: "*and so* [italics by J. M.] there is a legitimative [sic! L. S.] presumption that any of them . . . is true."

Davidson wrote "legitimate" and not "legitimative," but this may be just a typographical error. More importantly, Davidson's conclusion is a conditional: "and so there is a legitimate presumption that any of them, *if it coheres with most of the rest* [italics by L. S.], is true."

First reading. In Margolis's gloss the antecedent of the conditional is replaced by three dots: To charge Davidson with the fallacy of division, Margolis ascribes to Davidson the assertion of the conditional's consequent.

Second reading. Suppose the antecedent of the conditional is true. Even if its truth is not spelled out, the truth of the consequent is warranted by the rule of detachment. Margolis did not misread Davidson.

A second example may be useful for readers so firmly committed to one of these two readings that the other appears to be wholly unacceptable. It is written about Moses in Exodus 4:24: "And it came to pass by the way in the inn, that the Lord met him, and sought to kill him." As long as the interpretation's application in religious practice was predominant, the interpreter asked: What sin provoked God when he sought to kill his first prophet at a roadside inn? Motivated by a radically different application, Russell asked: What kind of a god is this who sought to kill his first prophet at a roadside inn?

Other readings and other interpretations can be applied to these examples. But we do not accept compromises between opposing views, unless both sides of a controversy are irrelevant to us. If we hold one view in a controversial interpretation, we start by arguing against the other, but soon thereafter we charge the opposite view with deliberate misconstruction or violence in interpreting. At this point, we are forced to admit that there is no convergence to the best interpretation. If this is the case, why do we argue against our opponents? And, if we don't succeed in convincing our opponents, why do we charge them so easily with violence in interpreting? Why do we charge them with dishonesty? After all, once we have admitted that there is no convergence to the best interpretation, we also admit that at least some interpretations are impervious to our arguments. So, why do we argue in these cases?

Margolis belongs to the generation of philosophers who over-heard the loudest whisper of a philosopher in the 1950s, that is, J. L. Austin's remark on seeing a colleague at Berkeley whom he could not convince about his views in epistemology: "That man is lying through his teeth." The issues in that controversy about sense-datum theory are not currently in the forefront of the discussion. The passions and the charges of dishonesty that it has generated are alien to us, but we don't see more light just because the heat has dis-sipated. We may not wish to participate in the controversy—at least in public—but the controversy has not been resolved. The contro-versy could serve as an example of the lack of convergence to the best interpretation. The psychological cause of the heat generated in that controversy or the tension between Margolis's two deeply held convictions is of no interest to me. But embedded in our very notion of interpretation and our understanding of the interpreting activity, there is room for the heat generated in a controversy and the tension between those two deeply held convictions. To show this, I provide here a sketch of our notion of interpretation and the interpreting activity.

THE HEREDITARY PROPERTY OF INTERPRETATIONS

If the flow of information directed at an audience is interrupted for lack of understanding of what was said, the questions that are raised can be answered either by an exact quotation or by a report in indi-rect speech on the content of what was said. The quotation merely replicates what was said, and it is useful only if the failure in understanding is due to a perceptual problem. The report provides the speaker's or an interpreter's understanding of what was said. Quoting doesn't presuppose the understanding of what is quoted. But a report in indirect speech on its content presupposes at least an attempt at understanding it. Such reports are interpretations.

"Interpreting" and "interpretation" have been used in a wide variety of other contexts. At this stage we must set aside natural contexts (e.g., "spots mean measles" or "clouds mean rain") and nonverbal contexts (e.g., an actor's interpretation of his role or a conductor's interpretation of a score). With one short detour, we shall discuss only interpretations that are reports in indirect speech of what was said or done.

In the large majority of cases, there is no need for an interpretation—we understand what was said or done immediately and without further inquiry. It may be objected: There is no clear distinction between understanding and interpreting, and we interpret even if the need for an interpretation does not arise. The answer is that even if the reader believes what is said in the objection, it is useful to focus first on cases where the need for an interpretation arises naturally.

Suppose that in answer to our questions our informant tells us what she believes to be the content of what was said or done. In judging her answer, we must distinguish among three different cases: (a) We acknowledge that the interpretation is about what is being interpreted and that it is the best available interpretation for a given purpose. (b) We acknowledge that the interpretation is about what is being interpreted, but it is not the best available interpretation for a given purpose. Such an interpretation is considered to be a misinterpretation or a wide of the mark interpretation. For example, if someone told us that Michelangelo's *Last Judgment* is about life and death in her native village, we would want to know about the interpreter's reasons for this strange claim. In the course of our discussion, she may convince us that her interpretation not only is within the range of acceptable interpretations for a given purpose, but it expresses—in an eccentric way—the best available interpretation of the fresco for that particular purpose. It is also possible that in our discussion we come to believe that this is indeed a misinterpretation or a wide of the mark interpretation. (c) We cannot acknowledge that an interpretation is about what is being interpreted. For example, if someone told us that Michelangelo's *Last Judgment* is a rectangular surface provided as a resting place for flying insects, we would reject this claim without further discussion. This is either an off-the-wall interpretation or no interpretation at all of the *Last Judgment.*

We must clearly distinguish the wide of the mark from the off-the-wall interpretations. An interpretation offered for a given purpose is rejected as a misinterpretation, if it is not the best available for that purpose. Misinterpretations are wide of the mark interpretations, but all such interpretations are at least on the wall. On the other hand, off-the-wall interpretations fail on a more fundamental level: They are not even acknowledged to be about their ostensible object. If we claim that the interpreter provided us with an off-the-wall interpretation, we must support our claim by showing that the interpreter has superimposed another object on the purported object of interpretation.

Wide of the mark and off-the-wall interpretations resemble each other in only one respect: The stories told in such interpretations often deserve to be evaluated independently of their ostensible goals. Occasionally we admire the creativity and subtlety at work in an interpretation, declare it to be good fiction, good literature, or even good philosophy, and at the same time reject it as a misinterpretation or an off-the-wall interpretation.

The attempt at understanding may be unsuccessful and its result unsatisfactory. But as long as the interpreter believes she has made an attempt, and her audience agrees that she has produced—instead of or in addition to a quotation—a report about what was said or done,[2] she has produced an interpretation. Interpreters may be insincere, for example, they may conceal in their report the result of their attempts and even contradict that result. But as long as we agree that their report is about what was said or done, they cannot be mistaken about their having produced an interpretation. Any interpretation may be replaced by another or discredited by another at a later time, but even if the result of an attempt at understanding turns out to be a misinterpretation or a wide of the mark interpretation—as long as it is not off-the-wall—we have no good reason for denying that it is an interpretation.

Concerning the notion of understanding, we must rely on our intuitions. Although I am not prepared to claim that this is a primitive notion that cannot be further analyzed, it should be mentioned that very often we are turning around in a very small circle when we speak about the notion of understanding. For example, understanding a story or understanding a joke is often explained as understanding the meaning of the story or the point of the joke. Such explanations are vacuous, and they do not provide an advance over our intuitions concerning the notion of understanding. Even if we agree with Kant that understanding and judgment rely on mother wit and their lack is stupidity,[3] we must add that native intelligence does not determine our understanding—if it did, we could expect a convergence to the best understanding and from there a convergence to the best interpretation.

Ordinarily we are confronted with interpretations that we accept without question. It is the questioning of an interpretation that requires explanation and not its acceptance.[4] The questioning may be triggered by the interpreter's tone of voice betraying uncertainty, by doubts about her understanding or judgment, by suspicions about her sincerity, and by a variety of other reasons motivating distrust of a given interpretation. Because a report even about a partially successful attempt at understanding yields an interpretation, the standards for what is an interpretation are quite low. It would seem this would be balanced by fairly high standards for the acceptance of interpretations. This is not the case. We accept the overwhelming majority of interpretations we are offered and question only cases where we have at least a motive leading to a reason for its rejection.

Reasons for the acceptance of interpretations are suggested only if we wish to allay doubt or calm suspicion about an interpretation, for example, "she was educated, and had many years of experience in this field," or "this is how her friends understood her behavior." The fact that reasons for accepting or rejecting interpretations are introduced only in exceptional cases has far-reaching consequences. If a speaker or agent is asked about what that person has said or done, we will get a report of his understanding of what is at issue. If we do not have reasons to doubt this report, we will accept it and pass it on to others who will hand it down further until doubt breaks off this process. As long as this chain remains unbroken, the self-understanding of a speaker or agent prevails. Within an unbroken chain, the content of self-understanding is a hereditary property of all later interpretations of the speakers' or agents' words and deeds.

Speakers and agents have at least psychological access to what they wanted to say or do, hence it is quite right that we should accept their interpretations; their acceptance is defeated only by good reasons for doubt. We seldom accept the self-interpretations of insane or insincere persons. In many other cases, we reject the speakers' or agents' self-interpretations. Those who go back on their word, break their promise, welsh on their bets, will not be forgiven if they claim that they did not mean what they said. In giving their word, they relied on a convention that discharges what they said from what they meant. Nor are we prepared to accept the speakers' or agents' interpretations if we can show that psychological access to the meaning of their words and the intention of their actions does not entail epistemic success: Their self-understanding may be insufficient, their vocabulary limited, and their judgment clouded. Typically, the speakers' or agents' self-understanding is disqualified if they are believed to be victims of self-deception. Whenever we are willing to claim that we know a relevant characteristic of the speaker or agent better than he himself knows, we refrain from accepting his self-interpretations.[5]

As long as the content of self-understanding is indeed a hereditary property of an unbroken chain of interpretations, the interpreting activity has a conservative, at times even an authoritarian bias. In such a chain, the authority is vested in the speaker, writer, or agent whose words and deeds are subject to interpretation. It is this authority that must be displaced by the interpreter who claims to know the speaker or agent better than that person knew him or herself. If the interpreter succeeds in displacing this authority, then that interpretation will be the beginning of another unbroken chain of interpretations.

At least since the beginning of modern science, the acceptance or rejection of an explanation is independent of the scientist's authority. "Newton said that" is not part of an explanation concerning one of the laws of physics. Concerning interpretations, however, the authority vested either in the speaker, writer, and agent or in the interpreter is constitutive of interpretations. In the small minority of cases where interpretations are controversial, claims of the following sort are sometimes entered in support of a given interpretation: "This was the legislative intent"; "this is how a certain poet, painter, composer, or philosopher understood his own work"; "this is how a certain critic, teacher, or trusted interpreter understood these words or deeds." Concerning religious documents, it is considered to be too pretentious to speculate about the presumed author's understanding of his own words; reference to the author's self-understanding is replaced in these cases by an appeal to the interpretive traditions of a given religious community. Because interpretive authority is constitutive of interpretations, the reasons for depriving the speaker, writer, or agent of authority over that person's own words and deeds and shifting it to an interpreter must become clear.

One reason for the shift of authority to the interpreter was mentioned above: The infant's parent, the patient's psychiatrist, and the battle's historian have good reasons for claiming that they know more about the beliefs and desires of the speakers, writers, or agents whose words and deeds are interpreted than they themselves knew. In these cases, interpreters are called on to provide an understanding of these words and deeds in a language that is richer than what was available to those they are interpreting; they bring to their task experience, professional competence, or knowledge that was unavailable to those they are interpreting. The shift of authority to the interpreter is supported in these cases by one of the two purposes of every interpretation: to provide an understanding of what was said or done. The need to provide such an understanding is but one constraint on interpreting.

We also construe what was said so as to demonstrate its value for a given purpose; this is the second constraint on interpreting. We not only wish to understand a religious or legal document, we also want to apply it in our religious or legal practice.[6] We not only wish to show what a historical document says, but also what it betrays—especially if what it betrays is of greater value for the understanding of a historical period than what it says. Concerning artworks, literary critics or art critics often take it for granted that their audience

understands what a given work says; their task is only to demonstrate its value as a work of art. Conflict between these two constraints yields an incentive for creativity and invention in interpreting. For example, if a document's literal interpretation undermines its value in religious or legal practice, a metaphorical,
ironical, or other nonliteral interpretation will be provided by the
interpreter.

In interpreting we provide understanding and we apply our
understanding for a given purpose. Understanding and application
must reinforce each other. If understanding and application are in
conflict, it is very often our understanding that is adjusted to the
application and not the other way around. When the literal understanding of the immoral behavior of the Greek gods was seen to be
in conflict with the Homeric poems' value as a religious document,
interpreters had a choice between a nonliteral understanding of
these poems and their rejection as religious documents. The reinterpretation of these poems as allegory in the sixth century B.C.E.[7] is
a case in point for the adjustment of the understanding of a document to its application.

Interpretations containing the speakers', writers', or agents'
self-understanding as a hereditary property are considered *natural
interpretations*. If the natural interpretation is unavailable, then the
interpreter is forced to offer his or her own understanding of what
is at issue. If it is accepted by others, it becomes the beginning of a
new chain of interpretations. Even if the natural interpretation
remains available, what is between the lines of a document is often
considered to be more important for its understanding and appreciation than what is in the lines. Also, in addition to or in place of the
natural interpretation, the interpreter's concern may be on a level
that is considered to be an extension of common sense.

Inquiries within any of the social sciences do not regard the
speakers', writers', or agents' consent to the interpretation of their
words or deeds either necessary or sufficient for accepting that
interpretation. Such inquiries imply an extension of commonsense
explanations, ordinarily restricted to the agents' beliefs and desires.
If what was said or done appears incoherent to common sense, an
extension of such explanations is warranted. Also, what is at issue
must be understood from the observer's rather than the agent's

viewpoint. For example, when a psychologist attributes uncon-
scious motivation to an agent, she must—at least initially—consider the agent's agreement with her interpretation irrelevant. Or,
when a historian or sociologist attributes conspicuous consumption
or class interest to agents, it is irrelevant that these very concepts
were unknown to the agents. Interpretations within the limits of
common sense do not compete with others that are only limited by
an extension of common sense. The two kinds of interpretations
have different purposes, they do not compete with each other and
they do not discredit each other.

To the extent that the interpreter adds to or replaces the self-
understanding of the speaker, writer, or agent, her own understanding of what was said or done displaces self-understanding. Because
the interpreter claims to know the speaker or agent better than he
knew himself, she must be prepared to defend her interpretation
against the charge that she has committed violence by usurping the
authority vested in those she is interpreting. To be sure, in addition
to the very few who believe that every interpretation commits violence,[8] only those who disagree with an interpretation would give
vent to such a complaint.

Our critics will agree with an interpretation if we can convince
them that it preserves the self-understanding of the speaker, writer,
or agent. Unless motivated by skeptical views in philosophy, objections against such natural interpretations need not be taken seriously. In such a case, the interpreter acts merely as a proxy for the
speaker, writer, or agent, by articulating only what he would say in
the given circumstances. But if the interpreter is not just a proxy for
those whose words and deeds are being interpreted, then how can
she establish a connection between her interpretation and what her
interpretation is about? She could argue, for example, that she
merely tries to articulate what these speakers, writers, or agents
would say about their own words and deeds, if they were in her circumstances. This establishes a connection between the interpretation and what the interpretation is about, but it will not convince
opponents in a controversial interpretation. For the opponents in a
controversy can both argue that they merely articulate what the
speaker would say about his own words.

In accepting the interpreter's view, we admit a connection

between an interpretation and those whose words or deeds are being interpreted. If we reject her view, we will judge the interpretation in one of two ways: either as an irrelevant story told about what is being interpreted, with a tenuous or no connection to those whose words or deeds are interpreted; or as a deliberate misconstruction of the self-understanding of those whose words or deeds are interpreted. Either way, the differences between opponents in a controversial interpretation cannot be negotiated.

Non-natural Interpretations

Just as most natural interpretations are accepted and transmitted to others, many non-natural interpretations are also accepted and passed on to others. But if an interpreter is asked to defend a non-natural interpretation, she must articulate her response to demands that are at cross-purposes. She must argue for her understanding of the words and deeds of others; claim that her interpretation is the best among the available alternatives for a given purpose; admit that she knows those she is interpreting better than they know themselves; defend her claims against the charge that she usurped the authority of those she is interpreting; and admit that there is no convergence to the best interpretation.

Every interpretation is offered as the best available alternative for a given purpose—the second item on this list merely spells out a normative claim implied by every interpretation. Depending on the circumstances, this list can be changed or extended in many different ways. But no matter how it is changed, the first and the fifth items are among the desiderata of the large majority of interpreters. They are at loggerheads. For in arguing we expect to convince all reasonable persons, but if we admit the lack of convergence to the best interpretation, we must choose between two unattractive alternatives. We may either come to believe that those we cannot convince are disingenuous or unreasonable—remember Austin's whisper—or we are led to admit that our arguments are at best good enough to convince those who have the same understanding of a given situation as we have. Our arguments carry conviction with the converted, but they fail to persuade the unconverted. So, why do we argue for our interpretations if we cannot expect the agreement of all reasonable persons? Why do we admit the lack of convergence to the best interpretation if we insist on arguing for our interpretations?

Contrary to Kant, it is not the lack of mother wit that clouds the judgment of some interpreters in an interpretive controversy. A given situation itself can be understood in more than one way, hence speakers or writers can differ in their diagnosis of that situation and the interpreters of that diagnosis may again differ. According to Paul Veyne,[9] ancient Greece had its believers in the gods of Mt. Olympus, its agnostics, its atheists—the shades of religious belief or disbelief known to us from our contemporary world were well represented. We have no good reason to doubt that they were also represented among the interpreters of their poets. Some believed that Homer and Hesiod told the truth about the gods, others believed that they told lies; some who believed that Homer and Hesiod told the truth, also argued that they told the literal truth; others argued that while they told the truth, what they said must be understood as allegories.[10] We are disengaged from these debates; in adopting one view, our choices are guided by aesthetic consideration. We argue for the allegorical or the literal interpretation of the homeric poems to demonstrate their value as literary artworks. The debate on the existence of the gods and their nature has been replaced long ago by a debate about aesthetic values. Heat is generated in both debates: those who are engaged in the debate consider their unconverted opponents unreasonable or lacking in mother wit. If we are not engaged in the debate, we consider the opinions and arguments presented on both sides as quaint or irrelevant.

INTERPRETATION AND THE ARTS: A SHORT DETOUR

The interpretation of artworks raises issues that are not regulated by the interpretive strategies used elsewhere. As mentioned before, I share the assumption that one and the same concept of interpretation is used in all fields of inquiry. But this does not imply that artworks must be treated as communications or as vehicles for messages between the artist and his or her audience. The role of intention in judging artworks has been debated in aesthetics for more than fifty years. I am a dyed-in-the-wool anti-intentionalist and a defender of Monroe Beardsley's contribution to the debate. But we must notice that the artworks best known to the authors of "The Intentional Fallacy" were literary. Concerning the literary arts, we all have a certain amount of expertise as part of our common linguistic heritage. We do not consider it a major accomplishment if we can continue with creditable results a literary artwork that remained a fragment; it requires greater expertise to add to an unfinished painting or musical composition with creditable results. If artworks are not treated as messages, but as poems and novels, art objects or compositions that must be interpreted, we will be less inclined to search for their creators' intentions.

To be sure, as long as our interests are historical or biographical and they are focused on poets, painters, and composers, we prefer the natural to the non-natural interpretation of what they have created. But if aesthetic interests are in the foreground of our concerns, our interpretations must be guided solely by the need of demonstrating the value of what they have created; the distinction between a natural and a non-natural interpretation cannot be maintained here. When poets, painters, or composers speak about what they have created, they compete on equal footing with their critics. Their interpretations are accepted only if they demonstrate the value of a poem, a painting or a musical composition better than other available interpretations.

"Criticism can talk, and all the arts are dumb"—Northrop Frye once said.[11] Literary critics have been more hospitable to the anti-intentionalist arguments that can be derived from this claim than art or music critics. Literary critics believe they have the expertise necessary to talk about the content of a poem without consulting with its author. Their attitude is not considered overbearing, even if they tell Shakespeare about the content of one of his sonnets. After all, not even the interpreters of the Bible or the Constitution defer to the presumed author or authors of the document they are interpreting when they talk about its content. Matters are different when critics speak about the works of painters or composers. The expertise necessary for talking about the content of their works or for demonstrating their value is not part of our common heritage. Critics who tried to tell them about the content of their works would be considered arrogant.[12] For this reason, it is understandable that art and music critics try to enlist all the help provided by painters and composers that sheds any light on the content of the works they are interpreting. But even they try to answer Beardsley's colloquially phrased question "What have we got here?" rather than the intentionalists' question "What is this supposed to be?"[13]

Anti-intentionalism does not warrant the currently fashionable practice of saying just about anything about artworks—as long as it is interesting. The danger is not that the interpreter produces a misinterpretation or a wide of the mark interpretation. For it is conceivable that such an interpretation brings out the value of a given artwork better than another interpretation that offers a superior understanding of that artwork. Fatal for the interpretive enterprise are only off-the-wall interpretations or the confusion between wide of the mark and off-the-wall interpretations.

In a now classic note,[14] Meyer Schapiro demonstrated that Heidegger was mistaken: The van Gogh paintings of shoes were not of peasant shoes but of the painter's own shoes. This much is admitted by all art critics and art historians: Heidegger has produced a wide of the mark interpretation. They are even ready to explain it away. After all, the metaphysical speculation that came in tow of the misinterpretation is interesting in its own right. But Schapiro's readers did not notice that Heidegger stands corrected not for a wide of the mark but for an off-the-wall interpretation. Whatever Heidegger said about the painting of a pair of shoes could be said about a pair of shoes but not about the painting. The philosopher, looking at a painting, superimposed his phantasies, free associations, and metaphysical speculations on the painting. There is no better judgment of the currently fashionable interpretive practices than Schapiro's remarks on Heidegger:

> Alas for him, the philosopher has indeed deceived himself. He has retained from his encounter with van Gogh's canvas a moving set of associations with peasants and the soil, which are not sustained by the picture itself. They are grounded rather in his own social outlook with its heavy pathos of the primordial and earthy. He has indeed "imagined everything and projected it into the

painting." He has experienced both too little and too much in his contact with the work.

The error lies not only in his projection, which replaces a close attention to the work of art. For even if he had seen a picture of a peasant woman's shoes, as he describes them, it would be a mistake to suppose that the truth he uncovered in the painting—the being of the shoes—is something given here once and for all and is unavailable to our perception of shoes outside the painting. I find nothing in Heidegger's fanciful description of the shoes pictured by van Gogh that could not have been imagined in looking at a real pair of peasants' shoes. Though he credits to art the power of giving to a represented pair of shoes that explicit appearance in which their being is disclosed—indeed "the universal essence of things," "world and earth in their counterplay"—this concept of the metaphysical power of art remains here a theoretical idea. The example on which he elaborates with strong conviction does not support that idea.

Schapiro's six-and-a-half-page-long note demonstrates the utter failure of all interpretive practices modeled on Heidegger's essay. Derrida noticed the note's importance. He must have understood that it threatened his own interpretive practice, for he tried to bury it underneath a tumble of words. Derrida's essay contains more than twenty times as many words as Schapiro's note.[15] The recently published Volume IV of Schapiro's *Selected Papers*[16] contains an addition: "Further Notes on Heidegger and van Gogh" (1994). Derrida is not mentioned in this additional note. On one reading of the controversy—and this is my preferred reading—his essay does not deserve an answer. On another reading, anything that could be said in answer to Derrida's interpretation of van Gogh's painting would be irrelevant.

In discussing Schapiro's critique of Heidegger's interpretation, Derrida changed the subject matter of the controversy. Schapiro talked about an artwork, van Gogh's representation of his own shoes; in Derrida's reading of Heidegger and Schapiro, the painting not only is a still life, an artwork, or a representation of reality. It is transformed into that kind of a self-contained object that not only admits Heidegger's interpretation but also creates agreement between Heidegger's and Schapiro's interpretations. This much will be granted: Just as some icons or relics were not only artworks, but served also within a religious practice, van Gogh's paintings of shoes are not only artworks, but are endowed with religious significance. Schapiro himself drew attention to the religious significance of those shoes in van Gogh's life, but when speaking about the painting, he spoke as an art historian about the representation of an object in a work of art—the painter's life and art are separated in both of his notes. Derrida blurs the distinction between van Gogh's life and art; as a philosopher, he not only meditates on the significance of the shoes in the painter's life but claims—allegedly, on Schapiro's authority—that the painting is a self-portrait of "van Gogh (alias J. C.)."[17] On this reading of the controversy, anything that could be said in answer to Derrida's transubstantiation of van Gogh's painting would be irrelevant.

Is Derrida's interpretation the best available interpretation? Or is it wide of the mark or off-the-wall? If we accept Derrida's interpretation as the best available interpretation, we erase the lines separating these three cases, and we blur the distinction between the painter's art and life. Because Derrida's supporters consider the difference among the three cases artificial, they would gladly pay this price for the acceptance of his interpretation. On the other hand, if we don't accept it as the best available interpretation, and we cannot show that Derrida superimposed another object on the purported object of interpretation, we would have to show that it is a wide of the mark interpretation. However, we cannot expect to convince our opponents that it is a wide of the mark interpretation unless they agreed that there is a fundamental difference between wide of the mark and off-the-wall interpretations. As Derrida's supporters don't accept that difference, they consider irrelevant anything that could be said in answer to his interpretation. They are mistaken.

If we erase the lines separating the three different cases, we obliterate the lines separating good works of art, bad works of art, and what are not at all works of art. What Derrida said about van Gogh's painting could be said about a devotional artwork, painted by a Sunday painter. The difference between bad artworks and what are not at all artworks is just as fundamental as the difference between wide of the mark and off-the-wall interpretations. In some cases, it is a mistake to admit as an artwork what is presented as a work of art. For example, pornography is often presented as art—critics must judge whether it is art, bad art, or not at all art. The judgment deserves to be accepted if it is based on the best available interpretation; it deserves to be rejected if it is based on a wide of the mark interpretation; it need not be taken seriously if it is based on an off-the-wall interpretation.

End of detour.

INTERMINABLE CONTROVERSIES

Phenomenalists and antiphenomenalists in epistemology, or intentionalists and anti-intentionalists in aesthetics have had their say. But the issues raised in these controversies have not been resolved. Philosophical debates find a satisfactory resolution if one and only one side has been discredited. However, when a debate has been going on for a long time without a satisfactory resolution, then three alternatives must be considered. Either both sides were mistaken, and their views must be rejected; both were right, but focused on different matters; or the two sides had different conceptions of the same matter, and the judgment about which side is considered to be right depends on the conception endorsed. The first two alternatives are familiar from Kant's discussion of the antinomy of pure reason. The third alternative raises a problem that even a Hegelian historical perspective finds intractable.

To be sure, some controversies are decided by a judgment of history. For example, last year's investment was deemed to be prudent to the majority of an estate's trustees; hindsight identifies it as reckless. Or, the political decisions leading to war seemed to be responsible to the majority of participants; hindsight identifies them as irresponsible. Could the participants who decided on these matters have had the foresight necessary to avoid failure? Such issues are settled by a judgment of the courts or of history.

Other controversies are not subject to the judgment of history. Such controversies seem to be interminable: We are not nearer to their resolutions than our predecessors, and our reasons and arguments are not better than theirs. In some cases, we recognize that we cannot reach our goal of convincing others by our arguments, and we avoid the controversy. Religious belief is a case in point. Participation in the controversy seems to be futile for many who have strong convictions on this matter. After all, both sides of the controversy appeal to the same facts, and the arguments on either side are continually recycled. Moreover, the effort invested in the controversy yielded rather meager results: The various shades of belief and disbelief we encounter in the world in which we live were already represented among our remote ancestors.

Interminable controversies are our best evidence that there is no convergence to the best interpretation. Two of the many questions such controversies raise are relevant to my topic: If we engage in arguing on behalf of the conceptions we endorse, what limits must be set for our arguments? Because we agree that there is no convergence to the best interpretation, we cannot argue to convince all reasonable persons; and if we don't wish to be intolerant, we must admit that reasonable persons hold views we oppose. On the other hand, it would be futile to argue to convince those who agree with our conceptions—we would be just arguing for the benefit of those who are already converted to our conceptions. The second question is about our discipline. The history of a discipline is the history of questions and their answers, of problems and their solutions. Mathematics or physics has a history. But, if our discipline contains interminable controversies, can we still claim that it has a history?

My answer to the second question will suggest an answer to the first; both answers will reveal an anti-Hegelian bent. The philosophical study of the history of philosophy is part of our tradition since Hegel, and it is part of our tradition regardless of any other philosophical views we hold. The study of the history of philosophy is currently more flourishing than ever. More and better books and essays are written in this field than ever before. Readers of recent work on Kant, for example, find it hard to believe that their teachers or the teachers of their teachers had even the faintest idea of Kant's achievements. Even philosophers uninterested in the history of their subject matter are in search of predecessors who agreed with their views. We look for confirmation of our own views, and we find it. The predecessor who anticipated our views retains his place in the history of philosophy; if he fails to confirm our views, he is relegated to the history of ideas. But we must notice that a history of philosophy that merely informs us about the anticipation of our own views is but an extension of our debates in contemporary philosophy. The content of such a study of the history of philosophy is determined by these debates. So, even if our discipline does have a history, that history cannot be gleaned from the philosophical study of the history of philosophy.

Philosophers who have the ambition to write the last philosophy—some philosophers have had that ambition at least since Hegel—find support in the claim that the history of philosophy consists of anticipations of their own views. If we don't have that ambition, it is easier to recognize that the philosophical study of the history of philosophy is an ahistorical study. Accordingly, we can either claim that our discipline does not have a history or that the history of ideas is the repository of our discipline's history. Neither claim seems very attractive. The interminable controversies favor the first choice, the changing fashions within our discipline favor the second.

The first choice is more surprising than the second. I have heard its defense from colleagues and former colleagues who are free from the Hegelian ambition to write the last philosophy, yet they are good Hegelians in their understanding of the history of philosophy. They are convinced that the history of philosophy contains the incompletely developed anticipations of their own or their contemporaries' views. The second choice treats the study of the history of our discipline with contempt; for the history of ideas records, but does not explain, the changes of fashion. The fashions indeed change within our field. In recent controversies, at one time phenomenalists and at another antiphenomenalists seemed to have the more convincing arguments; anti-intentionalism seemed to have been the fashion in aesthetics when the Romantic poets were neglected by the New Critics in the 1940s and 1950s, intentionalism when a later generation of critics had a renewed interest in these poets. If we wish to explain the change of fashions, we must return to the philosophical study of the history of philosophy—but this does not seem to be a viable solution. After all, we wanted to escape from the philosophical study of the history of philosophy to gain a historical view of our discipline.

Most readers will object that the picture presented here is inaccurate. Even if they are right, they will recognize that it is at least a plausible picture. The division into two branches—the philosophical study of the history of philosophy and the history of ideas—is not merely an invention of philosophers of the analytic tradition. The division projects unto the past a real divergence within contemporary philosophy: the analytic tradition and the Continental European tradition. The list of canonical figures that are fitted into or relegated outside of the philosophical study of the history of philosophy is different in the two traditions. "Philosophy has lost its way since . . ." or "Philosophy took a wrong turn after . . ." is a complaint common to both traditions, and both find it easy to dismiss the work of contemporaries who do not belong to their own tradition.

The two traditions represent different conceptions of philosophy, and it depends on our conception which side we consider to be right. Within each tradition, the other is regarded with suspicion. Other philosophical controversies are much older. Modern phenomenalism can be traced at least to Hume; anti-intentionalism can be attributed to Plato or ascribed to the Bible.[18] Compared with these debates, the controversy between the analytical and the Continental European tradition in philosophy is relatively recent. It could not have been predicted even at the beginning of the twentieth century. We cannot expect the judgment of history for a decision on this controversy—and it is primarily for this reason that it deserves to be called interminable.

Concerning interminable controversies, there is no difference between foresight and hindsight. The additional information that is provided by later developments does not contribute to the resolution of the controversy. When arguing for one side, we must establish that the claims entered for our side of the controversy are at least plausible. Earlier I asked: What limits must be set for our arguments in a situation where we admit that reasonable persons hold views we oppose? So far, I can give only one answer. We argue for the plausibility of the conception we endorse. This may be the best answer that can be given, but even a quick glance in the direction of interminable controversies will convince us that it is not a satisfactory answer. The controversy about religious belief is again a good example. In a crowded field, where each side is arguing only for the plausibility and not the truth of its own judgments, the views of the opposing side will appear to be implausible. The *odium theologicum* arises regardless of whether they argue for the truth or the plausibility of their beliefs.

INTERPRETATION AND PLAUSIBILITY

Interpretations are plausible—Margolis spelled out the implications of this thesis in great detail. His discussion of this thesis and its connection to relativism are among his many contributions to the theory of interpretation. Although the defense of Protagoras fills many pages of his books, he is also a Hegelian. According to one of my Hungarian colleagues who has considerably more sympathy with Hegel than I, "If Hegel were alive today, he would write what Margolis has written." Because this judgment was based solely on my comments at a Colloquium on Margolis's work a few years ago, I was surprised on hearing it, but I came to agree.

Margolis believes that his theory of interpretation about the arts and history is closely connected with his views in metaphysics and epistemology. It would be difficult to persuade me about this matter, because I share many of his views on interpreting but very few on First Philosophy. No doubt, the overarching view he has constructed from his—in many respects admirable—insights in almost all fields of philosophy is not only coherent but also plausible. Equally coherent and plausible are some of his opponents' views. He would, of course, agree that insights are but dark sayings if not supported by reason and argument. In some cases, the insight comes first, and we try to provide an argument for its support; in other cases, the insight is the result of an argument, but not necessarily of the same argument that is offered in its support.

Our insights in the theory of interpretation concerning the arts and history are usually guided by our intuitions, whereas our views concerning First Philosophy are ordinarily the results of arguments. Intuitions are of no help for the understanding of such claims as "to be is to be the value of a bound variable" or "the 'essence' of Dasein lies in its existence." Our students may become philosophical polyglots, but they will understand these claims as dark sayings if they cannot reproduce the arguments supporting them. They will come to appreciate both of these claims only if they produce their own theses in both philosophical languages and support them by their own arguments. The proficiency required for doing philosophy in a second philosophical language is on the same level that must be attained in the first philosophical language. Occasional tourists or recent immigrants into a second philosophical world do not reach that level. (Compared with the Scandinavian philosophers who are at home in both philosophical traditions, the more famous German or American philosophers mentioned by Margolis who have tried to build a bridge between the two traditions did not reach the level of proficiency required for this task.)

Contrary to Margolis, I do not believe that a reunion of different philosophical traditions is desirable. If the two traditions are locked in an interminable controversy, then the best we can hope for is that each learns about the other, but not much is lost if they ignore each other or are contemptuous of each other. Will their arguments improve, if they learn about each other? Analytic philosophers will not thereby gain intuitions that will lead them to insights in the theory of interpretation in art and history, nor will Continental European philosophers learn to develop arguments in support of their views in First Philosophy. Each side may learn to appreciate the plausibility of their opponents' views, but as long as they remain opponents, they must consider their own views more persuasive than their opponents' views. So, the door to the *odium philosophicum* remains open as long as they cannot convince their opponents.

Austin's whisper was an expression of the *odium philosophicum*. Its expression is not always pernicious. It has salutary effects if it prompts us to construct better arguments or better interpretations. Participants in a genuine philosophical controversy have different conceptions of what is at issue. The two readings of Margolis's gloss or the two readings of Exod. 4:24 are examples of such different conceptions. In some cases, the different conceptions are about one and the same issue; in others, the different conceptions bring about a change in the subject matter of what is at issue.

Participants in an interminable controversy are often unable to imagine the possibility of an alternative conception. Interminable controversies are certainly genuine controversies; even if we withdraw from them and become their spectators, we find it difficult to do justice to both alternatives. At the same time, we must profess that both views are plausible, for otherwise we would be arguing in a vacuum or preaching to the converted. So, even if we don't appreciate the views of our opponents, in claiming that their views are plausible, we prepare the ground for arguing for the plausibility of our own views.

Envoy

Margolis wishes to occupy a middle ground between the two traditions locked in an interminable controversy. From there he offers arguments against the views of his opponents on both sides. Even if some of the arguments against his opponents are less decisive than he thinks and he does not always succeed in demonstrating the profound arbitrariness of their philosophical projects, the wide-ranging investigations presented in his books provide a comprehensive view of our intellectual and artistic pursuits. His opponents will be prompted to provide a better defense of their own views. His friends will learn from his intuitions and reexamine their arguments before defending their own views. All will gain by arguing with his books.[19]

Notes

1. Joseph Margolis, *Interpretation Radical But Not Unruly: The New Puzzle of the Arts and History* (Berkeley and Los Angeles: University of California Press, 1995), p. 243.

2. If we cannot acknowledge that an interpretation is about what is being interpreted, then the interpreter merely told us a story that has to be evaluated independently of its ostensible goal. L. Stern, "Factual Constraints on Interpreting," *The Monist* 73 (1990): 205–21.

3. *Critique of Pure Reason,* A133, B172.

4. Compare with Tyler Burge, "Content Preservation," *Philosophical Review* 102 (1993): 457-88. My views on interpreting have been influenced by this paper. In my earlier writings, I relied on the Principle of Charity in interpreting. Its replacement by the Acceptance Principle, defended by Burge, led me to the hereditary property of interpretations.

5. Kant, *Critique of Pure Reason,* A314, B370; *Über eine Entdeckung, nach der alle neue Kritik der reinen Vernunft durch eine ältere entbehrlich gemacht werden soll* (1790) ed. Cassirer, VI:71.

6. L. Stern, "Two Constraints on Interpreting," *Philosophic Exchange* 18 (1987): 65–78.

7. Jean Pépin, *Mythe et allégorie: les origines grecques et les contestations judéo-chrétiennes,* 2d ed. (Paris: Etudes Augustiennes, 1976), p. 97.

8. Martin Heidegger, *Kant und das Problem der Metaphysik* (Frankfurt am Main: Vittorio Klosterman, 1929), p. 183; see also Ernst Panofsky, "Zum Problem der Beschreibung und Inhaltsdeutung von Werken der Bildenden Kunst," *Logos* 21 (1932): 103–19. As far as I know, this paper has not been published in a complete English translation.

9. Paul Veyne, *Les Grecs ont-ils cru à leurs mythes?* (Paris: Editions du Seuil, 1983).

10. Jean Pépin, *Mythe et allégorie,* pp. 85–214.

11. Northrop Frye, *Anatomy of Criticism* (Princeton, N.J.: Princeton University Press, 1957), p. 4.

12. Peter Kivy, *Music Alone* (Ithaca: Cornell University Press, 1990), pp. 124–46.

13. Monroe C. Beardsley, *Aesthetics: Problems in the Philosophy of Criticism,* 2d ed. (Indianapolis, Ind.: Hackett Publishing Company, 1981), p. 29.

14. Meyer Schapiro, "The Still Life as a Personal Object—A Note on Heidegger and van Gogh," in *The Reach of Mind: Essays in Memory of Kurt Goldstein,* ed. M. L. Simmel (New York: Springer Publishing Co., 1968), pp. 203–209. The quoted passage is from the 1994 reprint (see n. 16 below), pp. 138–39.

15. Jacques Derrida, *La vérité en peinture* (Paris: Flammarion, 1978), pp. 291–436.

16. Meyer Schapiro, *Theory and Philosophy of Art: Style, Artist, and Society* (New York: George Braziller, Inc., 1994).

17. Derrida, *La vérité en peinture,* p. 434.

18. L. Stern, "On Interpreting," *Journal of Aesthetics and Art Criticism* 39 (1980): 119–29.

19. I am grateful to László Baránszky, John Boler, and Peter Kivy for advice about this paper, and to Peter Klein for a detailed and forceful discussion.

Myth and the Logic of Interpretation

Noël Carroll

INTRODUCTION

One of Joseph Margolis's major discoveries in the area of philosophical aesthetics has been that in the realm of interpretation plausibility figures as an important gauge of the epistemic integrity of
critical statements, though I hasten to add that Professor Margolis
might not put it this way. Nevertheless, Margolis has at least
demonstrated that the pursuit of plausibility by critics need not
involve any lack of cognitive rigor. Moreover, an appreciation of
the importance of plausibility in interpretation is an eminently
useful therapy, enabling us to understand significant features of our
critical practices, including, notably, that we may acknowledge
unresolved critical debates without surrendering to the temptations
of critical nihilism (the view that anything goes) on the one hand or
skepticism on the other.

However, though I admire Margolis's emphasis on the importance of plausibility for understanding certain aspects of our interpretive practices, I am not convinced that in admitting the relevance
of plausibility to *some* or even to many of our critical disagreements, we need embrace the related doctrine that Margolis calls

robust relativism. Thus, the focus of this paper will be Margolis's argument for robust relativism, exclusively in terms of the claims made on behalf of robust relativism on the basis of the interpretation of artworks.

As is well known, Margolis has examined the nature of interpretation with respect to a wide gamut of cultural practices. Though he accords special pride of place to the interpretation of art, it is not his whole concern. Volumes would be required to discuss all Margolis's contributions to the theory of interpretation adequately. However, because I do not have volumes at my disposal, I will restrict my purview rather narrowly to the case for robust relativism as it emerges particularly with respect to artistic (or critical) interpretations. That is, I will be primarily concerned with the argument for robust relativism that derives from considerations of the nature of artworks and interpretations thereof.

Margolis has many arguments in favor of his brand of relativism and his across-the-board conception of interpretation. Some of these arguments—like the argument from symbiosis[1]—are metaphysical in nature and apply to practices of interpretation beyond the realm of aesthetics. But, for the purposes of this paper, I will not consider arguments for global relativism with respect to interpretation, but I will attend closely to what I believe are the special considerations that Margolis brings to bear when advancing the case for relativism on the basis of artistic interpretations.

On my reading of Margolis, the crux of his case for relativism with respect to critical interpretation of the arts is what might be called "the myth argument." This argument is primarily developed in chapter 7 (entitled "The Logic of Interpretation") of his book *Art and Philosophy*.[2] Because I believe that this is the most powerful argument that Margolis has in behalf of robust relativism in the aesthetic (as opposed to the metaphysical) realm and because I believe that this argument has received scant attention in the literature (despite its pivotal role in making the case for robust relativism in aesthetics), this essay will be devoted to understanding and criticizing the myth argument. By way of preview, let me say that I am skeptical about the success of this argument.

Of course, as I have already indicated, Margolis has other arguments for across-the-board relativism which, if they are compelling, could be applied to the case of artistic interpretation as an instance of a more general finding. Thus, even if I am able to deflect the conclusions that Margolis draws from the myth argument, the case for his brand of relativism with respect to artistic interpretation might be secured elsewhere in his system. Be that as it may, the thesis that I intend to evolve in what follows is that the relativism Margolis champions for artistic interpretation cannot be supported by the myth argument.

THE MYTH ARGUMENT

As I understand it, the doctrine in dispute is that critical interpretations are logically weak when compared with statements of fact.[3] This weakness is not methodological, but logical.[4] It amounts to the contention that interpretations characteristically take values other than truth or falsity. Plausibility might be one such value. Where interpretations are understood to take truth values, of two incompatible interpretations, at least one, if not both, must be false. However, if two such interpretations were taken to be plausible, both could be acceptable. Exchanging the value of truth for plausibility, we can then describe the two conflicting interpretations as nonconverging or incongruent (rather than as incompatible), and we can go on, with logical impunity, to say of two such nonconverging or incongruent, though rival or conflicting, interpretations that they may both be acceptable.[5]

So far, I take it, no one's hackles will be raised. Surely everyone will acknowledge that sometimes we find ourselves in a position epistemically where conflicting or apparently incompatible (that is, incongruent) critical conjectures seem plausible to the extent that one of the candidates does not lead us to preclude its competitor decisively. Nevertheless, the plot thickens once one realizes that for Margolis, this is not a "sometime" affair. Rather he seems, at times, to believe that *all* critical interpretations are logically weak and that finally not truth, but values such as plausibility, are the appropriate values with which to assess all artistic interpretations. How does he arrive at this conclusion? Again, in the isolated case of critical interpretation, his argument seems to rest upon his notion of cultural myths.

One feature of artworks that Margolis continually stresses is that "the nature of an artwork does not . . . permit us to draw a formal demarcation line between what is *in* a work and what is *outside it,* what may be descriptively true of it and what may be imputed to it only interpretively."[6] Furthermore, from this failure of demarcation (between what is inside and outside of the artwork), Margolis thinks his doctrine of nonconverging/incompatible interpretations follows. He writes: "the reason these judgments are weak depends . . . on the very nature of an artwork and on the impossibility of providing a principle for demarcating what is and what is not *in* a particular work. If one concedes the point, it becomes quite impossible to show that interpretive judgments can be true."[7]

Nevertheless, logically, the entailment here seems hasty. For even if we grant Margolis the premise that there is no principled way to demarcate what is "inside" or "outside" the artwork (an admittedly infelicitous set of metaphors), that in no way implies that in every case we will be forced to countenance the prospect of nonconverging/incompatible interpretations. For without further argumentation, I see no reason to believe that the assertion that " '*The Scarlet Letter* is about the costs of repression' is true" contradicts the contention that "We have no way to demarcate what is inside or outside *The Scarlet Letter.*" So, even if we concede that the boundaries of artworks are not determinately fixed, that does not logically entail that they will always support nonconverging/incompatible interpretations. In fact, the failure of demarcation alone does not seem to me to entail that we will ever confront nonconverging/incompatible interpretation.

Indeed, another reason to doubt that the failure of demarcation, which Margolis believes to be the essence of artworks, entails interpretive weakness in all cases is that some artworks, however resistant to demarcation, may altogether lack interpretations, and, therefore, lack nonconverging/incompatible ones as well.

Perhaps Margolis is aware of this lacuna. He admits that not all artworks require interpretations, and he agrees that not even all artworks that invite interpretations support plural, equally plausible, nonconverging and incompatible interpretations.[8] Rather he writes: "It is enough to concede that some artworks support such interpretations, that the nature of art entails the possibility and that extremely important artworks interest us in just this way."[9]

The remark here about important artworks is, of course, a red herring, because no reasons have been advanced to accept the correlation of nonconvergence with significance. Nor is it clear why the demarcation problem (a putatively essential feature of artworks) should secure the possibility of nonconvergence of interpretation nor why nonconvergence in some cases should entail the logical weakness of critical interpretations across the board.

Now as I understand Margolis, the possibility of nonconvergence comes to this: We cannot antecedently preclude the eligibility of nonconverging/incompatible artistic interpretations. But what might *antecedently* signify here? Surely, if we know an interpretation is true, we can preclude its contradictory a priori. Nor can Margolis block this contention by reference to his doctrine of relativism at this point in the argument, because the case for relativism should be the *conclusion* of this argument and not a premise in it.

Furthermore, as indicated already, I don't see the claim about logical weakness as following simply from the supposition that one cannot say what is and what is not *in* the artwork. So the putative recognition that there is a failure of demarcation with respect to artworks is not enough to secure Margolis's conclusion. It must be supplemented by something else. On my interpretation of Margolis's position, that something else is the myth argument.

It is useful to introduce the myth argument with an example. Consider a Catholic interpretation of a poem by Baudelaire as essayed by someone like Jacques Maritain. Such an interpretation may be advanced by the Catholic theologian on the grounds that inasmuch as Catholicism is a timelessly true doctrine, it is applicable to anything, including a poem by Baudelaire. However, Margolis ingeniously points out that, even if Catholicism is false, the Catholic interpretation of Baudelaire might still be acceptable, because, even if it is false, Catholicism may be nevertheless an actual cultural source of the poem in terms of patterns of imagery, feeling, and thought such that the interpretation may tell us something pertinent about both the author of the work and the audience that received it. Thus, a Catholic interpretation of a poem by Baudelaire might inform us about the thinking that went into making the poem and into the audience's understanding it, because Catholic *beliefs* saturated the culture of both the artist in question and his audience.

Quite clearly, Catholic interpretations of Dante's *Commedia* remain interesting to us, even if we reject Catholicism's claims to truth. For we have no problem with interpretations that advert to the claims of Catholicism with respect to Dante's *Commedia* for even if Catholicism is false, we can agree that Catholicism was a reigning and influential myth at the time of Dante and that the imagery of Catholicism shaped his *Commedia*. Thus, even if an interpreter advances a Catholic interpretation of Dante's *Commedia* on the basis of the purported truth of Catholicism, the interpretation may nevertheless still be motivated on other grounds—namely, as an interpretation that zeroes in on images and ideas that were culturally relevant to the production and the reception of Dante's *Commedia*.

The case for the Catholic interpretation of Dante is on a par with the case for a parallel interpretation of Baudelaire. Though presented by interpreters who might regard Catholicism as a veridical view of everything including Dante and Baudelaire, skeptics may still accept the interpretations on the grounds that Catholicism was a formative myth which may be hypothesized as having had a formative influence on Dante, Baudelaire, and their audiences. In such cases, a myth, like Catholicism, provides a source of imagery and ideas—an imaginative scheme—which saturates the outlooks of artists like Dante, Baudelaire, and their audiences, thereby shaping the communication nexus between production and reception, between utterance and uptake. Thus, Catholic interpretations may be warranted in these cases, not on the grounds of Catholicism's claims to truth, but on the basis of Catholicism as a cultural myth.

Furthermore, Margolis believes that it is instructive to approach psychoanalytic interpretations in the way in which we have just approached Catholic interpretations. A psychoanalytic critic may approach a novel like Stephen King's *Carrie* on the grounds that psychoanalysis, as the science of the mind, has something to say about all literature. But again this need not be our grounds for finding the interpretation useful. For psychoanalysis, among other things, is a widely disseminated myth in our culture, and it is reasonable to suppose that it, or some form of it, has seeped into King's consciousness, as well as that of his audiences. So, the psychoanalytic interpretation may manage to track imagery and beliefs—concerning, for example, repression—that are in fact relevant to the actual social context of communication in which *Carrie* figures. As Margolis notes: "The clue to the puzzle is that, though Freudian psychology claims respectable scientific status, the imagery of psychoanalysis is not at all restricted to the boundaries of the accompanying science; on the contrary, it is so much a part of our general culture that the imagination both of artists and semi-educated persons is saturated with it.[10]

Of course, many psychoanalytic interpretations apply to works produced before the invention of psychoanalysis. Think of Ernest Jones's *Hamlet and Oedipus* in which he contends that Hamlet's procrastination concerning Claudius is based in Hamlet's identification in guilt with Claudius as one who implemented Hamlet's own desires to do away with his father and to sleep with his mother. Jones precedes under the assumption that because psychoanalysis is true and because Shakespeare was an astute observer of human behavior, psychoanalysis is an appropriate theory with which to approach behavior astutely imagined. However, Margolis recommends that we may still find Jones's insights acceptable even if psychoanalysis is false because such interpretations may track culturally formative myths.

But how can such an interpretation track culturally formative myths in works designed prior to the advent of psychoanalysis? Margolis is not especially forthcoming about this, but I conjecture that he may have in mind that substantial elements of the imagery and ideas of psychoanalysis itself may, in fact, predate the formal discovery of psychoanalysis and that, as a result, that imagery and those ideas may be made salient by a psychoanalytic interpretation even if psychoanalytic theory is false. That is, psychoanalysis may be sensitive to the cultural imagery that gave rise to its own development.

Freud, himself, frequently delighted in connecting his ideas to commonly circulating cultural ideas—such as the idea that dreams have meanings—before welding those commonplaces into the fabric of his system. So when the scientific claims of psychoanalysis are suspended, psychoanalytic interpretations of artworks may still be safe from charges of anachronism, even if they apply to works produced prior to psychoanalysis, on the grounds that the psychoanalytic interpretation is still sensitive to "psychoanalytic" imagery and ideas—notably to the imagery and ideas, available in the pertinent culture prior to the discovery of psychoanalysis proper, which imagery and ideas, in fact, in part, gave rise to psychoanalysis.

A similar story might be told about deconstructive criticism, though Margolis does not do so. For example, it might be said that the deconstructionist might apply this mode of analysis on the grounds of its general philosophical probity. However, finding the operation of deconstruction in texts that predate deconstruction may be nevertheless supported historically, rather than by the philosophical claims of deconstruction. For at least insofar as deconstruction involves the undermining of logical contraries—such as "original" versus "copy"—one may argue that deconstruction has been available in the culture (to artists and their audiences) since at least the time of the Socratic dialogue. Thus, a deconstructive interpretation may inform us about the design of a work written before the crystallization of deconstruction as a philosophical stance, because such an interpretation will track what we might call a preexisting cultural predisposition to something that will evolve into deconstruction.

Professor Margolis wants to push a similar line about Marxist criticism. Like Catholic criticism and psychoanalytic criticism, it is a myth. He says: "We know a myth to be objective for criticism, though it may not be so for science, when the habits of thought, perception and imagination of a society or a substantial subpopulation—including of course productive artists—are educable in its terms, and when their responses to appropriate stimuli are generally predictable or congruent with such myths."[11]

Indeed, Margolis thinks that Buddhists may apply their own myths to Western works in the way that Catholicism may provide an interpretive framework for understanding Dante, though, as we shall see, this extrapolation from his earlier analyses of myths is hardly as straightforward as Margolis indicates.

Of course, myths in Margolis's sense need not be as comprehensive in scope as Catholicism, Marxism, Buddhism, and Freudianism. He thinks that the European perception of West African masks in terms of the emerging themes of cubism (the cubist myth?) is also an example.

But what is the connection between the admissibility of mythic frameworks of interpretation, whose admissibility hinges not on their truth but their cultural embeddedness, and the purported logical weakness of critical interpretation? Mythic frameworks are admissible irrespective of their truth claims. Interpretations, undertaken in accordance with these mythic frameworks, then, are admissible as well. However, often when these admissible mythic frameworks are taken together, they are incompatible or nonconverging. Catholicism, Marxism, and Freudianism, for example, cannot be conjoined, prima facie, without contradiction. Thus, the interpretations proffered under the aegis of each of these frameworks will also be nonconverging/incompatible, though, for the reasons already given, they will be admissible.

For Margolis, our inability to demarcate what is inside or outside the artwork mandates a certain critical tolerance. The demarcation problem is the problem, among other things, of not being able to say what contextual features—such as authorial intentions and audience expectations—are and are not in the work. Culturally available myths, therefore, are situated on the indeterminate boundaries of artworks. Critical tolerance, therefore, involves tolerance for culturally available myths. But, of course, the culturally available myths relevant to the interpretation of even a single artwork may be incompatible or nonconverging.

One interpretation may be Catholic and one may be Freudian in such a way that they are incompatible, yet both are, at the same time, contextually apposite as historically situated myths. And, of course, sets of interpretations drawn from sets of available, though incompatible, cultural myths may be incompatible /nonconverging as well. Thus, because it is always possible (and even likely?) that culturally available, though incompatible, myths may be pertinent to particular works, we cannot preclude the possibility of nonconverging/incompatible interpretations. For some incompatible myths may be relevant to the works in question.

Earlier I said that I did not see how the failure of our ability to demarcate what is inside and outside the artwork entailed the permanent possibility of nonconverging/incompatible interpretations. However, once we note that the demarcation problem can be connected directly to the availability of incompatible cultural myths (from which issue incompatible interpretations), the entailment may become more plausible. For if we cannot preclude nonconverging/incompatible myths on the grounds that they are "outside" and irrelevant to an artwork, then the nonconverging/incompatible interpretations that derive from them cannot be precluded either. The nature of art is such that, among other things, authorial intentions and audience expectations cannot be hived off as irrelevant to or outside the artwork, and with them comes a consideration of cultural myths that may shape authorial intentions and audience expectations and that may be incompatible /nonconverging.

Because, in principle, conflicting cultural myths are always available as the basis for interpretations of artworks, one cannot preclude the possibility of equally admissible, though nonconverging/incompatible, interpretations, such as, for example, Catholic and Marxist ones. Furthermore, because these interpretations are both admissible, the criterion of admissibility cannot be truth. If it were truth, the aforesaid rival interpretation would be straightforwardly incompatible. So the criterion must be something other than truth, like plausibility, because plausibility is what we invoke where we cannot invoke truth.[12] Moreover, the view that interpretations of artworks are plausible rather than true is the core of the doctrine Margolis calls robust relativism.

Margolis's relativism is robust, rather than radical, because in *Art and Philosophy* at least, it admits evaluation in terms of truth when it comes to descriptions, but only not to interpretations; whereas the leading forms of radical relativism would extend their relativism to every sort of claim. This, of course, is what opens radical relativism to charges of self-refutation. Robust relativism in acknowledging the applicability of truth to some claims, avoids charges of self-refutation; while, at the same time, Margolis's emphasis on plausibility does not herald an end to rational discourse about interpretations, because informed interpreters may assess candidate interpretations in light of rigorous standards of plausibility (such as according with what is descriptively true of the works in question). Thus, Margolis's version of robust relativism cannot be dismissed by raising the prospect of barbarians at the gate.

If this reconstruction of Margolis's argument is accurate, then the myth argument is a crucial—if not the crucial—way station to the doctrine of robust relativism. In what follows, I want to ask whether the myth argument is up to the role that Margolis assigns.

THE LIMITATIONS OF THE MYTH ARGUMENT

The strategy animating the myth argument is to reconstrue interpretations that ostensibly rely on the truth claims of certain systems of belief as interpretations concerning the cultural resources for the production and appreciation of the work in question. The insight that underlies this move is that the relevant interpretations may wrongly presume the truth of certain systems of beliefs, but may nevertheless, at the same time, be critically apposite, once suitably reconstrued inasmuch as those false systems of belief—in terms of imagery and ideas—may be historically relevant to the cultural context in which the work was created and received. Even if a Catholic interpretation of Dante's *Commedia* claims the truth of Catholicism as its warrant, such an interpretation might still be informative, because, even if Catholicism is false, the interpretation may track elements of the design of the work insofar as Catholicism, reconstrued as referring to a culturally relevant myth, was an undeniable influence on Dante and his audience. That is, the myth argument may recuperate various specimens of "deep interpretation"—such as Marxist and Freudian interpretations—as historical interpretations that are viable whether or not the pertinent systems of belief are true.[13]

That certain deep interpretations can be reconstrued or "reread" in this way is a useful observation, and I think that no one can deny that if, in the appropriate circumstances, a deep interpretation can be recuperated as a historical interpretation, then, in its reconstructed form, it may be admissible. Moreover, where a deep interpretation can be linked to prevailing images and ideas that exist in the relevant culture prior to the formalization of a system of belief, such as psychoanalysis, psychoanalytic interpretations may not be anachronistic. For they may still, perhaps inadvertently, afford historical insight, once they are reconceived or rewritten as sources of contextual information—about imagery and ideas—that, though they preexist psychoanalysis, have attained a certain cultural salience through their later integration into psychoanalysis.

In such cases, anyone who accepts historico-contextual criticism should have no principled objections to Margolis's recuperation of at least some deep interpretations. Admittedly, not everyone falls into this category. But anyone who is broadly historicist and who admits the relevance for interpretation of the historico-cultural backgrounds of the author and the audiences should find little to quibble with much of what Margolis has to say.

Of course, a great many contemporary schools of interpretation and theories of interpretation are historicist in certain respects, and, as a result, they should be willing to accept the myth re-reading that Margolis proposes for many cases of deep interpretation. For reconceived and/or rewritten as historical interpretations, the insights into the designs of certain artworks that these interpretations provide may be unobjectionable.

But, if this is our grounds for accepting myth interpretations, then this line of defense is notably limited. For if the strategy is predicated on recuperating deep interpretations as historical interpretations, then even reconstrued interpretations will only be acceptable where they meet the canons of historical interpretation.

That is, deep interpretations may only be recuperable as historical interpretations where it is feasible, on historical grounds, to believe that the myth presupposed by the deep interpretation could have been an influential myth in the cultural context in which the work was produced and received. Deep interpretations can only be reconceived as myth interpretations where one has grounds for maintaining that the myth in question belongs to the cognitive stock of the authors and audiences in question. As noted, this requirement may not be committed to the constraint that a formal system of beliefs, such as psychoanalysis, must be in play for psychoanalytic interpretations to track "psychoanalytic" ideas and imagery. But even in the case of "psychoanalytic" imagery and ideas *à la lettre,* it still must be the case that the ideas and imagery in question are historically grounded in the context of the production and reception of the work.

It is my conjecture that the myth argument is noncontroversial only so far as it abides by the historical constraint that deep interpretations can be re-read as myth interpretations only if it is legitimate to attribute the mythic imagery and ideas in question to the cultural context—which includes the authors and audiences—of the work under interpretation. If it is impossible historically to attribute the myths at issue to the pertinent cultural context, then one cannot recuperate a deep interpretation as a myth. For example, Lenin's theory of imperialism is not attributable to the Koran, because it could not have exerted any influence on the original producers and audiences of that work. And similarly, Trotsky's theory of combined development cannot be projected onto the *Gilgamesh* for the same reason.

It may be thought that I am making Margolis into more of an historicist than he wants or needs to be. But he does clinch his argument for the recuperation of psychoanalysis by saying that it saturates the imagination of our general culture both in terms of artists and audiences,[14] and the mention of artists here must commit him to the historical constraint to which I have been alluding. Nor is this a slip of the pen. For when Margolis discusses the grounds of objectivity for invoking myths in criticism, he again stresses that the myths in question must belong to the habits of thought of audiences *and* artists. He contends that the responses of the relevant artists that are congruent with said myths must be predictable (or, "retrodictable," I would presume).[15] And, of course, this requirement entails at least a limited form of historicism, viz., that myth interpretations be constrained to the extent that no myth that could not be part of the artist's cognitive stock is admissible.

I have referred to the preceding claims about artists to substantiate the claim that Margolis appears to embrace a certain level of historicism in his argument. Moreover, I think that he needs to endorse some, albeit limited, form of historicism for his analyses of the admissibility of Catholic, psychoanalytic, and Marxist interpretations to win wide assent. For the analyses seem unexceptionable just because they seem to be historically feasible. Nevertheless, if Margolis's reconstrual of myth interpretations rides on re-reading them as historical interpretations, historically constrained, then the work this strategy can do in the argument for robust relativism becomes suspect.

For if we reconstrue myth interpretations as historical interpretations—interpretations geared to the cultural context of the work—then those interpretations will only be acceptable where it can be shown that the myths in question are historically apposite. So, an initial observation to make is that conflicting myths not only are not always available, they are only available in accordance with certain historical constraints.

Moreover, once the claims advanced by such interpretations are reconstructed as historical observations, the issue of incompatibility between deep interpretations vanishes. For when a psychoanalytic interpretation is transformed into a historical interpretation about culturally motivated psychoanalytic themes that are relevant to the work, then it is no longer a psychoanalytic interpretation, properly so-called, and it is not at odds with a reconstrued Marxist interpretation that finds Marxist themes pertinent to the same work on historical grounds. For obviously a single consistent historical interpretation may track both psychoanalytic and marxist themes as relevant to understanding a given work without being self-contradictory.

Perhaps, in some cases, the work in question may be self-contradictory. I say *may* because a given author in regard to a given work may have successfully reconciled Freudianism and Marxism within that given work. But even where a work has not accommodated its potentially conflicting sources, an interpretation that notes those conflicting or even incompatible elements or sources is not itself logically self-contradictory. In remarking upon the contradictory forces in capitalism, a marxist need not have contradicted herself in the course of her analysis. So when deep interpretations are reconstrued as myth interpretations, the threat of incompatibility recedes, while, at the same time, because these interpretations are now historical interpretations, there is no pressure to retire truth values as applicable to them.

Likewise, what has been said about single historical interpretations—that remark upon the coexistence of Marxist and Freudian themes with respect to a given work—applies as well to the case where one critic, on historical grounds, isolates marxist themes with reference to a work where another critic emphasizes psychoanalytic themes, because, from an historical perspective, both interpretations can be true, and the truth of one does not preclude the truth of the other. Clearly, there can be artworks that are simultaneously inflected by both marxism and psychoanalysis. And clearly a historical interpretation or a set of historical interpretations that call attention to such conjunctions are not themselves locked in contradiction. Where such attributed conjunctions raise the prospect of incompatibility, the incompatibility, if there is any, pertains to the works in question and not to the historical interpretations that comment on the operation of these myths.

At one point, Margolis writes: "Artists cannot fail to be aware of the historical variety and contingency of the interpretive traditions through which their work is bound to move. Should we say, then, that their intentions are probably colored by that sensibility?"[16] I suspect that the point of this remark is that artists expect and perhaps even intend incompatible interpretations of their work. But surely the expectation of such interpretive variance and the intention to facilitate it by means of the construction of open texts is a very modern (modernist) phenomenon which should not be projected either historically within our own culture or indiscriminately to other cultures. It is doubtful that Bunyan had such modernist expectations. Thus, such modernist authorial expectations should not be taken as a grounds for generalizing an openness to the permanent possibility of incompatible or nonconverging interpretations. And, furthermore, in any case, where a text can be interpreted historically as designed to support incompatible audience responses, the interpretation itself is not inconsistent, and if there are incompatible interpretations of the work in the critical arena, they may be trumped by a historically motivated interpretation of the work as an open structure.

As mentioned earlier, the myths Margolis has in mind need not be as systematic of those connected with the deep interpretive practices of psychoanalysis or marxism. Cubism might serve as the relevant sort of myth, In one of his leading examples, Margolis says: ". . . The perception of West African masks came, with Picasso's *Demoiselles,* to be particularly informed first by themes of an emerging cubism; but by this time, such associations have either receded or have been entirely dissolved as far as the appreciation of West African art is concerned."[17] This is, I submit, a strange case for Margolis to include in the argument for robust relativism, because I think that the best explanation for the abandonment of the cubist interpretation of West African masks is that these interpretations were wrong from an historical point of view and were discarded as this became evident.

One example that Margolis includes among the cases of the Catholic, the psychoanalytic, and the marxist myths as an intuition pump is especially troubling. As noted previously, he appears to treat a Buddhist who brings his own myths to a Western work as on a par with the Catholic who interprets the *Commedia* by means of a Catholic myth. Margolis writes: "We should expect someone educated in a Buddhist society to construe the design of Western artworks in terms of the 'myths' that guide his own imagination."[18] Nevertheless, even if we would make such a psychological prediction about a Buddhist, it should be clear that in this case the Buddhist deep interpretation of a Western work (where the Western work has not been influenced by Buddhism) cannot be recuperated in the way that the Catholic deep interpretations were previously recuperated as historically grounded myth interpretations. For in the Buddhist case, the recuperation would not be historically constrained in the right way.

The Buddhist case, though placed on a continuum with cases of Catholic, Freudian, and Marxist interpretation, is quite different from them. It cannot be reconstructed as a historical interpretation. Perhaps it is on the strength of this example that Margolis goes on to hypothesize the general availability of incompatible interpretations. However, the skeptic can call a stop to the proceedings at this point by maintaining that in the case of the Buddhist we are dealing with myth projection and not myth interpretation, where there is a principled difference between the two. We accept reconstructed deep interpretations as recuperated myth interpretations where they can be shown to be historically intelligible. However, the Buddhist deep interpretation cannot be shown to be motivated by reference to the cultural context of the work in question. Consequently, the interpretation cannot be recuperated on the grounds that Margolis himself adduces in arguing for the ultimate critical admissibility of Catholic, psychoanalytic and marxist interpretations.

Using Margolis's own argumentative strategies as a template, we can in a principled way disallow him the case of Buddhist interpretation that he sketches. But if we can block this case and other cases of myth projection that resemble it, then the prospect of admissible incompatible interpretations diminishes. For cases of myth projection cannot be defended on the basis of the myth argument. Moreover, as we have seen, the myth argument itself does not get Margolis exactly what he needs to argue for robust relativism. For the myth argument reconceives deep interpretations as historical interpretations, and historical interpretations of the cultural context of the creation and reception of the work are not incompatible even if they remark upon historically conflicting or even incompatible themes that are relevant to understanding or appreciating a work.

The case of Buddhist interpretation, though only mentioned casually by Margolis, seems to me to be the actual linchpin of his argument for it will licit the introduction of any myth anywhere without appeal to historical verisimilitude. Roughly speaking, Margolis appears to intend to place this case before us on a slippery slope with his arguments about psychoanalysis and Catholicism. But there is a principled way to bring a halt to the slippage here. Insofar as the psychoanalytic and Catholic interpretations, once reconstrued, are palatable exactly because they are historically constrained, the Buddhist interpretation is radically different. It does not, without additional argument of the sort Margolis fails to provide, belong with the other cases, and, therefore, we may reject it, even while accepting much of the remainder of the myth argument. But without the Buddhist case, and cases like it, it seems to me that the myth argument will not support robust relativism.

On the face of it, the myth argument is meant to support the argument for robust relativism by demonstrating that there is a permanent possibility of nonconverging/incompatible interpretations with respect to artworks, because they are always open to incompatible deep interpretations. Moreover, this openness is related to the problem of demarcating the boundaries of artworks inasmuch as the grounds for these deep interpretations are contextual. Consequently, if artworks may admissibly support such incompatible interpretations, then truth cannot be the proper term of assessment for these interpretations. The admissibility of incompatible interpretations is absurd. So the criterion of admissibility must be logically weaker than truth. It must be something like plausibility.

However, if we recall the way in which Margolis has recuperated the relevant deep interpretations, I think we can agree that the argument falters. For it is not as deep interpretations that these interpretations are feasible but as historical interpretations. And as historical interpretations, as interpretations about the myths that are relevant to understanding the work as a cultural object, these interpretations, once recuperated, need not be incompatible *qua* interpretations.

Indeed, there is something slack about calling an interpretation of Stephen King a psychoanalytic interpretation where it has been reconstructed as an historical interpretation of Stephen King's psychoanalytic themes. And, in any case, an historical interpretation of Stephen King's psychoanalytic themes is compatible with a historical interpretation of Stephen King's marxist themes and with historical interpretations of his Catholic and Buddhist themes (if he has any), even if the conjunction of these interpretations might make King seem a bit confused.

That is, once deep interpretations are recuperated as historically grounded myth interpretations, they are no longer incompatible with each other just because the systems of belief from which they derive may be incompatible. And if the incompatibility problem is not in the offing, then the impulse to embrace plausibility as the name of the game disappears. Moreover, the incompatibility problem has not disappeared, because these interpretations are now to be conceived of as at best plausible, but because they have been recuperated as historical conjectures about the *beliefs* relevant to the creation and reception of the artworks. And, furthermore, as conjectures about beliefs, there is no reason to think that these conjectures cannot be assessed as true or false on historical grounds.

Margolis concedes that the tolerance he observes in critical interpretation "does not entail that any artwork can convincingly support plural, nonconverging interpretations. It means only that we cannot logically preclude the eligibility of such accounts. In practice, it may well be that only works of certain sorts will support divergent interpretations."[19] I would have thought that these concessions would be enough to undermine his claims about the logical weaknesses of critical interpretations. However, I surmise that Margolis resists this because of his faith in the permanent availability of myth interpretations. Thus, even if in practice we do not encounter many cases of apparent nonconvergence of the most radical sort, nevertheless, given the availability of myths, we can never preclude that cases of nonconvergence will not arise.

However, I do not think that faith in the permanent availability of nonconverging myths has the consequences Margolis postulates once we review the most persuasive formulation of the myth argument, because that formulation is only noncontroversial where deep interpretations and the like are reconstructed as historical interpretations of a kind that appeal to a brand of historical realism. But so reconstructed, the interpretations become assessable in the light of historical facts and constraints in such a way that they can, in principle, be assessed as true or false and, at least in some cases, this may also be determinable in practice. And that is enough to block the road to robust relativism, at least temporarily.

Of course, one thing that is strange about Margolis's argument is that he speaks as though psychoanalytic interpretations and Catholic interpretations are admissible once they are recuperated as myths. However that is not quite right. For these interpretations must be reconstructed, or rewritten, or re-read to recuperate whatever insight they may possess. It is really not the case that the Catholic interpretation and the psychoanalytic interpretations are what is admissible. They must be reconstrued as historical interpretations which are no longer correctly called "Catholic" or "psychoanalytic." And once they are reconstrued and presumably rewritten in the way Margolis suggests, they need no longer be incompatible because they have been turned into historical conjectures which at best may refer to states of affairs with possibly conflicting elements (such as fragments of influential but nonconverging Catholic and psychoanalytic doctrines). But given this, there is no reason to retire truth values in favor of the idiom of plausibility across the board.

Margolis likes to say that we do not discover aesthetic designs in artworks but impute designs to them. This way of talking relies on his conviction that we cannot demarcate what is and is not inside a work, thereby calling into question the notion that we find anything in artworks. But if this is what motivates the language of imputation, it should be noted that it does not lend credence to the argument for robust relativism, because even if we speak of imputation for this reason the imputation in question is historical imputation, constrained by realist considerations about what beliefs can be attributed to culturally situated artists and their audiences.

On my reconstruction of Margolis's argument, robust relativism presents itself to us as advisable once we come to appreciate the relevance of what might be called mythic reconstructions of deep interpretations to the practice of art criticism. But I have argued that, on the contrary, when we consider the strengths of the myth argument, we can agree with Margolis's diagnoses of the continued use of Catholic interpretations of Baudelaire, while eschewing robust relativism. We may, in short, accept his observations in the spirit of a sort of historical realism, a position that I herewith invite Margolis to embrace.

CONCLUSION

I have maintained that Margolis's subtle insights about the ways in which deep interpretations and the like can be reconstrued as myths will not support his brief on behalf of retiring truth and embracing values such as plausibility in the realm of critical interpretation. For the myth argument, where it is unobjectionable, relies upon effectively rewriting certain sorts of interpretation[20] as historical interpretations, and, as such, they afford no logical pressure—they raise no principled problem of nonconvergence/incompatibility—of the variety that would incline us toward robust relativism. The myth argument, in other words, does not compel us toward acceptance of the view that critical interpretations are logically weak. Of course, Margolis has other arguments for his preferred conclusion. They may succeed where the myth argument fails. But the rather narrow thesis of this paper has been to call into question the efficacy of the myth argument.

Moreover, though I have been complaining about the myth argument at length, it would be wrong to conclude that I think that it has not taught us something. I think that Margolis has revealed the basis (the basis in history) that explains why we continue to find use in things such as Catholic interpretations of Dante's *Commedia*.

In addition, though I do not believe that critical tolerance must extend as far as Margolis does, I think that by emphasizing the relevance of claims of plausibility to critical disputes, he has shown us why there is often the degree of tolerance about critical interpretations that there is. That is, to invert the order of things that Margolis advocates, *in practice* (rather than in theory), plausible claims are quite often the best we have before us. This is not a matter of logical necessity as Margolis contends, but only a reflection of our epistemic circumstances in certain cases. Yet even if one disagrees with the entirety of Margolis's account, his recognition of the relevance of plausibility to critical disputes has been a salutary philosophical advance and not the least of the many important contributions to aesthetics that he has made throughout his immensely productive and distinguished career.

NOTES

1. See, for example, Joseph Margolis's introduction to his *Interpretation Radical But Not Unruly: The New Puzzle of the Arts and History* (Berkeley: University of California Press, 1995).

2. Joseph Margolis, *Art and Philosophy* (Atlantic Highlands, N.J.: Humanities Press, 1980), pp. 145–64.

3. Ibid., p. 160.

4. Ibid.

5. In what follows, I shall refer to these interpretations as "nonconverging/incompatible" to signal that they are nonconverging by Margolis's lights, but if they were ascribed truth values, they would be *incompatible*.

6. Margolis, *Art and Philosophy,* pp. 146–47.

7. Ibid., p. 160.

8. Ibid., p. 151.

9. Ibid.

10. Ibid., p. 148.

11. Ibid., p. 152.

12. Ibid., p. 159.

13. For convenience, I have appropriated Arthur Danto's phrase—"deep interpretation"—here, but I have no commitments to his particular view of these interpretations. Dante uses the phrase in his article "Deep Interpretation" in his book *The Philosophical Disenfranchisement of Art* (New York: Columbia University Press, 1986).

14. Margolis, *Art and Philosophy,* p. 148.

15. Ibid., p. 152. Also, I should add that my presumption of retrodictability here is based on my belief that little sense of the sentence in question can be made with cases of dead artists, unless Margolis countenances retrodictability.

16. Ibid., p. 151.

17. Ibid., p. 149.

18. Ibid.

19. Ibid., p. 160.

20. It pays to remember that not all the controversial interpretations will be reconstruable as myths and will not be admissible on the basis of the myth argument.

Relativity, Intentionality, and the "Puzzle" of Interpretation

Gail Soffer

In *The Truth about Relativism and Reinterpreting Interpretation: The New Puzzle,* Joseph Margolis has elaborated a penetrating and provocative defense of relativism. Surprising as it may seem to some (including Margolis himself), his position has important points of contact with Husserlian phenomenology. In this essay, I explore the similarities between the two approaches, demonstrating the extent to which "classical" phenomenology is in fact "postmodern"; or, alternately, the consonance of the "postmodern" Margolis with the tradition. At the same time, I will identify and raise questions about certain important points on which Margolis clearly parts company with phenomenology. Let me begin by briefly reconstructing Margolis's position.

As must be expected from one of relativism's rare proponents, Margolis's conception of relativism is not the typical straw man of the absolutist's making. It eschews the usual subordination of truth to contingent subjective structures and, with this, the perennial self-referential paradoxes of relationalism. For example, if relativism is the view that truth is always "truth for x," then relativism can be true for the relativist but false for everyone else. Rather, according to Margolis's conception, relativism is the view that the principles of noncontradiction and excluded middle do not have unlimited applicability. In some domains, two judgments may be "true" which would be contradictory on the standard bivalent model; or they may be neither true nor false but some third value, for example, "undecided," "undecidable," "possible," "plausible." Thus, in a strange, roundabout way, Margolis's relativism preserves the notion of truth *tout court*, or "true for everyone." On his account, it is not that judgments are true for some subjects but false for others, but rather that some "incongruent" judgments are true (or valid) *tout court*, for everyone. This version of relativism differs from the standard one also in that it is a regional and not a totalizing view. It is intended only to limit the domain of applicability of bivalent logic, not to overthrow it altogether. Finally, Margolis is at pains to stress that relativism as he conceives it is ontological, and not only epistemic. It is not merely that opposing views may be defensible or undecidable by our best lights, the truth of the matter remaining veiled but unique and well defined. Rather, Margolis's claim is that even unveiled, truth and reality are vague, nebulous, dreamlike, pluriform, contradictory, defying our pathetically simplistic if reassuring most basic logical categories.

Clearly, a crucial question for Margolis's account is: *Which* domains, which types of phenomena, cannot be adequately characterized by traditional bivalent logic? The "strength" of his relativism, its radicalness and its plausibility, will depend largely on precisely where he believes the alternate logic is to be applied. A full-scale categorization of ontic regions into bivalent and multivalent domains is not contained in these two books. However, *Reinterpreting Interpretation* provides a decisive answer for a significant range of phenomena. Already in *The Truth about Relativism,* the realm of literary interpretation is a favorite hunting ground for examples of ontic nebulosity. Was Hamlet a just avenger or a self-seeking scoundrel? Virile or effeminate? Did Sherlock Holmes have a mole on his back? The blurriness of the text, the indeterminateness of the things themselves, seem self-evident here. This, Margolis holds, also places them beyond noncontradiction and *tertium non datur.* The reason, as he argues at the opening of *Reinterpreting Interpretation,* is that where reality is a flux (or what we have been terming a "nebula"), only human thought gives it a determinate form. Or, in his favorite formula, man is the measure. But human thought is historically contingent and manifold, hence the forms it impresses upon the textual nebula will be pluriform, various, and possibly contradictory, even though "true," "valid," and "real."

In *Reinterpreting Interpretation,* Margolis extends his relativism by claiming that bivalence and *tertium non datur* fail everywhere within the domain of cultural/intentional phenomena, including texts, works of art, historical narratives, and even history and persons themselves. Here the thesis of the flux is given an alternate formulation, stated in terms of the contrast between a history and a nature: cultural/intentional phenomena, Margolis holds, have no natures or static properties, only histories. Apart from interpretation, they are ontically nebulous and indeterminate. Human interpretation provides them with a certain degree of determinacy, a history that evolves over time. This history is indeterminate or plurally determined in places, but contains no invariant or necessary properties, nothing that could constitute a "nature." The possibility of repeated reference to the same phenomenon (e.g., the same text) is assured solely by the relative stability of social conventions and not by any absolute ontological invariance over time.

Yet although a self-described radical and critic of the philosophical canon, Margolis's analysis remains remarkably traditional in certain respects. It is true that he attacks any form of the view that there are determinate cultural/intentional phenomena (e.g., text, meaning, historical event, person) prior to or constant throughout interpretation itself. Opponents who fall into this category include not only traditional hermeneuticists such as Hirsch, with his notion of preinterpretatively determinate authorial intentions; but also structuralists such as Riffaterre, with his assertion of constant, preinterpretative textual structures. Even Gadamer comes under attack for holding that the values of classical Greece express universal and universally binding truths of human nature (a perhaps debatable interpretation of Gadamer). However, at the other end of the spectrum, Margolis resists the more radical tendencies of those would altogether abandon truth, justification, and validity in the cultural domain (Rorty), or who would completely collapse the distinction between fiction and reality (de Pan). In a startling burst of optimism, Margolis assures us in a chapter of *The Truth about Relativism* entitled "Order Restored" that every human society supports a well-entrenched practice of making truth-claims, and that there is little reason to doubt that physical science has made significant progress in discovering the nature of the actual world. Science discovers only "saliences," he qualifies, not true universals, principles with only an empirical, pragmatic justification, and no necessity or strict exceptionlessness. Still, even thus qualified, one might begin to suspect that this Protagorean successor to pragmatism is none other than pragmatism itself.

Another interesting feature of Margolis's complex relation to the tradition is the degree of consistency of his views with Husserlian phenomenology. Although Margolis himself cursorily dismisses Husserl as belonging to the despised archic camp, the parallels with traditional phenomenology, and the canonically Husserlian derivation of many of Margolis's basic theses, are unmistakable. The most obvious is the fundamental insight that reality itself is constituted by "interpretative" (or sense-bestowing) activity, that there is no reality prior to or apart from this activity. Because there does not seem to be any significant distinction for Margolis between interpretation and intentional activity (in the Husserlian sense), the thesis of the interpretative constitution of reality just is the phenomenological thesis of intentional constitution.

Further, Margolis's attacks on physicalism and fictionalism and his defense of the reality of intentional/cultural phenomena are also wholly consistent with a straightforward phenomenological approach. For example, when he argues against de Man that the distinction between fiction and reality remains unscathed by multivalence, his method is basically intentional analysis. He points out that what we *mean* by an historical event is different from what we mean by a fictional one. Historical events can be (or could have been) perceived; fictional ones can only imagined or represented. According to Margolis, if we derive our notion of reality from intentional acts themselves, then we must say that intentional/cultural phenomena are real and not fictions, despite their relative nebulosity or multivalence.

Indeed, even some aspects of Margolis's provocative loosening of the principles of traditional logic (especially the excluded middle) can be shown to have a solid phenomenological basis and to have been anticipated by Husserl's analysis of the lifeworld. A central aspect of this analysis is its emphasis on the indeterminacy and approximateness of the objects of ordinary lived experience, as opposed to the crystal line idealizations of the sciences. In consonance both with Margolis and with pragmatism, Husserl stresses that the determinateness of lifeworld phenomena is a function of the requirements of the relevant practical activity. An immediate consequence of this is the failure of the excluded middle in many cases. A lifeworld table, for example, does not have a mathematically exact shape or length, it is only roughly rectangular, roughly two feet long, determinate to the degree required by our ordinary practical ends. Because of this nebulosity, there will be a range of answers to the question, "What is the mathematically exact length of the table?" which will be neither true nor false. The mathematical-physical substruction of the table may have a precise length, such that all possible answers will be bivalently true or false (although even this is questionable, given the indeterminacies asserted by contemporary physics). However, the lifeworld phenomenon, the table, is imprecise in its very being and to hold otherwise is to substitute an idealization for the lived phenomenon itself. Indeed, although Husserl emphasizes the vagueness of lifeworld shapes and measures, the manner and degrees of nebulosity and indeterminateness of lifeworld phenomena are manifold and complex, giving rise to many failures of the excluded middle.[1]

A further important parallel to Husserl is Margolis's account of the strict sciences (such as logic, mathematics, physics) as domains where bivalence often holds, even though they, too, are in some sense intentional/cultural phenomena. Margolis's view is that these crystalline domains develop from within and are constructed upon the basis of ordinary, nebulous cultural/intentional phenomena. This view is strikingly reminiscent of Husserl's analysis in the *Crisis* of the lifeworld as the foundation of the world of science, and of vague, inexact, imperfectly intersubjective lifeworld truth as the foundation of exact, universally intersubjective, scientific truth.

However, let us not go too far. Certain significant divergences between Margolis and traditional phenomenology cannot be ignored, and in the remainder of this essay, I would like to explore some of these and to raise some questions about the plausibility of Margolis's views on these points.

The first is Margolis's claim of the failure not only of the excluded middle, but also of the principle of noncontradiction, especially for cultural/intentional phenomena. This aspect of Margolis's conception of "interpretative" truth clearly differs from Husserl's analysis of lifeworld truth, which scrupulously preserves the Aristotelian principle that the very same thing cannot both be and not be at the very same time and in the very same respect. Margolis motivates his position with examples from literary interpretation. The interpretation that Hamlet is a self-seeking scoundrel is "incongruent" with the interpretation that he is a just avenger. Yet both, Margolis suggests, may nonetheless be "true," in the sense of multivalent "interpretative" truth.

However, this formulation seems to me to raise questions. It is easy to concede that opposing interpretations of Hamlet may be plausible, interesting, coherent, valuable, and the like, and this is precisely because of the nebulosity of literary phenomena. But what would it mean to assert that, beyond all these attributes, diametrically opposing interpretations are also "true"? Ordinarily, a truth-assertion comports, in addition to coherence- and value-attributes, the exclusion of all logical opposites. But because here this is not the case, what could be the additional content of the truth-assertion in this context? In an earlier formulation of the relativist thesis, Margolis held that in domains such as literary interpretation, truth-predicates fail to apply altogether and should be substituted by non-bivalent predicates such as "interesting," "coherent," and so on.[2] This seems to me more plausible than the attempt to formulate a new conception of truth divorced from the notion of noncontradiction. Indeed, the difficulty of expounding this new notion of truth is clearly reflected in the consistently parasitic nature of Margolis's characterization of multivalence: Judgments may be "true" which would be contradictory according to the usual bivalent notion of truth. It is surprising that this allegedly foundational sense of truth—the sense on the basis of which the traditional bivalent sense is to be constructed by idealization—can be defined only parasitically and by way of a negation of the traditional conception itself and its logic.

Another more radical claim of Margolis, and another clear difference with Husserl, is his assertion that *nothing* remains constant throughout interpretative/intentional constitutive activity, that cultural phenomena possess *no* properties that endure through variations in interpreters and interpretations. This implies, for example, that there is no unitary authorial intention, there are no universal structures of the lifeworld, and no universal structures of human nature or subjectivity. All these claims stand in sharp contrast to Husserl's more traditional universalist position.

But are Margolis's more radical views phenomenologically warranted? Granted that reality, insofar as it is understood as phenomenal reality, has a nebulous, evanescent quality, does it not also have its fixed points and crystalline aspects, its features not subject to variation with mere changes in interpretation, and this even in the case of cultural phenomena? Margolis argues that this is impossible in principle, because form and stability are products of human interpretation alone, and human thought is the product of the contingencies of history. But is there not something of a paradox in this account? For history is alleged to be a product of interpretation, pluriform, beyond noncontradiction and excluded middle. How then can a flux, something with an indeterminate or plurally determined nature, "produce" or "condition" human thought? Is the language of causality and the attribution of causality to history consistent with the rejection of history's determinacy? In light of the principles of multivalence and "man is the measure," the "effect" of history on human thought will be determined not so much by *history* as by human *interpretations* of history, and will be possibly one thing, possibly the opposite, possibly both at the same time. Why cannot there be interpretations of history according to which it sometimes has a constant or insignificant effect on human thought, which leaves space for a measure of universality and constancy? Could not the universalist's interpretation of history also be "valid," in Margolis's sense?

For even if we grant Margolis that reality is intentionally/interpretatively constituted, we might still want to hold that some *cultural* aspects are constituted precisely so as to be invariant with changes in the contingencies of thought and interpretation. One plausible example of this from the domain of interpretation is authorial intention. According to Margolis, because authorial intention is constituted by our historically varying interpretations, it is ontologically and not merely epistemically beyond the logic of bivalence. But it seems to me that authorial intention is intentionally/interpretatively constituted precisely as something that is independent vicissitudes of interpretation. This is because a text is constituted as an embodiment of the intentional life of another person, and our understanding of this life is in turn based on our encounter with the dialogical other and our own self-experience of the determinacy of first-person intentional life. When each of us speaks or writes, we generally have something in view that we wish to communicate, and this "intended meaning" has a certain degree of determinacy and independence from the interpretations of others. Of course this determinacy is not perfect. There is always a foreground and a background to intentional life (what Husserl characterized as horizontality): Some things stand out clearly and explicitly, a potentially infinite number of other things are "there" but only in a receding or implicit way, only potentially explicit, and both explicitness and implicitness are qualities that admit all manner of degrees. At the far extreme, there could be instances of language without any prior or simultaneous intended meaning, as in a moment of inspiration, when a person speaks and first learns what he or she will say by hearing it and so becoming "reflective," or when a poet composes a poem but does not have reflective self-awareness of what he or she qua author meant to communicate. Arguably Gadamer, as well as Heidegger and Derrida, are correct to emphasize that there is some element of inspiration—of language "speaking through us"—in all writing and speech. Yet this does not eliminate the experience of intended meaning, and of the determinacy of this intended meaning, minimally in the sense of its distinctness from "significance," what someone else understood but not something one can recognize as what one meant (either explicitly or implicitly) to say.[3]

It is a phenomenologically ascertainable state of affairs that when we read a text, we generally attribute a (qualifiedly) determinate intentional life to the author. Of course our interpretations vary over time, and conflict with the interpretations of others. Yet through these varying interpretations, we intentionally/interpretatively constitute an authorial intention that in itself is relatively constant, independent, and determinate. Margolis is on safe ground with the example of Sherlock Holmes's mole: Few would argue that Doyle specifically and explicitly intended its presence or absence. However, it would be misguided to use this example as a completely general paradigm for the logic of intentional phenomena. What if we asked whether Holmes smoked a pipe or had a friend named Watson? Some authorial intentions are clearly determined and governed by bivalent logic, for all practical purposes. Thus it is highly questionable that the *entirety* of the textual/interpretative domain is subject to Margolis's form of relativism, rather than merely selected elements of it.

To bolster his opposition to even selectively univocal authorial intentions, Margolis, similarly to Gadamer, appeals to the historicity of interpretation, the inevitable interpenetration of understanding and application, and the consequent impossibility of univocally reconstructing the original. However, as I have argued in another place,[4] the historicity of the understanding and the real absence of consensus about authorial intentions are wholly consistent with authorial intentions that are interpretatively/intentionally constituted as determinate, constant, and univocal, and hence which, phenomenologically speaking, *are* univocal.

A clear indication that the historicity of the understanding does not in itself imply the nebulosity of truth is that even in the so-called strict sciences, human understanding is historically conditioned and evolving. Yet in these domains (as Margolis himself maintains), the principles of noncontradiction and *tertium non datur* remain valid. Thus, contrary to Margolis (and Gadamer), the crucial source of the conflict of interpretations in the hermeneutical/historical disciplines cannot be the insurmountable variety of meaning—constitutive subjective backgrounds or social conventions, and so some inherent difference among people. Were this the case, there would be no consensus in any domain, including the sciences. Rather, I believe that the greater lack of consensus in the hermeneutical disciplines is due to the greater inadequacy of the evidence, as measured against the standard of our implicit intentional claims. For example, in the case of authorial intention, the inconclusiveness of textual evidence results from the fact that the author is intentionally constituted as another person, even though our access to his or her intentional life is far more mediated than our access to the intentional life of a dia-

logical partner, or to our own. Thus, when our interpretation imputes certain intended thoughts to an author, this imputation is correlated with a manifold of behaviors, utterances, and further perceptions—including, as it were, imaginary dialogues—which delin-
eate further verifying or refuting evidence for the accuracy of the
interpretation.[5] This manifold belongs to the horizon of the interpretation and so is constitutive of its meaning. However, in the case
of a textual interpretation, many of the posited verification procedures are empirically impossible to carry out. The anthropologist
can reasonably confirm an interpretation of the intentional life of
another by speaking with the other in person and by witnessing the
physical and behavioral features of the other person's world. This is
impossible for most textual interpretations, despite the fact that the
claim to the accuracy of an interpretation of intended meaning
includes within it a claim to the possibility of confirmation of precisely this sort; for example, if this interpretation were proposed to
the author, the author would acknowledge it as correct, appear
honest in doing so, and so on. Rather, the claims here are counterfactual claims, the verification procedures can be carried out only in
imagination, and there is significant, meaning-constitutive evidence
which is forever beyond reach.

Margolis seems to exclude counterfactual, unverifiable claims
from the intentional constitution of our interpretations and to limit
the truth meaning—horizon to the factually verifiable criteria of
consistency and coherence. For only if what we mean by truth were
reduced to consistency and coherence, would the author's intended
meaning present itself as something not distinct from the manifold
of possible self-consistent interpretations of this meaning. However, it seems to me that this elimination of the counterfactual from
the horizon of truth is not in harmony with what actually happens
during the course of interpretation. It is precisely because the very
meaning of truth in the actual practice of interpretation contains
counterfactual implications, and because we can *imagine* convincing verification or refutation scenarios—imaginary, counterfactual dialogues, perceptions, and so forth—that we have the experience of being directed toward the "author's intended meaning" and
not some multiple object such as the "interpretation(s) consistent
with the whole text" or the "interpretation (s) that vanish(es)." Two

opposing reconstructions of a text may appear consistent with the text as a whole. But in the case of a determinate feature (e.g., Sherlock Holmes smoked a pipe), we presume that the author had at most one of these meanings in mind and that if we were able, for example, to question the author about it, we would learn that one is accurate, or that neither is, that the author was confused about the point at issue, and so on. The *true* reconstruction of authorial meaning is the one that would be confirmed by this further verification procedure. Thus, at most one of the two interpretations is true, even though we do not have access to the decisive evidence. Of course even dialogical evidence retains a relative degree of uncertainty and can be compatible with various hypotheses, although to a lesser degree than historical/textual evidence. In the end our directedness toward the "one" authorial meaning not only is based on the model of dialogical evidence but also and ultimately on our own experience of the (albeit qualified) determinacy of first-person intended meanings.

A similar argument can be made for the reconstruction of historical events. Granted that certain features of history may be phenomenologically nebulous, minimally in the sense of escaping the excluded middle, there remain other features that are constituted as relatively determinate, and here again essential counterfactual elements are included in the very meaning of truth, guaranteeing its univocity and constancy through variations in interpretation. For example, when we affirm that something "really" happened in the past, an essential part of what we mean is that, for example, if someone capable of perceiving the event had been there, that person would have witnessed it. This claim is in practice unverifiable, and yet it is precisely the counterfactual activity of the imagination that gives the experience of directedness toward something determinable and decidable, what "really" (bivalently) happened (e.g., something I would have seen if I had been there). Thus we have at once *evidential* indeterminacy (the evidence is insufficient to be conclusive across different interpretative backgrounds) but *intentional* determinacy (we remain directed toward a truth that is in principle but not in practice uniquely and intersubjectively determinable). For many aspects of historical narratives, counterfactuals remain truth-constitutive, the intentional/interpretative object remains distinct from the manifold of interpretations of it, and truth remains correlated to a set of (counterfactually realizable) perceptions exceeding nonbivalent consistency or value attributes.

Thus the real source of the failure of constancy and intersubjective consensus in interpretation is not primarily the different historical backgrounds of the interpreters, but the insurmountable inconclusiveness of the available evidence. Because the evidence is inconclusive, interpretations retain a degree of tentativeness and speculation, and it is in this space of uncertainty that diverse historically conditioned points of view have free play. We can fully agree with Margolis's claim of the essential undecidability of conflicting interpretations in many instances of literary and historical interpretation. This gives rise to a well-founded *epistemic* "relativism" (in Margolis's sense) in specific cases, a relativism that asserts that truth in the bivalent sense exceeds the bounds of human knowledge. However, there are difficulties in following Margolis's transition to an *ontological* relativism in all such cases. For the counterfactual activity of the imagination directs us toward a reality that can be determinate and univocal *beyond* the bounds and multiplicities of our interpretations, and it is not obvious why or how this imaginative, counterfactual activity is to be curtailed.

Prior to closing, I would like briefly to consider one final divergence between Margolis and Husserl, although perhaps this belongs more properly to the relativism than to the interpretation thematic: the problem of universal structures of the cultural- or life-world. Although Margolis's position seems, at least in places, to be emphatically antiuniversalist, it is well known that even in his latest period Husserl continued to uphold the universalist view. But we need to be careful here, for even Margolis's anti-universalism is qualified by his claim, for example, of the universality of constative discourse. In the end, he seems to be quite comfortable with the admission of "pragmatic" universals, which are not necessary or unexceptionless. Although it is not possible to enter into this question in detail here, it is my view that for most purposes, pragmatic universals are sufficient for Husserl's analysis as well. Yet a difficulty that Margolis, unlike Husserl, faces in this regard is the problem of justification: Precisely what is Margolis's *argument* that there are no necessary or exceptionless universals?

Margolis himself does not seem to find the need for an argument especially compelling. He often seems to take it that all "serious" contemporary philosophers, or at least all philosophers worthy of consideration, have already conceded this point, and, therefore, no further justification is necessary. Of course, this claim is true only if one circularly defines "worth" in terms of antiuniversalism. And even if it were true, it would not constitute much of an argument, especially in the absence of a full-blown consensus theory of truth with consequences of the most distasteful sort.

One antiuniversalist strand of reasoning suggested by Margolis is an empirical/pragmatic one. For example, empirical sciences such as anthropology and sociology demonstrate that there are no universal structures across all cultural- and life-worlds. But here again, this is a highly questionable claim. For although empirical studies uncover important sociological and historical divergences, arguably they also find certain universal features.

A further difficulty for Margolis's position (as Husserl clearly realized) is that because the sciences are founded upon the cultural/lifeworld or worlds, only if there are some universal structures of these worlds will it be possible to construct scientific knowledge with universal, cross-cultural intelligibility and validity. In the absence of universal structures, the sciences themselves will have no justification for claims to universal intersubjectivity. But then any empirical findings supporting antiuniversalist views in particular will themselves be of only limited intersubjectivity and subject to the logic of multivalence.

Finally, one begins to wonder whether the old reflexivity paradoxes have been laid to rest after all. For although Margolis artfully skirts many of these by rejecting relationalism and totalizing relativisms, there remains the question of the type of truth he would like to claim for his very own theories and his denial of universal lifeworld structures in particular. If his own philosophical analysis is supposed to fall under the same multivalent logic as cultural/intentional interpretative phenomena in general, then he would have to concede that "opposing" views may also be true. If, on the other hand, he is claiming a bivalent, univocal validity for his own theory, one wonders on what basis a philosophical theory (arguably as interpretative and historically conditioned as, e.g., literary interpretation) could be thought to escape the consequences of the flux.

In conclusion, Margolis's analysis of interpretation makes a decisively important contribution in expounding the need for alternate conceptions of truth and alternate logics in certain domains of phenomena, especially in the cultural/historical realm. His treatment of relativism as a regional thesis, and his assertion of the reality and fundamental character of cultural/intentional phenomena are also crucial philosophical insights. Some reservations remain about the precise manner in which phenomena are distributed between bi- and multivalence: Here a more finegrained analysis may be needed, and perhaps also a reconsideration of the extent of Margolis's debt to the tradition and the valid resources it offers for resolving interpretation's "new puzzles."

NOTES

1. A lengthier discussion of this point and of Husserl's relationship to relativism is contained in my *Husserl and the Question of Relativism, Phaenomenologica*, Vol. 122 (Dordrecht: Kluwer Academic), 1991.

2. Joseph Margolis, "Historicism, Universalism, and the Threat of Relativism," *Monist* 67 no. 3 (July 1984): 320.

3. I have developed this line of thinking in greater detail in "Gadamer, Hermeneutics, and Objectivity in Interpretation," *Praxis International* 12 no. 3 (October 1992): 231–68.

4. See ibid.

5. See Husserl's analysis of the phenomenological constitution of the other, *Cartesian Meditations,* trans. Dorion Cairns (Dordrecht: Martinus Nijhoff, 1960), §§ 49–54, especially § 52 (on the nature of verification of "interpretations" of the other's intentional life); *Cartesianische Meditationen und Pariser Vorträge,* ed. Stephan Strasser, *Husserliana,* Vol. I (The Hague: Martinus Nijhoff Publishers, 1950), §§ 49–54.

Interpretation and Objectivity

Peter McCormick

> Overcoming relational conceptions
> of truth is not equivalent to retiring
> or overcoming relativism.
> > —J. Margolis

> In any sense of "independence" I can
> understand, whether the sky is blue
> is independent of the way we talk.
> > —H. Putnam

> Every word is a doorway
> to a meeting, one often cancelled,
> and that's when a word is true: when
> it insists on the meeting.
> > —Yannis Ritsos

OLD WOMAN DRESSED IN BLACK

Some years after his return still again to the Greek island prison camps during the regime of the Colonels in the 1960s, and almost halfway through his extended 1956 dramatic soliloquy, "Moonlight

Sonata," the Greek poet Yannis Ritsos imagines "an old woman
dressed in black." The woman is describing a strange and elaborate
feeling to a young man sitting beside her in an old house in the
spring night as "a relentless moonlight streams through the two
windows."[1]

> From time to time, at the hour of dusk, I have the feeling
> that outside the windows the bear trainer is passing by with his
>   very aged, plodding bear. . . .
> and the bear, fatigued, marches within the wisdom of her
>   loneliness not knowing where she is going—
> she's grown heavy, she can no longer dance on her hind legs,
> she can no longer wear her little lace cap to entertain the
>   children, the idlers, the demanding,
> and the only thing she wants is to lie down on the ground,
> letting them step on her belly, playing her final game in this
>   way,
> manifesting her terrifying strength for resignation,
> her disobedience of the interests of others, the rings on her lips,
>   the needs of her teeth
> her disobedience of pain and of life
> with the sure alliance of death—even of a slow death—
> her ultimate disobedience of death with the continuity and the
>   knowledge of life
> going uphill with the knowledge and action beyond her slavery.
> But who can play this game to the very end? . . .

This image of the tired and aged female bear—her wisdom, her
strength for resignation, her disobedience, and something beyond
her slavery—reflects in important ways different strains in the
woman's own desires to leave her old house and to set out with the
young man in the moonlight that "will turn my hair gold once
more." At the end of this much celebrated poem, the young man
will leave alone, pause after awhile, laugh, and then mutter, "the
decadence of an epoch."

The fate of the woman in black, however, is left uncertain. "I
don't know if she finally went out," says the poet. And the poem's
readers are left to muse once again, as earlier in the readings and
later singings of Ritsos's *Epitaphios,* a poem publicly burned by the

Metaxas dictatorship then later set to music by Theodorakis, on the echoes of freedom and repression set ringing indistinctly by the muted similarities here between yet one more of Ritsos's women in black and an aged bear in chains, between Greece and her people, the Balkans and their violated and still tortured history even today.

In this essay, I would like to take Ritsos's poem here as an instance of the twentieth-century's poetry of suffering. And I would like to examine in what ways reasonably interpreting such poetry might be, properly speaking, objective. My central concern here will be to show why the objectivity of interpretation is problematic rather than to offer any sustained account of my own.

I begin with a further description of Ritsos's poetry to set up a contrast between two differing interpretations of that poetry. This contrast brings into focus the question as to how any interpretation of poetry can be objective. After setting out two different accounts of objectivity, one relativistic the other not, I then return to the poetry with the idea of particularizing these accounts and showing how interpreting such poetry objectively still calls for thought.

INTERPRETIVE DISAGREEMENTS

Part of the many-sided richness of Ritsos's sustained lyrical as well as dramatic soliloquy must also include its echoes of other mature twentieth-century Greek poetry since Cavafy, a poetry particularly sensitive to Greece's tragic history in the modern era. Perhaps one Such echo can be heard in a passage from "The Sacred Way," one of the many poems in the demotic tradition that the still now less well-known Angelos Sikelianos wrote before the full horrors of the German occupation engulfed the country and, in the autumn of 1941, provoked his great poem of prophetic wisdom, "Agraphon," with its single repetition as a final coda of the lines:

> a great pledge, mirror of the Eternal, but also,
> the Just One's harsh lightning-flash and hope![2]

"The Sacred Way" is a simpler poem than "Agraphon." Yet it manages to fuse elements of traditional folklore with evocations of the Greek myths and personal tragedy. On the long and crowded road to "the ruins of the Soul's temple at Eleusis," a gypsy leading two dancing bears in chains comes upon the poet and, tugging "fiercely at the chains," makes the bears dance.

> And the two bears
> rose on their hind legs heavily. One of them,
> the larger—clearly she was the mother—
> her head adorned with tassels of blue beads
> crowned by a white amulet, towered up
> suddenly enormous. . . .
> And the small bear at her side, like a big toy,
> like an innocent child, also rose up, submissive,
> not sensing yet the years of pain ahead
> or the bitterness of slavery mirrored
> in the burning eyes his mother turned on him.
>
> But because she, dead tired, was slow to dance,
> the gypsy, with a single dexterous jerk
> of the chain hanging from the young bear's nostril—
> bloody still from the ring that had pierced it
> perhaps a few days before—made the mother,
> groaning with pain, abruptly straighten up
> and then, her head turning toward her child,
> dance vigorously. . . .
> Then, as the gypsy
> at last went on his way, again dragging
> the slow-footed bears behind him, and vanished
> in the dusk, my heart prompted me once more
> to take the road that terminates among
> the ruins of the Soul's temple, at Eleusis.
> And as I walked my heart asked in anguish:
> "Will the time, the moment ever come when the bear's soul
> and the gypsy's and my own, that I call initiated,
>   will feast together?"
> And as I moved on, night fell,
> and again through the wound that fate had opened in me
> I felt the darkness flood my heart. . . . [3]

Although the poem ends with a barely heard murmur of assent in answer to the poet's question, readers of Sikelianos's "The

Sacred Way" are left once again, just as at the end of Ritsos's "Moonlight Sonata," with uncertainty about which of the poem's many implications for Greece's tragic history are to be taken as the central ones. Some readers may think of Sikelianos singing the forbidden national anthem under the eyes of the German occupiers mixed in with the mourners at the burial of the poet, Kostis Palamos in February 1943; others of Sikelianos reciting his own poem, "Palamos," at the graveside—"Blow bugles."[4] Still others may wonder at the vision here of a larger suffering than that of Greece, a suffering large enough to encompass the heart of the poet, the gypsy, and the bear.

Now, each of these poems invites searching reflection on its own terms. For the passages I have selected here need to be reinserted into their fuller contexts and then interpreted amply in those contexts. Moreover, nothing requires the reader to move beyond these individual poems to extract passages from each and then juxtapose them as I have done. Yet, part of what interpreters mean by the richness of Ritsos's postwar poem is its only vaguely intimated suggestion of Sikelianos's prewar, modernist work.

Ritsos's aged bear in "Moonlight Sonata" certainly plays an importantly different role than "the mother" in "The Sacred Way" where Sikelianos explicitly alludes to "the Great Goddess," "the Eternal Mother," "Demeter," "Alcmene," or "the Holy Virgin." Yet in each case the great and aged female bear is represented, in strong anthropomorphic terms that are at times almost sentimental, as aware of the pain and suffering of a slavery.

With Sikelianos's poem occasionally in mind, Ritsos's readers, not all of them Greek, might well recall the aftermath of the four-year Civil War—the massacres, the deportations, the denunciations, the betrayals, the settling of accounts. They might well remember all the horrors still to come after Ritsos composed this poem in 1956, during the years of hospitals and island prisons. And these interpreters might well claim that the two dramatic images of the chained dancing bears either passing by on a sacred road or in the nighttime fantasies of an old woman in black belong together.

We may then focus our discussion of interpretation and objectivity in this way. Suppose you claim, in an interpretive essay argued in your native modern Greek, that the figure of the chained dancing bear in Ritsos's "Moonlight Sonata" is, objectively speaking, an intentional allusion to the different but importantly similar figure of the larger chained dancing bear in Sikelianos's "The Sacred Way." And suppose I claim, in an interpretive essay written in English, that, whatever the persuasiveness of any eventual case you might make in attempts to justify your views, there can be, objectively speaking, no fact of the matter. For when what is at issue is the putative objectivity of a crucial element in an interpretation of fictional states of affairs like the ones presented in Ritsos's poem, an indeterminacy both ontological and epistemological ineluctably affects such matters.

These, of course, are both strong claims. You are committed to providing a thorough and convincing story about what is to count, in poetry, as an "intentional allusion." And you must also argue conclusively that what you count as an intentional allusion can be established "objectively speaking." In turn, I am willing to grant you some suitable (say, coherent, consistent, fruitful, etc.) account of "intentional allusion," thereby waiving the first question altogether. But, I take my stand on the second issue. And not only do I seem ready to argue against any construal of "objectively speaking" you might make, I also seem prepared to deny that you, or anyone else, can make such a case.

The issue between us then is not at the level of any first-order question about, for example, whether we have sufficient evidence of some sort or another to sustain your interpretation that, objectively speaking, Ritsos intended to allude to Sikelianos's "The Sacred Way." Rather, the question is a second-order one about whether the expression "objectively speaking" can objectively refer. And, whereas I want to espouse here some kind of relativism such that talk about objectivity must remain relative to a particular culture, or conceptual scheme, or language, or family of language uses, or whatever, you want to hold out for there being at least in some important cases certain ways the world is independent of our particular cultures, conceptual schemes, and so on.

On your view, once I grant that sufficient evidence is available to support strongly the interpretation that Ritsos intentionally alludes to Sikelianos, then, objectively speaking, it is the case that Ritsos indeed does so. On mine, when you put sufficient evidence on exhibit, then you have indeed justified your interpretation—but nothing more. For there is no additional objective fact of the matter beyond your now justified interpretation. What justifies your interpretation is sufficient to save your view from the vagaries of merely solipsistic interpretation (at least someone besides yourself can now find that evidence convincing, too). But it need not convince me. For there is no determinate fact of the matter to be discovered that would overrule my perhaps regrettable but tenacious relativistic tendencies.

Is there then no way round this dispute between us? Is there no way round some kind of a fundamental relativism about the objectivity of the interpretation of literary works of art? One fruitful way to investigate such general issues is to examine some particular questions about objectivity in recent work on the varieties, strengths, and weaknesses of philosophical forms of relativism. And this examination may well lead me to abandon my claims for the rationality of interpretation as radically relativistic and to concede in your favor that for interpretation to be rational even in the domain of the arts, interpretation must be objective in some basically nonrelativistic sense.

WEAK AND STRONG RELATIVISMS

Joseph Margolis has proposed a strong form of relativism that he believes can capture many fundamental results of contemporary philosophical inquiry without succumbing to the just as many fundamental problems with relativism over the course of philosophy's long history.[5] This strong form of relativism, moreover, also promises progress in a number of different domains such as moral philosophy, art and interpretation, philosophical psychology, and so on. Part of the promise here is a way out of the usual kinds of issues that arise about relativism and interpretation in the arts, for instance, the problem of reconciling divergent readings of Ritsos's poetry. A fair amount is at stake, then, in whether Margolis can succeed in making a strong form of relativism viable.

Margolis has relied on a number of strategies to elaborate this sophisticated relativism. He has taken up the diverse tasks of reconciling not just incongruent claims in different areas of philosophy but more largely in different domains of intellectual inquiry generally.[6]

Central to this work of exploring the dimensions of a strong relativism, one that can withstand both classical and contemporary criticism, has been a thorough and thoughtful reading of much contemporary work both in the English-speaking philosophical world and in European philosophical contexts as well. And one of the most important and fruitful strategies he has repeatedly deployed is the inventorying of salient features of apparently successful antirelativistic critiques, and then the devising of apparently viable strains of relativism that are immune to these treatments.

Although Margolis has drawn on a good deal of important contemporary work to pursue this strategy, he has examined with particular care the work of Hilary Putnam. Putnam's critiques of relativism have proved especially interesting because of their frequent variations—Putnam has changed his position repeatedly over the years, gradually working out very nuanced critiques of relativism. Moreover, Putnam has explicitly linked his critiques of relativism not just to continuing work in contemporary philosophy, but also to key figures in the history of philosophy, notably to Aristotle, Kant, and Peirce.[7] Margolis has taken issue with Putnam on both of these fronts, especially the former.

To the quite marked degree in which Margolis has been able to articulate his own robust relativism as a way of sidestepping the central features of the classical and contemporary attacks on relativism, his views remain centrally dialectical ones.[8] They arise, that is, not completely but in very large measure, out of opposition to the philosophical assumptions and preoccupations of attacks against relativism. This means of course that the operative elements in such opposed views as Putnam's need to be very carefully scrutinized if we are to take the critical measure of Margolis's own proposals.

We need to put on exhibit the picture Margolis gradually sketches of Putnam's critiques of relativism. I also want to show the different ways in which countering the presuppositions of those critiques generates some of the cardinal features of Margolis's formulations of his own version of a robust relativism. I then want to suggest that Margolis's sketch is, in the light of Putnam's own most recent work, importantly incomplete. The consequence is that, if

robust relativism is to continue to elude some of the strongest critiques that can be brought against it, several of the central features
of Margolis's concept of a robust relativism need reexamination,
especially the crucial notion of objectivity.

Putnam's repeated criticisms of relativism are long and varied. And,
although we will need to look at least briefly at some of the
nuances, I want to focus initially on the several major discussions
that Margolis highlights in his own attempts to defend a version of
relativism against its most able critics such as Putnam and, in the
process, provide a more perspicuous understanding of some strong
version of relativism. (Because an essential point of Margolis's own
attempts to establish a viable contemporary form of relativism follows from his virtuoso critiques of sophisticated classical and contemporary attacks against relativism, it is important to look at those
critiques carefully.)

If Margolis has gotten Putnam's views right, then his own version of relativism designed to incorporate defenses against just
those powerful criticisms becomes extremely persuasive. But has
Margolis gotten Putnam largely right? Perhaps not quite. But, if not
quite, then what philosophical consequences, if any, actually follow
for our concerns with interpretation and objectivity?

Margolis sees some of Putnam's earlier work as particularly
instructive. In Putnam's 1981 book, *Reason, Truth and History,*[9] for
example, Margolis has called repeated attention to an extended passage from "Two Conceptions of Rationality" where Putnam accuses
the relativist of failing to see that "some kind of objective 'rightness' exists." This objective rightness Putnam takes as "a presupposition of thought." The fuller passage, which Margolis cites,
reads as follows:

> The whole purpose of relativism, its very defining characteristic
> is . . . to deny the existence of any intelligible notion of objective
> "fit." Thus the relativist cannot understand talk about truth in
> terms of objective justification conditions. . . . The relativist must
> end by denying that a thought is about anything in either a realist
> or a nonrealist sense; for he cannot distinguish between thinking
> one's thought is about something and actually thinking about that

thing. In short, what the relativist fails to see is that it is a pre-supposition of thought itself that some kind of objective "right-ness" exists.[10]

Rich in nuances and presupposing wide acquaintance with an extensive literature, this passage remains persuasive for many philosophers today.

In his comment on these views, however, Margolis underlines four points he takes as serious deficiencies. First, the assumption here that paradoxes of self-reference must be part and parcel of any relativism worth the name has good historical support (Socrates versus Protagoras) but remains finally unconvincing. For Margolis thinks he can get round such paradoxes. Part of that task is formu-lating a strong version of relativism that sidesteps such paradoxes.

Second, the assumption that relativism entails the rejection of objectivity is left, at least here, without any supporting argument. While sidestepping any paradoxes of self-reference, Margolis wants to propound a version of relativism that would recover some central senses of objectivity and yet partly reconstruct that notion, too.

Moreover, the notion of objectivity that relativism is claimed to exclude relies here on a speculative doctrine that parses "objec-tivity" in the obscurer terms of "fitness." Yet, as Margolis is quick to remind us, the very notion of "fitness" to which Putnam wants to appeal in the interests of denoting what sense of objectivity is at issue here is one that Putnam himself has repeatedly criticized. Margolis's version of relativism would recover some other sense of objectivity than the strongly controversial notion here of objectivity as fitness.

Finally, the distinction on which this critique of relativism relies, namely, the line between "thinking one's thought is about something" and "thinking one's thought," is not clear. For once again Putnam himself has called into question the possibility of making what he called in 1987 "Dedekind cuts" between very sim-ilar matters, not just between the definition of real numbers in terms of rational ones but between the subjective and the objective.[11] Mar-golis wants to articulate a form of relativism that would incorporate just such a denial of clear-cut distinctions between subjective and objective. And this is the relativism that would resolve problems about divergent interpretive judgments of, say, Ritsos's poetry without succumbing to a defeasible form of relativism.

RELATIVISMS AND REALISMS

In responding to Putnam's critique of relativism then, Margolis sketches a more robust relativism. This doctrine is a strong relativism, one that would avoid paradoxes of self-reference while making a central place for nonspeculative construals of objectivity, yet one that would forego trying to make any sharp cut between objectivity and subjectivity.

More pertinent to our own concerns with interpretation and objectivity, however, is just how Margolis construes Putnam's understanding of relativism. On the evidence Margolis marshals here, Putnam takes relativism as centrally vulnerable to self-referential paradox, incorporating a controversial notion of objectivity, and committed to some clear-cut distinction between the objective and the subjective. Putnam directs his criticisms at each of these features. But Putnam's own nuances here suggest some hesitations. Why these hesitations?

Putnam's understanding of relativism in 1981 already represented, as Margolis reads the matter, a "reversal" of the position Putnam expounded earlier, for example, in 1978 in his paper on "Meaning and Knowledge."[12] Putnam had urged the view there that, regardless of some entities being no more than theoretical artifacts, the executive terms within two mature competing scientific theories "typically refer" when they are functioning explanatorily. Yet, at the same time, Putnam rejected any traditional correspondence relation holding between scientific statements and any world independent of the mind.

This tension forced Putnam, Margolis thinks, to give up "any pretence that the regulative principles [terms referring typically] . . . could yield, distributively, anything like a determinately confirmed (or converging) reference to given theoretical entities."[13] Putnam then went on to abandon his initial view in favor of a more nuanced perspective on the unconfirmability of sameness of reference for terms in competing explanatory theories. And these nuances are what brought Putnam to the hesitations about just which relativistic understandings of reference, objectivity, and subjectivity were to be his proper targets.

Besides looking at Putnam's earlier on relativism, however, Margolis also examines some later ones. In a key discussion in the third volume of his *Philosophical Papers*[14] from 1983, for example, Putnam tries to preserve some nuance in his understandings of relativism when urging a nonrelativistic position in the philosophy of science. There, Margolis sees Putnam trying "to separate the question of the nature of reality, of what there is, from the question of the nature of truth" (154). Margolis will go on to criticize this strategy roundly.

Putnam's concern is to hold metaphysical realism at bay. Yet his strategy, as Margolis sees it, leads him to a view about truth that entails a very strong commitment both to a bivalent logic and to some kind of Peircean optimism about eventually converging lines of inquiry based on Peirce's belief in some kind of "affinity" between mind and nature itself.[15] For in order to overcome any restrictive account of truth in terms of "verification" or confirmation or the selection of "right versions" or the like, Margolis thinks Putnam winds up after all with truth as correspondence.

Margolis puts it this way: "It is true, he [Putnam] would say, that 'the world' is not describable independently of our description" . . . but the revisability of any statement makes sense only in a logical space in which we hold (he would add) to the conception of objective truth (correspondence, in effect) which verificationism (positivism) and decidability (Dummett) and right versions (Goodman) do not and cannot make provision for" (154–55). We find ourselves then right back with questions about a putative line between the subjective and the objective.

Precisely here, with the question of whether any line can be drawn, is where Margolis wants to locate Putnam's Kantianism. And it is his Kantianism, Margolis claims, that keeps Putnam from imagining a more robust relativism.

Putnam thinks, at least on Margolis's account, that the various theories of reality our different practical philosophical inquiries cannot fail to support must "capture what is real" (155). But this view leads not so much to Kantian internal realism as to a Kantian "symbiosis of realist and idealist elements." When Putnam's views about objectivity and his pragmatic optimism are added to this Kantian "symbiosis," Margolis thinks Putnam becomes blind to the possibility that "realism (internal realism) and relativism are compatible." The key element in this incapacity is Putnam's largely implicit assumption that "a logic committed to bivalence or at least to *tertium non datur*" is both compatible with relativism and irreplaceable by anything else. The consequence is that Putnam cannot accept Margolis's own program of applying many valued logics to some domains and thereby "laying the necessary ground . . . to honor incongruent claims" (156).

The "secret argument" here is one that, on Margolis's reading, Putnam not only shares with Kant and Peirce but also with Husserl, Derrida, Popper, and Habermas. Margolis calls this argument the Enlightenment prejudice that:

> (a) humanity forms one inclusive inquiring community over the whole of time; (b) human reason, by which that inquiry is guided, remains essentially invariant over the length of its history; (c) cultural relativity, therefore, functions entirely benignly with respect to the longrun goals of objectivism (even within internalist constraints); and hence (d) a bivalent logic need never be abandoned during the diachronic run of approximations to objective truth. (160)

But, for Margolis, these beliefs all share a basic problem: They leave no place for the radical and pervasive phenomena of incommensurabilities, undecidabilities, and discontinuities so characteristic of our own era. And all these phenomena require a new attempt at understanding "what may be meant by objectivity or methodological rigor" in such conditions (160).

The problem with contemporary understandings of objectivity, then, even as we find them in Putnam's subtle formulations, are unreasonably and so far indissolubly linked to a bipolar logic. Even when sophisticated versions of reductive materialism and "uncompromising extensionalism" are, as also in Putnam's instance, rightly abandoned, Margolis thinks that the commitment to bivalence remains. This concern to safeguard the commitment to bivalence is what motivates Putnam's repeated opposition to relativism. And without effectively undermining this commitment, we cannot do justice to our understanding of an objectivity flexible enough to accommodate divergent interpretations of poetry like Ritsos's yet robust enough to withstand the familiar arguments against the usual forms of relativism.

STRONG RELATIVISM AND RELATIONALISM

Basic to the different attacks on relativism that Putnam has developed over the years out of this commitment to bivalence, Margolis believes, is Putnam's assumption that relationalism and relational conceptions of truth entail the defeat of relativism.

"Relationalism" here is the view that "true in L" can replace "true," where "L" designates "disjunctively one language or another, one world or another, or some such context of application" (98). Putnam purports to show that relativists of this ilk, namely relationalists, must fall prey to self-referential dilemmas and paradoxes. The reason is that these relationists must claim that what is "true in L(1)," say in your Greek interpretation of Ritsos, can be compared with what is "true in L(2)," say in my English interpretation of Ritsos. Claiming this, however, commits such relationalists to the further view that "there must be an idiom . . . available to us (and to the partisans of relationalism) in virtue of which distinctions relationalized to L(1) and L(2) are, there, truly assigned their truth values" (98). But this claim is what generates paradoxes of self-reference.

Precisely here, Margolis thinks, Putnam is mistaken. For Putnam first identifies all pertinent forms of relativism with relationalism.[16] Then, from the argument that all relationalist views succumb to self-referential paradoxes, Putnam generalizes mistakenly to the view that all relativisms are untenable. But, on the assumption that viable "nonrelativized (or, better, nonrelational or nonrelationalized)" conceptions of truth are available, Margolis would counter Putnam's move.

"Overcoming relational conceptions of truth," Margolis claims, "is not equivalent to retiring or overcoming relativism" (99). As Margolis sees things, Putnam effectively combines in his understanding of relationalism's conception of truth both epistemic and alethic elements. But, even when Putnam allows important qualifications in his own position where truth-values are ascribed in such a way as to allow for repeated revisions, the combination Putnam makes leads to fatal objections based on the paradoxes of self reference. By contrast, Margolis construes relativism in such a way as to avoid these fatal paradoxes to relationalism by separating "the meaning of 'true' and the epistemic appraisal of truth-claims" (67–68). For Margolis, relativism is not an epistemic claim but an alethic one. But this requires clarification.

One way to get clearer about just which elements in Putnam's critique of relativism Margolis wants to deny is to look more closely at Putnam's repeated criticisms of one widely remarked contemporary version of relativism, that of Richard Rorty.

Whether relativism can be avoided, Margolis thinks, depends on "whether first order truth claims and inquiries can be disciplined in ways that invite assessment of their comparative success (their perceived success) without implicating second order legitimating questions" (22). Rorty would dismiss this talk of first and second order issues outright. For Rorty thinks this way of taking relativism conceals a residual, and discredited, Kantian concern for transcendental arguments. Rorty wants, therefore, to disallow "legitimative second order questions about science, knowledge, truth, and the like" (57; 154). In fact, Rorty sometimes thinks relativism not only untenable; he thinks it unnecessary.

The basic difficulty Rorty finds in the usual talk of relativism is with legitimation. He thinks that we can have first order inquiries, namely scientific ones, without calling them that because talk of any legitimations of science (namely with the help of second order inquiries) is no longer viable. His reason for this claim is, as Margolis reads Rorty's *Philosophy and the Mirror of Nature*,[17] that "every would-be legitimation must be committed to privileged, cognitively transparent, ahistorical, context-free, universally exceptionless, timeless, linguistically understated, objective, a priori conditions governing meaning, truth, validity, values, and the like" (199). For Rorty we simply have to give up legitimation.

But Rorty's dismissal of legitimation cannot work. Rorty's quarrel is not really with legitimation. Rather, as his repeated concerns both to hold open some kind of talk about science and its priorities show, his quarrel is with the unacceptable ways in which legitimation is understood. In short, if we can change the description of legitimation so that the philosophical prejudices that trouble Rorty dissipate, then we can continue to talk about science after all.

Regardless of Rorty's occasional impatience with this kind of relativism in other places,[18] he seems to be plumping for some kind of cultural relativism. Or at least this is the way Rorty's frequent critic, Hilary Putnam, takes him there. Putnam goes on to criticize Rorty's relativism in several papers with a lengthy argument about the inconsistency of cultural relativism very much along the lines we have already seen.[19]

Now, whatever its intrinsic interest, this protracted discussion suggests to Margolis a distinction between two doctrines. This distinction fills out more fully his sketch both of Putnam and of certain central features in his own robust relativism.

The two conceptions of relativism in question here are the doctrine "that the same proposition can be at once both true or false," and the doctrine "that 'true' and 'false' are (alethically) relationalized to the insulated life and experience of one particular society (or person) or another" (58). The second view of course is stronger than the bare epistemic claim that "particular claims are (epistemically) decided in accord with whatever such life and experiment may recommend," a claim Margolis sees as trivially true.

Now, the stronger, second view is what Margolis sees Putnam attacking, namely, what Putnam himself calls "cultural relativity" and what Margolis calls more simply "relationalism." And it is precisely this strong view, one that incorporates alethic as well as epistemic elements, that Margolis wants to affirm. For this is the view he thinks that enables the robust relativist to sidestep the apparent contradictions between incongruent judgments in some areas of inquiry including aesthetics and our concerns with the objectivity of competing interpretations of such historically resonant lyric and dramatic poetry as that of Ritsos. But to see clearly what Margolis is denying, we still need a better hold on just what Putnam thinks he is attacking when he attacks Rorty's brand of relativism.

CAUSAL AND LOGICAL INDEPENDENCE

In a recent exchange between Rorty and Putnam, some of Putnam's own views about relativism come out quite clearly.[20] Rorty wants to put Putnam on the spot. Calling fresh attention to Putnam's 1983 article, "On Truth,"[21] Rorty points to Putnam's suggestion that there is a relation called "making true." The idea is that, unlike whatever relations that may or may not hold between some beliefs and others (for example, "justifying"), there is at least one relation that holds between belief and nonbelief, a relation called "making true." Rorty recalls that Davidson denies any such relation.[22] Davidson writes: "Nothing, however, no thing, makes sentences and theories true; not experience, not surface irritations, not the world, can make a sentence true."

Given that Putnam himself rejects the doctrine of any totality of objects existing independently of our descriptions, and hence his rejection as well of the idea that the word "object" is independent of language, Rorty is puzzled as to just what, if not "objects," could ever make statements true. In responding to this worry, Putnam glosses some of the views we have already caught sight of and brings us much closer to the subject of our concern with making good sense of the key expression, "objectively speaking" in accounts of rational interpretation.

Putnam disputes Rorty's reading here that objects cannot, in some sense, make our sentences true. (Note however that Putnam talks of sentences being true, which he thinks is the proper idiom, unlike Rorty who continues to talk of statements being true.) As Putnam reads the issue, what Davidson is attacking is not a particular doctrine about objects but about states of affairs. The point is that we must not inflate our ontology by thinking "that some sentences correspond one by one to things called 'states of affairs' " (432). The issue then is about states of affairs, not objects.

As for his own view, Putnam states very clearly "that whether a sentence is true or not typically depends on whether certain things or events satisfy the conditions for being described by that sentence—conditions which depend upon the ongoing activity of using and reforming language" (432).

Two points are important here for understanding Putnam's position more fully. First, Putnam insists that all our thinking is caught up in a continuous process of change, of what he calls both the using and the reforming of language. So any particular term, whether "object" or "state of affairs" or "event" or "thing," is going to be subject to shifts in its uses and hence in its meanings.

But, second, Putnam insists that the cardinal issue is not whether a particular term like "object" or whatever has a determinate meaning, but whether the determinate meaning it has is closed. The question is "whether notions like 'state of affairs' are conceived of as having a single determinate meaning, or an open and forever extendable family of uses—the same question that we must ask about 'object,' 'event,' etc." (432, n. 4). And, as he describes further in his Gifford Lectures,[23] different sentences can describe the same state of affairs just because notions like "state of affairs" can have such an extendable family of use.

Rorty's problem arises then not from substantive objections about whatever could make sentences true. Rather, the problem arises from how objects could make sentences true when objects are taken to be independent of our ways of talking. Putnam immediately highlights the general notion here of independence. He goes on to claim that in issues about truth what is at stake is the putative independence from our language about something that would make sentences true. And this kind of independence is "neither ordinary causal or ordinary logical independence" (433).

The point is an especially important one for our concerns with the putative objectivity of rational interpretations. To clarify, Putnam offers an extended example of how something can be the case independent in both causal and logical ways of the ways we talk.

> That the sky is blue is causally independent of the way we talk; for, with our language in place, we can certainly say that the sky would still be blue even if we did not use color words. . . . And the statement that the sky is blue is, in the ordinary sense of "logical independence," logically independent of any description that one might give of our use of color words. For these reasons, [unlike Rorty] I have avoided stating the thesis of conceptual relativity as a thesis

of the dependence of the way things are on the way we talk. . . . In any sense of "independence" I can understand, whether the sky is blue is independent of the way we talk. (433)

Putnam's point is not that what makes a sentence true is either causally or logically independent, or both, of the way we talk. Rather, what makes a sentence true is independent of the ways we talk in none of the above ways. "If language users had not evolved," Putnam adds, "there would still have been a world, but there would not have been any truths about the world" (433).

Just how what makes a sentence true is independent Putnam does not say directly. He does say however that recognizing that the sky is blue is independent in some way of how we talk. And the reason for Putnam is quite basic. No one way of describing the world can be privileged because we continue to reform language while using it. Nature does not lend itself to any unique description that is somewhere waiting to be discovered, a unique description that would say what nature is "in itself." As Putnam writes, "the 'in-itself' doesn't make sense."

Still, this view might seem to let the door open for the idea that, just because the world is not divisible into things describable in words of fixed uses (instead of ever expanding families of uses), we can never pin down at least some of the ways in which the world is divided. Yet Putnam closes this door emphatically—"it does not follow," he underlines, "that *when a particular use of 'object,' 'event,' etc., is already in place,* we cannot say how the particular statements we can make in that particular vocabulary relate to those particular objects" (434).

To support this strong claim, Putnam provides once again an example. He ask us to consider how things in a room can be counted in two different vocabularies, one using the vocabulary of objects, the other that of mereological sums of objects. This practice shows that, even when as here vocabularies are not semantically interdefinable, one can still talk variously about each vocabulary relating to the different things in the room. In short, "given a definite language in place and definite scheme of 'things,' the relation between 'words and things' is not at all indescribable; but it does not have a single meta-physically privileged description any more than the things do" (435).

This comes to the view that some things do make some sentences true—some things make assertions about them true. Yet what makes these sentences true cannot have unique, fixed, and closed meanings. Rather, what makes such sentences true both has a definite meaning where a particular use of the vocabulary at issue is already in place and keeps this definite meaning open to change in the ongoing continual uses and reforms of this vocabulary.[24] In that sense, what makes sentences true is not independent of language. But, as Putnam puts the matter persuasively, "the nature of the dependence changes as the kind of language games we invent changes" (435). And in these language games, as Putnam explains in Lecture IV of his Gifford Lectures, some things are right and wrong. For right and wrong in these activities, these language games, is not determined completely either by majority vote, or by consensus, or by convention.

Putnam has drawn some further conclusions about different forms of relativism from recent discussion, such as these with Rorty. Thus, again in his Gifford Lectures, he distinguishes carefully between various relativist positions—largely what he sees as standard forms of cultural relativism and first-person relativism—and a relativistic attitude. He thinks that the familiar forms of relativism as positions succumb to problems with consistency or with solipsism. The relativistic attitude, however, Putnam takes as indefeasible by rational argument and, in fact, ineliminable. While linking relativism with skepticism, he writes: "It is not that relativism and skepticism are unrefutable. Relativism and scepticism are all too easily refutable when they are stated as positions; but they never die, because the attitude of alienation from the world and from the community is not just a theory, and cannot be overcome by purely intellectual argument.[25]

Putnam favors at times this link between relativism and skepticism, for it allows him to endorse Stanley Cavell's views that skepticism is part of the human condition.[26] At other times, he also wants to link relativism with its opposite, foundationalism, as if relativism and foundationalism could be taken as manifestations of a similar phenomenon, of different attitudes toward a misplaced concern about metaphysical certainty or a "transcendental guarantee."

There is, however, no such thing. What is needed, so far as

Putnam is concerned, is something else altogether, something quite unexpected. To the relativist, Putnam says: "Some things are true and . . . some things are warranted and some things are reasonable, but of course we can only say so if we have an appropriate language. And we do have the language and we can and do say so, even though that language does not itself rest on any metaphysical guarantee like Reason."[27] But then the relativist quite understandably presses the issue. The relativist asks on just what such a language does rest if not on at least some kind of metaphysical guarantee. Putnam's surprising move is to answer with Wittgenstein— the language that enables us to say that some things are true, warranted, reasonable rests on—trust. Putnam quotes the *Philosophical Investigations* paragraphs 508 and 509:

508 What can I rely on?

509 I really want to say that the language game is only possible
     if one trusts something. (I did not say "can trust some-
     thing").

This trust, as Putnam takes the matter here in the light of Cavell's views, comes to curing our "inability to accept the world and to acknowledge other people, without the guarantees."[28] And because the inability is persistent, basing the language on trust comes to learning how "to live with both alienation and acknowledgment."[29] But can such a trust sufficiently justify claims that some interpretations are, objectively speaking, right, and others are, objectively speaking, wrong? Can the language of interpretive objectivity rest on trust alone?

INTERPRETATION, LANGUAGE, AND TRUTH

To see the pertinence of these points to our concerns with interpretation and objectivity, we may return to some of the poetry with which we began and to the questions about its interpretation that we initially formulated. However, consider this time not just excerpts from one of Yannis Ritsos's extended dramatic monologues such as

"Moonlight Sonata" and its possible echoes in some of the work of
Angelos Sikelianos's such as "The Sacred Way." Instead, consider
the full text of one of Ritsos's most celebrated short lyrics written
in the very difficult years of 1946–47 but only first published as part
of a collection entitled *Parentheses I,* compiled in the larger work
of Volume II of his poems.[30]

Ritsos joined the EAM (the National Liberation Front in
Greece) and went to northern Greece to do work in the theater there
and in Macedonia before returning to Athens. His activities resulted
in the banning of his published work, and then four very difficult
years during the first of two extended imprisonments from 1948–52
in different camps. His work was banned again under the
Papadopoulos dictatorship, and he was imprisoned in the camps
from 1967 to 1968, then hospitalized, then later confined to house
arrest.[31] During imprisonment, Ritsos wrote many short poems
which he hid in bottles and buried for safekeeping in hopes that
either he himself or at least one of the two or three of his prison
friends to whom he confided the secret could retrieve them much
later.[32] The short poem, in Kimon Friar's translation, reads:

The Meaning of Simplicity

I hide behind simple things that you may find me;
if you don't find me, you'll find the things,
you'll touch what my hand touches,
the imprints of our hands will merge.

The August moon glitters in the kitchen
like a pewter pot (it becomes like this because of what I tell you)
it lights up the empty house and the kneeling silence of the house—
always the silence remains kneeling.

Every word is a way out
for an encounter often cancelled,
and it's then a word is true, when it insists on the encounter.

Despite its uncharacteristically abstract title that immediately
puts his usual reader on guard, Ritsos's poem presents us with a dramatic scene very much like the scene in "Moonlight Sonata" in the
darkened house with the moonlight streaming through the window

and the long dramatic monologue of the woman in black. But much else is going on here that bears directly on our concern with questions about interpretation, relativism, and objectivity.

One way to make these connections is to reflect on the translator's own interpretive comment on this poem which we need to cite at length.

The poet informs us (parenthetically) that if the moon is glittering in the empty house like a pewter pot, this is because he has chosen to tell us so, thus warning us that the poem we are reading and its themes exist only in the words he had chosen. . . . "Every word," he tells us, "is a way out/for an encounter often cancelled," and in so telling us leaves us in doubt as to whether the "way out" is an opening toward that meeting or an escape from a meeting that, anyway, has been cancelled. But having once heeded the poet's parenthetical warning that we are entering a private house of words (where silence remains forever kneeling), where no two seemingly similar words for inhabitant and visitor ever denote or connote the same things or meanings, we must not be misled by the impasse of this encounter, because it is exactly the words themselves which are not only a bridge between each other, and so between ourselves, but also a bridge between ourselves and whatever they symbolize, whether things of the world inside each of us or outside us all. The imprints of our hands *will* merge, though not completely, for no two imprints are exactly alike, but sufficiently enough for an overall pattern to be discerned. The miracle is that communication is at all possible, and to the extent it is. The meaning of simplicity is complex. (412)

Now, part of what makes these interpretive comments suggestive for our own concerns here is their sharp focus on the last of the three stanzas where the poet treats of language and truth in a way that his earlier parenthetical comment about the glittering of the moon renders ambiguous. For another ambiguity comes clear besides the one Friar points out in the expression "every word is a way out." And this second ambiguity concerns truth.

"A word is true" when one has kept to it, when one keeps one's word, one's promise, and insists on what was promised, as here, on a meeting. But perhaps another suggestion is that "a word is true"

when words are used in such a way that things are made to be seen
as reflections of language only, when the glittering of the moon
becomes the glittering of a pewter pot just because someone says so.

Contrast for a moment the translation of the final stanza here in
Kimon Friar's version—

> Every word is a way out
> for an encounter often cancelled,
> and it's there a word is true, when it insists on the encounter
>
> (411–12)

—with the translation of the same stanza in Edmund Keeley's version—

> Every word is a doorway
> to a meeting, one often cancelled,
> and that's when a word is true: when it insists on the meeting.
>
> (125)

Keeley's version is, among other things, more concrete—
"doorway" for "a way out," "a meeting" for "an encounter." And
this difference subtly influences whatever awareness we may gradually come to of possible ambiguities here in the fuller expression,
"a word is true."

Now, worrying the Greek text of the poem would be foolish.
For both Keeley and Friar are distinguished translators of Greek
poetry with many years' experience in rendering Ritsos's poems
and those of other Greek poets into English. Moreover, each knew
Ritsos personally and had the benefit of discussing with Ritsos on
numerous occasions (before his death in November 1990 at the age
of eighty-one) the English translations of his poetry.

We should notice nonetheless the different versions of at least
one very important expression in the poem, the expression the poet
puts almost at the center of the poem, midway into the middle
stanza, and which the poet puts into parentheses in a collection of
poems he has entitled *Parentheses*. Where Keeley translates "(it
gets that way because of what I'm saying to you)," Friar has "(it
becomes like this because of what I tell you)."

The difference here seems quite small, even when we pin down the indefinite pronoun's referents to the moon's getting "like a tin-plated pot" and the moon's becoming "like a pewter pot." Yet the connections between the parenthetical remark and the ambiguous expression in the last stanza are important. The ambiguity comes out perhaps more strongly (although less artfully?) in Friar's more abstract renderings—"becoming" for "getting," "it's then a word is true" for "that's when a word is true."

When is a word true? On Keeley's version we may want to answer: just when the invitation, as it were, in the particular use of an expression in a conversation (I'm saying something about the moon, perhaps in response to what you've been saying) is accepted. Or, on Friar's version, we may want to answer instead: just when a possibility projected by the use of a particular expression is appre-hended ("I'm telling you something about the moon that I can't quite put into suitable words yet"), then actualized in a particular use of the expression ("You know, it's, well, it's—it's glittering!").

Besides the first answer's being more particular than the second one, the crucial difference here is between taking oneself as some-times committed ("it insists on," says the poet) to exploring the con-versational implications of certain actual linguistic uses, and taking oneself as sometimes committed to inventing possible linguistic instantiations for barely surmised abstract possibilities which are not yet linguistic in form (say, the suggestive gesture in the shadows lengthening on the prison camp's rock quarry). In the case here of difficult talk about a word or expression being true or false, con-trasting the two versions attentively suggests an opposition between determining the truth or falsity of an expression, usually by checking with the way things already are and determining the truth or falsity of an expression by telling a story about the way things are. Some people want to say an expression is true or false in a par-ticular context because of things happening to be one way or another—"that's the way it is," we sometimes say. Other people want to say an expression is true or false in a particular context because we make it that way—"there never was a world for her," Wallace Stevens wrote, "except the one she sang, and, singing, made."

LIKE A DOOR

Suppose, in concluding, we sharpen the discussion as we did at the outset, and imagine the two of us disagreeing all over again. This time, however, the disagreement is not about an interpretation—whether Ritsos in his "Moonlight Sonata" can be said, objectively speaking, to have alluded intentionally to Sikelianos's "The Sacred Way." Rather, we disagree this time about the nature of rational interpretation—just when, as in Ritsos's "The Meaning of Silence," interpretation holds a word to be true, objectively.

You say, with Edmund Keeley, it's when an expression, opening out "like a door" on what are often canceled meetings with the world, insists on the meeting with the world taking place. And, with Kimon Friar at my elbow, I say it's when an expression, "like a way out" for what are often cancelled encounters with the world, insists on the encounter taking place with language. Each of us—and the evidence here seems rather strong—may in fact be equally unhappy interpreters of Ritsos's beautiful work. But is there some way round, if not our glaring incapacities as reasonable interpreters of poetry, at least the disagreements between objectivity, about my interpretive relativism and your interpretive realism?

Notice that the disagreement here is only in part about a properly literary matter. In the earlier case of Ritsos's putative allusion to a passage in Sikelianos, we could have resolved the disagreement in a number of empirical ways. For example, we may have come upon correspondence, say letters Ritsos wrote in which he said that he had drawn on Sikelianos's "The Sacred Way." Or we may have come upon a draft Ritsos made of "Moonlight Sonata" that had the Sikelianos passage in the margins. Of course, we still would have been left with explaining the difficult matter of what intentional allusion comes to—How can what is an allusion be unintentional? But that, as we say for convenience, is a separate matter.

Here, the nature of the disagreement is such that no empirical strategy can be adequate for its resolution. What stands at issue is not a matter of fact at all. For the question is not whether Ritsos in some way intended the expression, "it's then a word is true," to be taken one way or another. Even if he took the expression to be ambiguous in just the way we were imagining—and this is implausible—there is no kind of empirical evidence that would allow either one of us to claim that Ritsos intended further that his intended ambiguity be parsed one way rather than another. For each of the understandings of interpretation we have relied on has modified Ritsos's own words in important ways—first by interpolating the notion of meetings with a world, and then by distinguishing meetings with a world from encounters with language.

In the case of the first disagreement where empirical evidence of some sort, did it exist, would be directly pertinent, we are in the familiar domain of literary history. But in the second case, where no empirical evidence of any sort could be pertinent just because what Ritsos wrote has been modified, we are in the less familiar domain of philosophy. The two domains are often, as here, closely related; but they are not the same. We can say more generally that the first extended example about Ritsos and Sikelianos occasions a literary disagreement about interpretation, whereas the second about hypothesizing the basis of ambiguities expressed in poetry occasions a philosophical disagreement about the nature of rational interpretation.

Our philosophical argument here concerns relationalism, relativism, and objectivity. The issue between us, clearly, is not whether two incongruent judgments must be construed as a contradiction. For the quarrel is not about whether Ritsos's "it's then a word is true" means X is true or not true. This would be a first-order dispute. And were we to disagree about this matter, then of course we would have to get clearer as to whether, in the domain of the interpretation of poetry, competing critical judgments always accommodate bivalent as opposed to multivalued logical commitments.

Our disagreement rather is about whether interpreting Ritsos's "it's then a word is true" refers mainly to something's always making a sentence true by virtue of this something's being the case in the world, or rather by this something's being the case in language. But at this level we are still dealing with first-order questions about whether and if so to what extent truth is a matter finally of linguistic conventions.

But we move to a second-order level just as soon as we notice that our disagreement about interpretation reaches to just how we are to talk of truth itself when we talk of what it is that makes something true. For here, unlike the situation so far, it appears that the true sentences we are concerned about in the sense of wanting to know just what it is that makes them true are not sentences about the nature or limits of linguistic conventions but true sentences about what makes sentences true.

We come then to our most basic disagreement about interpretation and objectivity. You say that what makes true sentences about sentences being true is, in particular contexts with particular vocabularies already in place, the give and take between the standing uses of families of language games and their ongoing reforms, in short a dynamic objectivity. And I say that what makes such self-referential sentences true is nothing other than the particular alethic options we choose together with consistency in their epistemic applications, in short, not any objectivity but subjective constructions. Can we decide this issue between us? Or is such an issue a matter of convention all over again? On the evidence of the issues Margolis and Putnam's ongoing discussions keep returning to, we have some more work to do before claiming to have resolved the complex matters involved in the putative objectivity of interpretation.

NOTES

1. *The Fourth Dimension: Selected Poems of Yannis Ritsos,* trans. R. Dalven (Boston: Godine, 1977), p. 57. Cf. "Moonlight Sonata," trans. P. Green and B. Bardsley in *Yannis Ritsos: The Fourth Dimension* (Princeton, N.J.: Princeton University Press, 1993), pp. 43–44.

2. In *Angelos Sikelianos: Selected Poems,* 2d bilingual edition, trans. and ed. E. Keeley and P. Sherrard (Evia, Greece: Denise Harvey [publisher], 1996), p. 139.

3. Ibid., pp. 101, 103, 105.

4. See the moving account in E. Keeley, *Modern Greek Poetry: Voice and Myth* (Princeton, N.J.: Princeton University Press, 1983), p. 42.

5. For a recent summary statement of Margolis's views, see his article, "Plain Talk about Interpretation on a Relativistic Model," and the two responses by Stephen Davies, "Relativism in Interpretation," and Robert Stecker, "Relativism about Interpretation," in *Journal of Aesthetics and Art Criticism* 53 (1995): 1–18.

6. Much of that work is on view in his trilogy, *The Persistence of Reality,* a

series of related investigations that explores different strategies of philosophical reconciliation under such provocative titles as *Pragmatism Without Foundations, Science Without Unity,* and *Texts Without Referents* (Cambridge, Mass.: Blackwells, 1986, 1987, and 1989, respectively). See also his *The Flux of History and the Flux of Science* (Berkeley: University of California Press, 1993), esp. pp. 195–96; and *Interpretation Radical But Not Unruly: The New Puzzle of the Arts and History* (Berkeley: University of California Press, 1995), passim.

7. See most recently the many essays in Putnam's *Realism with a Human Face,* ed. J. Conant (Cambridge, Mass.: Harvard University Press, 1990); *Words and Life,* ed. J. Conant (Cambridge, Mass.: Harvard University Press, 1994), and *Pragmatism: An Open Question* (Cambridge, Mass.: Blackwell, 1995).

8. See, for example, his accounts in *The Truth about Relativism* (Cambridge, Mass.: Blackwells, 1991), p. 62. This work is the most comprehensive of Margolis's investigations into kinds of relativism, and I will rely on it largely although not exclusively here. Further references to this book are incorporated in the body of the text.

9. Hilary Putnam, *Reason, Truth and History* (Cambridge: Cambridge University Press, 1981).

10. Putnam, cited in Margolis, *The Truth about Relativism,* p. 80. Talk about "fitness" here anticipates Putnam's reexamination of Nelson Goodman's views about truth. See, for example, Putnam's "Foreword to the Fourth Edition," in Goodman's *Fact, Fiction, and Forecast* (Cambridge, Mass.: Harvard University Press, 1983), pp. vii–xvi; and his "Irrealism and Deconstruction," in Renewing Philosophy (Cambridge, Mass.: Harvard University Press, 1992), pp. 134–57. Goodman's very important replies can be found in his "Comments" in *Starmaking: Realism, Anti-Realism, and Irrealism,* ed. P. McCormick (Cambridge, Mass.: MIT Press, 1996), pp. 229–34.

11. Cf. Putnam's Carus Lectures in his *The Many Faces of Reason* (Cambridge, Mass.: MIT Press, 1987), esp. pp. 26–40.

12. H. Putnam, *Meaning and the Moral Sciences* (London: Routledge, 1978), esp. pp. 20–34.

13. Margolis, *The Truth about Relativism,* p. 130.

14. (Cambridge: Cambridge University Press, 1983).

15. See Margolis, *The Truth about Relativism,* p. 155; and Peirce, *Collected Papers of Charles Sanders Peirce,* ed. C. Hartshorne and P. Weiss (Cambridge, Mass.: Harvard University Press, 1934), Vol. 5, para. 47, 603; cited in Margolis, p. 164. Cf. Putnam's "Introduction" to C. S. Peirce, *Reasoning and the Logic of Things,* ed. K. L. Ketner (Cambridge, Mass.: Harvard University Press, 1993).

16. In *The Truth about Relativism,* p. 56, Margolis cites Putnam's *The Many Faces of Reason,* pp. 16–22.

17. Richard Rorty, *Philosophy and the Mirror of Nature* (Princeton, N.J.: Princeton University Press, 1979).

18. Cf. Richard Rorty's American Philosophical Association Presidential Address that Margolis cites (59), "Pragmatism, Relativism, Irrationalism," in his

Consequences of Pragmatism (Minneapolis: University of Minnesota Press, 1982), pp. 160–75.

19. For a discussion of Putnam's criticisms of Rorty with full references, see C. G. Hartz, "What Putnam Should Have Said: An Alternative Reply to Rorty," and Putnam's "Reply to Carolyn Hartz" in *Erkenntnis* 34 (1991): 287–95 and 402–404, respectively.

20. See R. Rorty, "Putnam on Truth," and Putnam's response to Rorty as well as to two other critics in his "Truth, Activation Vectors and Possession Conditions for Concepts," in *Philosophy and Phenomenological Research* 52 (1992): passim. Cf. further criticism of Rorty's versions of relativism in Putnam's *Pragmatism* (Cambridge, Mass.: Blackwells, 1995), pp. 74–75.

21. In *How Many Questions,* ed. L. S. Cauman (Indianapolis: Hackett, 1983), p. 56.

22. Rorty cites Davidson's "The Very Idea of a Conceptual Scheme," in Davidson's *Inquiries into Truth and Interpretation* (Oxford: Oxford University Press, 1984), p. 194.

23. Hilary Putnam, *Renewing Philosophy* (Cambridge, Mass.: Harvard University Press, 1992).

24. Note, however, that although relying generally on the idea that meaning is use, Putnam is attentive to Wittgenstein's qualification in the *Philosophical Investigations*, para. 43, that in some cases the meaning of a word is not its use, a point Putnam stresses in his *Gifford Lectures* (Lecture VII).

25. Putnam, *Renewing Philosophy,* Lecture VIII, 164.

26. See J. Conant's discussion of the influence of some of Cavell's ideas on Putnam in H. Putnam, *Realism with a Human Face,* ed. J. Conant (Cambridge, Mass.: Harvard University Press, 1990), pp. lvii–lxxiv.

27. Putnam, *Renewing Philosophy,* p. 177.

28. Ibid., pp. 75 and 178. See also Putnam's preface, "Introducing Cavell," in *Pursuits of Reason* (Lubbock: Texas Technical University Press, 1992).

29. Putnam, *Renewing Philosophy,* Lecture VIII, 178.

30. See K. Myrsiadis's chronologies in *Yannis Ritsos: Selected Poems 1938–1988,* ed. K. Friar and K. Myrsiadis (Brockport, N.Y.: BOA, 1989). The translation is taken from p. 25.

31. For the historical and political backgrounds here on the aftermaths of the civil war and the regime of the colonels, see K. Clogg, *A Concise History of Greece* (Cambridge: Cambridge University Press, 1992), pp. 145–68.

32. See the helpful biographical information in Keeley, *Modern Greek Poetry* (Princeton, N.J.: Princeton University Press, 1983).

Interpretation, Relativism, and Culture: Four Questions for Margolis*

Michael Krausz

In several recent works, Joseph Margolis develops a strategy for accommodating a revised kind of realism and constructionism of cultural entities within a historicist framework. In *The Truth about Relativism* (1991), "Genres, Laws, Canons, Principles" (1992), and, more recently *The Flux of History and the Flux of Science* (1993), he rejects all forms of essentialism. Margolis embraces the theses of (1) cognitive intransparency, (2) the historicity of thinking, (3) the symbiosis of subject and object, and (4) the social constructionism of the self. Taken together, his theses suggest that there is no first philosophy. They lead to the general conclusion that there is no unique solution to interesting philosophical issues. He embraces:

> a strengthened adherence to the cognitive intransparency of the world; an increasingly radicalized sense of the historical nature and conditions of human existence; an insistence on the horizoned, pre-formed, fragmentary, biased cognitive and affective orientation of

---

*This is an expanded version of a paper delivered at the national meeting of the American Society for Aesthetics in Santa Barbara, California, on Thursday, 28 October 1993. Joseph Margolis commented on it, and this version incorporates some of the points made during the discussion. I am grateful for his amplifications on key points.

human life; the impossibility of extricating reason, inquiry, the
reflexive critique of any judgment or commitment from any of the
above conditions; the recognition of divergent and moderately
incommensurable conceptual schemes compatible with the survival of the race; the likelihood that our perceptual and critical
acquaintance with the world has been and continues to be heavily
overdetermined in theorizing and conceptualizing respects; the
realization that we cannot in principle distinguish between the constructed nature of our intelligible world and the "independent"
structure of the brute world; and the admission of the real-world
impossibility of ever judging, except under endogenous constraints, whether we are actually approaching closer to an understanding of all possible conceptual schemes or, using this scheme
or that, closer to the fixed Truth about the world. (1991, 6)

Margolis's so-called "fluxism"—in opposition to an invariant-
ism—is altogether global. That is, his view ranges from mathematics and formal studies to physics, chemistry, and biology; to
sociobiology, linguistics, and economics; to sociology and psychology; to politics and morality; and to the criticism and analysis of the
literatures and the arts. Simply put, for Margolis, all human activity
(including the activity of theorizing about these things) is historical
and therefore cultural.

Margolis is well known for his path-finding theories of relativism and interpretation especially as they apply in the arts, and he
takes the arts as something of a template for the understanding of
all things cultural. No doubt, historicist philosophers of science
such as Thomas Kuhn and Imre Lakatos have fueled Margolis's
vision in those areas.

Margolis rejects Aristotle's view that the real is necessarily
changeless and that whatever changes there are must in turn be embedded in a changeless order. He also rejects the corresponding Aristotelian view that knowledge must be about the changeless. Alterna-
tively, Margolis allies himself with Protagoras, the author of the
theory of the flux, or the theory that the world is in constant change
and that it has no constant structure. On Margolis's account, Protagoras held that knowledge could be claimed for some kind of grasp
of this changing order. Margolis holds that serious philosophers in the
late twentieth century in both the Anglo-American and Continental

European traditions are committed to some version of the double doctrine, namely: (1) The world is not constant. It does not have a constant and changeless structure. And (2) knowledge of that changing order, including logic, mathematics, science, morality, interpretation of the arts, or any other similar discipline, is possible.

Margolis holds that there are no invariant or exceptionless, changeless, timeless, universal principles for a thing properly to be a thing of its kind. For him, to use the same predicate does not commit one to an invariant order. One can use the same predicate in a world that is not invariant. The only account that makes sense to him is one that embeds the notions of sameness and difference in the interests and uses to which creatures put their intelligence. For Margolis, so-called Platonist accounts of universals do not actually bear on any operative discourse or intelligent behavior informed by it. Indeed, invoking changeless forms in a way that people can follow from case to case remains a mystery.

Correspondingly, principles, rules, genres, laws, and so on are abstractions from within some form of life, or practice, or *lebenswelt,* or *lebensform,* or something of that kind. When such forms of life change, the abstractions which arose from earlier enabling cases will have become detached and otiose with respect to new enabling cases. Discourse cannot be formalistically or algorithmically separated from its communicative contexts. Principles, natural kinds, laws, rules, genres, and other like notions should be reinterpreted in such a way that they save any reasonably well-defined discipline or science. Margolis's program—which he calls "an-archic," in contrast with the Aristotelian project—is progressive in the sense that it admits of theoretical advance; it allows for further accommodation of basic ideas such as objectivity, truth, and rationality in a reconstructed light.

Generally, Margolis holds that the intelligible world is articulated under certain conditions of history. What we impute as the real structure of the physical world is itself a function of the historical inquiry of human persons. Yet nature is interpreted in such a way that it does not answer to the "archic" model. On the an-archic model one can recover everything that is needed without losing anything. If one departs from the original archic model, it is just not the case that incoherence is inevitable.

One might object that the theory of the flux is itself subsumable under the archic model. For example, Heraclitus's theory of the flux can be seen as a specification of a higher order archē, an ahistorical principle. But this would be to misunderstand how radical Margolis's proposal is. Not only does he embrace the historicity of particular things, persons, interpreters, and objects of their interpretation. He holds further that the very frameworks or conceptual schemes in terms of which persons understand anything at all cannot be presumed to be fixed outside the context of theorizing to start with. This means that no sense can be made of archic principles, whether they be "the permanent" of Parmenides, or "the flux" of Heraclitus. Heraclitus is still too conservative for Margolis, and it is with this thought that Margolis seeks to reinstate his patron saint Protagoras, who was so summarily dismissed by his contemporaries and so ignored by ours. It was he who deeply threatened the archic tradition of his own time.

Further, according to Margolis's an-archic view, the cognizing subject and the cognized world are symbiotically related. Thus, Margolis moves neither from reality to knowledge (or from ontology to epistemology) as the ancients did, nor from knowledge to reality, as the idealists did. In the first case, he remarks that Aristotle does not tell us why we should suppose that the structure of the real world should be given priority over what it is we claim to know. Further, he notes that Kant's bifurcation of subject and object—which effectively denies the "unanalyzability" of the subject-object symbiosis—is precisely what makes it possible for Kant to theorize that there are *invariant* concepts of understanding in terms of which the world is understood. Rather, on Margolis's view, we postulate both the cognizing agent and the cognized world within a space of "critical reflection," as he puts it. They cannot be disjoined in the way that Kant attempts. The concepts under which we understand the world are themselves historical and changeable. Correspondingly, the knowing subject has no fixed structure, but is a center of cognitive activity which is open to change over time.

This view suggests the idea that human beings are social constructions and cannot be supposed to have invariant structures of understanding. Again, such a social constructionism runs counter to Kant's and Husserl's projects which, according to Margolis, pursued the epistemological counterpart of what Aristotle was doing in ontology. Namely, for them, at the end of inquiry there is a fixed set of concepts in terms of which our world is rendered intelligible. That account fails to come to terms with the fact that the concepts we use are used under certain conditions of historical preformation. Margolis holds that we cannot exit from this condition to claim to be moving in the direction of a unitary account of the changeless conditions of understanding. Correspondingly, human beings have no essential or fixed natures. Rather, they transform or make themselves. Generally, there is no collapse from object to subject nor from subject to object.

I should pause here to register a query. If the knower and the known are symbiotically related, as Margolis suggests, and if, consequently, what we take to be the objects of our knowledge are not thereby independent of our knowing them, what status are we to attach to the distinction between the real and the constructed? It would seem that that distinction between the real and the constructed would be internal to the symbiosis in question. But then how should we understand the distinction between knower and known (in symbiosis)? What sort of idiom would be required for such understanding?

One might well ask whether Margolis really does need to theorize about the status of the distinction between the knower and known, or between the real and the constructed. Might he not dismiss the matter, as, for example, Richard Rorty does, by suggesting that the very question of the status of such distinctions is nonsensical, a remnant of a bygone age of philosophy or metaphysics? Clearly, Margolis does not hold that we live in a postphilosophical or postmetaphysical (or, in parallel, a Dantoesque postartistic) age. His effort is avowedly reconstructive, so the Rortian route looks to Margolis rather like a copout. Well, what does Margolis say about the status of such distinctions?

Margolis says that the symbiosis of subject and object (or of word and world, or of the cognizing and cognized) is, in a special sense, a *myth*. It is a conceptual posit. It provides the space in which distributive claims can be made. Put otherwise, Margolis says that such myths provide the "context of all contexts," or the context in which all distributive claims can be made. Consequently, the thought that subject and object are symbiotically related cannot itself be a particular truth-claim, because particular truth-claims are posited within the space such a myth provides. On this account, the very distinction between epistemology and ontology depends on our being situated in relation to an organizing myth. This distinction is not given independently of a theoretical context, and it may be construed in different ways, depending on various mythic contexts. Yet, there cannot be plural myths from any one context. (In his Reply, Margolis will comment on this last remark.)

Because one is never in a privileged position independent of the context of all contexts, the claim of realism can be made only internally. Such a realism allows for such claims as that certain scientific theories enable us to intervene in nature, and so forth. However, to say that realism is internal rather than external to a subject-object symbiosis does not prohibit us from saying many of the same things about particular things that the naive or direct realist wants to say. On this account, the an-archic view admits the range of particular claims one might wish to make in an archic scheme and more, except, of course, for the modal claim of the flux that the archic scheme denies. Although the an-archic view allows that our survival depends on our contact with a real world, the specific details of that world are always a construction under the conditions of history. Further, this internal realism is not tantamount to idealism, for idealism denies the unanalyzable symbiosis between subject and object.

This sort of internal realism does not inhibit one from distinguishing the reality of the cultural world from the reality of the physical world. In the cultural world, as opposed to the physical world, humans are both the subject and the object of discourse. They are trying to understand *themselves*. This is a remark about a difference in the direction of respective inquiries and not about the natures of things independent of pertinent practices. Correspondingly, objectivity, neutrality, and cognate notions may be unpacked differently by the human sciences and by the physical sciences. The kind of neutrality that may obtain in the physical sciences may not obtain in the human sciences. Unpacking such notions on either side should be understood to be internal to the assumed subject-object symbiosis.

Now, one might ask what legitimates the symbiosis in question. Along Wittgensteinian lines, Margolis answers that it does not make sense to suppose that in a massive way human beings do not understand the form of life that they manifest in their lives. It is preposterous to suppose that we are not generally in touch with the physical and cultural orders. What we take to be the real structure of the world is systematically connected with the descriptions and explanations we take to be central.

One might suggest that there seems to be a problem about how one should talk about the symbiosis of subject and object as a *myth,* or the context of all contexts as a *myth.* Clearly, on Margolis's account all distributive claims have truth-value (or are truth-valued like), but pertinent myths are not; they are neither true nor false, nor are they subject to evidence or argumentation of the sort offered in support of distributive claims. Part of the reason for this is that, if all discourses are contexted, one cannot come to the limit of the space in which the truth-claims are made. And so it is impossible to speak about such discourse *as such* in terms that resemble how we speak about claims within the discourse. On Margolis's view, the mythic, as context for discursive claims, is not "foregrounded" for justification in the ways that discursive claims characteristically are. Being backgrounded, it remains unfathomed at any particular moment in the emergence of inquiry. We cannot speak about discourse from the outside, for any apparently successful attempt to do so will but expand the discourse and so we will have failed to speak from its "outside." But we are not left dumb at this stage, for there are ways of speaking about myths or the context of all contexts that are not truth-valued. That is, we may speak of their being more or less *amenable* to certain ways of thinking and acting; or more or less *perspicuous*; or more or less *apt*; or more or less *illuminating*; or more or less *useful* for one or another theoretical purpose. So we can theorize about the context of all contexts. Language has a discursive function concerned with truth-claims, and it has a mythic function beyond truth-claims. Although we need evidence for discursive claims, we do not, at least in the same ways, for mythic theorizing. In the latter, amenability, perspicuity, aptness, luminosity, usefulness, and further related pragmatic and aesthetic notions enter into consideration.

Margolis's way of understanding such "peripheral" knowledge, as we may call his myths, is not as strange as it might first appear.

We have encountered it, though in a different idiom, in R. G. Collingwood's theory of absolute presuppositions. In the context of a general theory of questions and answers, Collingwood distinguishes between relative and absolute presuppositions (1949). Relative presuppositions are those which answer questions within a systematic inquiry, and they give rise to further questions. But at the base of each systematic inquiry are absolute presuppositions or presuppositions that are absolute or fundamental or basic or constitutive of the given inquiry. And, as pertains to such an inquiry, they answer no questions at all. Collingwood says that only those presuppositions which are relative may be true or false. Yet absolute presuppositions may not be true or false, because they answer no questions. What Collingwood says about the justification of absolute presuppositions, given that we may not speak of them in terms of truth or falsity, is instructive here. He says, quite simply, that we may justify them by noting what they enable when pursuing a pertinent inquiry. Put otherwise, the justification is internal and pragmatic, and, *from within an inquiry,* it is not of a kind in which one has a genuine choice about acceptance or rejection. To change absolute presuppositions is to change one's inquiry. Further, the grounds of legitimation and rationality are holistically tied to the nature of a systematic inquiry to begin with. In this regard, we are reminded of Thomas Kuhn's treatment of the justifiability of a paradigm-based research program from the assumptions within such an inquiry. Like Collingwood's absolute presuppositions, Kuhn's paradigms provide the terms in which questions can be posed within respective inquiries.

We should note an important difference between Margolis's and Collingwood's views. Margolis does not think of discourse in the formally structured ways that Collingwood's hierarchy of questions and answers and his hierarchy of absolute and relative presuppositions suggest. Still, the instructive parallel here concerns the kind of legitimation that is appropriate for both Margolis's myths and Collingwood's absolute presuppositions, namely, it is internal, pragmatic, and aesthetic.

Something of the mystery of Margolis's suggestion that myths are unfathomable disappears when we recall Collingwood's thought that a historian of ideas may come to identify what for another inquirer served as absolute presuppositions. Indeed, that is just what Collingwood thought the proper job of the metaphysician (in his special sense) should be. That is, one's own guiding myths may remain peripherally clouded and incomplete to oneself at any stage of theorizing. But that does not mean that they, or appropriate portions of them, may not in principle be articulated from another historical viewpoint. Margolis's overriding point remains that, however successful one may be in offering anything like a history of Collingwoodian absolute presuppositions, the "logical space" in which they reside cannot be fully accounted, because such accounting itself remains constrained at every stage by the "biased cognitive and affective orientation of human life."

This is perhaps the place to consider the question of globalism. Might we perhaps detach middle-sized ordinary objects such as sticks and stones and mathematical entities and postulate a mythic context only for such highly encultured entities as language, literary or historical texts, scores, works of music and art, and the like? Is it really plausible to regard ordinary middle-sized objects such as sticks and stones or mathematical entities such as the number three as having intentional histories to start with, albeit of a different kind from other sorts of would-be cultural entities? Do all these entities really require a mythic context? Specifically, one might well argue that the existence of a multiplicity of geometries coheres nicely with a view that urges that formal systems are relativized to discrete assumptions and purposes which may vary over context and historical time. But when we consider such cases as resilient as arithmetical truths, like "Two plus two equals four," the invariance exhibited there seems stronger than that which a theory of the flux would seem to be able to accommodate. Of course, empirical theories of numbers are not new, and, fueled with Quinean arguments against necessary truths, one might well imagine the lines that a fluxist argument for arithmetical truths might pursue.

Margolis might well respond by saying that the suggestion that the thesis of the flux might be urged on a piecemeal basis is one that implicates an ontology which precisely is denied by his thesis of symbiosis. That is, the piecemeal/global issue can be pressed only on the condition that there are some domains whose objects answer to a realist construal and other domains whose objects answer to a constructionist construal. In short, realism can be articulated independently of constructionism and constructionism independently of realism. But on Margolis's view, these ontologies are not logically detachable. Rather, constructionism and realism are symbiotically related in such a way that the real is constructed and the constructed is real. To Margolis it makes no sense to say that the real is independent of the constructed or that the constructed is independent of the real. There is no construal of objects that can be parceled by domain. For Margolis, there is no way of articulating a piecemeal ontology on pain of denying the symbiosis in question. So, although the offered piecemeal strategy might appear to be benign to start with, the very acceptance of it terms assumes an ontology that significantly departs from Margolis's view. For Margolis the real and the constructed are symbiotized within a myth. Consequently, the context of all contexts cannot be inventoried at any particular stage of theorizing. And this ever-deferring strategy is certainly consistent with Margolis's general dictum: "no first philosophy."

So far I have been speaking of Margolis's fluxism, which is a mythic development of some of his earlier characterizations of relativism. Indeed, Margolis has come to see that relativism is perhaps a consequence of—even perhaps a side issue to—the sorts of questions touched upon above. But it is important for our purposes to consider his earlier, more restricted characterizations of relativism as a logical thesis.

Considering competing interpretations of a cultural entity (a poem, a work of visual art, or a work of music, for example), Margolis does not require closure or the elimination of all logical tension between competing interpretations. In this regard, Margolis's view contrasts with the views of Monroe Beardsley, E. D. Hirsch, and others who, however interesting and important their differences are, agree that ideally there ought to be full convergence with no logical tension. Of them, Margolis says that they have favored "exclusively correct and comprehensive interpretations; but none has *shown* why non-converging interpretations cannot be legitimately defended" (1980, 157).

Margolis capitalizes on the possibility that nonconverging interpretations can be legitimately defended, not as an interim or tolerable condition approaching an ideal condition of full convergence, but rather as a condition that is itself ideally admissible. Margolis holds that this condition reflects the nature of cultural entities and their interpretations. His view about the possibility that nonconvergence may be ideally admissible is tied to his view that one cannot clearly individuate a given work of art or a cultural entity; one cannot clearly say what is *in* a given work and what is not. He holds that cultural entities are ontically indeterminate.

Margolis holds that we should be as inclusive as possible about ideally admissible interpretations of cultural entities. Although he does not countenance contradictory pairs of interpretations (in a bipolar logic), he holds that characteristically bipolar values are inappropriately applied to interpretations of cultural entities. Rather, he invokes values other than truth (understood in a bipolar way), including plausibility, aptness, reasonableness, appropriateness, and the like. These are not to be understood as stand-ins for bipolar truth or falsity. Margolis holds that there is no reductive strategy in virtue of which such "plausibility-type" values are reducible to bipolar truth or falsity. With this caveat, he tolerates competition between so-called incongruent interpretations. Interpretations are incongruent if, on a bipolar logic, they would be contradictory; but on a many-valued logic they are not. This is part and parcel of what Margolis calls a relativistic logic.

Margolis's relativistic logic is closely tied to his view of the indeterminacy of cultural entities. He says,

> Nothing could be referentially fixed that did not exhibit a certain stability of nature; but how alterable (or by what means altered) the life of a person or the restored *Last Supper* or the oft-interpreted *Hamlet* or the theoretically intriguing *Fountain* or the marvelously elastic *Sarrasine* may be is *not* a matter that can be decided, or that is actually determined merely, by fixing such texts or artworks *as* the reidentifiable referents they are. (1989b, 241–42)

It is here that Margolis's account of imputational interpretation enters. About imputational interpretation, Margolis says,

> There is no reason why, granting that criticism proceeds in an orderly way, practices cannot be sustained in which aesthetic designs are rigorously *imputed* to particular works when they cannot be determinately *found* in them. Also, if they may be imputed rather than found, there is no reason why incompatible designs cannot be jointly defended. (1980, 160)

Insofar as attributes or features may be imputed to particular works in different ways in different circumstances, one wonders whether or not the results of such imputation are sufficiently divergent that one no longer has a basis for talking about different interpretations of *one* work as opposed to different interpretations of *different* works. In the latter case, the condition of competition between the two interpretations would not obtain. This latter condition would amount to an innocuous pluralism. But, Margolis wishes to capture the idea that under different imputations we may still talk of one work of art. (See his 1989b, for example.) This is possible on the condition that there is in place a soft notion of individuation (in contrast with identity) or "unicity." For example, we may say that the same self develops in the process of self-development, but the notion of self-development is not an oxymoron. As well, such unicity obtains for the individuation of a work of art: The "same" work is imputed and interpreted differently in different circumstances. At least such a condition as unicity is required for competition between two interpretations of a "given" work.

The question of unicity is closely tied to Margolis's view of the admissibility of incongruent interpretations, as evidenced in the parenthetical remarks in the following paragraph:

> Thus, musical interpretations A and B of Brahms's *Fourth Symphony* or literary interpretations A and B of *Hamlet* are incompatible in the straightforward sense that there is no interpretation C in which A and B can be combined. But that is not to say that A and B cannot both be plausible. (The equivocation on "A" and "B" is benign enough.) When, therefore, I say that "we allow seemingly incompatible accounts of a given work . . . to stand as confirmed," I mean to draw attention . . . to the fact that the accounts in question would be incompatible construed in terms of a model of truth and falsity, but are not incompatible construed in terms of plausibility. (1980, 164)

Margolis's claims about the indeterminacy of cultural entities and the contestability of the imputing terms for such entities significantly undercuts the nonimputationalist program that is committed to the idea that pertinent entities simply have certain properties independently of their interpretation and that such entities either do or do not have them. It undercuts the idea that in the long run, under ideal conditions, there must always be one right interpretation.

Yet what is to prevent one from imputing outlandish properties to cultural entities, and from countenancing outlandish interpretations of them? Margolis here turns to the idea of consensus or consensual memory of pertinent communities of practitioners. That is, leaning on his extensive work on social intentionality—as opposed to individual intentionality—he holds that, however muted, pertinent constraints are to be found in the norms, procedures, values, and other constituent features of Wittgensteinian forms of life. Yet there is no algorithmic procedure for applying these.

I wish now to raise a question of nomenclature and strategy. Margolis says, "It takes little imagination to see that admitting that judgments which are incompatible on the model of assigning truth-values (true and false) may be jointly defended in terms of the assignment of other values is tantamount to the adoption of a *form* of relativism" (1980, 160). Margolis has relished defending relativism against critics who have taken relativism to be something rather different from what Margolis takes it to be. One might ask why should Margolis call his position relativist? Does his heterodox construal of the term do any argumentative or strategic work for him? Is Margolis taking on extra rhetorical baggage which, in the end, might deflect one's attention from his insights about the indeterminacy of cultural entities, the contestability of their imputations, and the admissibility of incongruent interpretations?

In holding that his construal captures the spirit behind Protagoras's much misinterpreted view (the greatest misinterpreter being Plato), Margolis seeks to undo the bad press that relativism has gotten throughout its history. (See Margolis, 1989a.) This in itself may be an important issue, and it raises interesting questions about why and how it is that historians of ideas might have gotten it so wrong for so long. But, one wonders why Margolis ties this historical question so closely to his more textured substantive view.

The traditional criticism of relativism has been that it is either incoherent or false. So Margolis sets out to correct this criticism by indicating that the doctrine, appropriately adjusted *and* faithful to its original spirit, is neither incoherent nor false. But why not leave the adjustment as is, without invoking any putative historical connection between his view and classical relativism? Why cloud the case for incongruent interpretations with the difficulties associated with the history of relativism? As interesting as Margolis's suggestions are about relativism's original spirit, it remains historically contentious, still to be taken up as a separate research project in its own right. What philosophical pay-off is there for Margolis to tag his substantive view as relativist while actually arguing for his substantive view? Margolis's answer is that his relativistic logic just is part and parcel of the claim that "judgments which are incompatible on the model of assigning truth-values (true and false) may be jointly defended in terms of the assignment of other values is tantamount to the adoption of a *form* of relativism" (1980, 160). And that is not prey to the traditional criticisms of relativism.

Relativism is characteristically associated with the view that one may assign *contradictory* (bipolar) truth-values to interpretations of a given object-of-interpretation. Why stipulate that (non-bipolar) incongruence rather than (bipolar) contradiction should be characteristic of relativism? Why need Margolis take on the job of arguing for the propriety of construing relativism in this way? What difference would it make to his substantive view were one to trivialize the issue by just saying, "Well, if *that's* what relativism is, then, all right, have your relativism"?

If one were to insist that relativism should be understood as that thesis which allows for the possibility of assigning contradictory bipolar truth-values to competing interpretations, then Margolis's view would not be relativist. But again, why not leave aside this question of nomenclature, and affirm, rather, that what is important in Margolis's view is his allowance that there may be incongruent though not logically contradictory interpretations of a cultural object-of-interpretation? Is Margolis's argumentative strategy needlessly overburdened in this regard?

To all this Margolis could answer along the following lines: The admissibility of incongruent interpretations is not separable from the thesis of relativism, because relativism—in its most generous formulation—amounts to the rejection of a bipolar logic in pertinent practices. And one cannot make sense of the admissibility of incongruent interpretations without rejecting bipolar logic in such practices. In short, relativism is part and parcel of the thesis of incongruent interpretability. Relativism is no extra baggage.

We may now enumerate our four questions and sketch Margolis's answers to them.

First is the question of globalism. More pointedly, why not restrict the thesis of the flux to such cultural intentional entities as works of art, literature, language, and the like, but exclude other entities such as ordinary middle-sized objects (such as sticks and stones) or numbers (such as one, two, and three)? If Margolis were to answer that his globalism derives from his *general* denial of modal necessity, then we would ask why the denial of modal necessity must be general? More specifically, could one not deny modal necessity to all studies except, say, inquiries into middle-sized objects or mathematics and other formal studies?

Margolis answers that the thesis of the flux has to be global because the cognizing self and the cognized world are symbiotically related and that condition obtains irrespective of which universe of discourse is in question. Correspondingly, such universes are artifactually posited. It is within the context of the symbiosis that we distinguish cultural discourse from natural discourse from mathematical discourse, and so on. Specifically, Margolis distinguishes the cultural from the natural by observing that cultural entities intrinsically have intentional structures whereas natural entities do not. But their being posited in this way depends on the life of a society. However we parcel various types of entities, we are culturally endowed inquirers under changing historical circumstances. So the very observation that physical or mathematical entities lack intentionality is itself postulated in accord with an epistemic theory as to why the world has the kind of structure it does. The languages of mathematics, of the physical sciences, and of the cultural disciplines, are controlled by the same sort of symbiotizing conditions. Put otherwise, denying the globalism of the theory of the flux would be tantamount to affirming that the cognizing self and the cognized world are not symbiotized in some universe of discourse, and that such universes are not artifactually posited. On Margolis's view one gives up the idea of *de re* necessities: There are no necessary structures in the world. Yet this allows apparent necessities, seen as such from within the perspective of one's historical place. Accordingly, lawlike generalizations in science turn out to be idealizations within a designated idiom of inquiry. Whatever necessities that obtain are apparent and internal to a discourse that itself is not necessary. Whatever regularities appear in the ongoing inquiry of a society are, in this way, posited. Only *de re* necessity is denied. Specifically in the case of mathematics, Margolis holds that one manipulates uninterpreted formal systems and posited entities, assuming certain axioms, postulates, rule of derivation, and the like. They are comprised of completely artifactual games. Correspondingly, mathematical entities are nominalizations of mathematical predicables. Whatever claims we may make about the reality of such entities are made within the context of a symbiotized language that is posited in a historical circumstance. Although one may say that numbers are real, that cannot be taken to mean that they exist outside the horizon of one's state of inquiry at a particular historically constituted moment.

Second is the question of relative flux, or what I have on another occasion referred to as the molasses problem. That is, on the concession that all is fluxed, how can one be assured that there are sufficiently thick constraints on questions of rationality and the like to avoid arbitrariness? Margolis's answer centers around the notion of consensus and consensual memory. But what, precisely, is consensual memory? Is there such a thing as a mistaken consensual memory, and if so, on what independent basis could we identify such mistakes? Put otherwise, if all is fluxed, how can something be more fluxed than others? How can one make particular claims against a background of relative but not absolute invariance?

Margolis answers that, as regards newly considered distributive claims, appropriate discriminations can be made within the context of what pertinent fluxed practices hold to be more or less entrenched. Invariance is not required for the life of praxial activity. Margolis locates the grounds for discriminating between distributive claims within the consensual memory of pertinent practitioners under specifiable historical circumstances. To the question about mistaken consensual memory, Margolis answers that consensual memory is not criterial. It does not function in such a way as to determine which distributive claims are acceptable or not. This answer might seem paradoxical, for it might be thought that it was for the sake of discrimination of distributive claims that the point of consensual memory was invoked in the first place. But this is not so. For Margolis, consensual memory is always holistic and not criterial. What does the criterial work is what is invented within the space of consensual memory, which is to say, the actual functioning of practices. Consequently, there is no such thing as a mistaken consensual memory, on his view. Whether a memory is mistaken is a criterial matter and consensual memory does not operate that way. For Margolis, the question whether consensual memory may be mistaken does not arise. We should not be misled by what the term memory might suggest by a nonspecific usage. To be sure, memory claims are usually concerned with distributive claims. But this is not the case in Margolis's usage. Here one can be no more wrong about consensual memory than one can be wrong about what Wittgenstein took to be the whole body of beliefs taken massively. This is what Margolis calls consensual memory. Thus consensual memory does not operate in regard to such questions as whether a law is to be pronounced constitutional, or whether a revisionist account of the holocaust is acceptable, and so on.

Third is the question of the status of myths. That is, if the distinction between real and constructed is one internal to myths, it would seem that it would be inappropriate to ask whether myths are real or constructed (or indeed whether they are some combination of the two). But then what analogous ways of speaking of the status of myths are appropriate? Or, do such questions not arise at all?

Margolis answers that all distributive claims are contexted. And distributive discourse cannot provide its own discursive context. So there is an inherent informality about distributive discourse and its context. Yet, he says, we develop pictures of the inclusive context within which our distibutive discourse proceeds, although we cannot make truth-claims about such pictures. We cannot distributively talk about the context of discourse, for doing so would violate the conditions under which we could distibutively talk in the first place. In this way, there is a permanent limit to the inclusiveness of our distibutive discourse. We cannot escape this mythic dimension. At the same time, the mythic is not determinately there beyond the discursive barriers. Rather, the mythic is embedded in the discourse in every point in which we speak. Every utterance of a discursive sort implicates the inclusive universe of discourse in which it and every other such utterance belongs. We can speak of myths. Yet, the "context of all contexts" cannot itself be a determinate referent of distributive truth-valued discourse. We implicate it, but we can never invoke it so as to make it the object or subject of some further remark. One result of this picture is that it is impossible to give an account of what is general in the world in terms of *real* "generals" separate from the historical life of a particular community. That is, to say that something is like this rather than that draws upon the collective memory of a society rather than upon a preexistent Platonic order of things. Correspondingly, the Platonistic idiom of isolatable universals is, for Margolis, a nonstarter. It does not come to terms with the cognitive conditions under which we say that this is similar to that.

Fourth is the question of the nomenclature for the important thesis of multiple interpretability. That is, why call that thesis "relativist" rather than something more neutral such as "multiplist"? Why take on the extra philosophical baggage that the history of the term suggests?

Margolis answers that there is no reason why there should not be certain domains in which it would make sense to retire bivalent logic. If there are two or thirty reasonable interpretations of Hamlet, say, and, in confirming one we don't want to reject all others as false because they, on a bivalent logic, are incompatible with the one we accept then, Margolis suggests, we should retire bivalence in such cases. Margolis calls incongruent judgments those which, on a bivalent logic, would yield contradictions but no longer do so. In accord with a many-valued logic, one can agree to incongruent judgments. Margolis's account of incongruence takes the following negative form: X and Y are incongruent if, on a bipolar logic, they would be contradictory, but on a multivalent logic they are not. One wonders what, on a multivalued logic, the positive characterization of the relation between X and Y would look like. In any case, I have asked why we should call this substantive view "relativism."

Indeed, many people might well agree to retiring bipolar logic under these circumstances. But they might not agree to calling such retirement relativism or to associating it with the history of relativism, or having anything to do with relativism. Why should they?

Margolis answers that merely replacing bivalent logic is not sufficient for relativism. Indeed, in probabilistic logics one retires bivalence, but such logics are not on that account relativistic. Rather, relativism requires that under certain circumstances bivalent logic should be replaced by a many-valued logic, *and* that incongruent judgments can stand as confirmed. Of course, confirmation here should be understood in terms of aptness or reasonableness or something of the kind, rather than truth understood in a bivalent way Margolis holds that relativism requires both of those elements, and not just the first. And he holds that we should call this double condition relativism, because that is a solution to the problem which both Plato and Aristotle saw in Protagoras. It is not unreasonable, reasons Margolis, to say that this reconstruction is a resolution of the classic problem of relativism. We should therefore dub it a revised relativism, indeed a robust relativism.

Such are my four questions and responses to Margolis's answers. I look forward to his follow-up comments in this volume as he presses forward in articulating one of the pathbreaking philosophical projects of the present generation.

BIBLIOGRAPHY

Beardsley, Monroe. 1970. "The Authority of the Text." In *The Possibility of Criticism.* Detroit: Wayne State University Press.

Collingwood, R. G. 1949. *Essays on Metaphysics.* Oxford: Clarendon Press.

Hirsch, E. D. Jr. 1967. "In Defense of the Author." In *Validity in Interpretation.* New Haven: Yale University Press.

Margolis, Joseph. 1980. "Robust Relativism." In *Art and Philosophy: Conceptual Issues in Aesthetics.* Atlantic Highlands, N.J.: Humanities Press.

———. 1989a. "The Truth about Relativism." In *Relativism: Interpretation and Confrontation,* ed. Michael Krausz. South Bend, Ind.: Notre Dame University Press, pp. 232–55.

———. 1989b. "Reinterpreting Interpretation." *Journal of Aesthetics and Art Criticism* 47 (Summer): 237–51.

———. 1991. *The Truth about Relativism.* Oxford: Basil Blackwell.

Margolis, Joseph. 1992. "Genres, Laws, Canons, Principles." In *Rules and Conventions,* ed. Mette Hjort. Baltimore: Johns Hopkins University Press.

———. 1993. *The Flux of History and the Flux of Science.* Los Angeles: University of California Press.

PART II

Relativism

The Limits of Cognitive Relativism

Nicholas Rescher

COGNITIVE RELATIVISM

Relativism is the doctrine that people make their judgments by standards and criteria that have no inherent validity or cogency because their standing and status lies solely and wholly in the altogether "external" consideration of their acceptance by the group. The norms of different schools of thought differ, but those different norms are entirely on a par with one another.

In its general form, this relativist position has two prime components:

1. *Basis Diversity.* Judgments of the sort at issue—be it the true, or for that matter the good, the right, and so on—are always made relative to a potentially variable basis: a norm, standard, criterion, or evaluative perspective regarding acceptability that change from one group to another.
2. *Basis Egalitarianism.* Any and every basis of normative appraisal—any and every such standard of assessment—is intrinsically as good (valid, appropriate) as any other.

Egalitarian relativism in general holds that it is no more rational to opt for one alternative than for any of its rivals.

Relativism thus understood does not deny that those who have a particular commitment (who belong to a particular school or tendency of thought) do indeed have a standard of judgment of some sort. But it insists that only custom speaks for that standard—that it is nothing more than just another contingent characteristic of the cognitive position of that particular group. It is all a matter of the parochial allegiances of the community—there is no larger, group-transcending "position of impersonal rationality" on whose basis one particular standard could reasonably and appropriately be defended as inherently superior to any other. The cognitive relativist, in particular, insists that no actual or possible group of inquirers whatsoever is in a privileged epistemic position. Every group's resolutions in this regard are final; each is its own final arbiter. There is no higher court of appeal—no inherently cogent basis of cognitive acceptability that has any real claim to validity.

Such cognitive relativism holds that there is no inherently good reasons for thinking some possibilities to be better candidates for claims to truth (more probable or plausible). The cognitive relativist does not go so far as to join the nihilistic skeptic in *rejecting* the reality of truth—he simply denies that there is no such thing as a good reason for applying this idea in any particular case.

Relativism insists that the difference between fact and opinion may be all very nice in theory but simply unimplementable in practice. Whatever we may see as constituting "our knowledge" is simply a matter of opinion through and through. And one opinion is every bit as justified as any other. It's all just a matter of what people think. To believe anything else is no more than a recourse to the myth of the god's-eye point of view—a point of view which, in the very nature of things cannot possibly be ours.

Over the last century, indifferentist relativism of this sort has gathered strength from various modern intellectual projects. As the sciences of man developed in the nineteenth century—especially in historical and sociological studies—the idea increasingly gained acceptance that every culture and every era has its own characteristic fabric of thought and belief, each appropriate to and cogent for its own particular context. Historicist thinkers from Wilhelm

Dilthey onward have lent the aid and comfort of their authority to cultural relativism. And the aftermath of Darwinian biology reinforced this doctrinal tendency in giving currency to the idea that our human view of reality is formatively dependent on our characteristically human cognitive endowments—as opposed to those of other possible sorts of intelligent creatures. Not only are the data about the world that we can acquire something that comes to us courtesy of the biological endowment of our senses, but the inferences we can draw from those data will be analogously dependent on the biological endowment of our minds. Various turn-of-the-century philosophers of otherwise very diverse theoretical orientations—ranging from Nietzsche and Vaihinger to Henri Bergson and Samuel Alexander—all drew heavily on Darwinian inspirations to support a syncretist perspectivism of one sort or another. Under such inspiration, William James wrote:

> Were we lobsters, or bees, it might be that our organization would
> have led to our using quite different modes from these [actual
> ones] of apprehending our experiences. It *might* be too (we
> cannot dogmatically deny this) that such categories, unimagin-
> able by us today, would have proved on the whole as serviceable
> for handling our experiences mentally as those we actually use.[1]

Different cultures and different intellectual traditions, to say nothing of organically different sorts of creatures, will, so it is contended, describe and explain their experience—their world as they conceive it—in terms of concepts and categories of understanding substantially different from ours but in principle every bit as good. Anthropological and sociological investigations militated toward relativism on similar grounds. Moreover, psychologically inspired thinkers such as F. S. C. Schiller and John Dewey were also impelled in very much the same direction.

In this way, investigations in various modern fields of inquiry have conspired to provide aid and comfort for the partisans of cognitive relativism.

ALTERNATIVE MODES OF RATIONALITY?

Émile Durkheim was no doubt right in insisting that "all that constitutes reason, its principles and categories, is made (by particular societies operating) in the course of history."[2] But the fact that everyone's standards and criteria of rational cognition (etc.) are historically and culturally conditioned—our own of course included—certainly does not preclude their having a rationally binding stringency for those to whom they appertain, ourselves emphatically included. In conducting our affairs in this world—as in conducting our movements within it—we have no choice but to go on from where we are. If we are rational, then our standards and criteria of rationality presumably came to be ours precisely because we deem them to be (not necessarily the best possible in theory, but at any rate) the best available to us in practice on the basis of those considerations that we can conscientiously maintain.

But are the beliefs of primitive, prescientific cultures indeed less rational than ours? A resounding negative is maintained in Peter Winch's widely cited article on "Understanding a Primitive Society,"[3] which argues that Azande beliefs about witchcraft and oracles cannot be rejected as rationally inappropriate despite their clear violation of the evidential canons of modern Western scientific culture. But just here lies the problem. "Are those beliefs of theirs rational?" differs importantly from "Are those beliefs of theirs held rationally?" The answer you get depends on the question you ask. If we ask "Are those beliefs they hold rational?" we, of course, mean "*rational* on our understanding of the matter." And the answer here is clearly *no,* seeing that by hypothesis our sort of rationality does not figure in *their* thinking at all. The fact that they (presumably) deem their beliefs somehow "justified" by some considerations or other that they see as appropriate is going to cut no ice in *our* deliberations regarding the cogency of those beliefs. ("Are they being 'rational' by *their* lights?" is one thing and "Are they being rational by *our* lights?" another.) When *we* ask about the rational acceptability of those beliefs, we mean the issue to be considered from *our* point of view, and not from somebody else's!

The issues that arise at this juncture go back to the quarrel between E. E. Evans-Pritchard and Lucien Lévy-Bruhl. In his book on *Primitive Mentality*,[4] Lévy-Bruhl maintained that primitive people have a "pre-logical mentality." Against this view, Evans-Pritchard[5] argued that primitive people were perfectly "logical" all right, but simply used a logic *different* from ours. When, for example, the Nuer maintain that swamp light *is identical with* spirit, but deny that spirit *is identical with* swamp light, they are not being illogical, but simply have in view a logic of "identity" variant from that in vogue in Western cultures. The obvious trouble with this sort of thing is that nothing apart from bafflement and confusion can result from translating Nuer talk into *our* identity language if indeed it is the case that what is at issue in their thought and discourse nowise answers to our identity conception. Instead of translating the claim at issue as "Swamp light is identical with Spirit" and then going on to explain that "is identical with" does not really mean what it says because the ground rules that govern this idea are not applicable, an anthropologist would do well to reformulate or paraphrase (if need be) the claim at issue in such a way as to render intelligible what is actually going on. The fact that the Nuer have different (and to us strange-seeming) beliefs about "spirits" no more means that they have a logic different from ours than the fact that they communicate by drums mean that they have a telephone system different from ours.[6] To reemphasize: When we ask about logical acceptability, it is logical acceptability by *our* lights that is at issue.

Anthropologists do sometimes say that a certain society has a conception of rationality that is different from ours. But that is literally nonsense. Those others can no more have a conception of rationality that addresses an object different from ours than they can have a conception of iron that addresses an object different from ours, or a conception of elephants that addresses objects different from ours. If they are to conceive of *those* particular things at all, then their conception must substantially accord with ours. Iron objects are *by definition* what we take them to be; "elephant" is our word and *elephant* our conception. If you are not talking about *that*, then you are not talking about *elephants* at all. You have simply "changed the subject" and exited from the domain of the discussion. Similarly, if a conception of theirs (whatever it be) is not close to what *we* call rationality, then it just is not a conception of *rationality*—it does not address the topic that we are discussing when we put the theme of rationality on the agenda. Rationality as we ourselves see it is a matter of striving intelligently for appropriate resolutions—using *relevant* information and *cogent* principles of reasoning in the resolution of one's conjunctive and practical problems. If that is not what they are after, then it is not *rationality* that concerns them. The issues at stake in *our* deliberations have to be the issues as *we* construe them.

Of course, they may *think* that what we call pencils are chopsticks and use them as such. Or they may *think* books to be doorstops and use them as such. But that does not mean that they conceive pencils or books differently from us, or that they have a different conception of pencils and books. "They take pencils to be something we do not (namely chopsticks)" is fine as a way of talking. But "They believe pencils to be chopsticks" is nonsense unless it is glossed as: "They believe these sorts of things called 'pencils' to be chopsticks." And when this happens, then they do not conceive of pencils differently from ourselves, they just do not conceive of pencils at all. They simply do not have the (one and only) available conception of pencils—namely, ours. In such cases, if they do not have *our* concept, then they just do not have *the* concept.

There is no difficulty with the idea that "They implement and *apply* the conception of rationality differently from ourselves." After all, we implement and apply the idea of a medication very differently from the ancient Greeks, using medications they never dreamt of. But the matter stands differently with the *conception* of a medication. This remains what it always has been: "a substance used as a remedy for an ailment." When one ceases to operate with what answers to that conception, then (*ex hypothesi*) one is no longer dealing with medications at all. The discussion has moved on to other topics. To have "a *different* conception" of pencils or elephants or rational actions is simply not to have that conception at all. If they do not have *our* conception of scissors, they do not have *a* conception of scissors, full stop. For, when we ask about their dealings with scissors, it is our own conception that defines the terms of reference. If we recognize agents as rational at all, then we ourselves can make good rational sense of what they do! This is not because *we* are so talented and versatile, nor yet because the slogan "rationality is universal" gets it right. It is just because we could not and would not say that they are rational (could not and would not characterize the phenomena in this particular way) if we could not make rational sense of what they do.

So, it is literally nonsense to say, "The X's have a different conception of rationality from the one we have." For, if they do not have ours, they do not have any. It is, after all, rationality as we conceive of it that is at issue in this discussion of ours. Whatever analogue or functional equivalent there may be with which they are working, it just is not something that we, in our language, can call "a conception of rationality."

The pivotal fact lies in a "questioner's prerogative." Because the question "What is their mode of rationality?" is *ours,* so is the "rationality" that is at stake here. Thus, on the crucial issues— "What is rationality all about?" "What sorts of considerations characterize the rationality at issue?" "What is appropriately at stake?" —it is our own position that is determinative. When the questions are ours, the concepts that figure in them are ours as well. At this stage of establishing the constitutive ground rules of appropriateness for rationality, it is *our own position* that is decisive.

Gestalt switches are certainly possible, but they are just that: unpredictable leaps. We do not reason our way into them by the use of existing standards—if it were so it would be an implementation of the old standard that is at issue and not, as per hypothesis, a Gestalt switch. They are only seen as rational *ex post facto,* from the vantage point of the *then* prevailing "established" standard—that is, the new one. Consider the contention: "Surely there are no historically and culturally invariant principles of rationality. People's (altogether plausible) views about what is rational change with changes in place and time." The response here is yes and no. Of course, different people in different places and times conduct their "rational" affairs quite differently. But, at the level of basics, of first fundamentals, there is bound to be a uniformity. For, what all modes of "rationality" have in common is precisely this—they all qualify as "modes of rationality" under *our* conception of the matter (which, after all, is what we're talking about). At this level of delib-

eration, "questioner's prerogative" prevails, and our own conception of the matter becomes determinative.

It is helpful to contemplate some analogies. There are many
sorts of blades for knives. But, the fundamental principle that
knives have blades at all does not depend on how people choose to
make knives but on *our conception* of what a "knife" is. If the given
objects, whatever they might be, do not have *blades* then they are
not knives. It would, clearly, be the height of folly to go about in
another culture asking people "Must knives have blades?" The
answer is a foregone conclusion. A negative response would not
counterindicate the thesis at issue, but would simply betoken a
failure to comprehend.

Again, there are various quite different sorts of information that
people take as evidence to substantiate a claim. But "deeper" principles such as "Give more credence to that for which the evidence
is stronger" or "In inquiry, endeavor to expand and extend the evidence for your claims" do not depend on the evidential practices of
people, but on *our conception* of what evidence is all about. If
people do not proceed in ways that conform to these evidential conceptions and principles of ours, then their practices—whatever they
might be—are not *evidential* practices.

And so, in discussions about "alternative modes of rationality,"
we do indeed have a "higher standpoint" available to us—namely
our own. And this is rationally justified by the consideration that no
real alternative is open to us—we have to go on from where we are.
Accordingly, while one must recognize the reality of alternative
cognitive methodologies, one certainly need not see them as equally
valid with one's own. "You have your standards and I have mine.
There are alternatives." True enough. But this fact leaves me unaf-
fected. For, I myself have no real choice about it: I *must* judge matters by my own lights. (Even if I turn to you as a consultant, I must
ultimately appraise the acceptability of your recommendations on
my own terms.)

A FOOTHOLD OF ONE'S OWN: THE PRIMACY OF OUR OWN STANDARDS OF RATIONALITY

Despite its fashionable pervasiveness, however, cognitive relativism has serious and indeed gravely debilitating defects. And in the main, these inhere in its commitment to basis egalitarianism.

The crucial question, however, is not "Are there indeed different norms and standards of rationality?" where the answer is an immediate and emphatic "yes." (Just as *autres temps, autres moeurs,* so also, other cultures, other standards.) Rather, the salient question is "Are we well advised—perhaps even rationally obligated—to see all those various alternative norms and standards as equally appropriate, equally correct?" Must we adopt that Principle of Basis Egalitarianism: "All of the various standards of judgment have equivalent justifications. *Ours* is on an equal footing with *theirs* in point of acceptability. It is a matter of indifference which basis we adopt—each one is every bit as good (or poor) as the next"? And here the answer is an immediate and emphatic "no." There is no good and sufficient reason to see this principle as plausible. Basis indifferentism is daring and exciting—but also absurd. For, at this point we must turn relativism against itself by asking: *"Indifferent to whom?"* Certainly not to us! For, we have in place our own basis of rational judgment, and it speaks loud and clear on its own behalf. Nor yet by parity of reasoning is *ours* equally acceptable to *them.* From just what "angle of consideration" is it that claim to merit equivalency going to be made? Not from ours surely—for this, after all, is ours precisely because we deem it superior. And by parity of reasoning not from *theirs* either. (From God's? Perhaps. But he, of course, is not a party to the discussion—and if he were, then what price relativism?)

Perhaps from the point of view of the universe all experiential perspectives are of equivalent merit, and perhaps they are equal before the World Spirit—or even God. But we ourselves cannot assume the prerogative of these mighty potencies. We humans can no more contemplate information with our minds without having a perspectival stance than we can contemplate material objects with our bodily eyes without having a perspectival stance. We ourselves do and must occupy a particular position, with particular kinds of concerns and particular practical and intellectual tools for dealing with them. And for us, there indeed is one particular set of standards for making such appraisals and adjudications, namely, our own—the one we actually accept in the conditions and circumstances of our existences. (And were we to trade this set of standards in for another, then of course that other one would automatically become ours.)

In approving positions we have, of course, no alternative to doing so from the perspective of our cognitive posture—our own cognitive position and point of view. (It wouldn't *be* our point of view if we didn't use it as such.) We cannot cogently maintain a posture of indifference. Each thinker, each school, is bound to take a strongly negative stand toward its competitors: belittling their concerns, deploring their standards, downgrading their ideals, disliking their presuppositions, scorning their contentions, and so on.

Cognitive (or evaluative or aesthetic, etc.) standard-perspectives do not come to us ex nihilo. From the rational point of view such standards themselves require validation. And this process is itself something that is standard presupposing. For, of course, we cannot assess the adequacy of a standard-perspective in a vacuum, it must itself be supported with reference to standards of some sort. But in this world we are never totally bereft of such a basis: In the order of thought as in the world's physical order, we always have a position of some sort. By the time one gets to the point of being able to think at all, there is always a background of available experience against which to form one's ideas. And just there is where one has to start. It is precisely because a standard-deploying certain position is appropriate *from where we ourselves actually stand* that makes this particular position of ours appropriate *for us.*

The salient point is that we are entitled—indeed, rationally constrained—to see our own criteriological basis of rational judgment as rationally superior to the available alternatives. If we did not take this stance—if we did not deem our cognitive posture effectively optimal—then we could not sensibly see ourselves as rationally justified in adopting it. We cannot responsibly think that this variant scheme as co-meritorious with our own, because (if rational) it is precisely because we deem that scheme superior that we have made it ours. It would, ipso facto, fail to be our real position—contrary to hypothesis.

In the final analysis, one can and should turn the weapons of relativism against itself. If indeed each group has its own standards against which there is no further, external, higher appeal, then we ourselves have no viable alternative but to see our conception of rationality as decisive for any judgments that we conscientiously make on these matters.

If we are going to be rational we must take—and have no responsible choice but to take—the stance that our own standards (of truth, value, and choice) are the appropriate ones. Be it in employing or in evaluating them, we ourselves must see our own standards as definitive because just exactly this is what it is for them to *be* our own standards—their being our standards *consists in our seeing them in this light.* To say that we are not entitled to view our standards as definitive could be to our having standards at all. And, of course, someone who denies us this right—who says that we are not entitled to adopt those standards of ours—does no more than insist that it is by *his or her* standards (who else's) inappropriate for us to have these standards, and thus is simply pitting his or her standards against ours. We have to see our standards in an absolutistic light— as the uniquely right appropriately valid ones—because exactly this is what is at issue in their being our standards of authentic truth, value, or whatever. To insist that we should view them with indifference is to deny us the prospects of having any standards at all. Commitment at this level is simply unavoidable. Our cognitive or evaluative perspective would not be our perspective did we not deem it rationally superior to others.

Antirelativists often feel obliged to embark on a quixotic quest for "cognitive universals" at the level of substantive beliefs or cognitive procedures that all rational beings share in common. One can in principle contemplate two very different lines of approach here: (1) We find that certain types of creatures have somehow been predesignated as rational (by the World Spirit?), and we then inquire empirically into what it is that all these predeterminedly rational beings have in common. Or again, (2) we make use of our conception of what rationality is to characterize certain types of creatures as rational, and *then* ask (analytically) what it is that all of them *must* have in common simply in virtue of qualifying under this conception of ours. Clearly, the second approach is the only practicable one; it makes no sense to try to implement the first (seeing that we simply have no way to get in touch with the World Spirit).

However, when we proceed in this second way, the only commonalities we can get out are the ones that we put in. We must ask what features beings must possess in virtue of qualifying as the sort of creature that *we ourselves are prepared to accept as answering to our conception of "rationality."* Clearly, this approach puts that conception of ours at the forefront as the determinative pivot-point.

Recognizing that others see such matters differently from ourselves need not daunt us in attachment to our own views. It may give us "second thoughts"—may invite us to rethink—but this is not to move us to admit their standards but rather to make more careful and conscientious use of our own.

THE PRIMACY OF OUR OWN POSITION

When social scientists say that alien cultures have a different "rationality" from ourselves, what they generally mean (strictly speaking) is (1) that they have different *objectives* (for example, that we seek to control and change our environment to suit our purposes, whereas they tend to reconstitute their purposes to suit their environment—to endeavor to come into "harmony" with nature) and/or (2) that they use *problem-solving techniques* which are different from ours (for example, that we employ empirical investigation, evidence, science, whereas they use divination, omens, or oracles). But, if they pursue different sorts of ends by different sorts of means, they, perhaps, have a different thought style and a different intellectual ethos, but not a different *rationality.* The anthropologists' talk of different *rationality* is simply an overly dramatic (and also misleading) way of making a valid point—namely, that they do their intellectual problem-solving business in a way different from ours. But, those different processes of theirs do not mean that they have a different *rationality* any more then those blow-guns of theirs mean that they have a different *rifle.*

After all, it is *our conception* of rationality that fixes the "rules of the game" at issue when we pursue our deliberations about these matters. We have to play the rationality game by our ground rules, because it is exactly those ground rules that define and determine what "the rationality game" is that is at issue on our deliberations. If we were not playing the game on this basis, it would not be the rationality game that we were engaged in—it would not be *rationality* that is the subject of our concern. It is the determinative role of our own rationality standards that makes them absolute for us.

Rationality is in this regard like communication. What communication is, is the same everywhere and for everyone—inherent in the nature of the concept that is at issue. But, of course, it is only normal and natural that different people in different places and times would transact their communicative business very differently, because what is effective in one context may fail to be so in another. Similarly, *what rationality is,* is one thing (and one uniform thing from person to person within the framework of a meaningful discussion of the topic); but *what is rational* is something else again—something that is by no means uniform from person to person but variable with situation and circumstance.

To be sure, what makes our own conceptions authoritatively determinative in such matters is nothing special about us. Clearly, the Aristotelian cosmos is no longer with us—we are not the center of the world. But we certainly and inevitably are at the center *of our thought world.* Our inquiries have to be conducted within our frame of reference. We have to pose *our* questions in line with *our* ideas, to frame *our* perplexities by means of *our* concepts, to consider *our* issues in *our* terminology. If we ourselves are to classify someone as rational at all (and who else's attribution is now at issue?), then we must deem him qualified under the aegis of rationality *as we understand it.* If we ask about someone "Is she tall?" we are clearly asking about her height *as we conceive it.* What—if anything—she herself thinks about height is beside the point. And exactly the same situation holds with respect to rationality. A condition of "questioner's prerogative" prevails—it is the person who puts the issue on the table who sets the frame of reference for determining what that issue involves—it is, after all, *his* question. With all these questions about rationality, it is, of course, "rationality" *as we ourselves conceive of it* that is operative. The topic being ours, it is we who set the terms of reference for what is at issue. At this point "epistemic relativism" comes to a stop.

Paradoxically, it is precisely the inevitable relativization of *our* questions and concerns and puzzlements to *our* terms of reference that makes those particular terms of reference absolute in our own discussions. Being framed in our terminology, it is our terminology that is decisive for the questions that *we* raise and the inquiries that *we* conduct. If *we* ask if X is being rational in believing (or doing or evaluating) a certain thing, then the issue is clearly one of its being rational on the basis of the conception of rationality as *we* understand it. The governing absoluteness of our conception inheres in "questioner's prerogative"—in the fact that the questions and issues we address in our deliberations about rationality are in fact our own and that, because the questions are ours, it is our conceptions that are determinative for what is at issue. In this regard, our commitment to our own cognitive position is (or should be) unalloyed. We ourselves are bound to see our own (rationally adopted) standards as superior to the available alternatives—and are, presumably, rationally entitled to do so on the basis of the cognitive values we ourselves endorse.

To qualify those of an alien culture as fully rational, we must maintain both that they are conducting their inquiries intelligently by their own rules and also that in our sight these rules make good rational sense given their situation. It is ultimately "intelligent comportment" and "making sense" according to our standards of appraisal that makes what is at issue rationally invariant. The fact that *we* do (and must) apply *our* own idea of the matter is what makes for the universal element of rationality. What is universal about language use, namely, that to accredit another culture as rational at all is to accept it as being "rational" in *our* sense of the term—which may, to be sure, involve deciding whether their actions measure up to *their* standards. The absoluteness of (ideal) rationality is inherent in the very concept at issue.

AGAINST RELATIVISM

And so, although rationally appropriate knowledge claims and rationally appropriate actions and even criteria of appropriateness vary across times and cultures, the determinative principles of rationality do not. But this interesting circumstance does not so much reflect a fact about different times and cultures as the fact that what *counts* as a "standard of rationality" at all is something that rests with us, because we are the arbiters of the conceptual makeup of an issue within the framework of our discussions of the matter. What sort of thing we ourselves understand by "rationality" becomes determinative for our own discussions of the matter. And this uniform conception of "what rationality is" suffices to establish and render uniform those top-level, metacriteriological standards by whose means each of us can judge the rationality of another's resolutions relative to that other's own basis of appraisal. For those "deeper principles" of reason are inherent in the very conception of what is at issue. If you "violate" certain sorts of rules then—for merely *conceptual* reasons—you simply are not engaged in the evidential enterprise at all. The most basic principles of knifehood or evidence or rationality are "culture dependent" only in the sense that some cultures may not pursue a particular project (the cutting project, the evidence project, the rationality project) at all. It is not that they can pursue it in a different way—that they have learned how to make knives without blades, to evidentiate without grounds, or make rational deliberations without subscription to the fundamental principles we take as definitive of what rationality is all about. In such matters we do—inevitably and rightly as well—take our position to be pivotal.

These deliberations accordingly lead to a result that might be characterized as criteriological egocentrism. We can and indeed must see our own standards as optimal with respect to the available alternatives. If we did not so see them, then—insofar as we are rational—they would thereby cease to be our standards.

Indifferentist relativism insists that a choice between different bases of judgment must, if made at all, be based on extrarational considerations—taste, custom, fashion, or the like. But rationality simply blocks the path to this destination in its demand that we attune our judgments to the structure of available experiences and its insistence that doing anything else would be *irrational*. Relativism thus has its limits. The implications of our own conception of rationality, truth, and inquiry are absolutely decisive for our deliberations. We ourselves must be the arbiters of tenability when the discussion at issue is one that we are conducting. And so, we cannot at once maintain our own rational commitments as such while yet ceasing to regard them as results at which all rational inquirers who proceed appropriately also ought to arrive given the same circumstances. In this sort of way, the claims of rationality are inherently universal and, if you will, absolute.[7]

"But is it not possible for someone to go out and get another normative standard?" It certainly is. But on what basis would one do this? You might *force* me to change standards. Or you can, perhaps, brainwash me. But you cannot *rationally persuade* me. For rational persuasion at the normative level has to proceed in terms of norms that I accept, and, by the norms I actually have, my present standards are bound to prevail if I am rational in the first place.[8]

Thus, even while acknowledging that other judgments regarding matters of rationality may exist, we have no choice but to see our standards as appropriate for us. (In using someone else's with "no questions asked" we would, ipso facto, be making them ours!) To use another standard (categorically, not hypothetically) is to make it ours—to make it no longer *another* standard. Like "now" and "here," our standards follow us about no matter where we go. Of course, to see our own standards as the appropriate ones for us to use here and now is not to deny the prospect of a change of standards. But when this actually occurs, our stance toward the new standards is identical to our present stance toward the presently adopted ones. A commitment to the appropriateness of his present standards follows the rational man about like his own shadow.

Relativity ends where charity begins—at home. For, our discourse is governed by *our* conceptions which are absolute at any rate *for us*. It is care for the *concepts* involved that chastens the impetus to relativism with absolutistic constraints.

To be sure, this criteriological egocentrism can and should be tempered by a posture of criteriological humility. The wisdom of hindsight and the school of bitter experience teaches us the chastening lesson that our cognitive standards—and the judgments we base on them—are by no means necessarily perfect. All the same, we have no real alternative to using our standards—to doing the very best we can with the means at our disposal. Although we have to bear in mind the sobering thought that our best just may not be good enough, we are nevertheless bound to see the standards we have adopted in the pursuit of rationality as superior to the *available* alternatives and to regard ourselves as rationally entitled to do so here and now. (Future improvement "from within" can of course be envisioned along the above indicated lines.) To refrain from making this commitment is simply to opt out of the project of rational inquiry altogether. In the pursuit of rational cognition we must, as with any other pursuit, begin from where we are.

To acknowledge that other people hold views different from ours, and to concede the prospect that we may, even in the end, simply be unable to win them over by rational suasion, is emphatically not to accept an indifferentism to the effect that their views are just as valid or correct as ours are. To acquiesce in a situation where others think differently from oneself is neither to endorse their views nor to abandon one's own. In many departments of life—in matters of politics, philosophy, art, morality, and so on—we certainly do not take the position that the correctness of our own views is somehow undermined and their tenability compromised by the circumstance that others do not share them. And there is no good reason why we should see matters all that differently in matters of inquiry—or even evaluation.

THE ARBITRAMENT OF EXPERIENCE

A sensible pluralist will acknowledge not only that different people (groups or schools of thought) have different standards but that they can do so appropriately given their differential emplacement in the cognitive scheme of things. But of course it does not follow from this that the pluralist need be disloyal to his own standards (any more than it follows from my acknowledging that your spouse to be appropriate *for you* constitutes on my part an act of disloyalty toward my own). To concede that certain standards make good rational sense for someone in your shoes is not to say that they make sense for one, who is differently situated.

The stance espoused throughout the present discussion has quite emphatically been that of a *perspectival rationalism* (or *contextualism*). Such a preferentialist position combines a pluralistic acknowledgment of distinct alternatives with a recognition that a group's choice among them is *not* rationally indifferent, but rather constrained by the probative indications of the *experience* that provides them with both the evidential basis and the evaluative criteria for effecting a rational choice.

Of course, people's experience differs. Even if we are pluralists and accept a wide variety of normative positions as being (abstractly speaking) available, still, if we have a doctrinal position at all—that is, if we are actually committed to solving our cognitive and normative problems—we have no serious alternative to seeing our own position as rationally superior. Faced with various possible answers to our questions, the sensible and appropriate course is clearly to figure out, as best we can, which one it is that deserves our endorsement. But, of course, there is—or should be—a good rational basis for effecting such a choice, namely, normative perspective, whatever it might be, that is based on the probative indications of our own experience. For there indeed is an objectifying impetus to avert our problem—resolutions from becoming a mere matter of indifferent choice based on arbitrary preferences. And throughout the sphere of rational inquiry, this objectifying impetus lies in the appropriate use of the lessons of experience. Empiricism is our appropriate and optimal policy. We have to go on from where *we* are and proceed on the basis of our experiential endowment. For us, a perspectival egalitarianism makes no sense in making our decisions regarding theoretical, practical, or evaluative matters.

Different individuals, different eras, different societies all have different bodies of experience. This being so, then whether discordant thinkers are at issue is not *their* perspectival accommodation of their experience just as valid for them as ours is for us? No doubt, the answer here has to be affirmative. But it must be followed by an immediate "What of it?" The fact that others with different bodies of experience might resolve the matter differently is simply *irrelevant* to our own resolution of the issues. We have to go on from where *we* are and proceed on the basis of our perspective. For us, a perspectival egalitarianism makes no sense. Indifferentism is ruled out by the fact that it is experience that is the determinative factor, and for us, the experience at issue is *our* experience and cannot be someone else's.

In matters of cognition as elsewhere, our normative orientations do not come to us ex nihilo but emerge from experience. And in this world we are never totally bereft of an experiential basis: In the order of thought as in the world's physical order, we always have a position of some sort. By the time one gets to the point of being able to think at all, there is always a background of available experience against which to form one's ideas. And just there is where one has to start. It is precisely because a certain position is appropriate *from where we stand* that makes this particular position of ours appropriate for us. The posture that emerges from this way of approaching the issue is thus that of a contextualistic rationalism:

> Confronted with a pluralistic proliferation of alternative positions you have your acceptance-determination methodology, and I have mine. Yours leads you to endorse *P*; mine leads me to endorse not-*P*. Yours is just as valid for you (via your methodology of validating principles) as mine is for me. The situational differences of our contexts simply lead to different rational resolutions. And that's the end of the matter.

The fact that the cognitive venture viewed as a whole incorporates other positions does nothing to render a firm and fervent commitment to one's own position somehow infeasible, let alone improper.

For us, our own experience (vicarious experience included) is something unique—and uniquely compelling. You, to be sure, are in the same position—your experience is compelling, *for you*—but that's immaterial *to me*. "But isn't such an experiential absolutism just relativism by another name—is it not itself just a relativism of a particular sort—an experiential relativism?" Whatever relativity there may be is a relativization to evidence, so that relativism's characteristic element of indifference is lacking. It is just this, after all, that distinguishes indifferentist *relativism* from a rationalistic *contextualism*. And there is nothing *corrosive* about such a contribution. It does not dissolve any of our commitments. Its absolutism lies in the fact that, for us, our own experience is bound to be altogether compelling.

But does not a contextualistic pluralism put everyone's position on a par? Does it not underwrite the view that all the alternatives ultimately lie on the same level of acceptability? The question again is acceptable to whom? Rational inquiry as such maintains a certain olympian indifference—a noncommittal neutrality. However, this certainly does *not* mean that my position—need be just as acceptable to you as to me. A sensible version of contextualistic pluralism will flatly refuse to put everyone's position on a par—save from the unachievable olympian point of view of the community at large which is, of course, by its very nature unavailable to any single individual. For each individual stands fully and decidedly committed to his own orientation on the basis of his or her own experience, so that there is no question of a relativistic *indifferentism* in acknowledging the pivotal role of a cognitive perspective. A pluralism of contextually underwritten cognitive positions does not lend to indifferentism precisely because a normative position is in the very nature of things something that a sensible person cannot view with indifference.

It makes no sense to take the line that all normative perspectives are equally acceptable, because where experiential bases of judgment are at issue, the pattern of our own experience is—for us at any rate—altogether decisive. After all, rationality requires that we attune our beliefs and evaluations to the overall pattern of our experience. For us, our own experience is rationally compelling. We could not (rationally) deviate from its dictates—and it would really make no sense for us to want to do so. We can no more separate from the indications of our own experience than we could separate ourselves from our own shadows.

Such a position accordingly leaves no room for indifferentism. It pivots on the idea of *contextual* appropriateness—appropriateness in the context that is delimited and defined by the specific experiential circumstances of one's situation. Recognizing that pluralism prevails—that other standards are used by others—we nevertheless do and (appropriately) can deem our own standards of rational cognition as *appropriate* for ourselves. Even when conceding the prospect of someone's having another position, we cannot see it as appropriate for ourselves.

THE IMPETUS OF PURPOSE:
THE WARRANTING OF OUR POSITION

Our own cognitive position may be but one among many, yet if we came by it aright, it is one whose adoption is appropriate for us. The pivotal fact of the matter is that cognitive rationality is something purposive even though "theoretical" yet still it is, in a way, also "practical." For we require answers to our questions both to guide our actions in a difficult world and to respond to the information-requiring side of our nature.

Homo sapiens has evolved within nature to fill the ecological niche of an intelligent being. The demand for understanding, for a cognitive accommodation to one's environment, for "knowing one's way about" is one of the most fundamental requirements of the human condition. Humans are *Homo quaerens*. We have questions and want (nay, *need*) answers. The need for information, for cognitive orientation in our environment, is as pressing a human need as that for food itself. We are rational animals and must feed our minds even as we must feed our bodies. In pursuing information, as in pursuing food, we have to settle for the best we can get at the time. We have questions and need answers—the best answers we can get here and now, regardless of their imperfections.

With us, the imperative to understanding is something altogether basic: Things being as they are, we cannot function, let alone thrive, without knowledge of what goes on about us. The knowledge that orients our activities in this world is itself the most practical of things—a rational animal cannot feel at ease in situations of which it can make no cognitive sense. We have questions and want (nay, *need*) to have answers to them. And not just answers, but answers that cohere and fit together in an orderly way can alone satisfy a rational creature. This basic practical impetus to (coherent) information provides a fundamental imperative to cognitive intelligence.

We humans want and need our cognitive commitments to comprise an intelligible story, to give a comprehensive and coherent account of things. For us, cognitive satisfaction is unattainable on any other basis—the need for information, for knowledge to nourish the mind, is every bit as critical as the need for food to nourish the body. Cognitive vacuity or dissonance is as distressing to us as physical pain. Bafflement and ignorance—to give suspensions of judgment the somewhat harsher name that is their due-exact a substantial price from us. The quest for cognitive orientation in a difficult world represents a deeply practical requisite for us. That basic demand for information and understanding presses in upon us, and we must do (and are pragmatically justified in doing) what is needed for its satisfaction. For us, cognition is the most practical of matters: Knowledge itself fulfills an acute practical need.

And so, seeing that knowledge can only be obtained from a cognitive perspective, the fact *that* we need such a perspective—some one or other—can be taken as a given. But this, of course, still leaves open the issue of *which one*?

The appropriate answer here is rather straightforward. The proper perspective for us is that which—in the existing circumstances—most efficiently and effectively serves our purposes, which resolves our questions and furnishes our guidance with the most adequate and satisfactory way. Although many alternatives doubtless exist, the one that deserves—nay, rationally requires—our endorsement is that which best meets the needs of the existing situation as we face it. And this is going to be the perspective that is validated by our experience in that it most efficiently and effectively accommodates the concrete circumstances of our experiential situation.

"Facts are precisely what there is not," says Nietzsche, "only interpretations."[9] But this all-leveling perspective has its difficulties. For there are interpretations and interpretations—interpretations that resolve problems and interpretations that create difficulties. (If I interpret those grains of white sand as sugar and proceed accordingly, I shall encounter unpleasant consequences.)

To be sure, we do not occupy the vantage point of a god's-eye perspective. For us frail mortals, everything is a matter of judgment, of evidential availability, interpretation. But here we do have a guidance that is not of our making or wanting—the bitter school of actual experience. For where ideas are concerned humans may propose but nature disposes. Intelligent action may facilitate reaching our goals, but wishing and wanting is rarely of much help by itself.

What we have here, then, is an effectively *pragmatic* determination of the issue of the problem of perspectival selection and validation. There is an objectively optimal process of resolution through the adoption of that perspective that most efficiently and effectively accommodates the body of experience at our disposal.

To be sure, such a pragmatic /experiential validation of a particular cognitive perspective nowise *guarantees* the categorical correctness of the beliefs that ensue from it. All that it provides is that in following its strictures we will do as well as we can manage to in the circumstances. By allowing our beliefs by our experiences, we do all that we can to assure their adequacy to our needs within the setting of the situation that confronts us. As indicated above, beyond that point—the point of having done all that we reasonably can—a certain element of methodological optimism is called for, a rationally warrantable hope that once we have done all we can these best efforts of ours will prove to be good enough.

PLURALISM IS COMPATIBLE WITH COMMITMENT

But how, short of megalomania, can one take the objectivist stance that one's own view of what is rational is right—that it ought to be binding on everyone? How can I ask for this agreement between my position and that of "all sensible people"? Not, surely, because I seek to impose my standard on *them,* but because I do—or should! endeavor to take account of their standards in the course of shaping my own. Coordination is achieved not because I insist on their conforming to me, nor yet because I supremely adjust my views to theirs, but rather because I have made every *reasonable* effort to make mine only that which (as best I can tell) ought to be everyone's. In the end, I can thus insist that they should use the same standard that I do because it is on this very basis of a commitment to impersonal cogency that I have made that standard my own in the first place. One's commitment to one's own rational standards is—or ought to be—produced not by megalomania but by objectivity. It is a matter of seeking—to realize a situation where I can reasonably expect that others will see matters in the same light as myself because I have found my light in the illumination of theirs.

Thus, nothing stands in the way of a realization that ours is not inherently and inevitably the best conceptual scheme—a kind of *ne plus ultra*—and that we can *nevertheless* stand rationally committed to it. Consider how cognitive progress happens. We can admit THAT the scientists of the future will have a better science, an ampler and more adequate understanding of the natural universe, and thus a better conceptual scheme—though, admittedly, we cannot anticipate just HOW this is to be so. We need not take the stance that our own conceptual scheme is somehow the last word. Our recognition *that* our scheme is imperfect, though correct and appropriate in the interests of realism, is, to be sure, of rather limited use. A realization of the *en gros* deficiency of our conceptual machinery unhappily affords no help toward its emendation in matters of detail. A rational commitment to our position is just exactly a commitment to accepting its claims to be the proper basis for accepting its rulings as proper and appropriate. It is a matter of doing the best we can in the cause of responsible truth estimation—of carrying on the business of rational inquiry as best we can in the circumstances in which the world's realities have emplaced us.

Nevertheless, this realization of the presumptive suboptimality of our own cognitive proceedings plays a most useful role. It affords a *regulative* conception that preempts any claim to dogmatic finality, even if not a *constitutive* one that puts substantively informative data at our disposal. The presumption that there are other and perhaps better ventures of inquiry than ours is eminently salutary in blocking the path of the deplorably egocentric view that we ourselves some how stand at the cognitive center of things, occupying that pivotal position about which all else revolves. And here "internally" from our own cognitive posture we ourselves simply cannot consider other positions as genuinely on a par with our own in point of merit.

An experiential pluralism of cognitive positions is thus no impediment to a commitment to the pursuit of truth. There is no reason that the mere existence of different views and positions should leave us immobilized like the ass of Buridan between the alternatives. Nor are we left with the gray emptiness of equalitarianism that looks to all sides with neutrality and uncommitted indifference. In important matters such as inquiry (or evaluation, etc.), we cannot—and in good conscience should not—bring ourselves to view disagreement in the light of a "mere divergence of opinion."

It is, in the eyes of some, a disadvantage of pluralism that it supposedly undermines one's commitment to one's own position. But this is simply fallacious. There is no good reason why a recognition that others, circumstanced as they are, are inclined—and, indeed, rationally entitled *in their circumstances*—to hold a position of variance with ours should be construed to mean that we, circumstanced as we are, need feel any rational obligation to abandon our position. Once we have done our rational best to substantiate our position, the mere existence of alternatives needs give us no pause.

Jean-Paul Sartre deplored the attempt to secure rationally validated knowledge, which he saw as a way of avoiding responsibility for *making* something of oneself, for "choosing one's own project," seeing that the real truth is not something one can make up as one goes along but is something one regards as entitled to one's recognition (to a subordination of sorts on one's part). But this view turns the matter topsy-turvy. Not the pursuit of truth but its *abandonment* represents a failure of nerve and a crisis of confidence. The avoidance of responsibility lies in an indifferentism that sees merit everywhere and validity nowhere (or vice versa), thereby relieving us of any and all duty to investigate the issues in a serious, workmanlike way.

Admittedly, there are cognitive postures different from ours—different sorts of standards altogether. But what does that mean *for us*? What are *we* to do about it? Several stances toward those various bases are in theory open to us:

1. Accept none: reject ours;
2. Accept one: retain ours;
3. Accept several: conjoin others with ours;
4. "Rise above the conflict": say "a plague on all your houses" and take the path of idealization invoking the "ideal observer," the "wise man" of the Stoics, the "ideally rational agent" of the economists, or the like.

The first option is mere petulance—a matter of stalking off in "fox-and-grapes" fashion because we cannot have it all our own preferred way. The third option is infeasible: Different bases do not combine, they make mutually incompatible demands, and in *conjoining* them, we will not get something more comprehensive and complete—we will get a mess. The fourth option is utopian and unrealistic. We have no way to get there from here. Only the second alternative makes sense: to have the courage of our convictions and stand by our own guns. In *evaluating* contentions and positions (of any sort), we just have no plausible alternative to doing so from the perspective of our cognitive values—our own conscientiously adopted cognitive point of view.

To obtain informative guidance from inquiry, it is not enough to *contemplate* cognitive standards—be it as historical actualities or as theoretical possibilities. We must actually *commit* ourselves to one. We can only get viable answers to substantive questions if we do our inquiring in the doctrinalist manner—only if we are willing to "stick our necks out" and take a position that endorses some answers and rejects others, to be sure, in a principled way that is in line with standards for whose due validation we have made appropriate provisions. A perceptively grounded position is good enough for sensible individuals precisely because that position—determinative perspective of ours is by hypothesis OUR perspective.

IS TRUTH RELATIVE? A CRITIQUE OF MARGOLIS

What people *think* to be true is clearly something that is person variable and thus relative. We can take the line that "What is *true*?" is a question that different people can quite appropriately answer differently because of the interpersonal variability of available information. But what *truth* is all about is something that is—on the approach proposed here—altogether definite and fixed. In *our* discussion of the matter, it will be our conception of truth that is operative, so that we have to take the line that the question "What is *truth*?" is one on which different people should not think differently—that where two of them differ substantially, one of them has somehow gone wrong. The *evidentiation* at issue in the epistemic sector is interpersonally and intercommunally variable. But the *explanation* at issue in the conceptual sector is something one must (or ought to) see in a less relativistic light variability on the one side that does not make for variation on the other.

It is exactly here (so it seems to me) that Joseph Margolis's rather more formidable assessment of relativism encounters its most serious difficulty. After an illuminating critical analysis of various forms of relativism, he endorses a moderated version of the doctrine. His discussion here culminates as follows:

> What we may now characterize as a *robust* or moderate relativism is a substantive thesis about constraints [attributing the classical] truth values ["is true, is false"] ... in sectors or inquiry ... [where] we must fall back on logically weaker, many-valued claims (as of plausibility, reasonableness, aptness, and the like) if we are to salvage a measure of objectivity with respect to the inquiries of those sectors.[10]

Such an assessment wears on its sleeves an unwillingness to distinguish the internal assertive substance of a claim ("The cat is on the mat") from the claim-external epistemic qualification made by the claimant to reflect its evidentiary state ("*It is probable that* the cat is on the mat").

The salient point, however, is that "probably on the mat" is simply no place for the cat to be. Two separable and indeed separate items are at issue, and two different questions are being answered:

Q. Where is the cat?
A. On the mat.
Q. How sure are you of this?
A. Reasonably sure.

One question relates to the location of the cat; the other to the status of the grounding or evidentiation of our claims about this. And only the latter has a status that is subject to relativistically degreelike qualification.

Questions about the structure of reality admit only of resolving answers within the true/false dichotomy, even where they have a degreelike position in the certainty spectrum. Accordingly, Margolis runs (so it seems to me) into difficulty when he maintains:

> The strongest substantive reason for advocating relativism rests ... with the finding that we cannot uniquely fix the structure of

reality just where we are justified in insistence on the objective and realist import of our cognitive claims. . . . There are no areas of inquiry usually cast in bipolar [true/false] terms that are adversely affected by replacing such values with relativistic values.[11]

What is going on here is (to all appearances) a conflation of the more duality at issue with *semantical* status (true/false) with the more flexible characterization of the *cognitive* status of claims ("I am [or we are] inclined to believe [be reasonably confident, absolutely certain, etc.] that p''). Indeed, we cannot "fix the structure of reality" where we *feel* justified, but this does not preclude us from seeing it as fixed where we *are* justified. Degrees of confidence are indeed person-relative and variable. But truth status is not. Even mere opinions are still opinions about the facts. And even merely to conjecture that p is to conjecture that p *is true,* is not to think that p *is conjecturally true.* The dimension of epistemic qualification enters into the *external semantical status* of claims, not to their *internal assertoric constitution.* And differences in evidentiation do not make for differences in truth-value.

And so (it seems to me) we cannot or should not with Margolis speak of "the space of relativistic truth-values" as somehow not bipolar. The truth-status of claims is not pluralized by the fact that different people can have different views about it. Smallish evidence that p is true is not firm evidence that p is smallishly true. Admittedly many of our truth claims are no more than that—mere claims or estimates. But there are contentions for which—given the operative ground rules—we can stake greater claims, particularly insofar as we render them vague. With G. E. Moore's "this is a human hand," with the classical "The cat is on the mat" in its experiential immediacy, and with "yon tree is higher than an inch and less high than a mile," one need not be all that diffident. Such claims are themselves sufficiently modest so that there is room for not more than a neurotic doubt as to how "the structure of reality" is fixed.

Moreover, even if we are relativists regarding *evidence,* we need not be so regarding *evidentiation.* Once I learn what evidentiation is about, I can no longer reasonably believe that q constitutes evidence for p for Jones but not for Smith. They may or may not *realize* this. But evidentiation works in such a way that what is evidence for the goose is evidence for the gander. To be sure, people's *views* of evidentiation may vary. But if they have a concept of evidence at all, it is one that they will deem "objective" in the sense of rejecting the idea that evidentiation is person variable. Of course, *information* does vary from person to person. So I may lack evidence that you have. But if it is *evidence* that is at issue, that is something we have to see as person—indifferent. The sort of nonobjectivism that is defensible seems to me to be far weaker than that which Margolis espouses.

Insofar as Margolis is intent to be an evidential relativist, we must be with him all the way. But if he wants to be a semantical relativist of truth-value in general, we have good reason to hold back.

ON PURSUING "THE TRUTH"

Regrettably, many people have—under the influence of relativism—simply given up on the truth. The very idea of "the truth" is of small interest to various theorists nowadays. Heidegger, for one, regarded those so-called absolute truths as no more than "remnants of Christian theology in the problem—field of philosophy."[12] Of themselves, truth and falsity, correctness and incorrectness, adequacy and inadequacy, reason and unreason, sense and nonsense approached as issues of logic, semantic theory, or epistemological explication—simply do not interest the hermeneuticist. He wants to know what role the *ideas* about these issues have in the sphere of authentic human experience; he does not ask about what these ideas *mean* but about what people *do* with them. Truth as such is something he is eager to abandon. And he is not alone. In stressing the pluralism of philosophizing, William James wrote:

> *The* Truth: what a perfect idol of the rationalistic mind! I read in an old letter—from a gifted friend who died too young—these words: "In everything, in science, art, morals, and religion, there *must* be one system that is right and *every* other wrong." How characteristic of the enthusiasm of a certain stage of young! At twenty-one we rise to such a challenge and expect to find the

system. It never occurs to most of us even later that the question "What is *the* Truth?" is no real question (being irrelative to all conditions) and that the whole notion of *the* truth is an abstraction from the fact of truths in the plural.[13]

Inspired by James, various contemporary pragmatists are quite prepared to abandon concern for truth.

But this reaction is gravely misguided. Epistemological pluralism has no substantive consequences for the nature of truth as such. The fact that "our truth," the truth as we see it, is not necessarily that of others—that it is no more than the best *estimate* of the real truth that we ourselves are able to make should not disillusion us in our inquiries and should not discourage us in "the pursuit of truth." In inquiry, as in other departments of human endeavor, we are well advised simply to do the best we can. Realizing that there are no guarantees we have little sensible choice—*pro tem* at least—but to deem the best we can do as good enough.

Recognizing that others see matters differently in contexts of inquiry need not daunt us in attachment to our own views of the matter. There is clearly no conflict between our commitment to the truth as we see it and a recognition that the adoption of a variant probative perspective leads others to see the truth differently. Given that we ourselves occupy our perspective, we are bound to see *our* truth as *the* truth. But we nevertheless can and do recognize that others who operate in different times and conditions see matters in a different light. The circumstance that different people see something differently does not destroy or degrade the thing as such.

The fact is that relativism misconstrues the significance of unavailable consensus. For, after all, consensus as such is neither a means to nor an effect of people's commitment to rational cogency. We have to come to terms with the epistemic realities, which include:

- the diversity in people's experiences and cognitive situations
- the variation of "available data"
- an underdetermination of facts by data
- the variability of people's cognitive values (evidential security, simplicity, etc.)

- the variation of cognitive methodology and the epistemic "state of the art."

Such factors make for a difference in the beliefs, judgments, and evaluations even of otherwise "perfectly rational" people. Short of a biological and situational cloning that equips every inquirer with exactly the same cognitive basis for the formation of opinion, it is clear that consensus is unrealizable.

Rationality can be counted upon to lead to *consensus* only in situations of uniform experience—which are, obviously, also in general not realized. In the circumstances in which we labor in this world, consensuality is neither a requisite for nor a consequence of rationality in the conduct of inquiry. Nor is it a practicable goal. All our factual claims are made in a setting of place and time, in the context of cultural and observational states of the art. But their being provisional and contextual claims to truth does not metamorphose them into claim to conditional and contextual truth. The flaw of relativism is that it conflates the status of our truth-claims with their *substance*.

We have no choice but to pursue *the* truth by way of cultivating *our* truth; we have no direct access to truth unmediated by the epistemological resources of rational inquiry. And, given the ground rules of rational inquiry, this means that one's view of the truth is bound to be linked to one's cognitive situation. To say that this is not good enough and to give up on our truth—to declare petulantly that if we cannot have *the* absolute, capital-T Truth that of its very nature constrains everyone's allegiance, then we will not accept anything at all—is automatically to get nothing and to abandon the pursuit of truth as such. It is foolishness to reject an orientation-bound position as not worth having in a domain where a position is only to be had on this basis. The only truth-claims worth staking are those which can be seen as rational on the standards that we ourselves endorse.

THE ACHILLES HEEL OF RELATIVISM

But are we really entitled—rationally entitled—to place such reliance on our own standards? Assuming that we indeed have done what reason—as best we can understand it—demands for their substantiation (and this is a long story best reserved for another occasion), the answer is and has to be an emphatic *yes*. Inquirers should not and need not be intimidated by the fact of disagreement—it makes perfectly good sense for a person to do the best possible toward securing evidentiated beliefs and justifiable choices without undue worry about whether or not others disagree.

There is nothing admirable in relativism's inclination to noncommittal detachment with its concomitant reluctance to trust one's personal judgment in matters of human significance. Relativism reflects a regrettable unpreparedness to take intellectual responsibility—to say: "I've investigated the matter as best I can, and this is the result at which I've arrived. Here I stand, I can do no other. If you wish to stand with me, then welcome to you; if not, then please show me how my position is untenable." They represent recourse to an uncritical open-mindedness that comes down to empty-mindedness. In matters of rational inquiry, as in politics and religion, one does well to prefer someone who has views and sticks by them to those who reject the whole project or (equally wrongly) try to ride off in every direction at once.

The decisive weakness of a philosophical relativism with its commitment to basis egalitarianism in matters of cognition lies deep in the nature of the human condition. It emerges as follows: The characteristic stance of relativism is to insist on the *rational indifference* of alternatives. Be it contentions, beliefs, doctrines, practices, customs, or whatever that are at issue, the relativist insists that "it just doesn't matter" in point of rationality. People are led to adopt one alternative over another by *extrarational* considerations (custom, habituation, fashion, or whatever); from the rational point of view there is nothing to choose—all the alternatives stand on the same footing. The fatal flaw of this position roots in the fact that our claims, beliefs, doctrines, practices, customs, all belong to identifiable departments of purposive human endeavor—identifiable domains, disciplines, and the like. For all (or virtually all) human enterprises are at bottom teleological-conducted with some sort of end or objective in view. In particular, the cognitive enterprise of rational inquiry has the mission of providing implementable information about our natural and artificial environments—information that we can use to orient ourselves cognitively and practically in the world. After all, explanation, prediction, and effective intervention constitute definitive enterprise-characterizing goals of science. (And the moral enterprise is also purposive, its mission being to define, teach, and encourage modes of action that bring the behavior of individuals into alignment with the best overall interests of the group.) Human endeavors in general have an inherent teleology seeing that homo sapiens is a goal-pursuing creature. Now in this context, the crucial fact is that some claims, beliefs, doctrines, practices, customs, and so on, are bound to serve the purposes of their domain better than others. For it is pretty much inevitable that in any goal-oriented enterprise, some alternative ways of proceeding serve better than others with respect to the relevant range of purpose, proving themselves more efficient and effective in point of goal-realization. And in the teleological, contexts *thereby* establish themselves as rationally appropriate with respect to the issues. It lies in the nature of the thing that the quintessentially rational thing to do is to give precedence and priority to those alternatives which are more effective with respect to the range of purposes at issue.

There is no doubt that such a position qualifies as a version of "pragmatism." But it is crucially important to note that it is *not* a version of practicalism. It stands committed to the primacy of purpose, but it certainly does not endorse the idea that the only possible (or only valid) sort of human purpose is that of the type traditionally characterized as "practical"—for example, one that is geared to the physical and "material" well-being of people. Purposive enterprises are as diverse and varied as the whole spectrum of legitimate human purpose, and such purposes can relate not only to the "material" but also to the "spiritual" side of people (their knowledge, artistic sensibility, social dispositions, etc.). To decipher the position from the classical range of specifically practical purposes such a pragmatism might perhaps better be characterized as *functionalism*.

Such a functionalist perspective is decisive in its impetus against relativism. For relativism with its commitment to basic egalitarianism is flatly indifferentistic. Presented with alternatives of the sort at issue (cognitive, moral, etc.), the relativist insists that at bottom it just doesn't matter—at any rate as far as the rationality of the issue is concerned. But once we see the issues in a purposive perspective, this line just doesn't work. In a purposive context, alternatives are not in general portrayable as rationally indifferent. Rationality not only permits but demands giving preference—to purposively effectual alternatives over the rest (at any rate as long as other things are anything like equal). It is quintessentially rational to prefer what works.

To the relativist one must grant *pluralism*—the lack of uniformity and the availability of alternatives. But this concession does not "give away the store," because it does not authorize irrationalistic indifferentism. On the contrary, two higher level metanorms—to wit, conformity to one's standards and conduciveness to one's goals—operate so as to assure a purchase hold for rational appropriateness at the procedural level (even though they do not otherwise engender substantive uniformity).

As this line of reflection indicates, relativism stubs its toe against the pervasively purposive nature of the human situation, the fact that our proceedings—be it in inquiry, interpersonal interaction or whatever—fall within the scope of purposive ventures that have an end in view. This teleological aspect provides a basis for rationality in a way that puts relativism into a thoroughly problematic and dubious light.[14]

NOTES

1. William James, *Pragmatism* (New York: Longman, Green & Co., 1907), p. 171. The basic line of thought goes back to the ancient skeptics. Compare Sextus Empiricus, *Outlines of Pyrrhonism,* vol. 1, pp. 54, 59–60, 97, and passim.

2. This view has become axiomatic for the entire "sociology of knowledge."

3. Peter Winch, "Understanding a Primitive Society," *American Philosophical Quarterly* 1 (1964): 307–24; reprinted in B. R. Wilson, ed., *Rationality* (Oxford: Clarendon Press,, 1970).

4. Lucien Lévy-Bruhl, *Primitive Mentality* (1921; London: Macmillan,, 1923).

5. E. E. Evans-Pritchard, *Witchcraft, Oracles and Magic among the Azandi* (Oxford, 1937); idem, *Nuer Religion* (Oxford: Oxford University Press, 1956).

6. The relevant issues are interestingly treated in John Kekes's book, *A Justification of Rationality* (Albany, N.Y.: State University of New York Press, 1976), pp. 137–49.

7. For an interesting critique of cognitive relativism that is akin in spirit though different in orientation from that of the present section see Lenn E. Goodman "Six Dogmas of Relativism," in Marcello Dascal, ed., Cultural *Relativism and Philosophy* (Leiden: E. J. Brill, 1991), pp. 77–102.

8. To be sure, someone could convince me that my understanding of the implications of my standards is incomplete and lead me to an internally motivated revision of my rational proceedings, amending those standards from within with a view to greater systemic coherence.

9. *The Will to Power,* trans. Walter Kaufmann and R. J. Hollingdale (New York: Random House, 1967), p. 481.

10. Joseph Margolis, "The Truth about Relativism" in Michael Krausz, ed., *Relativism: Interpretation and Confrontation* (Notre Dame: University of Notre Dame Press, 1989), pp. 25051.

11. Ibid., p. 252.

12. "Reste von christlicher Theologie innerhalb der philosophischen Problematik" (Martin Heidegger, *Sein und Zeit* [Leipzig: Kröner Verlag, 1923], p. 230).

13. William James, "Pragmatism and Humanism," in *Writings,* ed. by John J. McDermott (New York: Modern Library, 1967), p. 450.

14. I am grateful to Charles Taliaferro for some constructive comments on an earlier version of this discussion.

Folk Epistemology as Relativism

Tom Rockmore

"Un Français qui arrive à Londres trouve les choses bien changées en philosophie comme dans tout le reste. Il a laissé le monde plein; il le trouve vide. A Paris, on voit l'univers composé de tourbillons de matière subtile; à Londres, on ne voit rien de cela. Chez nous, c'est la pression de la lune qui cause le flux de la mer; chez les Anglais, c'est la mer qui gravite vers la lune, de façon que, quand vous croyez que la lune devrait nous donner marée haute, ces Messieurs croient qu'on doit avoir marée basse; ce qui malheureusement ne peut se vérifier, car il aurait fallu, pour s'en éclaircir, examiner la lune et les marées au premier instant de la création."

—Voltaire, *Lettres philosophiques*

This is an essay in relativism understood, by analogy with folk psychology, as folk epistemology. Most of us, when we are not being philosophers, accept a relativist view of knowledge. For we are willing to admit, if pressed, that our claims to know are not absolute and certainly not independent of the conditions under which they are raised, of the convictions on which they rest, or even of who we are.

162

EPISTEMOLOGICAL ABSOLUTISM AND RELATIVISM

The idea that knowledge is any sense relative, for instance, to time and place, as well as to human reason or human cognitive capacities is at least as old as Protagoras. But beginning with Plato, it was long ago rejected in the philosophical tradition. Modern philosophy can be regarded as a particularly interesting effort, extending over several centuries, to work out a concept of reason as pure, calculative, and not relative, as self-contained or self-grounding.[1] This effort, which extends from Descartes forward, can now be seen to have failed or to give signs of having failed. Current rejections of the transparency thesis, or cognitive privilege, the move toward antirealism, the apparent failure of foundationalism in any form, the claim that the concern with reference central to analytic philosophy has mainly resulted in a deconstruction of the problem that it has not otherwise solved,[2] the attacks on transcendental arguments, and so on are signs of this failure. This failure, which is largely that of modern philosophy itself, either leaves in its wake skepticism or a rival view of reason understood as relative to human being as well as a cultural and historical background, what I am here calling relativism.

Our present task is to rethink this alternative idea of reason that is the other side of the Cartesian theory. When we do so, I believe that we arrive at a view of knowledge rather similar to that held on reflection by nonphilosophers who are unlikely to see the need of committing either to normative claims of knowledge as absolute or to absolute claims for reason as the necessary means to absolute claims to know. Relativism, as I see it, is not some exotic view, or rather, it is a view that is exotic only with respect to the kind of claims that philosophers too often make, such as assertions of apodicticity and the like.

What is relativism? The term "relativism" has been understood in many different ways. Richard Rorty suggests that " 'Relativism' is the view that every belief on a certain topic, or perhaps about *any* topic, is as good as every other."[3] Yet this is merely a straw man, as Rorty himself suggests, a view that no one holds or has probably ever held. It is not a view that helps us to understand what a viable form of relativism looks like, even in outline.

It is useful to anticipate the kind of claim that I want to make. It is often said that so-called first-order claims are relative to second-order justifications. In my view, the enunciative, constative, or assertoric discourse present in every human society is not meaningful as such but meaningful in the society in which it occurs. Claims for objectivity are not questionable but must be located by saying relative to what. The answer can only be something like relative to observations by human beings dependent on the sort of conceptual framework prevalent at the present time. It is, then, one thing to claim that we have genuine invariances and another thing altogether to claim that such invariances as we have are relative to a given framework that is itself not necessarily invariant but subject to historical change. First-order claims are not intrinsically meaningful, but meaningful relative to a framework that, although it justifies them, may or may not be able to justify itself.

Relativism can be understood as what happens to our understanding of epistemology when we deny the traditional normative philosophical view of knowledge as absolute, as unlimited or nonperspectival. The advantage of the relativist approach to knowledge is that as soon as one acknowledges that claims to know are in fact limited, there is no end of identifiable, limiting factors to be explored. A relativist thus is in the position of not being able to tie up all the loose ends in a tidy theory. Yet what a relativist lacks in tidiness is more than made up in the ability to describe the knowing process as it is, as distinguished from an ideal that exists only in the mind of the philosopher.

Relativism, as I see it, is a name for the way we go about getting what we call knowledge in the everyday world. There is, then, a distinction between a practical description of what we know and how we know it and a theoretical claim of what knowledge must look like to be worthy of the name. This distinction opposes representatives of two different epistemological perspectives that for present purposes we can call epistemological absolutists and epistemological relativists. Epistemological absolutists maintain a normative idea of knowledge without limits whatsoever, which implies a concept of reason adequate to this task. Epistemological relativists, on the contrary, acknowledge that claims to know are relative in various ways, to us, to our object, to a conceptual scheme, and so on.

Epistemological absolutism is the majoritarian view in the philosophical tradition. Historically, relativism, the minoritarian view, has long been in disrepute, roughly since Plato's well-known attack on Protagoras's theory, or at least on the theory attributed to him. Plato's epistemological absolutism is clear in his defense of a view of knowledge as not relative in any sense, say, with respect to time, place, or subject, but absolute in every sense. From the epistemological perspective that Plato exemplifies, relativism, whether understood as *Weltanschauungsphilosophie,* which relates claims to know to a given society or form of life, or historicism, which relates claims to know to history, is usually regarded as either identical with or leading ineluctably to skepticism, as in Husserl's position.[4]

Relativism, although not under that name, is widely present in the philosophical tradition. An example is Aristotle's well-known view that knowledge is a function of the object and that practical theory, what we would now call social and political theory, is, for that reason, necessarily approximative. Husserl, who defends a version of the familiar, Cartesian, absolute conception of knowledge, appeals to Augustine's idea, taken up separately by Montaigne[5] and Descartes,[6] that knowledge depends on a return into oneself.[7] Yet Augustine offers a stunning argument for relativism in his analysis of time. According to Augustine, the difference between future and past is not absolute but relative to the present.[8]

If relativism is understood as the denial of immediate claims to know in favor of the view that knowledge is based on a conceptual scheme, then with the exception of such defenders of indefeasible perceptual claims as Roderick Chisholm, we are all relativists. The relevant problem is not whether and how to avoid relativism, because it now seems that we cannot do so, but rather which form of relativism to defend. Now some writers, who acknowledge that we require a conceptual framework, are nonetheless nostalgic for a version of the Kantian or even the Cartesian view on the grounds that there is at most one such framework. The battle has recently been joined between proponents of a single, inalterable conceptual framework and proponents of multiple frameworks. The burden of this paper is to show that because more than one such framework is possible, claims to know are doubly relative, that is, relative in respect to alternative conceptual frameworks or epistemological perspectives that, in turn, are historically relative.

FOUNDATIONALISM AND RELATIVISM

Not enough has been said about the relativist implications following from American pragmatism. Among the classical American pragmatists, this issue is perhaps most directly joined in Dewey's attack on the idea of certainty as a central theme in the philosophical tradition[9] and less directly in Peirce's claim that knowledge is what the informed community of scientists thinks that it is. More recently, the issue of relativism has been clearly raised in two ways: through the failure of epistemological foundationalism and in discussion of the philosophy of science.

The failure of foundationalism is significant. After Descartes and throughout the modern period, foundationalism has continued to serve as the main strategy to make out the traditional claim for knowledge in the full sense, which Descartes famously identifies with apodicticity. Among contemporaries, Richard Rorty has prominently tried to draw the lesson following from the failure of foundationalism. Like the young Hegelians who thought that Hegel had brought philosophy to a peak and to an end, Rorty holds that philosophy peaks and ends in analytic philosophy, understood as the epitome of the philosophical tradition.

The shortest formulation of his view is the claim that, because foundationalism fails, philosophy as such fails. Basing himself on the ideas of W. V O. Quine, Wilfrid Sellars and others, Rorty holds that foundationalism has now irrevocably failed. For epistemology, we can substitute edifying conversation[10] that, however, always and necessarily falls below the demonstration of claims to know that would require a viable form of foundationalism. For this reason, Rorty even goes so far as to abandon the idea of truth.[11]

Rorty apparently sees himself as a modern Socrates who knows only that he does not know. Yet his skeptical pessimism goes farther than the Socratic variety, because he also knows that he cannot know. Although Rorty willingly enters into conversation, he knows, as his illustrious predecessor did not, that philosophical conversation never surpasses the exchange of opinions to become knowledge. On Rorty's view of things, the problem with philosophy is that it never gets beyond relativism as he understands it, because in the philosophical arena, any opinion is as good as any other one.

From this angle of vision, Rorty is a modern skeptic. His skepticism follows from his unjustified tendency to identify philosophy, analytic philosophy, and foundationalism. Yet obviously his skeptical conclusion can be avoided by taking a weaker line. It does not follow that knowledge is impossible if foundationalism fails. It only follows that a particular normative view of knowledge that has long bewitched an entire tradition fails. If we cannot demonstrate our absolute claims to knowledge, there is nothing wrong with viewing them as relative. If we concede that foundationalism has now failed and that there is little hope of finding a viable species of the genus, then we can still understand knowledge in another, weaker sense as relative.

KANT AND RELATIVISM

Rorty's epistemological despair concerns the realization of the influential Cartesian view of knowledge. Descartes, who insists that each of us possesses common sense, also distrusts it. The idea motivating the foundationalist epistemological strategy is to provide knowledge free of any dependence on a conceptual or historical framework. In the early Cartesian version of the causal theory of perception, ideas in the mind are true and are seen as such when we apply the twin criteria of clarity and distinctness. Although these items of knowledge come into the mind at a given time and place, they do not depend on either.

Kant carries further the causal theory of perception as well as the view that knowledge is independent of time and place. Denying the claim to immediate knowledge, he argues that objects of perception and knowledge, which he does not distinguish, are mediated by a conceptual framework that he claims to deduce. According to Kant, knowledge is possible if and only if there is a conceptual scheme that can be demonstrated prior to and apart from experience.

In his attempted deduction, Kant is reacting to Aristotle who, he claims, provides a mere rhapsody in virtue of the failure to deduce the categorial framework. Neither Kant nor Aristotle is usually considered as a relativist. Yet if not Aristotle, who insists on intuitive knowledge in his theory of scientific first principles, at least Kant is com-

mitted to relativism understood as the denial of any claim to immediate knowledge. For the critical philosophy, immediate knowledge is
impossible, because knowledge requires as its condition the application of the categorial framework to the content of experience. If relativism is understood as the relativization of claims to know to a form
of mediation, in Kant's case to a categorial framework, then Kant is
already committed to a form of relativism.

LINGUISTIC RELATIVITY

Diametrically opposed, Kantian and anti-Kantian views of knowledge have emerged in recent discussions of science. Working independently, Kuhn and Feyerabend follow Kant in arguing that knowledge is relative to a conceptual framework, but break with him in
maintaining that there are different, incompatible conceptual
schemes. Reacting to the views of Kuhn, Feyerabend, and others,
Davidson maintains a version of the Kantian view according to which
the very idea of an alternative conceptual scheme is incoherent.

   Problems of translation and commensurability are currently in the
wind. MacIntyre suggests that claims of incommensurability and
untranslatibility are always false.[12] Yet Kuhn and Feyerabend rely
independently on ideas of incommensurability to question the compatibility of alternative conceptual frameworks. In ancient thought, the
idea of incommensurability was already troubling. It seemed to indicate an intrinsic limit to what is or even could be known. If number is
associated with the real, and if what is to be known can only be known
through a mathematical representation, then knowability and mathematical commensurability converge. Conversely, what cannot be represented mathematically, what is incommensurable, cannot be known.
The idea of incommensurability leads, hence, to a form of skepticism.

   Similarly, skepticism has sometimes been said to follow from
the admission of different possible perspectives that, in virtue of
their incommensurability, cannot be expressed in terms of each
other. It is as if, in denying various proposed instances of reduction,
say, the reduction of biology to physics, in admitting the legitimacy
of biological and physicalist perspectives, we, therefore, commit to
skepticism with respect to the object of knowledge.

The idea of different, incompatible perspectives that Davidson proscribes is a staple of social science. In cultural anthropology, the well-known effort to avoid ethnocentrism is a tacit admission of other possible perspectives, of angles of vision radically different from what the anthropologist carries into the field. Whorf has introduced a related idea into sociolinguistics. Languages are often held to carry with them a general view of the world. In a famous paper, Whorf asserts the existence of irreducible and fundamental differences between different languages and, in terms of these differences, in related views of the world. Whorf is aware of the relativistic consequences of his argument, because he argues straightforwardly that language organizes experience and that differences in linguistic background lead, in the presence of similar evidence, to different views of the universe. He writes:

> . . . language produces an organization of experience. We are inclined to think of language simply as a technique of expression, and not to realize that language first of all is a classification and arrangement of the stream of sensory experience which results in a certain world-order. . . . In other words, language does in a cruder but also in a broader and more versatile way the same thing that science does. . . . We are thus introduced to a new principle of relativity, which holds that all observers are not led by the same physical evidence to the same picture of the universe, unless their linguistic backgrounds are similar, or can in some way be calibrated.[13]

For Whorf, language not only serves to formulate but also in a rather Kantian manner to provide form to its content. The content not only is not directly accessible but is further formed by the linguistic instrument, or medium, through which it becomes accessible. If the linguistic instrument shapes its object, and if different languages impart different "shapes" to the same or similar contents, the result is a certain linguistic relativity

Whorf's idea of linguistic relativity is very suggestive. It appears even obvious to those among us who are at least bilingual, those whose particular linguistic background allows access to experience from two or more linguistic perspectives. Bilinguals and polyglots uniformly report the subjective feeling of being able or at least impelled as it were to say certain things in certain ways in some languages but not in others. Although it is always possible with suitable qualification to designate in a given language what comes more naturally or more easily in another language, translation often, perhaps always, induces a displacement.

Whorf's theory of linguistic relativity elicits resistance most frequently from monoglots who tend to deny the existence of what they do not and cannot directly experience. Others are troubled by the idea of two or more incompatible, but equally valid perspectives. At the limit, supposing that German, say, differs basically from Hopi, we can at least imagine separate German and Hopi theories of physics. This suggests that different linguistic backgrounds point toward and are rooted in different worlds or at least largely different interpretations of the same world.

This consequence of linguistic relativity is often seen as disturbing. In response, some writers insist on the idea of a single, common, intersubjective world of experience prior to and independent of our various scientific and linguistic approaches to it. Philosophers who hold that language provides a true picture of the world, who study language to understand the world,[14] are committed to the idea that there is only one world and one truth about it, not different worlds and different truths. They balk at the idea of linguistic relativity while holding fast to the indemonstrable conviction that to analyze language is to analyze the way the world is.

KUHN, FEYERABEND, AND DAVIDSON

Whorf's theory straightforwardly suggests that there are in fact different, incompatible views of the universe based in linguistically incommensurable backgrounds or conceptual frameworks. According to Whorf, language only does in a cruder way what science also does, namely provide a conceptual framework. The scientific equivalent of Whorf's linguistic relativism has emerged independently in the efforts of Kuhn and Feyerabend to comprehend the evolution of scientific theory.

Philosophy of science, which meditates on science from a metatheoretical plane, is not the same as science itself. A relativistic understanding of science, concerning the philosophical grasp of science, is different from the appeal to relativism within scientific theory, most famously in the theory of relativity. The recent emergence of relativism in philosophy of science that is unrelated, say, to the nature of physical theory, concerns the effort to make sense of how science grows and develops.

The relativistic perspective clashes with holism, or roughly the view that statements are not meaningful in isolation but rather in respect to the total view. According to Quine, loosely following Duhem,[15] science presents a conceptual framework for the interpretation of different items of possible experience. Science is like a worldview or overall perspective with the difference that scientists working from different linguistic backgrounds presumably surpass their linguistic backgrounds to adhere to similar scientific theories. The process of understanding a given item of experience requires its translation into or domestication within a single, overall scientific framework.

If there is at most a single encompassing scheme, commitment to holism has been seen, for instance by Davidson, as in principle excluding the very idea of an incompatible conceptual framework, precisely what is suggested in a Whorfean linguistic relativism. Like Descartes, who insists that we all have the same common sense and, by implication, the same commonsense perspective, Davidson maintains that we finally share a single conceptual framework, if not on the everyday level of folk psychology, at least within the scientific community.

A Davidsonian analysis excludes the idea of linguistic relativity following from the existence of incompatible conceptual frameworks at the price of freeing what is to be depicted from the language that depicts it. In this theory, the conceptual framework is prior to and apart from the language in which it is expressed. Like Kant, who held that there was a single a priori categorial framework, Davidson is committed to a similar view. The difference is that whereas Kant, the critical philosopher, tried, and all observers agree, failed to deduce his categorial. framework,[16] Quine and his followers, including Davidson, are content to claim that there is such a framework that they neither characterize nor justify.

A similar point can also be made about Chomskean linguistics, where the insistence on deep rules suggests a single categorial structure for all languages.[17] Yet despite much discussion, the nature of the supposed deep structure has never been described, and its existence, which is mainly "deduced" in a Kantian manner as a condition of language acquisition, has never been demonstrated.

ALTERNATIVE CONCEPTUAL SCHEMES

"Relativism" can be understood in different ways, for instance, as admitting the idea of alternative conceptual schemes. To deny that there can be more than a single conceptual scheme is to deny the possibility of this kind of relativism. The disagreement between partisans of a single or of multiple conceptual schemes often opposes abstract analyses to concrete studies of the phenomena. It is, then, not surprising that the idea that the process of knowledge consists in a conflict between incompatible perspectives, each of which can be said to be true, arises within studies of the history of science.

The concept of multiple conceptual schemes, the scientific analogue of Whorfian linguistic relativity, was reintroduced independently by Thomas Kuhn and Paul Feyerabend. Kuhn's well-known theory develops an analysis of scientific change against the background of a series of alternative paradigms or conceptual schemes. The idea of an alternative paradigm, although not under that name, is widely anticipated in the prior discussion, for instance, in Hegel's description of experiential knowledge as a succession of attitudes of thought to objectivity,[18] in Robin Collingwood's distinction of different ideas of nature,[19] in Gaston Bachelard's view of an epistemological break (*coupure épistémologique*) that Louis Althusser makes the basis of his reading of Marx's development,[20] and so on.

According to Kuhn, the development of science reflects the choice among different scientific paradigms that succeed each other in particular circumstances as the dominant metaphor tending to organize the scientific research at a given point in time. Kuhn, who correlates different paradigms with different scientific traditions, draws the conclusion that scientists working in different scientific traditions "work in different worlds."[21] Because for Kuhn, where Priestley saw "dephlogisticated air," Lavoisier saw oxygen,[22] in effect their respective views followed from and depended on different conceptual frameworks.

Kuhn's distinction between different, incompatible scientific paradigms is reinforced in Feyerabend's independent analysis of the change in scientific vocabulary over time. Working from a different perspective, he argues against meaning invariance in successive theories. According to Feyerabend, who seems to appeal to something like a Wittgensteinian theory of meaning in use, meaning can be shown to vary between successive theories, or points of view. Later theories are not only different; they also use the old vocabulary in new ways that eliminate old meanings.

Kuhn and Feyerabend argue for the existence of specifiably different, incommensurable conceptual schemes through the analysis of scientific practice. They reproduce within science the problem of alternative perspectives that arises within Whorf's linguistic relativism. Relativism is not in itself dangerous as long as it can be confined to the linguistic background. It is sometimes said that Chinese-speaking physicists have a special affinity for recent developments in microphysics. To the best of my knowledge, no one suggests a Chinese theory of physics or a view of modern physics rooted in the Chinese linguistic background. Yet when different paradigms are no longer confined to language, but appear within science itself, this appears to threaten the scientific enterprise. Science, on this view, cannot tolerate multiple points of view, different perspectives on experience.

KANT'S SINGLE CONCEPTUAL SCHEME

The idea of a single scientific framework animates the views of Descartes and Leibniz. It still guides the critical philosophy, whose official aim is to demonstrate the conditions of the possibility of knowledge whatsoever. For Kant, the very possibility of knowledge requires us to deduce a universally valid categorial framework. He holds that this same framework is valid without restriction for all observers and in all times and places. Despite his interest in history,[23] his own epistemological analysis is resolutely antihistorical. In his anthropology, he studies what nature has made of human beings and envisages what we can make of nature.[24] And he insists that we have not yet begun to think for ourselves, that is, to think critically. Yet he continues to insist that there is a single, invariant conceptual scheme that is not subject to historical change.

In the critical philosophy, the well-known categorial framework functions like a Cartesian foundation to guarantee the possibility of knowledge that is not relative to different points of view. Despite other differences, Descartes and Kant agree that science cannot tolerate a different perspective nor take up a historical point of view. Descartes has no conception of history that he regards as a mere fable. Kant, who has a better historical sense, is unable to bring together his nascent view of history and his theory of knowledge, his view of human development, or the development of the human species in time through the internalization of the moral law, and his twin theories of morality and pure reason as basically atemporal and devoid of any point of view.[25]

Yet if reason is not ahistorical but historical, as Hegel argues, then the very idea of the deduction of a single categorial framework on an a priori basis must give way to a notion of impure reason in context or spirit.[26] Although Hegel in turn continues to insist on a fixed categorial framework,[27] it is only a short step from the denial that the philosophical instrument is pure reason itself, a familiar fiction that lies at the heart of the critical philosophy, to the elaboration of alternative conceptual frameworks.

DAVIDSON AND ALTERNATIVE CONCEPTUAL SCHEMES

The possibility of conceptual alternatives, of other points of view, is central to the very idea of relativism. Arguments indicating the possibility of alternative conceptual frameworks have sometimes been perceived as a threat to the very idea of objective knowledge that has long been understood as rejecting the very idea of different, incompatible perspectives, such as the wave and corpuscular theories of light, or alternative interpretations of quantum mechanics. Davidson has recently been one of the most prominent opponents of alternative conceptual schemes.[28] In an influential paper, he examines what he calls, in a Kantian turn of phrase, the very idea of a conceptual scheme.[29]

The title of his paper is misleading, because Davidson would be misunderstood as denying that there is a conceptual scheme. His point is that there is not more than one such scheme; hence there is no reasonable alternative to the familiar framework offered by contemporary science. Davidson's rejection of the idea of alternative conceptual frameworks is combined with a restricted form of relativism. In his defense of Tarski's convention T, he insists that a truth theory is credible as a theory of interpretation only if it is relative to speaker and time.[30] Yet his own relativism stops well short of admitting the kind of relativism following from alternative frameworks favored by, say, Whorf, Kuhn, and Feyerabend.

Davidson's paper draws two unrelated conclusions: First, alternative conceptual frameworks cannot intelligibly be defended. This conclusion would be misconstrued as the claim that everyone shares the same scheme. Davidson does not want to hold, contrary to fact, that we all agree, although he does want to maintain that when we disagree, there is a rational way of adjudicating the difference. He wants, then, to deny such radical views as Goodman's assertion that all forms of inquiry are roughly on the same level[31] and Feyerabend's extreme assertion that voodoo is as good as quantum mechanics.[32] Second, he concludes that we can retain the idea of objective truth while giving up the idea of "an uninterpreted reality, something outside all schemes and science."[33] He concedes, then, Whorf's point that our conceptual framework shapes the content of experience while denying that the framework is basically linguistic.

These conclusions are unrelated and perhaps incompatible. There seems no way to argue that there is anything like an uninterpreted reality to which we fit our views, as presupposed in various versions of the correspondence view of truth. This point has been widely recognized in recent attention to antirealism by Dummett, and, following him, Rorty. Yet to acknowledge that our conception of the world influences our perception of it is to come close, perilously close, from Davidson's perspective perhaps too close for comfort, to the view that different conceptual frameworks yield different worlds.

Davidson, who does not argue for his conclusion that objective truth can be severed from the idea of an uninterpreted world, concentrates on denying the possibility of more than one framework. His denial rests on an analogy between conceptual schemes and languages. For Davidson, following Quine, the test of differences is a failure, or difficulty, of translation. Alternative conceptual schemes are like different languages that are not intertranslatable. He maintains that, because there are no such cases, the idea of alternative conceptual schemes is unintelligible.

In a trivial sense, Davidson obviously does not want to deny that alternative conceptual frameworks are possible. Nothing he says mitigates against the distinction between, say, folk psychology and his favored scientific perspective. Here he is close to someone like Sellars who distinguishes between what most people think and the informed or scientific observer.[34] When there is a difference, it is rational to prefer the scientific view. On the contrary, Davidson wants to affirm that there is only a single correct scientific scheme of things. In this respect, he perhaps unwittingly follows the Hegelian idea that there is only a single science, in Hegel's language a single system, because only one systematic analysis of the world can be correct.[35]

Davidson's view is deeply problematic. If we admit that there is only a single scheme and that our language organizes our experience in the form of a conceptual scheme, he is unable to show that our scheme, in his terminology, our language, is true. What does it mean to say that English is true? Or French? Or that both express a scheme that is true? Why is this more than an unjustified assumption? Descartes so distrusted common sense that he resorted to foundationalism to justify claims to know. Davidson seems to accept common sense at face value, as when he identifies the belief that a sentence is true with the claim that it is.[36] In so doing, he overlooks the distinction, as old as Plato, between opinion and truth.

Davidson's analogy between conceptual schemes and languages, the basis of his argument against alternative schemes, is problematic. Here we need not address Quine's theory of translation, upon which Davidson relies. Suffice it to say that Davidson's application of this Quinean theory is a classical example of the substitution of theoretical discussion for practical analysis, in this case discussion of the problem of translation without addressing any examples at all.

There are at least three problems with Davidson's effort to rule out alternative schemes through the analogy between translation and interpretation. First, there are no untranslatable languages, languages that cannot be rendered into one another. Yet if, as I suggested above, translation induces displacement, then it follows that there could well be alternative conceptual frameworks that, although translatable among themselves, would be irreducibly different. Otherwise stated, there is an important dissimilarity between conceptual schemes and languages that cannot be captured through the device of translation.[37]

Second, we can only know that there is a problem of translation if there is someone competent in both languages who can point it out. It follows that were there incompatible schemes, the incompatibility would only be apparent to someone who could participate in, or partake of, both simultaneously. Such an incompatibility would not be apparent to someone like Davidson who doubts the very possibility of any framework other than his own. Yet it would be incorrect to infer from one's own epistemological deficit that the distinction is in question cannot be made out. For instance, from the fact that one is color blind, it does not follow that there is no distinction between red and green.

Third, there are in fact different, incompatible conceptual frameworks, such as the analysis of combustion prior to and after the discovery of oxygen, and so on. Although this may be disagreeable to Davidson in virtue of his commitment to a single scientific perspective, I do not see how this fact can reasonably be denied. It is striking that Davidson chooses to respond to the careful, concrete analyses of particular cases offered by Whorf, Feyerabend, and Kuhn through a theoretical argument meant to deny their very possibility. Yet to convince us that he is correct, Davidson needs to do more than to formulate a transcendental or pseudotranscendental argument; for he must show us concretely where the others have gone astray. And this he fails to do.

SOME CONSTRAINTS ON
EPISTEMOLOGICAL RELATIVISM

Davidson's effort to show that there cannot be incompatible conceptual frameworks fails, because they in fact exist. The problem is not that the very idea of alternative frameworks is unintelligible; the problem is rather how, because they exist, we can make out claims for knowledge, objectivity, and truth. In other words, we need to understand the resources of relativism with respect to alternative frameworks for an adequate theory of knowledge.

A start in this direction can be made by adopting three principles. First, we need to avoid transcendental arguments about what can possibly be the case to concentrate on how we come into contact with and know our world as given in experience. Transcendental arguments typically eschew description for the effort to deduce a result. Kant, who is the main source of the transcendental mode of argumentation, reflects an unlimited confidence in his capacity to elicit the conditions of knowledge, not only for human beings, but for all rational beings. In an unguarded passage, he goes so far as to claim that were one to change anything, anything at all, in his theory, all human reason would totter.[38] Yet although many observers thought that his general approach was correct, no one, not even K. L. Reinhold, his closest immediate follower, accepted the argument as formulated in the *Critique of Pure Reason*. In a word, despite the undoubted interest of the critical philosophy, there have never been more than a very few who thought it possible to deduce or otherwise univocally to specify the conditions of knowledge.

Second, we need to start from the first-person perspective, from the angle of vision of the perceptual subject, understood not as an epistemological placeholder, such as a cogito or a transcendental unity of apperception, but as a human being. Yet as soon as we acknowledge that claims to know are relative to the human observer, then we need to take into account the context in which the person is rooted, including the criteria that he or she applies within the knowing process, the relation of various claims to know with respect to the discussion underway, the preceding tradition, and so on.

Third, enunciative, constative, or assertoric discourse that is present in every human society must be grasped against the conceptual background in which it occurs. The point is not to attack objectivity as such but rather to locate any claims to objectivity by saying relative to what. The answer can only be something like relative to observations of human beings dependent on the sort of conceptual framework prevalent at the present time.

At a minimum, and from the first-person perspective, a description of the knowing process must relate claims to know to the conceptual framework tending to legitimate them, and the framework to the wider historical background. Davidson's analysis of the very idea of a conceptual scheme is not meaningful in itself, but with respect to his prior acceptance of the generally Quinean framework he presupposes and the continuing controversy concerning alternative frameworks. Davidson, who denies the existence of alternative conceptual frameworks, effectively absolutizes the Quinean approach he accepts while simultaneously devaluing other philosophical alternatives, indeed, other alternative philosophical frameworks.

The history of thought reveals the succession of different conceptual frameworks or perspectives on reality as revealed in experience. Our views of experience are inevitably colored by the lenses of the scheme we accept. At this late date, it seems difficult to deny that there are different possible perspectives and equally difficult even to imagine a perspective that is none or is all at the same time, what Putnam, following Descartes, calls a god's-eye view.[39] Claims for objectivity and truth can only be made in relation to a particular framework, perspective, form of life, society, and so on. Yet we must be doubly aware that we cannot finally justify any particular framework and that the framework of the moment is indeed only that. For like the stages of society, our conceptual categories only seem to be stable although they are in fact historical variables.

ALTERNATIVE CONCEPTUAL SCHEMES AND RELATIVISM

Different views of relativism rely on different conceptual frameworks. The present view favors description of how we go about knowing our world and ourselves as given in experience as opposed to transcendental arguments about what is possible. It further favors adoption of a first-person perspective, reliance on a conception of the subject as a real human being, and the reinterpretation of enunciative, constative, and assertoric discourse basic to claims for knowledge within a real context. In this view, first-order claims to know are not self-demonstrating, but demonstrable, to the extent that demonstration is possible, through the relation to second-order discourse presupposing a conceptual matrix that may or may not be a historical variable. In other words, claims to know are never neutral or free of context but always relative to one or another conceptual framework in respect to which they are intelligible.

Davidson's argument against alternative conceptual schemes presupposes that science rests on a single conceptual scheme to which there is and can be no alternative. This abstract argument is refuted by the existence of alternative conceptual frameworks within physical theory. The presence of alternative conceptual schemes is even more frequent within philosophy. Indeed, the philosophical tradition has been insightfully understood as a clash of different, incompatible frameworks yielding different interpretations of the world as given in experience. Such differences cannot finally be adjudicated within philosophy, because they rest, as Fichte and James independently point out, on prephilosophical commitments. It follows that, reputedly like psychoanalysis, philosophical arguments are not terminable but interminable.[40]

This pluralistic conception of philosophic truth is opposed by those thinkers who conceive of the philosophical tradition, sometimes by analogy with physical science, as a single whole. Although various philosophers have from time to time understood philosophy as a unitary science, most recently Husserl, this regulative ideal has never been realized in practice. Hegel, who was strongly committed to this goal, failed to realize it for he was unable to take up into his theory ideas that were inconsistent with it.[41] Even the most closely monitored movements, those committed to a single author or a single conceptual approach, typically represent a series of related, but different views, as in Marxism. As we approach the end of this century, analytic philosophy, to which Davidson belongs, has never appeared less united.

The effort to argue that there cannot be more than a single

scheme, which fails for science, is even less promising for philosophy. Different philosophical theories clearly advance different conceptual frameworks. At this late date, there seems to be no way to argue that there is only a single possible philosophical scheme. In fact, all philosophical theories, Davidson's included, are doubly relative: to other arguments that appear within the preceding discussion and to what they intend to understand, the world as given in experience. The conceptual framework adopted at a given moment in the discussion is dependent on the prior discussion, from which it is inseparable. We cannot free the philosophical discussion from its dependency on the history of philosophy. Philosophical theories must be relativized to the philosophical tradition.

MARGOLIS ON ROBUST RELATIVISM AND RELATIONISM

Relativism has had few defenders recently although, as I have made clear, there are reasons to believe that the time is ripe to defend it. Nothing I have said until now commits me to a defense of so-called deep relativism that is usually regarded as enmeshed in insuperable difficulties of self-reference. I want now to extend my view to test its viability when it is interpreted as deep relativism. To do so, I will confront my view with that of Joseph Margolis, whose own theory of robust relativism turns on a distinction between relativism and what he calls relationalism.

Margolis's view of robust relativism can be fairly regarded as an effort to refute Davidson's and similar attacks on the kinds of relativism usually attributed to Whorf, Kuhn, and Feyerabend without falling into the paradoxes arising from deep relativism, which Margolis calls relationalism. In response, my strategy will be to show that what is known as relationalism can avoid the paradoxes in question, to show further that Margolis's form of relativism is itself committed to relationalism, and finally to show that no form of relativism can avoid relationalism.

Margolis's argument distinguishes between what he calls robust relativism that he accepts and relationalism—sickly relativism?—which he rejects.[42] According to Margolis, we "cannot escape the self-referential paradoxes, *if* one espouses deep relativism rather than robust relativism."[43] He maintains that there are many forms of deep relativism, but all produce a self-referential paradoxes. He further maintains that self-referential paradoxes arise when the claim of true is replaced by the claim of true in L.[44]

If I understand him correctly, Margolis regards claims such as true in L as intrinsically paradoxical. Yet there is nothing paradoxical about the perfectly general claim, typical of first-order discourse, that, say, on the basis of criteria I now accept, the information known to me, and so on, that is with respect to my present scheme of things, I accept one or another view of relativism. And there is nothing wrong with the straightforward claim that in terms of my understanding of the stock market, I think this is a good time to sell or not to sell. Finally, there is nothing wrong with the ordinary statement that on the way to the office I think I saw someone I know.

These ordinary claims are typical of so-called first-order discourse. Each of these claims depends on second order, or metadiscourse, for their intelligibility. None of these claims is acceptable in itself or self-justifying without an appeal to a further conceptual framework. Now there is nothing unusual about this remark. It is a fair description of how we usually operate, that is, how we go about things on the folk level of knowledge when we are not in the widespread philosophical mode that leads, mistakenly in my view, to believe that we can go beyond a given conceptual framework to knowledge itself. If, in practice, we are willing to relativize truth claims to actual agents and specific times, as indeed we must, then we admit relationalism as Margolis defines it.

In my view, there is nothing parlous about relationalism, because it describes the way that we ordinarily cope with our world. Margolis is unsuccessful in avoiding relationalism. The main message of his book is that robust relativism is possible, plausible, and favored at the present time.[45] This is suspiciously close to the assertion that his own robust relativism is justifiable with respect to where we are in the discussion of knowledge, in particular of relativism at the present time. In fact, he could hardly have argued in another manner without opting for the kind of transcendental analysis he strives to avoid. It seems, then, that Margolis cannot make out his view of relativism without answering the question:

Relative to what? The answer, ultimately, has to be relative to the preceding discussion and, beyond that, to history. Yet this is deep relativism.

CONCLUSION: RELATIVISM AND THE HISTORICAL FRAMEWORK

The moral of this essay is that if not in theory at least in practice claims for knowledge can without contradiction be relativized to a historically relative conceptual framework. I will conclude by making the converse claim that, if not in theory, at least in practice claims for knowledge cannot be separated from the historical framework in which they are embedded. Because there are and cannot be neutral claims, because the very idea of a neutral perspective is no more than a useful fiction, we do not and cannot avoid or escape from the historical framework. If this is correct, then all claims to know, including this one, are relative and eventually subject to modification with respect to the historical background. For if we maintain the well-known vertical framework, then it is neither philosophy nor physics but history that is the master science. Claims to know as well as their analysis are always embedded within the historical flux.

NOTES

1. For a recent version of this argument, see Stephen Toulmin, *Cosmopolis: The Hidden Agenda of Modernity* (New York: Free Press, 1990).

2. See Hilary Putnam, *Realism with a Human Face,* ed. James Conant (Cambridge, Mass.: Harvard University Press, 1990), p. 51.

3. Richard Rorty, "Relativism, Power, and Philosophy," in *Consequences of Pragmatism* (Minneapolis: University of Minnesota Press, 1982), p. 166.

4. See "Philosophy as Rigorous Science," in Edmund Husserl, *Phenomenology and the Crisis of Philosophy,* trans. Quentin Lauer (New York: Harper and Row, 1965), pp. 71–192.

5. As early as the first page of his *Essays,* he insists that he is himself its subject. See Michel Montaigne, *Essais,* ed. Pierre Michel (Paris: Librairie générale française, 1972), I: 23.

6. Descartes's theory can be understood as continuing Montaigne's con-

centration on himself. The difference is that whereas, on this basis, Montaigne draws a skeptical conclusion, most notably in his "Apology for Raymond Sebond," Descartes argues for apodictic knowledge.

7. See Augustine, *De vera religione,* p. 39, n. 2, cited in Edmund Husserl, *Cartesian Meditations,* trans. Dorion Cairns (The Hague: Martinus Nijhoff, 1960), p. 157.

8. See Augustine, *The Confessions of St. Augustine,* trans. Edward B. Pusey (New York: Washington Square Press, 1961), XI: 223–39.

9. See John Dewey, *The Quest for Certainty* (New York: Putnam, 1960).

10. See Richard Rorty, *Philosophy and the Mirror of Nature* (Princeton, N.J.: Princeton University Press, 1979).

11. See Richard Rorty, *Contingency, Irony, and Solidarity* (Cambridge: Cambridge University Press, 1989), p. 5.

12. See Alasdair MacIntyre, *Three Rival Versions of Moral Inquiry: Encyclopedia, Genealogy and Tradition* (Notre Dame, Ind.: Notre Dame University Press, 1990).

13. B. L. Whorf, "The Punctual and Segmentative Aspects of Verbs in Hopi," in *Language, Thought, and Reality: Selected Writings of Benjamin Lee Whorf,* ed. J. B. Carroll (Cambridge: Technology Press of MIT, 1956), p. 55.

14. See, e.g., "The Method of Truth in Metaphysics," in Donald Davidson, *Inquiries into Truth and Interpretation* (Oxford: Clarendon Press, 1984).

15. According to Margolis, Quine and Duhem defend very different views of holism. See Joseph Margolis, *Science without Unity: Reconciling the Human and the Natural Sciences* (Oxford: Blackwell, 1987), p. 111.

16. For an argument that it is not possible to deduce a categorial framework of the Kantian type, see Stephan Körner, *Categorial Frameworks* (Oxford: Blackwell, 1970).

17. See Noam Chomsky, *Language and Mind* (New York: Harcourt Brace, 1968).

18. See G. W. F. Hegel, *The Encyclopedia Logic, Part I of the Encyclopedia of the Philosophical Sciences,* trans. T. F. Geraets, W. A. Suchting, and H. S. Harris (Hackett, Ind.: Indianapolis, 1992), pp. 65–124.

19. See R. G. Collingwood, *The Idea of Nature* (Oxford: Oxford University Press, 1960).

20. See Louis Althusser, *For Marx,* trans. Ben Brewster (New York: Vintage, 1970).

21. Thomas Kuhn, *The Structure of Scientific Revolutions* (Chicago: University of Chicago Press, 1970), p. 134.

22. See Kuhn, *Structure of Scientific Revolutions,* p. 118.

23. See, e.g., "Idea for a Universal History with a Cosmopolitan Intent," and "Speculative Beginning of Human History," in Kant, *Perpetual Peace and Other Essays,* pp. 29–40, 49–60.

24. See Immanuel Kant, *Anthropologie in pragmatischer Hinsicht,* Vol. 10 in *Kants Werke,* ed. W. Weischedel (Frankfurt a.M.: Insel Verlag, 1956–64).

25. Kant is unable to integrate his interest in history with his epistemological analysis. For this argument, see Tom Rockmore, "Subjectivity and the Ontology of History," *Monist* 74, no. 2 (April 1991): 188–205.

26. This is a main theme in all his writings. See G. W. F. Hegel, *Phenomenology of Spirit,* trans. A. V. Miller (Oxford: Oxford University Press, 1977), chap. 6: "Spirit," 263–409.

27. See G. W. F. Hegel, *Hegel's Science of Logic,* trans. A. V. Miller (Atlantic Highlands, N.J.: Humanities Press, 1989).

28. For detailed criticism of Davidson's attack on the very idea of alternative conceptual schemes, see chap. 2: "Conceptual Schemes," in Nicholas Rescher, *Empirical Inquiry* (Totowa, N.J.: Rowman and Littlefield, 1982), pp. 27–60.

29. See "On the Very Idea of a Conceptual Scheme," in Donald Davidson, *Inquiries into Truth and Interpretation* (Oxford: Oxford University Press, 1984), pp. 183–98.

30. See Donald Davidson, *Inquiries into Truth and Interpretation* (New York: Oxford University Press, 1991), p. 74.

31. See Nelson Goodman, *Ways of Worldmaking* (Indianapolis, Ind.: Hackett, 1978).

32. See Paul Feyerabend, *Against Method* (London: Verso, 1978), pp. 48–53.

33. Davidson, *Inquiries into Truth and Interpretation,* p. 198.

34. See "Philosophy and the Scientific Image of Man," in Wilfrid Sellars, *Science, Perception and Reality* (London: Routledge and Kegan Paul, 1968).

35. Hegel, *The Difference between Fichte's and Schelling's System of Philosophy,* trans. Walter Cerf and H. S. Harris (Albany: SUNY Press, 1977).

36. Davidson writes: "I propose that we take the fact that speakers of a language hold a sentence to be true (under observed circumstances) as primafacie evidence that the sentence is true under those circumstances." Davidson, *Inquiries into Truth and Interpretation,* p. 152.

37. For this argument, see Henri Bergson, *An Introduction to Metaphysics,* trans. T. E. Hulme (Indianapolis, Ind.: LLA, 1965).

38. See Immanuel Kant, *Kritik der reinen Vernunft,* B xxxvii.

39. See Hilary Putnam, *Realism with a Human Face,* ed. James Conant (Cambridge: Harvard University Press, 1990), pp. 5, 7, 8, 9.

40. For this argument, see Nicholas Rescher, *The Strife of Systems* (Pittsburgh, Pa.: University of Pittsburgh Press, 1979).

41. See Tom Rockmore, *Hegel et la tradition philosophique allemande* (Brussels: Editions Ousia, 1993).

42. See Joseph Margolis, *The Truth about Relativism* (Oxford: Blackwells, 1991), pp. 8–9.

43. See ibid., p. 201.

44. See ibid., p. 98.

45. See ibid., p. 219.

Pragmatism and Culture

Richard Shusterman

And Joseph said this is the interpretation thereof.
—Genesis, 40:12

I

Pragmatist philosophy celebrates the idea of culture. It not only recognizes that culture is both an essential value and the ineliminable matrix of human life; it further insists that philosophy itself is the product of culture, changing with cultural change. Philosophy's methods, aims, and problems reflect those of the culture that shapes it. Even its concepts like truth, knowledge, identity, means, and ends get their concrete significance from the roles they play in a culture's (historically changing) language games. Like other rich traditions, pragmatism presents no monolithic school but rather a variety of approaches. In this essay, I shall characterize and contrast two different pragmatist approaches to culture. One I dub the descriptive-metaphysical approach, the other the reconstructive-poetic approach.

The first is particularly concerned with the ontology of culture, with second-order, metaphysical questions of legitimation: questions about what sort of objects cultural discourse is grounded on and what allows or guarantees the coherence of cultural discourse in conditions of change. This approach can be seen as largely Kantian—a quest for the conditions of possibility of coherent discourse. The second approach is less concerned with the metaphysical grounding and logical legitimation of our cultural discourse than with employing and revising it to address concrete problems and to overcome obstacles that block the road of inquiry. More Hegelian than Kantian, it legitimates (and challenges) not by transcendental arguments of "conditions of possibility," but by composing polemical narratives and advocatory depictions, by suggesting new ways of thinking and talking of cultural phenomena.

The first approach has its source in Peirce and is most fully and cogently developed in the work of Joseph Margolis. The other, inspired by Dewey, is represented (in rather different ways) by Richard Rorty's advocacy of new vocabularies and by my own legitimating narrative-polemic for popular art and nondiscursive somatic understanding.[1] Must pragmatism choose between them or can they be reconciled so that one will simply complement the other? If such reconciliation is possible, it is because these two approaches share pragmatism's major themes. Let us then begin with these shared themes.

II

As both Dewey and Peirce remarked, pragmatism is inspired by Darwin's idea of evolution. It is not simply that the world, including the world of human thought, develops and changes over time; it is also that such development is contingent rather than necessary. The universe is not only plastic but variant, the product of chance probabilities. Human thought and action are evolutionary response to the world and play central part in reshaping that world. The very concept of reality, Peirce famously urged, is a social product implying a community of inquirers focused on the same object of inquiry. William James similarly insisted that the very concepts with which we experience the world reflect humanity's past valuations or interpretations of experience and that the trace of the human is everywhere. In Quine's more contemporary formulation, reality is a blend of fact and convention that cannot be factored into its pure separate components. Finally, there is pragmatism's strong fallibilism and antifoundationalism. No representation or alleged fact enjoys apodictic incorrigible certainty; any belief is open to revision by further inquiry; no cognitive act enjoys absolute privilege. For besides the permanent possibility of error, there is the possibility that conceptual change will render a past belief irrelevant and even incoherent.

In the technical vocabulary of Margolis, these themes are described as variance, flux, contingency, the lack of cognitive transparency and privilege, and the socially constructed nature of human culture, including human selves. His recent book on interpretation begins by formulating them in the following five doctrines:

1. Reality is cognitively *intransparent*: that is, all discourse about the world is mediated by our conceptual schemes [and no single perception or scheme can claim apodictic privilege or necessity].
2. The structure of reality and the structure of human thought are inextricably *symbiotized*: that is, there is no principled means by which to decide correctly what the "mind" contributes to what we take to be the world's real structure or what the "brute" world contributes.
3. Thinking has a history, is *historicized*: that is, all the supposed fixities, invariances, necessities, universalities of thinking and world . . . are contingent artifacts of the historical existence of different societies . . . [and are] under the constraint of changeable history.
4. The structure of our thinking is *preformed* and self-modifying: that is, tacitly formed by antecedent enculturing processes that we cannot entirely fathom, though by participating in these same processes (as we must) we alter them. . . .
5. The phenomena and entities of human culture are *socially constituted* or *constructed,* have no "natures," . . . are only histories: that is, persons and selves, artworks, artifacts, texts, actions, institutions, societies, words and sentences,

and the like cannot be characterized as failing under "natural kinds" . . . having assignably fixed essences or [explainable] by reference merely to . . . physical things. (I, 2–3, 7)

Although these doctrines may strike some philosophers as quite radical, they find support from various quarters outside pragmatism. Kantianism already argued for intransparency and symbiosis, though insisting on the fixity and necessity of a certain conceptual scheme and of the noumenal world. Varieties of historicism and sociological theory (e.g., nonessentialist Marxisms and Pierre Bourdieu) provide support for theses three and five, while thesis four is central to the wide range of philosophies that have embraced the interpretive turn. More generally, the acute time-consciousness that has grown from the birth of modernity to the breathless confusion of postmodern transformations has made us (and not merely us philosophers) particularly aware of change, flux, and the constructed, artifactual character of ourselves and the so-called natural.

Though the general worldview emerging from the conjunction of these pragmatist doctrines is, of course, more radical than its individual components, this vision is far from unfamiliar. It almost seems part of the unreflective common sense of postmodern experience. The question is whether it can survive philosophical reflection, whether it can be maintained against the philosophical critique that in giving up fixed objects and unchanging essences one abandons the possibility of coherent discourse and thus of real knowledge.

The pragmatist defense of flux therefore concentrates not on adducing the presence of change, but in combatting the deeply entrenched philosophical view that at least some independent, invariant objects and essences are necessary to ground discourse and thus guarantee the possibility of truth and knowledge which themselves depend on discourse. Because this view seeks foundations in an invariant, autonomous reality apart from human practices, let me call it invariant realism. Such realism can, of course, allow for change; otherwise it would be implausible. It merely insists that something (some form of foundational atoms, as it were) remains invariant. Such realism has always dominated philosophical thinking, and its abandonment has usually been taken to entail a vitiating skepticism. Both forms of pragmatism—the descriptive-metaphysics of Margolis and the reconstructive-poetic approach I prefer—challenge the argument that invariant realism deserves its dominance because it is in fact conceptually necessary for the very possibility of coherent discourse and knowledge.

In challenging invariant realism, pragmatism deploys at least three central strategies. The first is shared by the descriptive and reconstructive approaches, while the two others are more closely linked to reconstruction. Let us start with the shared strategy.

1. It challenges invariant realism's claim that coherent discourse and knowledge are impossible without invariant objects to serve as the shared objects of discourse and objective truth. Invariant realism's argument is that without fixed objects to ground our referential discourse, there is no way to reidentify anything as the same thing, and thus there is no way of establishing reference that is stable enough to sustain discourse on a common object. But without the possibility of a common object of discourse, an object that can be reidentified (hence sustained) for more than one utterance, the very notions of discourse and shared knowledge are rendered impossible. Since coherent discourse and knowledge are, however, achieved, then the conclusion is that there must be some invariant objects.

Margolis's central strategy in *Interpretation: Radical But Not Unruly* is to challenge this argument by showing how pragmatist philosophies of the flux can allow for reidentification of particular objects without presuming their fixity. There is no need, he argues, to prove that there is variance. Since change is surely evident and history seems open to further change, the burden of proof rests on those who insist invariance is instead necessary for coherent discourse.

The key maneuver is to show how we can individuate and reidentify an object as the same object without denying that that object has in fact changed radically and without appealing to a core of essential properties that always remain stable throughout all the changes of the object. Margolis's crucial tactic is to distinguish the referential fixity of an object—that is, the fixity necessary for establishing that object as an object of discourse—from the substantive fixity of that which is thereby discursively identified or referred to. "The referential (grammatical) fixity of a text is a matter quite distinct from the substantive fixity of what may be thus fixed." Although "nothing could be referentially fixed that did not exhibit a certain stability of nature," stability is different from complete invariance and the nature and range of the existent or needed stability is left wide open" (I, 34). Margolis makes a related distinction regarding the oneness traditionally required of an object; to speak of an object, all one needs is grammatical unity or "unicity," not real substantive unity of that which is individuated and reidentified through such minimal unicity (I, 33). In this way, we can say of a particular object that it lacks substantive unity yet still regard it as constituting a single object through its unicity.

My reconstructive pragmatism employs the same strategy of distinguishing between logico-referential issues and substantive ones. In arguing against the need "to posit a fixed independent meaning as the work's identity in order to guarantee identity of reference for its critical discussion," I wrote in *Pragmatist Aesthetics*:[2]

> The key is to distinguish the logical issue of referential identification from the substantive issue of the nature, properties, or meaning of what has been identified. Certainly, however much we allow our interpretations of a work to differ, we must allow for the reidentification of the same work in order to talk about "the" work (and indeed "its" different reception) at all. The ordinary referential and predicative functions of discourse simply require this bare logico-grammatical identity of individuation. But such identity does not entail that what is identified on different occasions is completely or even substantially the same. For practical purposes of discourse, we can agree that we are talking about the same thing while differing radically as to what the substantive nature of that thing is, whether it's a bird, a plane, or indeed Superman. . . . In distinguishing between referential and substantive identity, we can similarly distinguish between change *in* the object interpreted and change *of* the object interpreted, where the former need not (but can, if sufficiently extreme) involve the latter. (PA, 93–94)

But how, one might persist, is this referential identity achieved and sustained if it cannot rely on a fixed substantive identity? The answer that Margolis and I give is essentially the same: Reference is achieved and sustained simply through the culture's linguistic practices of individuation and identification, which can supply enough propositional agreement to allow us to focus on or frame common, if vaguely specified, object, without committing us to the precise, substantive content of that object. As I wrote in *Pragmatist Aesthetics,* "Agreement about referential identity can be secured by agreeing on a certain minimum number of identifying descriptions, or it can be (and most often is) simply assumed by our deeply entrenched cultural habits of individuation" (PA, 94). As Margolis puts it, "What ensures the success of discourse . . . are the collective resources of a natural-language community's habits of life" (I, 75). In short, Margolis and I regard artworks, texts, and even human selves as cultural entities that are constituted and identified as the individuals they are by the social and linguistic practices of the culture they serve. Their identities thus can change as these practices change, but given the stability of our linguistic practices, such cultural artifacts can be "relatively stable" (I, 45; PA, 94).

III

What then is the difference between Margolis's descriptive-metaphysical pragmatism and the reconstructive-poetic pragmatism I favor? Part of the difference is in reconstruction's advocacy of two other strategies for challenging the claim of the necessity of invariance. One is a genealogical, reconstructive narrative that undermines the claim of invariance (and by extension other undesirable claims) by explaining the historical motives that generate its power. The other strategy is simply the creation of new linguistic means, new vocabularies or ways of talking, which by the very fact of their variance yet coherence challenge the doctrine of invariance.

Another important difference, however, is Margolis's great concern with ontologizing the cultural and linguistic practices that allow individuation and reference. He is intent on claiming that "some form of cultural realism would be required" to ground our linguistic practices, to give them a logical coherence or rigor (I, 25). He is preoccupied with providing a *metaphysics* of cultural objects, for determining the precise mode of being of the referents of cultural discourse. Although he opposes fixity in the identity of such objects, he is much concerned with fixing their ontological status and for sharply distinguishing the status of these cultural referents from that of natural objects. Although he insists that cultural objects have no natural nature but only histories (i.e., they are not natural kinds), he gives them a metaphysical nature as "Intentional objects."

Cultural objects he insists are special entities that "differ from natural objects essentially in possessing Intentional properties"; and though as yet unrealized, his aim is "a full account of the ontology of artworks or cultural phenomena in general" (I, 46). The apparent motive for this concern for the metaphysics of cultural referents is that cultural discourse would be incoherent without the positing of entities to which such discourse refers and without an account of the metaphysical nature of such entities.

Reconstructive pragmatism is hardly interested in these metaphysical questions. It embraces the idea that our reality is plastic and contingent and largely structured by human discourse and action. But it doesn't see the point of trying to ground cultural discourse in an elaborate metaphysics of cultural objects when the ground of those very cultural objects is simply, by Margolis's own account, those same discursive cultural practices that metaphysics seeks to ground. If a culture's linguistic practices are, as Wittgenstein and Margolis argue, the bedrock for all justification and grounding, what need do we have to construct a metaphysics to render these practices coherent? Is it not enough proof that they work in practice? How does elaborating a metaphysics of Intentional entities either improve or justify linguistic practice, when language itself is invoked to explain the Intentional ("language is its paradigm," I, 52)?

To borrow an image of Wittgenstein, there is no need to elaborate clouds of metaphysics, if their justificatory or explanatory function is already condensed effectively in drops of grammar. In other words, there is no crucial legitimative reason, after adducing the concrete linguistic means by which reference is secured, to plunge ourselves into metaphysical theories of the objects referred to.

Such metaphysical analyses had much more point and legitimative function when reality was conceived in terms of fixed or necessary essences on which language depended and which it sought to mirror. For in that case, once we achieved an adequate metaphysical account of the real, it would always remain valid and effective as a criterion for assessing ordinary understanding. However, once reality (at least in its human, cultural dimension) is grasped as historical contingent flux that is itself the symbiotic product of language, the value of elaborating a metaphysics becomes questionable. For here the metaphysical picture neither can ground our changing linguistic phenomena nor can predict or illuminate their changes. Margolis's metaphysics by being historicist can at least accommodate linguistic and cultural change and is in this way far superior to nonhistoricist metaphysics of culture. But for radical pragmatism, the question remains, what useful explanatory or legitimative work does such a language-grounded metaphysical system perform that is not already gained by simply recognizing that language structures human thought and practice and that it changes over time through contingent developments and in variant ways?

One could, of course, defend the project of a systematic historicist metaphysics of culture by simply saying that philosophy traditionally demands a metaphysics of everything, so that even if metaphysics has lost its old grounding legitimative role, it must be pursued nevertheless as a central philosophical undertaking. For what could philosophy be without metaphysical systems? However, if we recognize that philosophy itself is a cultural practice and we take the full measure of Margolis's insistence on cultural flux, there is reason to allow that philosophy itself can change and has already changed, and that we are moving slowly but surely beyond the age of metaphysical systems. Margolis's extremely elastic, contingent, and historicized metaphysics can be seen as a progressive station on the way to this new age of philosophy, though with its face largely turned backward to the metaphysical concerns of the past.

There is yet another way to argue for the usefulness of elaborating a historicized, linguisticized metaphysics of culture *à la* Margolis. Our linguistic practices are extremely complex and confusing; hence their metaphysical import is obscure and requires a systematic metaphysics to provide a perspicuous representation of the reality and objects constituted by language. This argument is perhaps the most persuasive. But the question remains whether Margolis's metaphysical systematization, with its complex terms of art like "the Intentional" and its subtle distinctions of the "lingual" from the "linguistic," is indeed more perspicuous than the linguistic practices it seeks to capture and more enlightening than the vivid images of flux and the plastic universe. This raises the further question of what is the standard or variety of perspicuity one seeks, as well as the question of perspicuity for whom. Is it perspicuity for academic specialists in metaphysics or perspicuity for intelligent readers who want to understand their cultural world?

Reconstructive pragmatism does, however, recognize other reasons for going beyond our actual concrete linguistic practices. These reasons are not concerned with the metaphysical grounding of actual practice but with its improvement. This reconstructive improvement is pursued by actively pursuing change in our linguistic practices by composing narratives to undermine the myth of fixity that would encourage a linguistic status quo, but also by proposing new vocabularies or new ways of talking about certain things that concretely show how coherent linguistic change is possible by actually effecting such change. These strategies of narration and of novel, performative characterization are why I portray reconstructive pragmatism as narrative-poetic in contrast to the descriptive-metaphysical pragmatism of Margolis. Let us briefly consider how these reconstructive strategies are used to challenge the metaphysical doctrine of invariance.

IV

The pragmatist strategy of deploying genealogical narrative to undermine the philosophy of fixity finds perhaps its most famous and influential exemplification in John Dewey's critical account of philosophy's traditional "quest for certainty."[3] According to Dewey, primitive man's deep desire to "escape from peril" in an unmanageable "world of hazards" generated a religious attitude of appeasement and conformity to the transcendent powers assumed to control the humanly unmanageable flux of nature. This primitive religious disposition for fixity and certainty was the underlying inspiration for "philosophy's search for the immutable," a search that would eventually substitute absolute being and its fixed, rational laws for the gods and their capricious acts and verdicts (QC, 3, 21).

To appreciate the power of this strategy of genealogical narrative, one must get at least some sense of the scope of the story. I
therefore am obliged to quote at some length from Dewey's account
of how "insecurity generates the quest for certainty" and fixity, thus
creating a long philosophical prejudice of privileging the theory of
the immutable over practice within the flux.

> Absence of arts of regulation diverted the search for security into
> irrelevant modes of practice, into rite and cult. . . . Gradually
> there was a differentiation of two realms, one higher, consisting
> of the powers which determine human destiny in all important
> affairs. With this religion was concerned. The other consisted of
> the prosaic matters in which man relied upon his own skill and his
> matter-of-fact insight. Philosophy inherited the idea of this divi-
> sion. . . . Because of the growth of mathematics, there arose also
> the ideal of a purely rational knowledge, intrinsically solid and
> worthy and the means by which intimations of rationality within
> changing phenomena could be comprehended within science. For
> the intellectual class the stay and consolation, the warrant of cer-
> tainty, provided by religion was henceforth found in intellectual
> demonstration of the reality of the objects of an ideal realm.
> (QC, 202)

The Greeks, therefore, institutionalized a distinction between
the certainty of theory and the flux of practice.

> Practical action . . . belongs in the realm of generation and decay,
> a realm inferior in value as in Being. . . . Because ultimate Being
> or reality is fixed, permanent, admitting of no change or variation,
> it may be grasped by rational intuition and set forth in rational,
> that is, universal and necessary demonstration . . . the unalterably
> fixed and the absolutely certain are one. (QC, 16)

After the Greeks, the identification of certainty with im-
mutability was reinforced and extended into ethical matters by
Christianity. "The authority of ultimate Being was, moreover, represented on earth by the Church; that which in its nature tran-
scended intellect was made known by a revelation of which the
Church was the interpreter and guardian" (QC, 202–203). Dewey

concludes that although the discoveries of modern science have undermined our belief in fixity with respect to practical and material matters, the habit of fixity and certainty still pervades our philosophical thinking and drives us to search for absolute values, immutable categories, unchanging entities, and eternal laws.

By this compelling, tendentious narrative, Dewey discredits the philosophical prejudice for fixity by tracing it to emotions of insecurity, primitive religion, undeveloped science, and rigid Christian dogmatism. The view that knowledge and discourse require invariant objects is shown to rest not on logical compulsions but on compulsive primitive fears.

The same type of narrative strategy can, of course, be used to challenge other entrenched philosophical views. Dewey deploys it to undermine the privileging oppositions of theory/practice and ends/means, which, apart from their connection with the quest for certainty, are shown to stem from class hierarchies in ancient Greece and the primitive conditions of labor there. In *Pragmatist Aesthetics* (chaps. 7–8), I similarly employ the reconstructive narrative strategy in challenging the rigid privileging dichotomy of high art versus popular art. By relating historically how today's high art was once viewed (and often condemned) as popular, I show that this distinction marks not permanent, essential aesthetic qualities but changing and alterable social conditions. By tracing the power and aura of high art to its conservative, undemocratic sources in court aristocracy and high church "otherworldliness," I also discredit its claim to be the exclusive aesthetic vehicle of progressive social value.

Such genealogical narrative may taint the image of high art but does not suffice for aesthetic legitimation of the popular. Here reconstructive pragmatism of culture needs another tool: the third strategy I mentioned for challenging invariance. This strategy involves linguistic innovation, either inventing new vocabularies or applying familiar vocabularies to things not formerly described in such terms. To give rap cultural legitimation as art, I therefore analyzed it in culturally valued aesthetic and philosophical terms in which it had never been discussed. To speak of it in such new, better ways can help effect a new cultural valuation. For cultural or aesthetic value is not permanently, ontologically fixed, but rather the product of changing human practices informed by language. Of course, philosophical talk alone cannot in itself give popular art full social legitimation. That would require also change in the discourse and institutional practices of other, more socially powerful, groups.

The logic behind this reconstructive challenge to invariance is simple. By actually effecting coherent linguistic change, by adding to the flux, it manifests that language varies yet maintains coherence through change. Nor is such linguistic change merely linguistic; it can amount to a substantive change in our cultural world. Take, for example, the new linguistic terms of "sexual harassment" and "stalking." These terms are not simply faithful descriptions of previous, invariant forms of behavior that were already immoral or criminal; instead, such locutions reconstruct sexual relations to create these new criminal acts. Early in this century as in the remote past, ardent but unrequited lovers were not stalking, sexual criminals, even if they could be rather annoying. Changes in sexual language, like the changes of PC-discourse, have effected substantive cultural change, a change in actual social relations whose effects go well beyond language and even reach the most basic, nondiscursive sensual dimensions of our experience. The sexual ambience has been radically altered (at least on American campuses); thus not even the apparent permanence of sex escapes invariance.

V

Having described pragmatism's three strategies for challenging the necessity of invariance to ground our discourse and cultural world, I shall conclude by reviewing, *in nuce,* the relation between Margolis's descriptive-metaphysical pragmatism and the reconstructive-poetic pragmatism I favor. While Margolis concentrates on the first strategy and on metaphysical representations of linguistic practice, reconstructive pragmatism goes beyond the logical solution of the first strategy. It offers the strategies of new narratives and ways of talking that not only expose the questionable motives and sources of invariance but contribute themselves to new, variant linguistic practices that can improve our culture.

Margolis is a fine philosophical poet in his own right. But he confines his new locutions to what he calls second-order philosophical discourse, to his technical terms of art like "unicity," "Intentional," and "lingual," and he insists on marking a clear distinction between first- and second-order discourse, criticizing pragmatists such as Rorty and Stanley Fish for denying a role for second-order projects. Reconstructive pragmatism, as I construe and practice it, recognizes a functional distinction between these levels of discourse, but it insists on considerable seepage and flexibility between them. It also insists that philosophy's poetic efforts of innovative discourse should be directed at first-order discourse, not simply at higher grounding or justificational levels of inquiry.

Reconstructive pragmatism is actively interventionist, aimed at effecting—not merely representing or metaphysically accommodating—cultural change. It seeks more than a philosophical account of culture, but substantive cultural improvement. Its first stage of argument, which it shares with Margolis, is this: If the world is partly the result of human linguistic practices, then it can in part be changed by changing those practices. Margolis seems satisfied with this important conclusion and devotes himself to patiently, skillfully showing how such change is compatible with the rigors of referential discourse and how it can be embodied in an ontology of historicized, variant, vague but still identifiable cultural entities. But reconstructive pragmatism is not so simply satisfied and pursues its argument further: If our cultural world is altered by changing linguistic practices, why should not philosophy play a more active role in such change by advocating linguistic reforms, by advancing new ways of talking that would improve the concrete practices of our actual life world and not merely the second order, philosophical practices of ontologically representing it?

There is a familiar objection to reconstructive pragmatism: In taking such an activist role, philosophy abandons its essential posture of disinterested neutrality and its defining role of interpreting rather than changing the world. But this objection is easily countered. First, much of classic philosophy (e.g., Plato's theory of art or Locke's theory of government) is far from disinterested and devoid of reformatory agendas. Second, on the view of culture's flux I share with Margolis, philosophy, like any cultural product, is variant and open to change. So even if it once displayed Olympian neutrality, it need not maintain this posture. The crucial question, for the pragmatist, is only one of cost accounting: whether the gains of philosophical activism outweigh the advantages of philosophical neutrality. I think they do, not only because of my skepticism of putative philosophical neutrality, but also because the stakes of our cultural struggles are too important to be neutral about.

Let me close by addressing a question I raised at the outset. Although I have contrasted the descriptive-metaphysical and reconstructive-poetic as rival forms of pragmatism, are they indeed incompatible, and must we choose only one between them? I would like to think that the approaches can be reconciled and used to complement each other. Endorsing the general metaphysical and epistemological themes expressed in Margolis's notion of the world of flux, I would find it hard to refute the elaborate ontology of cultural entities that he proposes. I hope and trust it is adequate to whatever metaphysical tasks he constructed it for. But practically speaking, for the reconstructive pragmatist, such ontological exercises seem relatively pointless, for reasons already delineated. In any case, they leave me cold, so I choose to do other things.

Margolis might protest this cavalier dismissal of ontology, arguing that I must address the question of the entities of discourse. Otherwise, he would claim, discourse itself remains incoherent and ungrounded, and the cultural world is reduced to *façons de parler.* But I just don't see how his ontological constructions of the flux, which explicitly rest on discursive practice, provide any more robust grounding than those discursive practices themselves. Moreover, the refusal to ontologize the lifeworld is hardly tantamount to treating it as a mere *façon de parler.* Discursive practices involve actions and objects as well as words, and there is also, I would argue, an important nondiscursive (though discursively alterable) dimension to the lifeworld, expressed, for example, in immediate somatic experience.

This questioning of the ubiquity of text and interpretation is another place where my pragmatism differs from Margolis's.[4] But rather than pursuing this new issue here, I prefer to end with a chord of reconciliation. For, to make a personal confession, I might never have found my way to reconstructive pragmatism, had I not encountered Margolis's pragmatist metaphysics. Nor would I have ever been so free to pursue my flaky new topics of reconstruction in the classroom, if Margolis—my senior, exemplary departmental colleague—had not been there to take care of the traditional business of metaphysics.

Despite my own lack of zeal for his ontological efforts, I can imagine how a pragmatist could be a Margolian metaphysician in the morning (particularly if he's a very early riser) and a reconstructive poet in the afternoon. Philosophy and pragmatism should be big enough for both enterprises and tolerant enough to allow their independent cultivation. I hope Margolis thinks so as well.

NOTES

1. See Margolis's trilogy, *The Persistence of Reality,* including *Pragmatism without Foundations, Science without Unity,* and *Texts without Referents* (Oxford: Blackwell, 1986, 1987, 1989). See also his recent books, *The Flux of History and the Flux of Science* (Berkeley: University of California Press, 1993) and *Interpretation: Radical But Not Unruly* (Berkeley: University of California Press, 1994). I shall be citing extensively from this book, using the abbreviation "I." See Richard Rorty's *Contingency, Irony, and Solidarity* (Cambridge: Cambridge University Press, 1989); and Richard Shusterman, *Pragmatist Aesthetics* (Oxford: Blackwell, 1992), henceforth abbreviated PA; and *Practicing Philosophy: Pragmatism and the Philosophical Life* (New York: Routledge, 1997), henceforth PP.

2. I already made the point in an earlier essay, "Interpretation, Intention, and Truth," *Journal of Aesthetics and Art Criticism* 47 (1988): 399–411, which included a critique of Margolis's earlier theory of interpretation that posited a core of fixity in descriptive properties of a work that were contrasted with interpretive properties and served as the necessary substratum for the latter.

3. See John Dewey, *The Quest for Certainty, 1929* (Carbondale: Southern Illinois University Press, 1984), henceforth cited as QC.

4. For my arguments against the ubiquity of interpretation and a crucial nondiscursive, somatic dimension of experience, see the chapter "Beneath Interpretation," in *Pragmatist Aesthetics* and "Somatic Experience: Foundation or Reconstruction?" in PP, chap. 6. Margolis's affirmations of the ubiquity of interpretation and the complete textualism of the self are most apparent in the first and final chapters of *Interpretation: Radical But Not Unruly.*

Ontology Historicized:
From Natural History
to Cultural Evolution

Marx W. Wartofsky

The American Museum of Natural History plays a special role in the childhood of native New Yorkers. At its entrance stands a monument to late nineteenth-century American racism and to our distinctive national adaptation of the "white man's burden"—a self-congratulatory form of British imperialist ideology. On a horse, erect and in a commanding posture, turned slightly to the right, left hand on the reins, sits Teddy Roosevelt at his "Rough-Rider" best. Walking alongside him on the right, slightly to the rear in respectful subordination, is a Native American chief (to judge by his war bonnet); and on the left walks an African-American, dressed (if one may surmise) in plantation work clothes, suitably stripped to the waist.

So much for American history. Inside, as one entered, there once was a charging herd of trumpeting elephants (now replaced by the huge skeleton of a brontosaurus); and in the lower level entrance hall (still in place) is a one hundred-foot-long war canoe filled with amazingly lifelike Haida warriors of the Pacific Northwest. As one headed for the animal dioramas, frozen in the stillness of their glass-enclosed worlds, one passed an historical diorama of Nieuw Amsterdam: Mayor Peter Stuyvesant (old anti-Semitic peg-leg Pete himself) trading with some Manhattan tribesman at what is now Battery Park. Geological displays, fossils, a giant whale suspended from the ceiling, hugely magnified models of one-celled animals splendid in their symmetries, the cross-section of a two-thousand-year-old Sequoia, with historic dates marked on its concentric rings; and in the old days, the standard progression from rude, apelike Australopithecus and Neanderthal to handsome, rugged Cro-Magnon. Natural history and human history, geological and biological and cultural evolution stood side by side, or rather in progressing array, as generations of schoolchildren trooped past in class visits, disgorged from scores of yellow buses, or pouring in from the subway entrance leading directly to the museum, on Saturdays and Sundays.

For me, in my prephilosophical concept formation, the effect was vivid and has remained permanent. Nature and culture; mineral, vegetable, and animal; natural fact and artifact formed one continuous, though internally segmented, whole. I knew about evolution, as a child-ape to man, eohippus to modern horse, displays on both—and I also knew about culture-clay pots, weapons, tools, totem poles, vivid "native" costumes, and so on. I (being leftwise precocious) also knew about Marx, about social progress and the class struggle in its well-ordered historical periods (slavery, feudalism, capitalism, socialism). And, being art-wise precocious, an intended painter by age twelve, I also knew about the history of art and of the progression of periods and styles.

What I didn't know about yet was emergence, nonreductive and eliminative materialisms, physicalism, intentionality, persons—not even, yet, about sense-data, the correspondence theory of truth, the mindbody problem, metaphysics, epistemology. As a child, I was in the philosophical Garden of Eden, before the Fall. I had a rather nicely systematic ontology, with closure, and all things large or small, living or dead, thinking or dumb, fell into their places well, in the categorical schemata provided by the American Museum of Natural History, my native language-frameworks (English and Yiddish, both Indo-European), the canons of my representational practices in viewing and making pictures. In short, my *praxis* yielded an ontology (or as we say now, ontological commitments) derived from, or rather immanent in (because tacit) my "form of life." The values assigned to my variables, whether lexical, praxical, or logical, were those suitable for a nice Jewish intellectual-artistic kid of the 1940s, from a combined left-wing atheist and orthodox religious

background. My ontology was seamless, comfortable, uncompli-
cated though complex, unproblematic, unquestioned, and so far as I
felt or knew, coherent.

It was, ahead of its time, an historicized ontology: Things didn't
just exist, atemporally and essentially, and neither did minds.
Rather, they came into being at their appropriate time, in their
appropriate niche, out of what preceded them. This went beyond the
Museum and on into the Planetarium adjacent. My historical
ontology included the universe, stars, galaxies, our own solar
system or others. I remember a book borrowed on two-week loan
from the local branch of the Brooklyn Public Library, and duly
renewed twice (the then-limit), entitled *Atoms, Men and Stars*,
which had me all excited about cosmic continuities from micro-to-
macrocosm. Only a little later, I learned to my satisfaction about the
hypothesized evolution of the atomic elements themselves. Of
course! What could have been more obvious?

Substitute for this particular historical world of child-praxis, the
contextualized, theorized praxis of the scientific-philosophical community of seventeenth-century Europe: a different story, a different
ontology. Still, it was one familiar to me even as a child, inherited in
the characteristic models of the physical-geometrical-mathematical
sciences as I learned them in school, and well fitted to the ubiquitous
embodied mechanism in the object-world around me. Or again, substitute the ontologies of early medieval Europe, or of the Islamic and
Jewish philosophies of the eleventh or twelfth centuries, with their
neoplatonic or Plotinean hierarchies of Being, from the lowest to the
highest, God at the apex, choirs of angels, souls in various stages of
spiritual ascent, terrestrial and celestial regions qualitatively ordered,
sulfurous, earthy, aqueous, airy, fiery, crystalline. Where we do not
know the specific practices and cultures, the philosophical ontologies give us heuristic clues as to what to look for, as the jawbone of
the dinosaur leads us to reconstruct the animal's skeletal structure, its
diet, its ambience, the ecology within which such a jawbone would
have fit. So, too, the tools, shards, the fossilized seeds, burnt animal
bones, petrified ordure at prehistoric sites are the traces from which
we attempt to reconstruct a way of life, a way of thought. When all
we have—and when we have as much as—cave paintings of the
Magdalenian, then, as Max Raphael pointed out, we cannot recon-

struct the ideology or the ontology from the praxis; we have instead to retrodict the praxis from the symbolic forms themselves. Where we have both—*Annales* history and history of ideas, history of philosophy—we need to be cautious in presupposing simple causal connections, one way or the other, from so-called base to so-called superstructure, or back again. How we construct our world in thought may be a function of how we live, but the question is whether we can separate how we live from how we construct our world, or how we can *know* how we live, what to correlate with what, independently of our self-representations, our thoughts, our "ontologies," in their reflective articulation.

The thesis introduced here narratively, locally, personally, conjecturally, is that ontologies are historical constructs, not simply in the sense of forms of thought, categorical schemes of language, or choices of values for variables in our logical space—thus, not simply explicit ideational—philosophical constructions in the theoretical mode (though also and most familiarly these); but also immanent praxical formations of an "objective" ambient world, an *Umwelt,* of my own, your own, our shared "lived experience," *Erlebnis, praxis, Dasein*—that is to say, *culture.* Ontology is robustly viewed here: This is not just the world I *think*, in my representational practice, in the mode of articulated self-consciousness in which my culture is an object of my reflection, but the world I exist and act in and make or remake in my activity. In this world, I am not an entity "in" this world, as a pea in a pod, a marble in a box, but as a constitutive (constituting and constituted) aspect of that world, an integral though distinguishable part of its "reality."[1]

The ontological distinctiveness of my kind of world-being, my kind of daily existence (*Dasein* in its prephilosophical everyday connotation in prephilosophical everyday German), is, perhaps paradoxically, that it (this kind of daily existence) is or *I* (who am this existence, daily) am the kind of being that is both "of" this world, and can also take itself to be "in" this world, separating it off as other, as object. That is to say, I am a reflective and self-reflective being, conscious of myself as being conscious, conscious of my consciousness, conscious that I can think about my consciousness, *selbst-bewusstes selbst-Bewusstsein,* in Hegel's thorny but precise reflexive grammatical construction. How does this happen? How, out of what we naturalistically or materialistically presuppose as an inchoate mass of potentialities, does there somehow come into being an "I," an achieved "ego," or if not an "I," then minimally, a self-reflective being with a cumulative historical self-awareness, a memory of self-continuity—"self" here not yet in any substantive sense of *a* self, but as the grammatical (and ontological) reflexive, the "token-reflexive" *x* of Reichenbach's logic (which he did not know, positivist that he was, were also the token reflexives of Hegel's phenomenology of mind: "here," "now," but not yet "I," not yet Russell's "egocentric particulars"). *The* "self," as Ego, comes later, an historical or developmental achievement, a matter of cultivation, education—in short, of culture. Thus (to anticipate) the self as "I" emerges with the emergence of culture, or in the enculturation of an individual human consciousness, within a pre-existing human culture.

All this heavy going is prologue, then, for a consideration of an historical ontology, companion to what I have elsewhere and earlier described as an historical epistemology.[2] Both together, ontology and epistemology historicized, constitute the systematic philosophical framework for an account of culture, of the sort of entity or process a culture is, of the kinds of cognitive practices or ways of knowing that make up a culture, and of the kind of change or development we may characterize as cultural evolution. Neither an historical epistemology nor an historical ontology is really new to philosophy. Both are at least implicit, and often explicit in the work of such philosophers as Hegel, Vico, Marx, Peirce, Dewey, Cassirer, Bachelard, Vygotsky, Foucault, inter alia. Some such views are foreshadowed, or cry for articulation in the work of evolutionary epistemologists such as Campbell and Shimony, in the evolutionary psychology of Janet or Baldwin, and in the genetic psychology of Piaget. Philosophical receptivity to such historicized epistemology and ontology is prepared for, even if not yet acceded to in the ontological relativity of Quine, in Goodman's "Ways of Worldmaking," in Wittgenstein's "forms of life/forms of language" insight, and among pluralist pragmatists, constructivists, historicists, emergentists in general (e.g., C. Judson Herrick, Roy Wood Sellars, F. J. E. Woodbridge, G. H. Mead, E. B. McGilvary, Sir Samuel Alexander, among an older generation, and more, recently). Finally, one needs to mention the generations of Marxist philosophers, psychologists, anthropologists, laboring in the shadows of Stalinist dogmatism, who tried to formulate a dialectical theory of the growth of knowledge and of culture. Here, Bogdanov, Vygotsky and Luria, and Rubinshtein, and, more recently, Lektorsky, deserve mention.

Here, I will focus on one exuberant growth on this old vine, namely, the "praxism" and "emergent materialism" of Joseph Margolis, and in particular, his metaphysics of culture and his conception of cultural emergents. More narrowly still, I will address principally Margolis's later thoughts, in the final volume of his trilogy, *The Persistence of Reality*,[3] and only obliquely some of the earlier arguments (e.g., in the chapter on "The Nature and Identity of Cultural Entities," in his *Persons and Minds* [1978]). This will be less a discussion of Margolis, however, than an exploitation of the opportunity of this Festschrift, to find out what I have been thinking about this myself. For I have been thinking about it, in the context of the project of an historical epistemology as an account of cognitive evolution, and thereby, of cultural evolution more generally.

One brief paragraph about that, by way of background, another one about Margolis, and we can then go on to the business at hand.

Historical epistemology is the thesis that it not only is the content of our knowledge that changes, historically, but also the modes of cognition themselves, the "ways of knowing,"[4] indeed, what counts as knowledge and further that such epistemological changes take place in some complex but systematic relation to changes in our modes of social, technological, scientific, and artistic practices. I have worried this thesis for the better part of two decades, now, publishing parts of it and sitting on the rest (to hatch soon, hopefully). What goes along with it is the thesis of ontology as an account of the world we inhabit—"our" world—as a coherent or systematically unified ambience which contains or exhibits not only all of our doings and undertakings and reasoned or well-imagined reconstructions of these, but everything else as well, that is, a nature not of our making, but which constitutes the domain of our (past, actual, and possible) activity. A realist ontology would ostensibly demarcate a world (a universe? a reality?), which is what it is, independent of our knowledge, or possible knowledge of it, but also including us, our practices and our thoughts.

Now this is, on the face of it, a self-refuting constraint. For if the world *contains* our knowledge of it as one of its constituents (as it must, if it is not to be a question-begging and evasive realism that is ontologically incomplete), then it *cannot* be *what it is,* independent of or apart from our knowledge of it. In a trivial and minimal sense, if our knowledge changes (as it does historically, and even biographically, day by day) then, a fortiori, this changes the world by so much, at least. In this weak sense, the world is "changed" by changes in one of its constituent parts, its cognitive component, so to speak. But this is not really what is at issue in a traditional realist ontology, because the rest of the world apart from its mental or cognitive component remains what it is, independent of any knowledge of it by this component consciousness. A picture of the world doesn't affect what it is a picture of, except perhaps in the perception or understanding of that world, by virtue of its representation.

But now, suppose we construe our "knowledge" not simply as the reflective, ideational reconstruction of the experienced or lived-in world, in thought. If instead, "knowledge" as cognitive praxis includes the processes and outcomes of our human, conscious, intentional, intelligent, norm-driven, practical as well as theoretical activities, then, cities, irrigation projects, environmental pollution, deforestation, reforestation, mining, agriculture, war, energy consumption, architecture, road building, the history of art, the proliferation of languages, and language change, the rise and fall of states and empires—all, all become "objective" (or objectified) knowledge, knowledge revealed in its expressed modes, that part of "the world" given over to culture, its constituents and its processes. How a cognitively transformed nature—that is, culture—is to be counted ontologically—whether as "physical" or something else—becomes a rather prissy sort of consideration.

Certainly, it is "nature," the "physical world" transformed by human thought and action, *made* teleological, shaped to human purposes and needs. Aristotle took care of this neatly by supposing that culture (what he called "art" or *techne*) was nature "made over" by human action-second nature, so to speak. His "nature"/"art" distinction makes it clear where the ontological continuity is. Ontological distinctions between a virgin nature, untouched by human hands, and its derivations in artifacts, are settled at one stroke, leaving modern agonies about "realism" entirely *hors de combat.*

But Aristotle is no historical epistemologist, and certainly not an historical or constructivist ontologist, neither about the domain of nature, nor about that of culture, of human *poiesis* and *praxis*. An historical ontology proper would countenance transformations in the objects of knowledge themselves, by virtue of the cognitive practices that take them (or make them) as *their* objects. The object of knowledge itself (including here the "real," taken to be as objectively physical as one likes, the precultural "given" of our world-activity) *becomes* an historicized object, a "cultural emergent," and it becomes transformed by our practices of inquiry or experiment, by the economic or technological or artistic uses we make of this object. This is as true of the objects of scientific inquiry—the so-called theoretical entities to which we assign ontological status in our physical sciences—as it is of the "objects" we produce in our agriculture: "domestic" corn, wheat, "cultivated" fruits or vegetables—that is, objects created by that "cultivation," which is the earliest etymological sense of the term "culture" as in "agriculture," "viniculture," and so on.

Ontology is historical, or becomes historicized not simply in the sense that our ontologies—our ontological *theories* or *constructions*—change historically, in science, in mathematics, in philosophy, in politics, but more significantly, that the worlds of our practice, the structures of our reality change. There seems to be no problem with that, insofar as the "reality" we are talking about is the socially constructed or transformed world of our practices. There are questions, of course, as to what counts as an ontological feature of such a social or historical reality, categorically, and what is a merely phenomenal change or transition within some abiding or historically invariant ontological category. Thus, for example, persons or languages or obligations or tools may be considered as ontologically invariant types across the variable historical domains of social human reality, whereas the development of hand tools or historical changes in the normative content of obligations may be local transformations through such ontological invariance. In any case, the ontological categories of this made world (or these made worlds) are themselves relatively invariant, and come into being with the origins and development of human culture. That is, the categories themselves are cultural emergents and cannot be said to "exist" in nature prior to human culture.

However, can the same notion of an historicized ontology be said to pertain to precultural, prehuman "nature," to the physical or material world itself? Weren't there atoms before the advent of atomic theory or of the practices of experimental physics? Do atoms "emerge" only as we give them birth, first in the speculative imagination, then as hard, massy particles, then as "clouds" of electrical point charges or fields "around" ("encircling?" "held together by?" "statistically distributed about?") a nucleus? Or do whatever we *now* construe as "atoms" exist as what they are, through all variations in the models or representations of them in physics? Or are they ineluctably nothing but artifacts of measurement, and of theories and processes of measurement (the "theoretical entities" or "intervening variables" or "hypothetical constructs" of an earlier debate over ontology in the philosophy of science)? Can we conceive of ontological changes in the nature of matter through its own history, such that the laws of physics change over time, as C. S. Peirce already conjectured? Is an historicized ontology pertinent to any temporally variable realities, other than those constituted by human practices and knowledge? Or does it address only the kinds of entities that are paradigmatically "historical": cultural entities, in their emergence, transformation, passing away.

I have tried to address some of these questions elsewhere,[5] but only initially. I pose them here critically, trying to tease out what an historical ontology could be if one were to seek a reasonable and illuminating account of it.

This, then, is a current *problematique* for me. Happily, it is one for Margolis as well. His attempts to resolve it are subtle, philosophically responsible, and generally well informed (though his sources and philosophical references, as well as his manner of posing the questions, is quite different from mine). His is one of the few attempts, at least in the Anglo-American tradition (broadly conceived), to work out a contemporary "metaphysics of culture" as he calls it, and to build it upon the notion of cultural emergents. I turn then to Margolis, with a prefatory personal word as befits a Festschrift. (Better here, *in medias res,* than at the beginning, or in a footnote, where the integrity and continuity of the personal and the philosophical would be lost to the ritual artifices of their required separation in our learned writings.)

Margolis is a prolific writer and thinker, on occasion a prolix one, but mainly a knotty, subtle, literary, and courageous one. He attests to his own philosophical quest, in the recent trilogy (*The Persistence of Reality*) as a kind of *Bildungsroman,* and also even suggests the *Comédie humaine* as a model, the sweeping throng of philosophers who crowd its pages analogous to the multifaceted characters of Balzac's great work. I have (in public in my comments at an APA symposium on the trilogy) accused Margolis of greater hubris still—of attempting to replay Hegel's *Phenomenology of Mind* in modern philosophical dress, with a new cast of characters. That work is, of course, the philosophical *Bildungsroman* of all *Bildungsromane,* thus, an eminent model for all narratives of voyages of self-discovery.

Margolis is nothing if not immodest. However the triple negatives play out in the preceding sentence, I mean no affront by this, but rather an acknowledgment of Margolis's grand ambition in the work, or in the continuity of his work. There is, at the same time, a healthy modesty that reveals itself in the close, detailed attention Margolis pays to the work of many, many (many, many) others. The dialectic of his argument grows in the colloquy with these others, and as he writes, "the philosophical argument is the dialogue of historicized and contexted theories."[6]

I think so, too. But I confess that, even though I have always been deeply committed to historical context and the critical engagement of my contemporaries, I have lost patience with the reconstruction and critique of their arguments in haste to get on with my own, constructively. Margolis and I come out of a graduate program saturated with historical consciousness (in our time, but no longer), namely, the Columbia Philosophy Department, where we were graduate students together. Some of this still shows, I imagine, though our commitments to historicity and context have proceeded in very different ways. There is a reconvergence, I suspect, and I expressed some of this in the editor's preface to Margolis's *Persons and Minds* (1978)—a preface I coauthored with Robert S. Cohen, as the book appeared in our series, *Boston Studies in the Philosophy of Science.*

In the present essay, I take Margolis up on only two points, but they are central ones:

1. The relation, in any coherent ontology, between nature and culture;
2. "Praxism" in Margolis's account of an historical/social epistemology adequate to an account of culture as an emergent entity.

Margolis's discussion of the relation(s) of nature and culture is so ramified, and so widely distributed over the volumes not only of his recent trilogy, but in *Persons and Minds* (1978), in *Culture and Cultural Entities* (1984), and elsewhere that I will not pretend to do it justice (nor admit to doing it an injustice) here. It's not my job to tell the readers all about it. Let them read for themselves! I will pick out only a few relevant themes for my own exploitation. First, Margolis's argument is that there is no ontological privilege to be granted to nature, over culture, (though he doesn't use the term nature so much as "the physical world" or "the physical," which he distinguishes from the "material"). The argument is neat and well elaborated. In short, "reality" pertains no less to the ontological status of persons or minds than it does to spatio-temporal, that is, physically "determinate" entities. One difference is that cultural entities are essentially interpreted entities, that is, intentionalistic in that their "being" is, in a sense, in their being understood (or "understood-as"), thus, objects for minds, caught up in language or in conceptual webs. Margolis writes, "Cultural realism is essentially hermeneutic."[7] However, the cultural isn't pre-given, ontologically; it *pre*-supposes what Margolis calls embodiment, incarnation. So any cultural particular (ontologically grounded in the existence of persons, because no persons = no culture) is at the same time, an embodied particular, incarnate in some physical particular, as the statue, Michelangelo's *Pietà,* is incarnate in a particular block of marble. Thus, in Margolis's argument, the natural world is presupposed by the very existence of cultural entities, because they are (*ex hypothesi,* for Margolis, at any rate) cultural emergents, and necessarily embodied particulars. This assures us, at least, of a kind of realism by presupposition: *If* cultural entities are emergents, then there must be some precultural domain they emerge *from* (barring emergence ex nihilo, an interesting alternative at that!).

Note that this is not an epistemological, but an ontological argument: It's not that the object of *knowledge* exists independently of its *being known,* that is, mind-independently in that sense; but rather that what must be mind-independent is whatever it is that is premental, and not merely contingently so, but necessarily so, as the origin or genesis of mentality itself. ("Mental" is okay as shorthand for "cultural," because the latter is defined relative to interpretation, and interpretation without an interpreting [cognitive/mental] subject has not yet been conjured up by Platonistic semioticians—or has it?)

The physicalist reductionist would want to argue against emergence, to the effect that a properly "scientific" ("scientific image"?) account of culture would adequately describe/explain all its allegedly distinctive phenomena, without residue, at the level of physical entities or processes. (This usually is accompanied by promissory notes about suitably ramified and developed physical sciences of the future.) "Culture" would simply be, naturalistically, the physical world in one of its many ways of being.

Not so, says nonreductive, emergent materialist Margolis. He writes:

> Attempts at explaining the emergence of the culturally complex *reflexively* concede the cultural, and then speculate on what *could have led* to its emergence from simpler, subcultural or *pre*cultural phenomena; but no attempt can be made that will not prove reductive that shows that the cultural is actually *not* conceptually more complex than the domain from which it emerges.[8]

Translating the triple negative, we have: Any account that reduces the complexity of the cultural to the simplicity of the physical is reductive (tautology), or: the cultural emergent is irreducibly more complex than what it emerges from (definition). It is, of course, hard to disagree, and being of an emergentist mind myself (a long-standing Hegelian-Marxist, Deweyan, Woodbridgean, R. W. Sellarsian dialectical emergentist, by creed), I can only welcome this kind of account of the ontological priority of nature over culture, as well as the ontological irreducibility of emergent levels to their generic components. There is even the hint of an "historical" ontology here, in a trivial or degraded sense: Ontology of a temporally prior physical nature without minds, persons, culture is transformed by the genesis of the emergent reality of cultural entities, all requiring their hermeneutic status as essential to their distinctive kind of being. But, of course, there is nothing "historic" about the relation between an ontology of nature without culture and an ontology of a cultural world emergent from this nature.

At best, we simply have two ontologies, which we take to be temporally, or even developmentally sequential: one precedes or is the ontological precondition for the other. But there is here no historic moment of transition from one to the other, nor have we as yet introduced any historicity *within* each of these ontologies, that is, no historic changes in natural ontology or in cultural ontology. But what exactly would it mean for there to be a *historical* ontology of nature? Or of culture?

One thing it could mean is simply a history of ontologies: insofar as "ontology" connotes a theory (explicit or tacit) of what there is, or the presuppositions or beliefs that exhibit themselves in our practices (unreflective or merely enacted ontologies), one could reconstruct either a history of such explicit—say, philosophically articulated—theories of being, or else tease out the historical development of embedded or praxical ontologies, reconstructing these by hypothesis from an inquiry into, and interpretation of various cultural practices, for example, religious rituals, languages or grammars, political behavior, artworks, and so on. Similarly, one could do a history of epistemology, as a special aspect of a more general history of philosophy, or of ideas. But neither of these is what I mean by ontology or epistemology historicized.

Let's stick with the ontology here, and in particular, the ontology of nature, and of culture, and the ontological question of the transition or transformation of a natural into a cultural ontology. We already have a theory about the transition, in Margolis's Metaphysics of Culture: Culture is an *emergent* from nature. An historical ontology has to do more than simply describe the ontological features of the natural world and distinguish those features (e.g., intentionality, mentality) which separate the cultural world from it, and it has to do even more than give a conceptual account of emergence in categorial terms, that is, an account of irreducibility. Insofar as it is really historicized, an ontological theory has to show, or explain, or propose how physical reality undergoes fundamental changes in its very structure, or in the nature, of the entities or processes that characterize it. It would not be enough, for example, to talk about physical changes *within* a given ontological framework, because any physical process entails changes of many sorts (e.g., in the values of kinetic or dynamic variables in physics, in physical or biological structure, etc.). But then the question emerges (pardon the verb) about what is to count as an ontological category or as a change of ontology. At what level do we count changes as ontological, and in what way are such changes (once we have sorted them out) "historical"?

One clue, within natural ontology, is the often cited "emergence" of living systems from lifeless matter, that is, of the biological from the prebiological physical. Another concerns the evolution of physical matter itself in "Big-Bang" cosmological scenarios—that is, the "emergence" of certain previously nonexisting physical structures, for example, the atomic elements. In both cases, what has been "added" to the existing reality is something taken to be fundamentally, that is, *ontologically* new. What comes into being is not simply another rearrangement or organization of the physical "base-entities"—molecules, constituted by combinations of atomic elements in the case of the emergence of life itself; or some primal matter/radiation in the space-time case of the emergence of the atomic system. Rather, what is added is an "emergent" with properties irreducible to those of the "lower" or more basic level. In emergentist accounts, this is sometimes described as a difference (a "qualitative" difference) in structural complexity or type of organization, which requires new laws to express its invariance through transformation, to account for its distinctive processes. If one had an account of the two ontologies—of nature and of culture, of the "base" level and the "emergent" level—then one would have no more than a sequence, or perhaps the beginnings of a taxonomy of "species" of ontology, arranged in the order of their chronological appearance, or in the relation of ontological priority or causal derivation. But we would be without any explanatory theory of the "evolution of (ontological) species" (to speak in terms of the biological analogy). We would not be able to explain (nor as yet even have posed to ourselves to problem of explaining) the processes or mechanisms by which the emergent (cultural) ontology originates out of its physical preconditions, without resorting to a *deus ex*

machina or some mysterious, ineffable, and inexplicable spon-
taneity to account for the origin of a new, ontological "species."

In the paradigmatic case of biological evolution, Wallace and
Darwin, among others, provided such a theory of the transition, that
is, of the "origin of species." But is an emergent biological species
a case of *ontological* change? One is prompted to declare "obviously not!" And I think this is correct. But *why* obviously not? Why
is the transition from nonliving matter to life a change in ontology,
and biological speciation not? Why would the creation of the
atomic system, from the first hydrogen atom (or indeed, *its* origina-
tion, if we speculate about that, say as a statistically spontaneous
event) count as ontological innovation, and the transition from radi-
ation to matter, or back again, count only as an intraontological
change? Is ontological relativity a matter not only of which ontologies we adopt (or live by, in our varying historical practices, say),
but also a matter of what will count as an ontological category in the
first place?

In the case at hand, of the *transition* from nature to culture, or
as we may more specifically say, from biology to culture, what we
will decide to take as distinctive ontological categories will pretty
much determine whether or not we can speak of an historicized
ontology at all. For if culture is simply biology rearranged, and
mind is a particularly complex arrangement of the sensibility of
neural systems in certain vertebrate organisms, and culture is the
particular nest-building or dam-building propensity of some such
gregarious organisms, who, instead of the efficient pheromones of
the insect-world, are limited to vocal emissions or physical
scratches as means of communication, why then, there's no
problem of "irreducibility." Biology is generous and sporting in its
variability. "Intentionality" is the particular pathological delusion of
this neural-sensibility, which is a kind of overspilling of unused ner-
vous energies, in periods of relative disuse of vital species functions. (How to account for the "mental activity" of theorists who
explain all this to us, then? Well, the most economical hypothesis is
that, like the mind-body problem, it lies beyond the capacity of such
neural systems to "know," i.e., to achieve the refractory state that
follows successful use of the neurons.)

"Culture" thus reduced, the law of parsimony triumphs in the domain of ontology: No unnecessary multiplication of entities has taken place. But this common and current reductionism is arrent nonsense for reasons so patent and numerous that the persistence of the reductionist party, in philosophy at least, is hard to account for. In the neural sciences, as in biology, reductionism has a strong heuristic value as a methodological imperative. It is exceptionally fruitful there, in guiding research programs and laying open to critical question established "higher level" theories. The slippery slope almost always begins with the facile extension of methodological heuristic to ontological assertion, and where ontology simply recapitulates methodology, we have the relativization of ontology (or of ontologies) to the variety of practices and conjectural mental experiments that mark the present and the history of the natural and cultural sciences. ("Cultural sciences" may serve here as equivalent for the *Geisteswissenschaften,* though "human sciences" is sometimes used, confusingly I think; and so is "mental sciences.") Scientific reductionists (e.g., E. O. Wilson, Desmond Morris, David Huebel) almost always slide from heuristic and methodological to ontological and eliminative reductionisms, and are gleefully followed on the road to confusion by technically proficient and conceptually naive philosophers. Oh well.

Having gotten that off, let me say that, among the antireductionists, Margolis gives as fair and rich an argument for the irreducibility of persons and minds, hence, of culture, as one could hope for, and I simply point at it, in the works mentioned. This then, is not an argument, but rather, arm-waving and declaiming. I start my argument after all this is over.

How does the ontological *transition* take place? What turns nature into culture, what *generates* mind, personhood, language, human consciousness, and self-consciousness? What is the history of this momentous ontological transformation? We cannot *presuppose* mind as a condition for the existence of culture, nor a preexisting culture as the condition for the emergence of mind. Out of what animal, that is, biological activities, could human-consciousness arise? That's ontological question number one, without which the project of an *historical* ontology couldn't even be appropriately formulated. Question number two concerns those changes in the cultural ontology itself which come about by virtue of the remaking of the natural *and* cultural worlds by cultural agents. Here, the earlier question occurs again: What would count as an *ontological* change within the domain of culture? Or is "culture" as such an ontological category within which changes may occur and history unfold, but which remains ontologically, that is, transhistorically, invariant?

Two alternatives suggest themselves: (1) The cultural is an ontologically invariant category. It *emerges* historically from nature, and historical ontology therefore pertains only to such categorical processes of change, paradigmatically, from nonliving to living nature, and from living nature to culture. Of course, to agree with Margolis, "types" don't emerge, except by virtue of the emergence of tokens of the type, so culture *as such* emerges only in terms of the concrete and particular cultural *emergents* that identify it. (2) As the alternative, the cultural domain is itself ontologically *variable* and has a history of the emergence of new kinds of entities, structures, processes which may be said to constitute a second-level historical ontology within this cultural domain itself.

To move very quickly here, before too many difficult questions occur to the reader, we may assert that the fundamental constitutive element of the domain of culture is that activity characteristic of the entities which, collectively, make up this level of being—namely, the *praxis* of cognitive agents, that is, of persons with minds, in their engagement with each other and with the world. This gets us neatly, if hurriedly, to my second Margolis topic, his *praxism* so-called; and also, in this connection, to my historicized epistemology and its (you should pardon the expression) ontological implications.

Here, as often in this essay, I offer promissory notes, chits to be cashed in against what I hope to lay out in detail elsewhere (or have laid out, in some initial detail, elsewhere). But first, what does Margolis's *praxism* offer, and why is it so relevant here?

Margolis *praxism* (his own term, not mine. I hate it because it *sounds* ugly) is, perhaps unsurprisingly, close to Marx's conception of praxis, and a conscious adaptation of it, and at the same time, is regarded by him as an alternative formulation of pragmatism.[9] It is an account of the paradigmatic activity that makes culture culture, that is, the cognitive activity of persons, or for short, thinking. Praxism, therefore, is a theory of cognitive practice, inquiry and cognitive acquisition, thus a theory of knowledge, thus, an epistemological theory; but at the same time, it is an ontologically oriented theory about the constitutive modes of activity that define a certain kind of being, that is, culture.

Margolis, in attempting to disassociate himself from the "doctrinal commitments" that make Hegel's and Marx's versions of praxis incompatible with pragmatism, makes use of an unnecessarily violent rhetoric of rejection, phrased equivocally in conditionals: "Let it be said as directly as possible that those grand doctrines, so easily extracted from the canonical texts, are utterly preposterous and utterly indefensible . . . *if* they are, so to say, the authentic train schedule for the actual odyssey of Geist or of its global materialist replacements, then Hegel and Marx deserve all the contempt that has been so cordially heaped on them."[10] "Our own concern, of course, is only to recover a workable conception of *praxis* that escapes (with or without Hegel's or Marx's blessing) all the conceptually indigestible isms enumerated above."[11]

Well all right, we won't blame Margolis for the excesses of Stalinism, just because he adopts the Marx-laden term, *praxis*. And we will recall that Sidney Hook the Earlier (prenuclear) took Marx to *be* a pragmatist, not only compatible with pragmatism, and that Richard Bernstein noted the affinities of *Praxis* and *Action* as well. I was accused, in a review of my work some years ago, of contaminating the philosophy of science with the use of the term *praxis*. And from its initiation until its recent sad demise, I was on the editorial board of a journal called *Praxis International*. So we're with you, Joe, but where are you taking us?

Praxism is accorded an elaborate characterization by Margolis, which includes fifteen features, which I will list seriatim and in abbreviated form here: *Praxism* rejects the reducibility of persons to things, or of behavior to physical events, hence all forms of physical reductionism; it affirms the symbiosis of the individual and the societal, in human life; it "admits the individual and the societal,[12] in human life; it "admits the historicity of human nature—denies any essential or fixed nature to human beings, therefore, and holds that human beings transform themselves by their own labor and activity. Further, praxism repudiates a priorism, logocentrism, all forms of cognitive privilege; it "accommodates discontinuities and incommensurabilities among large movements of conceptual change," and "accommodates the ineliminability of pluralism and relativism in the confrontation of alternative conceptual schemes." Again, it denies any split between the theoretical and practical, sees thinking as purposive and normative, and "concedes the historicized preformation of man's conceptual horizons" and sees thinking as related to contexts of material life (productive, reproductive, biological, social). Further, Praxism construes human thinking as objective, that is, as "addressed to the real, mind-independent world," and so forth.

At the end, we are told that *praxism* is congruent with Marx's conception of praxis, as expressed in the *Theses on Feuerbach,* especially theses II, IV, VIII, and XI.

Margolis wants to *add* to this long litany the explicitly pragmatic idea that praxism "attributes objectivity or objective truth to thinking as a practical rather than a theoretical matter,"[13] borrowing Marx's own language from Thesis II. And at long last, the fifteenth condition sees all claims to objectivity, all realist epistemologies then, as "artifactually relativized," that is, historically and praxically contextual and framework bound.

Margolis has created a very heaven for the historical epistemologists and historical ontologists! Like heaven, the conditions for the realization of all these conditions are impossible to fulfill. But they are, after all, heuristic, ideal conditions, consummations devoutly to be wished. Now what we need is a theory of culture, of human practice and human thinking, that translates these normative desiderata into an account of how such emergents arise in the actual course of things. How does the *praxis* that praxism describes come into being? One would have to show, in a plausible way, based on as much scientific, anthropological, historical evidence and argument as one can muster, but primarily based on a conceptual analysis of human cognitive practices, how such a nonreductive, that is, physically irreducible phenomenon could come into being from a precognitive, precultural nature. One would need to give a detailed argument as to what a "historicized human nature" *is,* not just claim programatically that there *is* one. How, in fact, is thinking related to contexts of practical life, in given historical cases? How does the relativity of claims to objectivity play out in the history of the sciences or in contemporary debates (e.g., in the Einstein-Bohr debates about the [ontological] completeness of the Quantum Theory)? What role, in specific and concrete terms, does the production and use of artifacts play in the self-transformation of human beings? And so forth.

In effect, Margolis's *praxism* may serve as the sketch of a research program in the philosophical and historical understanding of culture and of human thought.

Backtrack a moment: Marx scribbled the *Theses on Feuerbach* and put them aside, together with the 1845 *German Ideology,* which he wrote with Engels (consigning this work, as we are told by Marx, to the "gnawing criticism of the mice"). But the fact is that the German Ideology, in the opening sections on "historical materialism," is a theory about the emergence of culture. The *Economic-Philosophic Manuscripts of 1844–45* (first published in 1932), and large sections of the *Grundrisse* of 1857–59 (first published, in any accessible form, in 1959) *were* Marx's attempts to formulate a theory of human cognitive practice, in its socially embodied forms, in economic production, in social and political life, and in its explicit theoretical forms, in ideology and in the science of political economy. However incomplete, or skewed, or historically limited, or wrong these efforts may be, they are the efforts of a philosopher coming to terms with the demands of a theory of praxis, that is, of (practical and theoretical) human cognitive activity in its applications to the "real world."

Insofar as this activity is a socially embedded and historically developing activity, insofar as it constitutes a world of nature transformed in the image of humanly perceived ends, insofar as the activity and its products create the lifeworld of the human species, we may characterize the outcome of this activity as cultural evolution, emergent from and transcending natural history.

I think this is not too distant from the Margolis project. I call such an account of cultural evolution "historical epistemology" and link it to an historicized ontology. Margolis calls it *praxism.* They are not the same response, nor exactly the same project either. But in a world of disjoint reflections, bounced back from shards of a smashed mirror, I'll welcome any help I can get, especially when it comes from an old friend.

NOTES

1. Cf. J. Dewey, on the relation of art to its "conditions of origin and operation in experience": "Mountain peaks do not float unsupported; they do not even rest upon the earth. They are the earth in one of its manifest operations." *Art as Experience* (1934; reprint, New York: Perigree Books, 1980), p. 3.

2. Cf. Marx W. Wartofsky, "Epistemology Historicized," in *Naturalistic Epistemology, Boston Studies and the Philosophy of Science,* Vol. 100, eds. Abner Shimony and Debra Nails (Dordrecht and Boston: D. Reidel, 1987), pp. 357–77; "Art History and Perception," in *Perceiving Pictures,* ed. John Fisher (Philadelphia: Temple University Press, 1980); "The Mind's Eye and the Hand's Brain: Toward an Historical Epistemology of Medicine," in *Science, Ethics and Medicine,* Vol. I, *The Foundations of Ethics and Its Relation to Science,* ed. H. T. Engelhardt Jr. and D. Callahan (Hastings-on-Hudson: Hastings Center, 1976), pp. 167–94; "Perception, Representation and the Forms of Action," in *Aistheisis—Essays on the Philosophy of Perception, Ajatus* 36, Yearbook of the Philosophical Society of Finland, ed. J. Manninen (Helsinki: 1976), 20–43; and *Models: Representation and the Scientific Understanding* (Dordrecht and Boston: D. Reidel, 1979), xxviii + 369, esp. Introduction, 13–26.

3. Joseph Margolis, *The Persistence of Reality,* Vols. I–III (New York and Oxford: Basil Blackwell, 1986–89).

4. The phrase "ways of knowing" is one I like, and I hope it isn't already patented (e.g., by some cultural anthropologist or other). It parallels "ways of seeing," which I had already decided on as the title of a forthcoming book (on the historical epistemology of visual cognition); but then discovered as the title of John Berger's (interesting and relevant) book and BBC series. Oh well.

5. "Three Stages of Constitution: Historical Changes in the Ontological Status of the Scientific Object," manuscript.

6. Joseph Margolis, *Texts without Referents,* Vol. III of *The Persistence of Reality,* p. xi.

7. Ibid., p. 224.

8. Ibid., p. 202.

9. Ibid., p. 102.

10. Ibid., p. 120.

11. Ibid., p. 121.

12. Ibid., p. 124.

13. Ibid., p. 128.

PART III

The Metaphysics of Culture

Margolis and the
Metaphysics of Culture

Dale Jacquette

INTRODUCTION

The concepts of mind, art, and artifacts are brought together under
a single set of ontic principles in Margolis's metaphysics of culture.
The framework in which Margolis offers his theory recognizes that
tools, machines, languages, art objects, genres, movements, institutions, and civilizations can only be understood as purposive expressions of thought. Margolis thereby relates the philosophy of mind to
the philosophy of history, language, art, and technology in a way
that is unique among contemporary philosophers.[1]

Most impressive in Margolis's program is the balance he has
achieved between the clear bold statement of general principles and
the critical investigation of data from many different disciplines.
Margolis's systematic exposition of his original contributions to
philosophy moreover is enriched by a thorough detailed knowledge
of the history of philosophy and science, from ancient to modern
and postmodern thought, in both analytic and continental traditions.
Margolis has pursued the implications of his philosophy of mind in
developing a rich and extensive account of cultural entities, including approaches to the theory of realism and relativism, epistemology and philosophy of science, the analysis of interpretation,

semantics and philosophy of language, ethics and moral theory, and the philosophy of history.[2]

At the outset I wish to emphasize my agreement with much of the basic framework in which Margolis has cast his metaphysics of culture. My interest in Margolis's philosophy of mind and art derives from the fact that I am so convinced of the rightness of his project in general terms that I can envision no tenable alternative. Margolis is an oasis in the desert landscape of materialist-mechanist eliminativism and reductivism. There are few other thinkers who have recognized and in their work taken to heart the important truth that language, art, and artifacts, culture in all its manifestations, must be understood as expressions of thought, and that therefore a satisfactory linguistic and aesthetic philosophy can only follow from a correct philosophy of mind. This central underlying assumption of Margolis's metaphysics of culture is so obvious to me that I believe no philosophy of language or art can possibly succeed unless it is conceived within the broad outlines which Margolis in the forefront of contemporary philosophers has repeatedly urged.[3]

THREE COMPONENTS OF MARGOLIS'S METAPHYSICS OF CULTURE

Margolis's theory has three main components. We can think of these as beginning with a core of principles relatively specific to the concepts of mind, art, and artifacts, embedded in two successively more encompassing philosophical doctrines. The latter not only have implications for persons and artworks, but, in the first instance, for entities of any kind, and, in the second, for any and every theory, thesis, principle, and thought. The core consists of a set of distinctions and propositions by which Margolis defines his conception of persons, artworks, and artifacts as materially embodied culturally emergent entities. This set of principles in turn is contained within a more general metaphysical commitment to an interpretation of C. S. Peirce's type-token distinction, with application to both cultural and extracultural. entities. Finally, all thought, including his own theoretization about the metaphysics of culture, falls under the aegis for Margolis of a still larger partially metaphilosophical cultural historicism or contextualism.[4]

If the analogy is not taken so far as to deny Margolis more originality than that of combining preextant ideas in an unusual way, we
might think epigrammatically of Margolis's three-tiered metaphysics of culture as combining Spinoza's dual aspect theory of
mind with Brentano's thesis of intentionality as the mark of the
mental, subordinated by Peirce's theory of thirdness and the type-
token distinction, and finally by something like Feyerabend's cultural historicism. (See Figure 1.)

In previous explorations of Margolis's work, "Margolis on
Emergence and Embodiment" and "The Type-Token Distinction in
Margolis's Aesthetics," I critically examined the first two parts of
what I have described as Margolis's three-tiered theory.[5] There I
dealt specifically with problems arising for Margolis's concept of
the material embodiment of culturally emergent entities, and his
application of the type-token distinction in accounting for the generation, reproduction, diversity of presentations, and extinction of
artworks. My earlier attempts to clarify and evaluate Margolis's
treatment of these ideas can be seen as efforts to work from the
inside toward the periphery of his complex metaphysics of culture.
Now in what follows I shall try to complete my analysis of Margolis's theory by dealing specifically with the historicism or contextualism in which the ontology of persons, artworks, and artifacts
as materially embodied culturally emergent entities under the type-
token distinction is conceived. In this way, I want to continue my
sounding of Margolis's system at its foundations by raising questions about the most fundamental metaphysical concepts on which
he has built his philosophy.

I shall argue that solutions to certain problems about the
ontology of cultural entities entailed by Margolis's metaphysics of
culture are unnecessarily complicated, ontically prodigal, and explanatorily less appealing than an alternative. The point of advancing such criticism is not to refute Margolis's theory but to identify one respect in which the ontology of cultural entities that he has
promoted can be enhanced. I offer, in place of Margolis's typetoken
distinction packaged in his historical contextualism, a more traditional kind-instance distinction packaged in an ontically neutral
intensionalist semantic reference and predication theory. The recommendations I reach are intended to show how Margolis's theory,

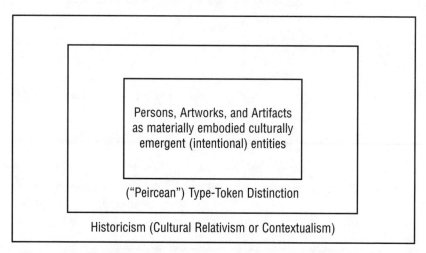

Fig. 1. Margolis's Three-Tiered Metaphysics of Culture

some parts of which I fully accept, might be better served by a non-standard philosophy of language compatible with the main lines of his ontology, to which Margolis need not be unreceptive [6]

MATERIALLY EMBODIED CULTURALLY EMERGENT ENTITIES

To explain the concepts of person, art, and artifact, Margolis offers a third choice between traditional (Cartesian) ontically dualist and (Platonic) realist, and reductively materialist, ontologies. His theory advances an attribute dualism of distinct material and intentional properties in place of an ontic dualism of distinct material and immaterial substances.[7]

Persons, artworks, and artifacts are materially embodied, but not reducible to and therefore not identical with their material embodiments. They are distinct from the physical stuff in which they are embodied because they have intentional properties that cannot be explained in physical, material, or mechanical terms in a purely extensional idiom. Margolis presents physically realized or incarnate functionalist identity criteria for culturally emergent entities, and defines the individuating incarnate functions for cultural entities as irreducible intrinsic psychological and derivative linguistic, aesthetic, and instrumental intentionalities.[8]

In *Persons and Minds: The Prospects of Nonreductive Materialism,* Margolis articulates the following seven-part definition of "embodiment":

> The meaning of "embodiment" has already been given. But the necessary and sufficient conditions for one particular's being embodied in another may be stated more explicitly [than] before: (i) two particulars thus related are not identical; (ii) the existence of the embodied particular presupposes the existence of the embodying particular; (iii) the embodied particular possesses some (at least) of the properties of the embodying particular; (iv) the embodied particular possesses properties that the embodying particular does not possess; (v) the embodied particular possesses properties of a kind that the embodying particular cannot possess; (vi) the individuation of the embodied particular presupposes the existence of some embodying particular; (vii) the embodying particular is not a proper part of the embodied particular.[9]

The statement of the concept's conditions makes it clear that Margolis thinks of embodiment as something like the material foundation of a cultural entity from which it is nevertheless distinct. The difference between the material in which a person, artwork, or artifact is embodied, and from which it emerges, the property "of a kind that the embodying particular cannot possess" is the intentionality of thought and its expression. (Condition [iv] may be unnecessary in light of condition [v], from which it follows a fortiori, and condition [i] is eliminable in favor of [v], if Leibnizian identity principles are invoked.)

In "Margolis on Emergence and Embodiment," I argue that Margolis's statement of the conditions for the concept of embodiment are subject to a damaging counterexample. Briefly, I claim that there are particulars that satisfy Margolis's seven conditions, but that intuitively are not embodied one in the other. I offer a naive formulation of the objection, followed by more refined variations. The latter are intended to track possible revisions of the conditions that might be put forward in response to less sophisticated objections. The first problem concerns a valley located between two mountains, for which it appears Margolis's seven conditions are met in such a way as to make the valley embodied in one of the mountains. Margolis's definition seems to be satisfied by the problem case because: (1) the valley is not identical with the mountain; (2) the existence of the valley presupposes the existence of the mountain (the valley would not exist if the mountain did not exist); (3) the valley and mountain share at least some properties (a common slope); (4) (entailed by [5]); (5) there are some properties that the valley possesses, but that the mountain cannot possess (being overall convex); (6) the individuation of the valley presupposes the individuation, and hence the existence, of the mountain; (7) the mountain is not a proper part of the valley (since the opposite side of the mountain extends beyond the valley).[10]

The difficulty is not that a valley satisfying Margolis's conditions for embodiment is not a person, artwork, or artifact. Margolis allows the possibility of materially embodied entities that are not also culturally emergent—the two categories overlap—in extension, but are conceptually distinct. The counterexample rather calls attention to a mereological inadequacy in what are supposed to be necessary and sufficient conditions for embodiment. The entire valley intuitively is not materially embodied in the entire mountain, but at most a proper part of the valley is materially embodied in a proper part of the mountain. Yet Margolis's definition implies without further qualification that the valley is embodied in the mountain.

The more sophisticated revisions of the counterexample are intended to meet two anticipated revisions of Margolis's conditions. The first involves a restatement of condition (v), reflecting the fact that for Margolis it is the intentionality of thought and its purposive expression that distinguishes emergent entities from their material embodiments. The reformulated condition states:

(v′) The embodied particular possesses at least some intentional properties which the embodying particular cannot possess.

This is ineffective, because the mereological problem remains for a valley made into or regarded as an environmental found object artwork. An artwork *Valley* has the derivative intentional property of artistic expression, in somewhat the way, though (gratuitously) on a larger scale, as Marcel Duchamp's *Bottlerack* and other so-called ready made artworks. The artwork *Valley* intuitively is still at most only partially materially embodied in a proper part of the mountain, despite satisfying Margolis's seven conditions, with (v') substituted for (v).

The second method of amending Margolis's definition is to add an eighth condition to exclude counterexamples in which an embodied particular has physical or material properties the embodying particular lacks. It requires that:

(viii) The embodied particular possesses no physical or material properties which are not also properties of the embodying particular.

Although this condition avoids the naive and intentionally expressive found object valley and mountain counterexamples, it is too strong. Consider a stone with a charcoal drawing sketched on it. The stone is part of the drawing's material embodiment, because the drawing cannot float free in space, but must adhere to a surface. If condition (viii) is added, it appears to follow that the drawing's physical property of being totally destroyed when it is scrubbed from the stone applies to the drawing's material embodiment. Nevertheless, if the stone remains, then the drawing's material embodiment is not totally destroyed when the drawing is destroyed. There is a relevant analogy in the case of the death or total destruction of persons, when proper parts of their surviving corpses are not totally destroyed.

The point of the counterexamples is not to overturn Margolis's theory of materially embodied culturally emergent entities, but to suggest that some further more complicated revision of the stated conditions for the concept of embodiment is needed. The conditions Margolis offers seem insufficient. There are particulars like the valley and mountain that satisfy all seven clauses, but that intuitively are not embodied one in the other. The counterexample shows the need to tighten up the definition and close the loophole. Previously, I could see no plausible solution. I concluded that a satisfactory reformulation of the concept of embodiment would need to be articulated before Margolis's theory of persons, artworks, and artifacts as materially embodied culturally emergent entities could be accepted.

Now, although I remain convinced that the counterexamples I had posed are lethal to Margolis's original statement of the conditions for embodiment, I believe the possibility for an adequate revision of the definition is at hand. I want to suggest a way of closing the gap by which the valley and mountain counterexamples can be avoided through a principled application of the distinction between what I shall call *constitutive* and *extraconstitutive* properties. There are properties that determine an object's nature independently of its ontic status, and others that imply an object's mode of ontic categorization. The former are constitutive, because properties of this sort, such as being red, round, five centimeters in diameter, and the like, go to constitute an object as the particular object it is. The latter kinds of properties categorize the ontic mode of an object constituted in a certain way, such as being existent, nonexistent, possible, impossible, and the like, and are therefore appropriately called extraconstitutive. The distinction makes it possible to reinforce superadded condition (viii) so as to avoid the charcoal drawing on stone and dead person and corpse counterexamples. The amended condition can be given in this form:

(viii*) The embodied particular possesses no constitutive physical or material properties which are not also properties of the embodying particular.

This version preserves the virtues without the faults of (viii). The condition is immune to naive and intentional valley or *Valley* and mountain counterexamples in the manner of (viii), as previously explained. But it also avoids the charcoal drawing on stone and dead person and corpse counterexamples. For that family of cases, the physical or material property of being totally destroyed, which the embodied particular does not share with its embodiment, is extraconstitutive rather than constitutive. This is seen at once in the fact that the property of being totally destroyed implies that the object no longer exists. The charcoal and corpse scenarios satisfy (viii), but not (viii*). This means that they cannot stand as counterexamples to an expansion of Margolis's seven necessary and sufficient conditions for embodiment, supplemented as proposed by (viii*). As yet, I have been unable to discover or devise any more subtle objections to the reformulated definition of the concept of embodiment, so I am provisionally inclined to conclude that the proposed analysis offers a more bulletproof basis for Margolis's thesis that persons, artworks, and artifacts are materially embodied culturally emergent entities.[11]

EXISTENT TOKENS OF REAL NONEXISTENT TYPES

To account for identity relations among cultural entities, Margolis introduces a realist interpretation of the typetoken distinction. With this distinction, he tries to demystify neglected philosophical problems about the metaphysics of culture. These concern such topics as the exact relations between multiple instances of artworks, copies, reproductions, translations, scores, recordings, performances, alternative instrumentations, and mechanical replication by phonograph, tape, and other information media, printing press, woodblock, etching plate, lithography, and photography.

As with the definition of 'embodiment,' Margolis isolates seven characteristics of tokens and types.

> We may summarize the ontological peculiarities of the type/token distinction in the following way: (i) types and tokens are individuated as particulars; (ii) types and tokens are not separable and cannot exist separately from one another; (iii) types are instantiated by tokens and "token" is an ellipsis for "token-of-a-type"; (iv) types and tokens may be generated and destroyed in the sense that actual tokens of a novel type may be generated and destroyed, and whatever contingencies may be necessary for the generation of actual tokens may be destroyed or disabled; (v) types are actual abstract particulars only in the sense that a set of actual entities may be individuated as tokens of a particular type; (vi) it is incoherent to speak of comparing the properties of actual token- and type-particulars as opposed to comparing the properties of actual particular tokens-of-a-type; (vii) reference to types as particulars serves exclusively to facilitate reference to actual and possible tokens-of-a-type. These distinctions are sufficient to

set off the type/token concept from the kind/instance concept and the set/member concept.[12]

The account is (nonplatonically) realist because types are said to be real, though not necessarily existent, abstract particulars. The distinction is in some ways Aristotelian and reflects an Aristotelian kind of realism, because types lack independent reality and are real only insofar as they inhere in corresponding existent tokens. In other respects, however, Margolis's ontology goes beyond the Platonic-Aristotelian dichotomy, by incorporating a version of Peirce's type-token distinction.[13] Types are created, destroyed, and identified or individuated heuristically as devices to facilitate reference to particular spatiotemporal tokens-of-a-type. Margolis writes: "We may speak of type artworks as particulars because they are heuristically introduced for purposes of individuation, but cannot exist except in the sense in which particular tokens of particular type artworks exist."[14] And: "There are no tokens except tokens-of-a-type. The very process of individuating tokens entails individuating types; that is, it entails individuating different sets of particulars as the sets of alternative tokens of this or that type."[15] The difference between the type-token distinction and the kind-instance or set-member distinction as Margolis conceives it is chiefly that, unlike types, sets and kinds or universals exist even if their members or instances do not, and are neither created nor destroyed.[16]

Margolis wields the type-token distinction in several ways. He uses it to explain the creation or invention of new styles and genres of art, the destruction or loss of art, and the metaphysical linkages between art replications and their causal instrumentalities. The problems here are distinguishable but directly interrelated. There are no types without tokens, and tokens are always tokens-of-a-type, although types and tokens may be of several kinds. When an artwork is mechanically reproduced, its multiple instantiations, even under constraints of accidental or deliberate artistic variation, can satisfy intuitive identity conditions if its replicas are tokens of an identifiable type. Degrees of tolerance for numerically different tokens of an identical artwork can be established on this basis, in accord with what Margolis regards as sound pretheoretical classifications. Musical events may be denoted token performances of a single composition type identified and individuated by reference to a particular score (despite innovative direction or flubbed notes); prints or etchings drawn from a single woodblock or copper plate (with or without coloration, correction, minor additions or deletions) may be seen as the issue of an identical artwork individuated by reference to the materials and historical circumstances of production or the artist's intent. The situation is similar for multiple publication and translations into other languages of literature, films and still photographs made from a single negative, statues or pottery cast from a single form.[17] Margolis writes:

> Printings properly pulled from Dürer's etching plate for *Melancholia I* are instances of *that* etching; but *bona fide* instances of *Melancholia I* need not share all relevant properties, since plural printings, printings that show a touching up of the plate, or printings that are themselves touched up may be genuine instances of *Melancholia I* and still differ markedly from one another—at least to the sensitive eye.[18]

The creation and destruction of art and art types is explained by the theory in terms of the creation and destruction of particular tokens-of-a-type. Usually a new type of art emerges as the result of the creation of a token of that type. This activity, manipulating artistic media to produce an actual token artwork of a novel type, precludes any analysis of types as omnitemporal or atemporal universals or kinds. Margolis maintains: "If, in painting *Les Demoiselles d'Avignon,* Picasso created a new kind of painting, it would appear he could not have done so *by using oils.*"[19] Later he adds: "If we further grant that . . . in creating a new kind of painting with *Les Demoiselles,* Picasso applied paint to canvas, we see that it is at least normally the case that one does not create a new kind of . . . painting without . . . making a particular . . . painting."[20] Types are created by creating novel particulars (or instructions, scores, or the like, for creating novel particulars) that are at once tokens of the new type. When Picasso paints *Les Demoiselles,* he simultaneously manufactures a new particular artwork and the new type of which the painting is a token, giving rise to a nouveau genre or style of art. It is implausible to think of *Les Demoiselles* floating about in a Platonic heaven before

Picasso paints it. Picasso does not merely copy or instantiate a pre-fabricated form by his brushstrokes, but creates a token that simultaneously makes real the type to which the token belongs.

The contrary presumably occurs when an art type dies out or disappears. All tokens of the type are destroyed, and there remain no instructions by which they might be resurrected. Margolis does not deal expansively with the problems of art type destruction, but the possibility clearly follows from the ontological dependence of types on tokens, and the contingent existence of the particular tokens of any type. This is acknowledged in Margolis's statement in condition (iv) above that "types and tokens may be generated and destroyed in the sense that actual tokens of a novel type may be generated and destroyed, and whatever contingencies may be necessary for the generation of actual tokens may be destroyed or disabled."

Art extinction is like extinction in natural history. It may be equally unfortunate from an ecological or humanistic point of view when a species or artwork disappears from the face of the earth. If all recordings of Mozart's *Requiem* are destroyed, the type itself of which they are tokens vanishes when every copy of the score and all knowledge or memory of how to play it is eradicated. If every white Siberian tiger dies, the (Aristotelian or Peircean) type need not be lost as long as there remain genetic DNA instructions in Siberian tiger tissue samples (or Siberian tiger ova and spermatozoa frozen in liquid nitrogen), and the knowledge of how to decode the information for gene expression to produce more Siberian tigers. Art styles and techniques, like plant and animal species, are permanently lost when the tokens of their respective types and the knowhow to produce them disappear.

Margolis's approach goes beyond previous investigations in doing justice to our prephilosophical procedures in identifying, individuating, and classifying artworks. But even his use of the term "kind" switches back and forth from a Platonic sense in which kinds are universal, to an Aristotelian sense in which kinds are nonuniversal types inhering only in tokens under the type-token distinction.[21] Ordinary language is probably equivocal in just this way, indicating that strict adherence to everyday linguistic conventions cannot be the final arbiter of adequacy for a metaphysics of culture. One method of testing Margolis's theory, however, is to compare its consequences against those of more traditional ontologies. Is it necessary to suppose with Margolis that there are particular abstract types in addition to concrete particulars and universal kinds? We need independent justification for the introduction of types and tokens-of-types alongside particulars and universals in the ontology of art. Why are types needed?[22]

The answer Margolis gives is that types are not necessarily or absolutely needed, but are heuristically introduced for convenience of individuation in the classification and evaluation of art. Heuristic purposes vary and are subjectively relative to the interests of those who individuate, classify, and evaluate cultural artifacts. There is a type "Prints of Dürer's *Melancholia I*," because collectors and art historians are interested in identifying certain particulars as causally connected with and originating from the artist's hand. There is (presumably) no type "Prints of *Melancholia I* and Arthur Schopenhauer and the Eiffel Tower," because it happens that no one has any heuristic interest in identifying particulars as tokens of such a peculiar hybrid conjunctive type. The need for types is derivative and depends on the need to identify and individuate particulars as tokens of types according to multiple classificatory schemes sustained by a variety of heuristic interests. Accordingly, we must ask whether these interests might also be served by more standard ontological categories than Margolis's abstract particular types and concrete particular tokens-of-types.

Artworks can be grouped together in different ways for different reasons. The gray-brown high analytic cubist paintings of Picasso and Braque are nearly indistinguishable to all but the expert, and obviously belong together in some aesthetic-metaphysical category. The multiple original prints pulled from the etching plate for Dürer's *Melancholia I* are intuitively instances of an identical artwork, and similarly belong together in some perhaps quite different kind of aestheticmetaphysical category. Margolis attempts to justify the introduction of certain types as the aesthetic-metaphysical category required for these heuristic classificatory purposes. The argument is that types and tokens-of-types are needed because (1) the only possible alternative postulates universals and their instantiations in a traditional Platonist ontology; but (2) universals cannot possibly satisfy the intuitive requirements for aesthetic-metaphysical categories in the heuristic classification of cultural artifacts; because (3) universals, unlike types, are neither created nor destroyed.[23]

Picasso creates or invents a new art style or genre when he paints *Les Demoiselles d'Avignon.* He produces something in real time using real materials that does not have the timeless eternal existence of Plato's Forms. Dürer's etching *Melancholia I,* and indeed his entire oeuvre, unlike any universal, can be entirely destroyed, when the prints and copies and etching plate are destroyed, and his masterpiece lost to the world. Margolis concludes:

> What is important here may not be immediately evident. But if the chef can be said to create (invent) a new (kind of) soup, and if universals cannot be created or destroyed, then, in creating a kind of soup, a chef must be creating something other than a universal. . . . There is only one solution *if* we mean to speak this way. It must be possible to instantiate particulars . . . as well as to instantiate universals or properties. I suggest that the term "type"—in all contexts in which the type/token ambiguity arises —signifies abstract particulars of a kind that can be instantiated.[24]

Yet, surprisingly, Margolis offers no demonstration that instantiable abstract particular types and tokens-of-types are the only or even the best solution to the problem of explaining these ordinary ways of speaking, and satisfying the need for an aesthetic-metaphysical category in the heuristic classification of art and artifacts. Nor does he take up the question whether an alternative kind of category might work as well. Because Margolis already accepts particulars and universals into his ontology as well as tokens and types, a theory that accounts for the same phenomena by reference to universals rather than types is explanatorily and ontically more economical.

To appreciate the limitations of Margolis's rationale, consider an exactly parallel situation in the philosophy of mathematics. Proofs are produced by mathematicians who work with pencil and paper or computers. They exist as cultural entities, and are replicated in textbooks, on blackboards, and in students' notebooks. These might all disappear, like the prints, copies, and plate of Dürer's etching. But a Platonic realist would not for that reason admit that the proof itself had ceased to exist. As a real mathematical entity, it exists timelessly to be rediscovered, or expressed in new ways or different notations. This is not to deny that the mathematician *in some sense* invents the proof, though it may be more accurate to hold that what is created in the discovery or rediscovery of the proof is a certain particular mode of expression of an abstract truth. The formulation of the proof worked out in pencil or chalk is a concrete particular object, the proof itself universal. By analogy, in the ontology of art it might be said that Picasso creates an instantiation of *Les Demoiselles d'Avignon,* which itself is a timeless universal, or that by painting the canvas he instantiates an even more general or higher order Platonic universal (the primitive-modern), and thereby provokes, inspires, or causally induces others to do so, too. The claim that Picasso creates both an artwork and a new kind of art is not denied. But the facts about his artistic activity are reinterpreted in the vocabulary of a more streamlined philosophical theory, leaving the commonsense judgments of ordinary language untouched.[25]

The Platonic realist or universalist ontology has other advantages in comparison with Margolis's type-token account. There is a difficulty for Margolis's ontology as it confronts a number of puzzles about artwork genidentity and extinction. Consider what might be said about the destruction and recreation of art that falls somewhere between abstract mathematical proofs and particular copies of Dürer's etchings.

Suppose that the great pyramids of the Egyptians, Greeks, Toltecs, Aztecs, and Maya were all destroyed, and that, as is virtually the case today, the blueprints, instructions, memory, or other knowledge of how to build such structures also disappeared. Margolis's concept of type requires us to say that by these contingencies the art type "pyramid" is destroyed along with its tokens. If at some later date the art of pyramid building is rediscovered, the theory in principle might imply either that a new architectural type, genidentically distinct from the original, has emerged by creation or invention, or that the old and new pyramids are tokens of a single historically discontinuous type.

Choice among types is heuristic. But what is gained by reference to types that could not equally be provided by appeal to universals and instantiations in a categorically more economical Pla-

tonic realist ontology? We can say that the original and rediscovered pyramids are concrete historically discontinuous instantiations
of the same universal. In this way, we admit that for a time no particular pyramids existed, although the form or abstract idea of
pyramid remains in timeless universal existence, waiting to be
rediscovered and reinstantiated. Because types lack reality when
their tokens do not exist, Margolis's type-token theory is committed
to holding that during the interval of time when pyramid tokens and
the blueprint engineering instructions to produce them are nonexistent, the type itself is no longer real.

In the dark ages before pyramids are reinvented, the pyramid
type, according to Margolis's Peircean inherence theory, is unreal.
But this does not agree with ordinary ways of speaking. "The
pyramid" does not come into and go out of reality, any more than
the number π or Gödel's theorem. The discrepancy is especially
clear in this case, because a pyramid is a solid geometrical figure,
which (on a Platonic realist theory of universals) may be instantiated or imitated in various media, including stone monuments. It is
more plausible to suppose that Dürer's etching (the type, in Margolis's terminology, of which prints and even burin-incised plates
are tokens) is created at a certain time and eventually destroyed. As
Dürer himself writes in his (1525) *Unterweisung der Messung*: "Art
is easily lost, but—although it may be only with difficulty and after
a long time has elapsed—it is rediscovered." But this is less obviously true for the most general artistically instantiable geometrical
shapes and artifact kinds such as the pyramid at the opposite extreme from autographic art.[26]

Now we are embarked on a progression of categories, a slippery
slope, if you like, in which universals explain the genidentity or
destruction and resurgence of art more plausibly than Margolis's
types. The next step is to discount the philosophical importance of
detail and complexity in a work like Dürer's etching when compared with pyramids. It is unlikely that another artist could instantiate Dürer's etching with all its minutiae as precisely as the master,
or in the way that makes almost any pyramid an instantiation of *the*
pyramid, though skillful art forgers might be said to do just that. Yet
in another logically possible world, there could occur as many multiple instantiations of "the *Melancholia I*" as there are of "the

pyramid" in the actual world. These would not all be instantiations *per se* of Dürer's *Melancholia I,* but neither are all instantions of "the bed" instantiations *per se* of Dürer's bed. The point is that the complexity and specificity of Dürer's etching in comparison with the generality of the basic pyramid shape seems inessential to the question whether both are best understood as the instantiation of a universal, rather than as tokens of types. (Plato was familiar with the difficulties of ambiguous specificity in the characterization of Forms, as we know from his dialogue the *Parmenides.*[27])

The type-token distinction is also less competent than the traditional Platonic theory of universals in handling problems of art extinction and rediscovery or reinvention. Suppose that all recordings and scores of Mozart's *Requiem* were to be destroyed, but that one musician or an entire orchestra and choral ensemble remembers how to perform the piece, and if prompted might even be able to write out the score exactly. It would seem strained to say that the *Requiem* at this stage is already lost to the world, though it is perhaps on the brink. The traditional realist or universalist theory implies that the music itself, unlike its instantiations, is neither created nor destroyed. Margolis, in accord with the type-token distinction, seems compelled on the contrary to hold that once the scores, recordings, and actual performances are destroyed, the type, the *Requiem* itself, is lost, despite the fact that living musicians could restore the piece from behavioral disposition or memory.

Margolis might respond that the musician's memories or dispositions to perform Mozart's work are in some sense instructions for producing it and that the type survives in these. This is reminiscent of Wittgenstein's assertion in the *Tractatus Logico-Philosophicus* (4.014): "The gramophone record, *the musical thought,* the score, the waves of sound, all stand to one another in that pictorial relation, which holds between language and the world."[28] But memories and behavioral dispositions, although they may in Wittgenstein's terminology share an internal logical structure with a musical score, sound waves produced at a performance, and the grooves in a record or magnetic patterns on a plastic tape or disk, in Margolis's sense of the word are not tokens of the artwork. The memory of an artwork is not itself an artwork. The type is lost with its tokens, and the memory of the *Requiem* or even of how to play the *Requiem* is

Albrecht Dürer, *Melancholia 1* (1514). Print reproduced with the permission of the Herbert F. Johnson Museum of Art, Cornell University, bequest of William P. Chapman Jr., Class of 1895.

no more an actual token of the artwork than a mirror's reflection of Dürer's *Melancholia I* is a token of *Melancholia I* (though again it may have what Wittgenstein would call the very same logical structure or internal pictorial relation).

If we stretch the meaning of the term to allow that the memory of an artwork can also be one of its tokens, another problem remains. Assume that future musicians happen to produce, a score or live performance that is indistinguishable from Mozart's *Requiem*. Imagine that this occurs many years after the disappearance of its last actual token instantiation, including the last memory of Mozart's composition. This simultaneously produces a token-of-the-type *and* a type of which it is the token. It is a different token than any that had previously existed. But is it the same or a different type?

Types are introduced heuristically to identify and individuate tokens-of-types, so within reason we can say what we like. The dilemma is this: If we conclude that the type created along with the token is different than the original type before all its tokens were eliminated, then there is no sound justification for identifying the new work as the *Requiem,* and the use of the name for both would be strictly equivocal. This is unsatisfactory, because intuitively what the musicians regardless of intent have unknowingly produced is a token or instantiation of (what we would call) Mozart's music.[29] The performers are not inventing something entirely new that merely bears a remarkable resemblance to the original score, if their restoration corresponds exactly note-for-note and accent-for-accent. But the types cannot be identical on Margolis's theory, because by hypothesis the original type is completely destroyed along with its tokens.

This is not a problem for a Platonic realist or universals theory, because the same universals are always available for real world instantiation or reinstantiation. But only a deviant (certainly non-Aristotelian, non-Peircean) -metaphysics of coming-to-be and passing-away could permit the same type to suffer temporally discontinuous reality, undergoing total extinction only to resurface at a later time as the very same individual. Annihilation is not an accidental genidentity-preserving change, because a thing's nature or essence is standardly defined in terms of those properties without which it ceases to be.[30]

Margolis's Historical Contextualism

We began with the core of Margolis's metaphysics of culture, working outward from the thesis that persons, artworks, and artifacts are materially embodied culturally emergent entities to a more comprehensive level at which the identity and categories of cultural objects are subject to a version of the type-token distinction. Cultural tokens are creatures of dual attributes, according to Margolis. They are irreducible to the physical substratum in which they are embodied by virtue of their intrinsic or derivative intentional properties. They possess the intentionality of thought or its purposive expression, and belong to or fall under real though nonexistent heuristic cultural types that are generated and destroyed by the coming into existence of at least one or passing out of existence of all corresponding concrete tokens.[31]

Within this structure of concepts we have seen that, other things being equal, Margolis's application of the type-token distinction might reasonably be challenged by an unfavorable comparison with simpler and more economical traditional categorizations of kinds and instances. Yet Margolis's metaphysics of culture can be defended at least to a plausible extent against the criticisms mounted thus far. The material embodiment cultural emergence thesis, surrounded by the more comprehensive type-token distinction, is in turn enveloped in an even more comprehensive partially metaphilosophical historicism or historical contextualism. Here is a representative statement from *The Flux of History and the Flux of Science*, in which Margolis acknowledges:

> . . . (1) that reference and predication are inherently historicized; (2) that individuation and reidentification are ineliminably context bound and logically informal; (3) that predicative similarity is a function of the consensual practices of viable societies and cannot be confirmed in any more reliable way; (4) that theoretical discourse is inseparable from a given society's social praxis, through which it fixes effective reference and predication; (5) that the rational structure of science is inseparable from its history; (6) that numerically distinct referents may be successfully individuated and identified though they lack fixed natures and have (or

"are") only histories; (7) that the "nature" of such referents may change, or (as with selves) may be changed reflexively, in altering their histories, without adversely affecting their numerical identity; (8) that the identity of individuated things persisting through change depends in all instances on a society's narratized memory of how it has individuated and identified such referents at earlier times; (9) that bivalence and alternative logics are open to empirical choice on the basis of fitting the distinctive judgments a given domain can effectively support; (10) that all interpreted *de re* and *de dicto* necessities may be opposed without self-contradiction; (11) that the structure of human thought and reason and logic are, in a measure, artifacts of a society's linguistic history; (12) that human persons or selves are social constructions that emerge with the symbiotized natural world and a society's historical and linguistic traditions; and (13) that all formerly affirmed invariances bearing on the foregoing and related distinctions hold only within the tacit horizon of a given society's conceptual imagination.[32]

The cultural relativist reply to these objections on behalf of Margolis's theory is that it is ahistorical and acontextual to speak of the recurrence of an art type after the extinction of all its corresponding tokens. The objection presupposes a modal *apriorism* incompatible with Margolis's historicism. Margolis regards all heuristic predications and classifications by type as thoroughly historically contexted. The inference is that when every token of a previously real type has ceased to exist, when all exemplars and the knowledge to produce them have disappeared, the historical context in which predications of and classifications by the former type can intelligibly be made will also no longer obtain. Margolis limits type predications and classifications even for philosophers stationed outside the fray who may want to consider the possibilities of cultural entities from an imagined transcendent perspective for purely theoretical purposes, as a metaphysically impermissible uncontexted view *sub specie aeterni* from nowhere.[33]

Contextualism enables Margolis to forestall the counterexamples. There is no point in disputing Margolis's metaphysics of culture by entertaining thought experiments in which an art type is created, then completely dies out with the destruction of all its tokens, and is later restored or rediscovered. Margolis can counter such criticisms with an ingenious dilemma. If a type persists in any form, however dimly or remotely, then the type is not actually destroyed. If on the other hand the type is entirely eliminated, then the historical context in which predications of and classifications by that type is also passé. Thus, Margolis cannot take seriously the possibility that the very same type, a culture-bound heuristic device for categorizing cultural phenomena, could entirely disappear and then reoccur. At most, an homonymous term, undetached from the historical context in which it derives its ambivalent meanings, could equivocally be given to designate a new type for relevantly similar token cultural entities as for those which had previously existed and since become extinct.

Margolis's historicism raises profound metaphilosophical questions. It implies among other things that there can be no adequate conception of transcendent *a priori* logical modalities. What is possible, impossible, necessary, or contingent is just as historically contexted for Margolis as Impressionism or the baroque. There is no higher context-free ground from which philosophers can evaluate a theory's credentials. This applies as well to Margolis's own metaphysics of culture in its application of the material embodiment cultural emergence thesis and type-token distinction, for which he cannot consistently claim absolute truth. Margolis's cultural relativism nevertheless might be thought to serve as a bulwark against certain pedestrian criticisms such as those involved in the philosophical comparison of kind-instance versus type-token categories for purportedly context-free elimination and recurrence of (the tokens of) a particular type.[34]

Whether Margolis's historical contextualism with its implications for modality and other traditional philosophical transcendentalia is ultimately acceptable or not is a difficult subject. But in one way the question is irrelevant to the criticism of Margolis's interpretation and use of the type-token distinction. The fact that Margolis jackets the core of his metaphysics of culture with a cultural historicism means that no element of the core can be effectively internally criticized by posing counterexamples that presuppose an ahistorical or acontextual argumentative standpoint.

There is nevertheless a way of recapturing the force of the

objection to Margolis's application of the type-token distinction without violating his historical contextualism. The important ingredients of a context-sensitive counterexample are these. We recall that even for Margolis the mere memory of a token of a type is not enough to preserve the token from nonexistence or the corresponding type from nonreality.[35] When the tokens of a type no longer exist, and there no longer exists the ability or disposition to produce more tokens, the type has been annihilated, lingering memory of its tokens notwithstanding. To do justice to ordinary usage, which Margolis sometimes takes as a goal of adequate theoretization, it would arguably be unsatisfactory to distinguish different historical contexts in the logically most finegrained way, by identifying a different one for every discriminable instant of time. This would make nonsense of attempts to discern temporally enduring historical periods such as Impressionism, the baroque, or the Napoleonic era. It is incumbent on historical contextualism to allow for heuristic groupings of relevantly similar but nonidentical (often but not necessarily strictly temporally contiguous) historical episodes as belonging to the very same historical context. From these assumptions, it is easy to see that Margolis's theory remains subject to modified criticisms concerning the extinction and recurrence of cultural entities that are better understood as instances of a kind, rather than as tokens of a type.

Suppose, as a modest refinement of the previous counterexample, that a lone survivor of the classical baroque lives through the destruction of each and every token of the baroque aesthetic type, including all artworks, artifacts, architecture, graphic representations, musical scores, treatises, and so on, and the death of all persons who previously had the ability or disposition to produce baroque works. The survivor has none of these talents, and as we can readily imagine, for reasons of neurophysiological disability or the like, cannot even whistle or hum a baroque tune, sketch a baroque façade, or compose a baroque verse. Thus, there are no baroque tokens left, so that on Margolis's theory it seems obligatory to declare the disappearance of the baroque and the unreality of the baroque type. Some years go by. The survivor witnesses several changes of artistic styles, and finally, after a long hiatus, a musician produces a beautiful chamber piece reminiscent of Mozart's *Eine*

Kleine Nachtmusik. The survivor hears the first performance, and, alone among the audience, recognizes the similarity of style, and proclaims to an uncomprehending world that the musician has produced a new composition heralding the return of the baroque.

The survivor appears to have spoken truly, and by hypothesis is the only one who, as contexted chance has it, is in an epistemically justified position to know. Margolis, on the contrary, must denounce this labeling of the new production, after the elimination of the classical baroque, as equivocal at best. The piece cannot be truly baroque, because the historical context of the baroque ended with the passing of the baroque type into nonreality with the destruction of all existent tokens of the type. Yet I see nothing conceptually mistaken about attributing to the style represented by the musician's composition an unwitting revival or rediscovery of the baroque. This seems in fact the most natural way to describe what we are asked to imagine has occurred. No one but the survivor of the previous instantiation of the baroque could have recognized it as such, and no one else could have used the kind-term "baroque" correctly rather than equivocally in this way. The survivor remembers what the baroque is like even after, according to Margolis's application of the type-token distinction, the baroque type has vanished from reality with the disappearance of all corresponding tokens.

If the counterexample seems far-fetched from Margolis's intent to describe the practical heuristics of historically contexted type-attributions, we must remind ourselves that the point is a conceptual one concerning the philosophical adequacy of Margolis's analysis in all conceivable applications. The criticism is an internal objection to Margolis's metaphysics of culture, because the imaginability of the example admittedly is itself historically contexted. But because we can conceive of the thought experiment as it has been described, and because we are trying to determine its implications for our own purposes from the standpoint of the historical context within which we are evaluating Margolis's theory, the counterexample without contradicting his historicism seems both legitimate and genuinely problematic for Margolis. The historicist defense of Margolis's type-token distinction against the recurrence counterexamples succeeds only if it is implausibly assumed that our conclusions about another historical context must be limited in the same ways as the target context which is the object of our reflections and hypotheses. But I see no reason whatsoever to suppose that this must be true, and I preemptively denounce any such inference as an instance of the historicist fallacy.[36]

There are other related categories of counterexamples that apply with equal force against Margolis's metaphysics of culture insofar as it relies on the type-token rather than kind-instance distinction. These have to do with third-party cultural type or kind attributions to different culturally isolated societies for which cultural interaction, diffusion, or transmission of ideas can be effectively discounted (pyramid temple building in Aztec and Egyptian cultures), and scenarios in which it seems reasonable to suppose that entire historical contexts are relevantly replicated (Nietzschean eternal recurrences or self-enclosed discontinguous cultural historical cycles).

Whether or not an historical context can correctly be said to have recurred after an interruption is entirely a heuristic matter to be decided by the reasonable interests and demands of classification and explanation. This is true especially in view of the fact that the most fine-grained basis for individuating historical contexts, as we have observed, precludes attempts to individuate enduring dynamic historical contexts. It follows as an immediate consequence on Margolis's terms that some eras, epochs, periods, ages, and historical contexts conceivably might recur after having vanished from the world stage, or that they might occur simultaneously in culturally isolated societies. This putative possibility cannot be readily explained on Margolis's interpretation of the type-token distinction, though it is more simply, economically, and plausibly modeled as the multiple instantiation or reinstantiation of a subsistent kind. If relevantly identical historical contexts can recur, then we should expect Margolis's theory to allow that there can equally recur relevantly identically historically contexted relevantly identical types, even after intervals in which all tokens of the type have been entirely eliminated. But what historical context serves to situate the recurrence of historical contexts?

Finally, the historicist ploy can be turned against itself. If Margolis's contextualism disallows pronouncements of a type's imagined recurrence after its total extinction, then by rights the same considerations should prohibit the type's imagined total extinction. Who in such an historically contexted event could possibly be in a position to judge that the type has been extinguished? If there is anyone who can recognize that a type, say, the baroque, has disappeared, then by this historicist dilemma, the type paradoxically has not actually disappeared. There is no one who in the hypothetical historical context can truly witness the passing of the type, just as there is no one who can truly witness its return. When a type is gone, it is so completely gone that no one situated in that context can know it; no one can miss it or regret or rejoice in its departure. If anyone still recognizes the type well enough to have any of these attitudes toward it, then the type persists and has at least some lingering degree of real presence.

This may be the symptom of a deep confusion in Margolis's concept of type. Margolis permits himself to describe the destruction of types in general terms as though from an uncontexted vantage point, although (inconsistently, I should think) he insists on historical contextualist grounds that the imagined recurrence of a type after its total obliteration cannot intelligibly be described in general terms as though from an uncontexted vantage point. If we cannot coherently hypothesize in general terms the contexted return in time of a previously annihilated type, then so much the worse for contexted types. But equally then also we cannot coherently hypothesize in general terms a type's contexted destruction in time. Yet Margolis needs the possibility of the contexted destruction of types for his interpretation of the type-token distinction, as when he says, in condition (iv): "types and tokens may be generated and destroyed."

The implication is that Margolis's historical contextualism cannot consistently be used in defending the type-token distinction as he has defined it against type extinction and recurrence counterexamples. The effort to neutralize such counterexamples works only on pain of denying the intelligibility of Margolis's essential claim that a type is destroyed or rendered unreal when all of its tokens are destroyed. If a contexted type cannot coherently be described in general terms as recurring after its destruction, then it also cannot coherently be described in general terms in the first place as being destroyed. But if contexted types cannot be destroyed, then what sense does it make to say that they are created?

What then is the difference between uncreated indestructible types and Platonic kinds?

SEMANTIC PROPOSAL FOR ONTIC NEUTRALITY OF CULTURAL KINDS

The type-token distinction can be made to do most of the work Margolis requires of it. But it strains under the effort of tying to handle recherché cases involving the elimination and recurrence of tokens of the same presumptive type, multiple occurrences in culturally disconnected historical contexts, eternal recurrence, and cyclical historical contexts. These problems make Margolis's metaphysics theoretically less commendable than traditional kind-instance categories, unless there is some compensating advantage offered by the type-token distinction.

Margolis prefers types and tokens to kinds and instances because he accepts certain intuitive claims about the origin and demise of classificatory cultural categories and thinks these are better explained by the type-token than by the kind-instance distinction. Things (mostly) fit together nicely, and ontological baggage is kept to a minimum. We have already seen that there are drawbacks to types in accounting for the recurrence of destroyed types, and that historical contextualism does not preclude recurrence unless it also precludes destruction. The kind-instance distinction can also be used to explain not only the origin and destruction, but also the recurrence of cultural entity categories. Kinds are not created or destroyed, but their instantiations can come and go, and, unlike types, come back again. Artists "create" new kinds only metaphorically in the sense of creating influential instances of (at some level of generality) previously uninstantiated kinds.

Other things being equal, ontic commitment to real but nonexistent types is more economical than to Platonically existent or subsistent kinds. Margolis might find it worth tolerating a few implausible consequences (especially for contrived counterexamples unlikely to be encountered in actual applications), if by doing so he can avoid commitment to a domain of entities inflated by existent universal kinds as opposed to real but nonexistent general types (though Margolis's ontic largesse condones kinds as well as types). If Margolis follows Ockham's razor in preferring tokens and types to instances and kinds, at least for the sake of achieving overall parsimony in the metaphysics of cultural entities, his attitude is fully in agreement with much of contemporary ontic minimalism and naturalism.[37]

But if the main theoretical advantage of Margolis's type-token distinction is its ontic commitment to a smaller sheer number of existent entities than required by the kind-instance distinction, then an even more salutary economy can be derived from a nonstandard nonplatonic interpretation of the kind-instance distinction, without sacrifice of explanatory simplicity. For this purpose, I recommend substituting for Margolis's type-token distinction housed within his historicist shell, a version of the kind-instance distinction housed within an ontically neutral intensional semantic shell. There are several nonextensional logics, reference and predication theories, from which to choose. Intended object theory logics as intensional systems in which it is possible to refer to and truly predicate properties of nonexistent objects enable a metaphysics to include kinds without commitment to their existence.[38] Ontically neutral reference to kinds supports whatever theoretical predications a more traditional Platonic realist ontology finds useful in classification and explanation. But a theory of kinds need not inflate the realm of existents beyond necessity, because beingless kinds in an intensionalist semantic framework fulfill all the desired philosophical functions of abstract entities without assuming any ontic burden. The virtues of kinds over types in accounting for the extinction and resurrection of certain cultural categories are preserved even if kinds lack existence, reality, or being altogether, if they are available as (mind-independent) intended objects for reference and true predication in an extraontological semantic domain.[39]

From this standpoint it can now be seen that the preceding apparent endorsement of Platonism was nothing more than a critical foil for raising difficulties about Margolis's type-token distinction by contrast with the kind-instance distinction and that no ontic commitment to Platonic realism is thereby intended or implied. The following diagram indicates a modification of Margolis's three-tiered metaphysics of cultural entities. The intentionalist dual-aspect or property dualist core is preserved (with only the minor revisions

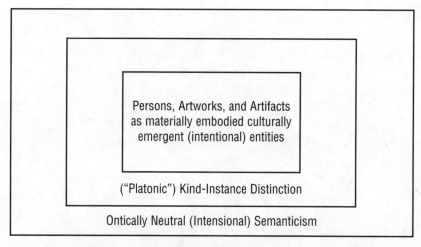

Fig. 2. Proposal for a Modified Three-Tiered Metaphysics of Culture

recommended for the definition of the concept of embodiment), but the historically contexted type-token distinction is replaced by an intensional ontically neutral semanticized kind-instance distinction.

DIRECTIONS FOR AN ONTOLOGY OF CULTURAL ENTITIES

The philosophy of mind and culture I find most attractive is inspired by Margolis, and might be described as a revisionary development of his central ideas. With the minor reservations I have already explained, I wholeheartedly accept the core of Margolis's theory. The intentionality of thought and its purposive expression in persons, artworks, and artifacts as dual-attribute materially embodied culturally emergent entities strikes me as true in all essentials.[40]

I have argued that Margolis's definition of embodiment can be improved, and I have suggested a way of doing this, by invoking a distinction between constitutive and extraconstitutive properties and supplementing Margolis's seven conditions with an eighth clause that the embodied particular possesses no specifically constitutive physical or material properties that are not also properties of the embodying particular. I favor an account of emergence that empha-

sizes the intrinsic intentionality of mind and the derivative intentionality of expressions of thought in language, art, and artifacts.[41]

As a response to problems in explaining the imaginable elimination and recurrence of cultural entities under Margolis's type-
token distinction, I have advocated a return to the kind-instance distinction, and, as compensation for introducing abstract kinds in
place of types into the ontology, I have proposed substituting for
Margolis's historicism an ontically neutral semantics for reference
to and true predication of properties to kinds. This may be just as
well, because I have argued that Margolis's historicism does not
adequately or even consistently shield his application of the type-
token distinction from the recurrence of cultural types counterexamples anyway. If forced to choose, I prefer populating ontology
with existent kinds to involvement in the historicist controversy.
But the ontically neutral intensionalist semantics I endorse grate-
fully allows theoretical explanatory access to kinds via reference
and true predication without ontic commitment.

It is the outermost tier in Margolis's metaphysics of culture, its
historical contextualism, with which I am most uncomfortable. That
humans generally and we as philosophers in particular are historically situated is indisputable; that our historical situation as thinkers
inescapably limits the truth or generality of our conclusions is by no
means as evident. Margolis has not adopted historical contextualism merely as an expedient for dealing with puzzles occasioned
by his use of the type-token distinction. He regards relativism properly understood as justified by a number of telling considerations,
and perhaps sees its coherence with and bolstering of the type-token
distinction as further proof of its importance. But the solution is
problematic, and there is an alternative that secures the same advantages without the drawbacks.

Where I have raised difficulties, I have pointed in another direction for a parallel development of ideas faithful at least to the core
of Margolis's metaphysics of culture. The proposal I offer reduces
ontological commitment, for ontically neutral reference to and true
predication of properties to abstract kinds accomplishes all that is
required in accounting for the peculiarities of cultural entities
without swelling the ranks of ontology. Margolis, I believe, will
continue to prefer the type-token ambiguity and historical contex-

tualism. Certainly his system is rich enough and Margolis adroit enough in exploiting its resources to provide answers to objections that I may not have anticipated. My purpose in any case is not to dissuade Margolis from the path he has chosen, because, like Margolis, I celebrate the variety of approaches to philosophical problems. By presenting a more familiar if less scenic route under a nonstandard interpretation, I only hope to have highlighted what is distinctive about Margolis's metaphysics of culture.[42]

NOTES

1. Joseph Margolis, *Culture and Cultural Entities: Toward a New Unity of Science* (Dordrecht: D. Reidel Publishing Company, 1984); *Persons and Minds: The Prospects of Nonreductive Materialism,* Boston Studies in the Philosophy of Science, 57 (Dordrecht: D. Reidel Publishing Company, 1978); *Philosophy of Psychology* (Englewood Cliffs, N.J.: Prentice Hall, Inc., 1984).

2. Margolis, *Values and Conduct* (Oxford: Clarendon Press, 1971); *Knowledge and Existence: An Introduction to Philosophical Problems* (New York: Oxford University Press, 1973); *Negativities: The Limits of Life* (Columbus: Charles Merrill, 1975); *Pragmatism without Foundations: Reconciling Relativism and Realism* (Oxford: Basil Blackwell, 1986); *Texts without Referents: Reconciling Science and Narrative* (Oxford: Basil Blackwell, 1989); *Life without Principles: Reconciling Theory and Practice* (Oxford: Basil Blackwell, 1996); *The Flux of History and the Flux of Science* (Berkeley: University of California Press, 1993); *Interpretation, Radical But Not Unruly: The New Puzzle of the Arts and History* (Berkeley: University of California Press, 1995).

3. Margolis, *The Language of Art and Art Criticism: Analytic Questions in Aesthetics* (Detroit, Mich.: Wayne State University Press, 1965); *Art and Philosophy* (Atlantic Highlands, N.J.: Humanities Press, 1980); "The Identity of a Work of Art," *Mind* 68 (1959): 34–50; "Works of Art as Physically Embodied and Culturally Emergent Entities," *British Journal of Aesthetics* 14 (1974): 187–96; "The Ontological Peculiarity of Works of Art," *Journal of Aesthetics and Art Criticism* 36 (1977): 45–50; "A Strategy for a Philosophy of Art," *Journal of Aesthetics and Art Criticism* 37 (1979): 445–54; "Artworks and the History of Production," *Communication and Cognition* 17 (1984): 89–106; "Constraints on the Metaphysics of Culture," *Review of Metaphysics* 39 (1986): 653–73.

4. Margolis in no single source to date weaves together all three of these themes. The closest he comes to offering a complete picture of his three-tiered metaphysics of culture is in those parts of his writings on cultural entities that also gesture toward a radical historicism and in his more recent studies of historical contextualism and cultural relativism that take issue with eliminative and reductive analyses of mind and cultural entities.

5. Dale Jacquette, "Margolis on Emergence and Embodiment," *Journal of Aesthetics and Art Criticism* 44 (1986): 257–61. A French translation appears as "Émergence et incorporation selon Margolis," *Philosophiques* 13 (1986): 53–63. Margolis's reply follows in the subsequent issue, under the title, "Pour réhabiliter la notion d'incorporation des entités culturelles: Réponse à Dale Jacquette," *Philosophiques* 13 (1986): 333–43; Jacquette, "The Type-Token Distinction in Margolis's Aesthetics," *Journal of Aesthetics and Art Criticism* 52 (1994): 299–307. See note 41 below.

6. I think it likely that Margolis would find an intensionalist semantic framework for the metaphysics of culture acceptable because of his remarks about the irreducibility of intensional linguistic contexts. See *Philosophy of Psychology*, esp. pp. 13–15. Margolis regards the prospects for developing nonstandard reference and predication semantics as germane to his radical historicism. See the quotation from his *The Flux of History and the Flux of Science* attached to note 32 below.

7. *Persons and Minds*, pp. 1–19, 234–36; "Works of Art as Physically Embodied and Culturally Emergent Entities," pp. 187–89.

8. *Art and Philosophy*, pp. 23–24; *Persons and Minds*, pp. 24–25; *Philosophy of Psychology*, 24–33, 52–55; *Culture and Cultural Entities*, pp. 6–7, 124–25.

9. *Persons and Minds*, p. 234.

10. Jacquette, "Margolis on Emergence and Embodiment," esp. pp. 258–60.

11. The distinction between constitutive and extraconstitutive properties is roughly that by which Kant refutes ontological proofs for the existence of God in his 100 gold thalers argument. The 100 gold thalers are constituted by the constitutive properties of being gold, coins of a certain denomination, and 100 in number. The question of whether the 100 gold thalers exist goes beyond the question of how the objects are constituted, and if extraconstitutive properties like existence or nonexistence enter into the nature or determination of an object, then, as Kant maintains, the very same existent (nonexistent) object could not intelligibly be imagined to be nonexistent (existent). If the same restriction is applied to the concept of God, then God's nature or essence cannot be constituted by, and hence cannot entail, the extraconstitutive property of existence. The distinction in more recent intentionalist philosophy is associated with the Graz School of Alexius Meinong. The division between constitutive and extraconstitutive properties was suggested to Meinong by his student and collaborator Ernst Mally. Meinong, *Über Möglichkeit und Wahrscheinlichkeit: Beiträge zur Gegenstandstheorie und Erkenntnistheorie* (Leipzig: Verlag von Johann Ambrosius Barth, 1915), rpt., *Alexius Meinong Gesamtausgabe*, ed. Rudolf Haller and Rudolf Kindinger, in collaboration with Roderick M. Chisholm, VI, pp. 176–77. J. N. Findlay, *Meinong's Theory of Objects and Values*, 2d ed. (London: Oxford University Press), p. 176. See Jacquette, "Meinong's Doctrine of the Modal Moment," *Grazer Philosophische Studien* 25–26 (1985–1986): 423–38; "Meinongian Logic and Anselm's Ontological Proof for the Existence of God," *Philosophical Forum* 25 (1994): 231–40.

12. *Art and Philosophy,* p. 20. The passage originally appears in "The Ontological Peculiarity of Works of Art," p. 47. Margolis traces his version of the type-token distinction to C. L. Stevenson, "On 'What is a Poem?' " *Philosophical Review* 66 (1957): 330–33; and ultimately to C. S. Peirce's semiotic, *The Collected Papers of Charles Sanders Peirce,* ed. Charles Hartshorne and Paul Weiss (Cambridge: Harvard University Press, 1939), Vol. IV. Margolis also mentions Stevenson's essay, "Interpretation and Evaluation in Aesthetics," in *Philosophical Analysis,* ed. Max Black (Ithaca: Cornell University Press, 1950); and Richard Rudner's criticism of C. I. Lewis, in "The Ontological Status of the Esthetic Object," *Philosophy and Phenomenological Research* 10 (1950): 380–88. See *The Language of Art and Art Criticism,* pp. 51 and 184, n. 6.

13. Note that Margolis more recently speaks in Peircean terms of the "reality" of "nonexistent" types (of existent tokens). This subtlety derives from Margolis's interpretation of Peirce's concept of metaphysical "thirdness." See Margolis, "The Passing of Peirce's Realism," *Transactions of the Charles S. Peirce Society* 29 (1993): 293–330. But in his original formulations of the distinction, appearing in *Art and Philosophy,* p. 20, and "The Ontological Peculiarity of Works of Art," p. 47, Margolis refers without special qualification simply to the "existence" of tokens and types. See, for example, his condition (ii): "types and tokens are not separable and cannot exist separately from one another" (emphases added). My previous criticisms in "The Type-Token Distinction in Margolis's Aesthetics" were based on his earlier statement of the distinction, in which his later separation of existence and reality was not emphasized. Margolis's new distinction is not merely a terminological variant of the first version, but as far as I can see my objections carry over from one vocabulary to the other without loss of argumentative force.

14. *Art and Philosophy,* p. 23.

15. Ibid. and *Persons and Minds,* p. 235.

16. *Culture and Cultural Entities,* p. 14; *Persons and Minds,* pp. 231–32; *Art and Philosophy,* p. 17; "The Ontological Peculiarity of Works of Art," pp. 45–46.

17. *The Language of Art and Art Criticism,* p. 53: "Reproductions correspond either to copy tokens, as in plural sculpture castings or etchings from the same plate, or to translation tokens, as in reduced-scale color lithographs of great paintings," *Art and Philosophy,* pp. 17–23.

18. *Art and Philosophy,* p. 18.

19. Ibid., p. 17.

20. Ibid., p. 18.

21. Ibid., p. 17: "In painting *Les Demoiselles d'Avignon,* Picasso created a new kind of painting" (informal "nonuniversal" sense in which kinds like types can be created or destroyed); p. 20: "These distinctions are sufficient to set off the type/token concept from the kind/instance concept" (technical "universal" sense in which kinds unlike types cannot be created or destroyed).

22. *The Language of Art and Art Criticism,* pp. 62–63: "We have not really described the actual ways in which we individuate works of art; we have, rather,

constructed an alternative language for individuating, a language that parallels our actual usage, exhibits its logical features more clearly, but a language that is hardly more convenient."

23. Supra note 16.

24. *Art and Philosophy*, p. 17. See *Persons and Minds*, pp. 231–32. "The Ontological Peculiarities of Works of Art," p. 45. Margolis's culinary example derives from Jack Glickman, "Creativity in the Arts," in *Culture and Art*, ed. Lars Aagaard-Mogensen (Atlantic Highlands, N.J.: Humanities Press, 1977), pp. 140–42. *The Language of Art and Art Criticism*, p. 63: "The scheme we have applied has the double advantage of clarifying the order of our range of usage in terms of the tokentype distinction (which is of primary interest in speaking of individuating works of art) and of marking the fundamental problem of ambiguity with which we must come to grips in describing, interpreting, and, ultimately, in evaluating, works of art."

25. *The Language of Art and Art Criticism*, pp. 62–63.

26. Margolis, "Numerical Identity and Reference in the Arts," *British Journal of Aesthetics* 10 (1970): 138–46; "On Disputes about the Ontological Status of a Work of Art," *British Journal of Aesthetics* 8 (1968): 147–54. See Nelson Goodman, *Languages of Art: An Approach to the Theory of Symbols* (Oxford: Oxford University Press, 1969), pp. 148–208, for an account of the strict notational identity criteria for artworks which Margolis attacks. Lucian Krukowski, "Artworks That End and Objects That Endure," *Journal of Aesthetics and Art Criticism* 40 (1981): 187–97.

27. Plato, *Parmenides*, pp. 130–34.

28. Ludwig Wittgenstein, *Tractatus Logico-Philosophicus*, ed. C. K. Ogden (London: Routledge & Kegan Paul, Ltd., 1922), 4.014 (emphasis added). See also 4.0141.

29. We should not be distracted by the question of whether the music written by the imaginary future musicians should be referred to as Mozart's *Requiem*. The names by which an artwork is designated are generally irrelevant to its identity, as we know from changing and evolving nomenclatures and corrections of mistaken attributions in art history. The artists who redo these masterpieces in any case might even refer to them by the same names. The imaginary future musicians could conceivably designate their compositions "Mozart's *Requiem*" in honor of Mozart, dimly recognized through the mists of time as having been a great composer, without knowing whether or not Mozart himself ever attempted to write a requiem or what it might have sounded like.

30. Aristotle, *Metaphysics* Δ 1025^{a}15–35; Z 1029^{b}1–1030^{b}13. Saul A. Kripke, *Naming and Necessity* (Cambridge: Harvard University Press, 1980), p. 48: "When we think of a property as essential to an object we usually mean that it is true of that object in any case where it would have existed."

31. Margolis, "Emergence," *Philosophical Forum* 17 (1986), esp. 287–92; "Nature, Culture, and Persons," *Theory and Decision* 13 (1981): 311–29. *Culture and Cultural Entities*, pp. 157–59. Types and tokens-of-types are ontological cat-

egories that are themselves historically contingent culturally emergent entities on Margolis's theory. Types lack reality in the absence of heuristic interests, and heuristic interests obtain only through the historically contingent cultural emergence of persons with minds. This fact about the origin of types unavoidably entails their historical contextuality.

32. Margolis, *The Flux of History and the Flux of Science,* pp. 140–41. These propositions are first cautiously introduced in these terms: "We have been able to show—or take for granted, where the matter can hardly be contested—that certain heterodox notions are not in the least incoherent or self-contradictory or self-defeating" (140). Then Margolis states, "We have earned the right to proceed beyond those notions and to build upon them" (140). On 141, he pulls out all the stops: "Surely, this tally defines an absolutely breathtaking vista that goes utterly contrary to the 'canon' (both ancient and modern) that claims that the denial of the real invariances, of thought and reality yields only contradiction and insuperable paradox. Not only are (1)–(13) individually coherent, they are coherent when taken together. They afford a foundation, therefore, for a novel theory of history. . . . There is no developed theory of history that fits the entire set of (1)–(13). *And that is just what we are after!*" (Margolis's emphasis). Compare Margolis, "The Truth about Relativism," in *Relativism: Interpretation and Confrontation,* ed. Michael Krausz (Notre Dame: Notre Dame University Press, 1989), p. 6, where in similar terms he endorses: "an increasingly radicalized sense of the historical nature and conditions of human existence; an insistence on the horizoned, preformed, fragmentary, biased cognitive and affective orientation of human life; the impossibility of extricating reason, inquiry, the reflexive critique of any judgment or commitment from any of the above conditions; the recognition of divergent and moderately incommensurable conceptual schemes . . . the realization that we cannot in principle distinguish between the constructed nature of our intelligible world and the 'independent' structure of the brute world."

33. Margolis discusses some of the metaphilosophical implications of his historical contextualism or historicism in *Pragmatism without Foundations,* 199–201. See 199: "We are led to a most intriguing consideration. To adopt a thorough-going historicism, along the somewhat radicalized lines sketched, is to acknowledge that, in every cognitive undertaking, we are in the grip of conceptual schemes whose systematic boundaries, essential rules of internal orderliness, relationship to the world independent of our linguistic access, relationship to other similar such conceptual schemes, propensity and capacity for change and evolution, we cannot ever finally fix or fully fathom." *The Truth about Relativism,* pp. 16–17, 57–67. A similar objection is made by Thomas Nagel, *The View from Nowhere* (New York: Oxford University Press, 1986).

34. Margolis implies a disclaimer of absolute truth for his own metaphysics when he remarks, as in "The Truth about Relativism," quoted in the previous note, that we can never determine whether any particular conceptual scheme approaches "an understanding of all possible conceptual schemes" or the "fixed Truth about the world." Yet he permits an exception to rescue historicism or cul-

tural relativism from the standard charge of internal inconsistency by relativists who deny that the truth of relativism is itself more than relativistically true. See *Pragmatism without Foundations,* p. 21: "Put very simply, the point is that relativizing truth claims to evidence so that they are not detachable in an evidentiary sense is not, in itself, a relativistic commitment." The problem is discussed at length in *The Truth about Relativism,* pp. 54–68. For both astute and obtuse criticisms of historicism, see Karl Popper, *The Poverty of Historicism* (New York: Harper & Row, 1964). Margolis answers Popper in *The Flux of History and the Flux of Science,* pp. 67–71, 74–77, and *The Truth about Relativism,* pp. 24–39.

35. We can infer from Margolis's seven conditions for the token-type distinction that the reality of types is dependent on the existence of appropriate corresponding tokens of the type, and that the mere memory of such tokens is insufficient for the reality of types. In particular, Margolis presumably would not allow that the new soup of his example remains real when all its instances, recipes, and knowledge of how to make it are destroyed, merely on the grounds that someone remembers that there was once such a soup, or even on the dispositional ability to recognize its taste if counterfactually it were to be experienced. If Siberian tigers become extinct, and all the species' tokens, including tissue and DNA samples or other information for reproduction, are destroyed, it would be highly implausible to say that the Siberian tiger genetic type still survives merely because a zoologist remembers having seen one and would recognize it as such if counterfactually another were to appear.

36. It seems unobjectionable that I can truly say of Neandertals that they were hominids, even though Neandertals, themselves lacked the concepts of being a Neandertal and being a hominid. Margolis nimbly makes such otherwise apparently ahistorical judgments and provides a philosophical foundation for even more extreme attributions of this kind, when, for example, he explains the extension of our linguistic capacities to nonhuman animals in accounting for their mental states. See *Persons and Minds,* pp. 146–70; *Culture and Cultural Entities,* pp. 42–63.

37. Margolis rightly presses the demand for adequate explanation of psychological and other cultural phenomena before invoking the principle of theoretical economy in choosing between reductive and nonreductive ontologies. See *Persons and Minds,* pp. 28–33.

38. See *inter alia* Terence Parsons, *Nonexistent Objects* (New Haven, Conn.: Yale University Press, 1980); Richard Routley, *Exploring Meinong's Jungle and Beyond,* interim ed. (Canberra: Australian National University Philosophical Monographs, 1981); Jacquette, *Meinongian Logic: The Semantics of Existence and Nonexistence* (Berlin and New York: Walter de Gruyter and Co., Inc., 1996); "Modal Meinongian Logic," *Logique et Analyse* pp. 125–26 (1989): 113–30; "Object Theory Foundations for Intensional Logic," *Acta Analytica* 13 (1995): 33–63.

39. I explore the advantages of ontic neutrality in an intensional semantics for some abstract (mind-independent) intended objects in Jacquette, "Virtual

Relations," *Idealist Studies* 25 (1995): 141–54. I do not say that Margolis could not accommodate an ontically neutral intensionalist semantics somewhere within or as a complementary fourth component added to his currently three-tiered metaphysics of culture. My claim is only that an ontically neutral intensionalist semantics substituted for Margolis's historical contextualism more simply and economically explains the phenomena to which Margolis's theory is addressed by permitting nonexistent kinds to be introduced in place of types and that it does so at no ontological expense, without commitment to cultural relativism, contextualism, or historicism.

40. For an extended defense of property dualism largely in agreement with Margolis's metaphysics, see Jacquette, *Philosophy of Mind* (Englewood Cliffs, N.J.: Prentice Hall, Inc., 1994); "Adventures in the Chinese Room," *Philosophy and Phenomenological Research* 49 (1989): 605–23; "Searle's Intentionality Thesis," *Synthese* 80 (1989): 267–75; "Fear and Loathing (and Other Intentional States) in Searle's Chinese Room," *Philosophical Psychology* 3 (1990): 287–304; "Intentionality and Stich's Theory of Brain Sentence Syntax," *Philosophical Quarterly* 40 (1990): 169–82.

41. Jacquette, "Pollock on Token Physicalism, Agent Materialism, and Strong Artificial Intelligence," *International Studies in the Philosophy of Science* 7 (1993): 127–40, upholds Margolis's concept of the emergence of intentionality against a more diluted account of part-whole supervenience.

42. I wish to thank Philip Alperson for permission to reprint portions of my essays, "Margolis on Emergence and Embodiment" and "The Type-Token Distinction in Margolis's Aesthetics" from *Journal of Aesthetics and Art Criticism.* A version of "Margolis on Emergence and Embodiment" was presented to the American Society for Aesthetics, Eastern Division, State University of New York at Buffalo, Buffalo, N.Y., 24 March 1984. A version of "The Type-Token Distinction in Margolis's Aesthetics" was presented to the American Society for Aesthetics, Eastern Division, Rhode Island School of Design, Providence, R.I., 19 March 1993. An abbreviated prototype of the present paper, "Margolis and the Metaphysics of Culture," was presented as an invited talk at a colloquium in which Margolis participated at the American Society for Aesthetics, Santa Barbara, Calif., 27–30 October 1993. I am grateful to Margolis for critical and clarificatory comments and for ongoing discussions in correspondence.

Some Thoughts on
Time, History, and Flux

J. N. Mohanty

I

One must distinguish between: (1) everything is in time, and (2) everything is in the process of change. It has often been taken as self-evident that (2) follows (1). But (2) follows from (1) only on the further assumption that time is one-dimensional and consists of a series of perishing instants. (I am not even sure if this assumption suffices for deriving [2] from [1]; although it certainly is necessary.) But duration is also a modality of time, and to endure is a mode of being in time, so that something can be in time without being a flux in which nothing abides. It does not necessarily follow from (1) that nothing is ever the same; that identification and reidentification of a thing can only be ontologically misleading, even if pragmatically useful (as the Buddhists held).

Two kinds of philosophical moves are possible at this point: one descriptive, the other revisionary. The revisionary move starts with the premise that everything is in flux and argues that any ontology that admits abiding things must be abandoned. The descriptive move starts with the fact that in the world as we experience it we perceive things (and persons) that we recognize as being the same; so it holds that there must be some things that are temporal in the sense of abiding and enduring, even if not everlasting. Unless an independent argument which does not beg the issue is advanced for its premise, I would prefer the descriptive over the revisionary move.

But on what ground is the premise "everything is in flux" to be justified? Not on the basis of (ordinary) experience, for we do not perceive, relate, act upon bits of flux, but rather upon things that can be again and that we can recognize and identify as being the same. The only arguments known to me are the one advanced by the Buddhists and the one making use of elementary particle physics. It can be shown, I believe, that neither of these two arguments can prove that things—all things—are in flux. They both would be under the obligation to show why and how things that abide could consist of elementary particles that do not abide.

II

If (2) does not follow from (1), it is also questionable if (1) is true in any nontrivial sense. To begin with, (1) should be distinguished from (1*) all experience is temporal. An experience may be temporal while the object of that experience may not be. But what is it to be temporal or to be in time? Clearly, something is in time or is temporal (these two, again, need to be distinguished, though for the present I would do without undertaking that work), if predicates such as "came into being at time t_n," "goes out of existence at time t_n," can be meaningfully predicated of it. Of an experience—a perception, a memory, an imagination, a thought, for example—one can always meaningfully ask "when did it occur, at what point of time, and when did it cease to exist?" But there are objects precisely of those experiences—a proposition, a theorem, a number, an arithmetical truth, a theory—of which such questions cannot be meaningfully asked. A locution such as "The Pythagorean theorem began in the year ——, month —— and day ——, at such and such hour and such and such minute" is not false; it is meaningless. The question "When did the number 0 begin to exist?" makes no sense. Some objects then are not in time, not in the sense that to say they are in time is false, but in the sense that ascribing temporal predicates of them does not make sense.

I should add here, without stopping to take up these matters in this essay, that there are various sorts of objects insofar as their relation to time is concerned. These are:

- those, like the ones mentioned in the preceding paragraph, in which case questions of beginning and end just do not make sense;
- those to which a beginning is ascribed, but no end (ask, "when did Shakespeare write *Macbeth*?" but not, "when will Shakespeare's *Macbeth* cease to exist?"); and
- those to which a beginning cannot be assigned, but an end can be (compare the question "when did you begin to be ignorant of Quantum Mechanics?" with "when did you cease to be ignorant of Quantum Mechanics?")

But in the case of each such object, its experience is temporal. We then have to face up to a most serious question: "How do experiences which are intrinsically temporal, present objects which are not temporal (in the aforementioned sense)?"

III

There is no one unique conception of "time" to which, according to some philosophers, all experiences and all objects belong. One must, at least, distinguish between:

(a) the cosmological time to which supposedly all Nature belongs;

(b) physical time, meaning by this the time of physics;

(c) historical time in which the history of humankind takes place; and

(d) the inner, phenomenologically lived time in which the internal stream of consciousness flows.

But if we do not presume to know what real time is, or even what real time is under any of (a), (b), and (c), then under each of these headings, we are faced with various possibilities. Under (a), for example, we may have the Greek conception of circular time or Newtonian infinite linear time. Likewise, under (b), we may have Newtonian time (which is also the time of Newtonian physics) or the conception of time implied by the space-time geometry of relativity theory, the second law of thermodynamics and the indeterminacy principle of quantum mechanics. For some, the very distinction between (a) and (b) would have to be given up. Consider now (c): Unless we have one universal history of humankind, there need be no talk about one historical time. If there were many histories, there would have to be a plurality of times (as Foucault was led to suggest), and between these times one could affirm temporal relations only by violating categorial laws which prevent mixing up temporal predicates from different domains. What I am suggesting is that the concept of time of a domain is co-constituted with that domain, and we do not have available—as Kant, Bergson, or the physicists would have us believe—one concept of time in terms of which we could nontrivially assert that everything is temporal; so, we then have to ask, "temporal" *in which* sense? Thus, monistic and absolutistic claims on behalf of either (a) or (b) or (c) would fail: (a) is incurably cultural, (b) is theoretical, and (c) differentiates itself in terms of a plurality of histories.

Only (d) promises to present a monistic framework—not for all things, but for all experiences. All experiences regarded as immanent within the mental life of an experiencing self are in this immanent lived time with its retention-protention-now structure. For the present, it is not important that Husserl's exact description of this structure be true. As a matter of fact, he modified his version several times. What is important is that there is such an immanent temporality to be distinguished from both the world-time, the time of physics, and historical time. But this immanent time does not comprehend physical objects, historical events, or ideal entities such as numbers, rather it comprehends our experiences of all transcendent objects, also of all immanent objects such as acts, sensory data, thinking, imagining, remembering, and so forth regarded not as events occurring in nature, but as belonging to a stream of experience constituting the mental life of a transcendental ego.

We still do not have a satisfactory formulation of the thesis "all things are in time."

IV

From both (1) and (2), we must sharply distinguish (3) All things are historical.

If (1) does not entail (2), and if neither (1) nor (2) seems to be true, for what cannot be formulated as a thesis cannot be taken to be true, and this holds good of (1), nor does (1)—even together with (2)—entail (3), then what could one mean by saying that all things are historical?

Being in time or being temporal is a necessary, but not sufficient, condition of being historical. What else must be added to temporality to make historicality possible? One answer, widely accepted in contemporary philosophy, would run something like this: The possibility of history or of being in history lies in the historicity of being. Unless one accepts the thesis, pressed by Karl Löwith among others, that mundane history is a reflection of *Heilsgeschichte,* there is no clear meaning to be assigned to the locution "historicity of being" other than the straightforward "being of history." In that case, the answer is trivial, for it amounts to saying that the possibility of history lies in the being of history. A more substantive and plausible answer is: History is possible, because of the historicity of human existence, of what Heidegger calls *Dasein.* From this point of view, only what pertains to human existence in the general human world, society, and culture has history and nature can be said to have history only insofar as it is nature for man— insofar as it is the subject matter of natural science which is historical in the straightforward sense of being a human project and a human accomplishment. It is then appropriate to say that culture is historical and nature is also historical insofar as it enters into culture or has been, as Marx said, humanized. So, (3) needs to be modified into: (3*) All things of human significance are historical. Only under the assumption that "all things" and "all things of human significance" are coextensive, would (3) still be true, but that assumption needs justification in a nontrivial manner. But neither (3) nor (3*) entails (2): to be historical is not *eo ipso* to be in a process of change. The idea of history involves both change and endurance, besides the idea of human significance. Obviously, I am now speaking not of history as a science (as what is done by historians, let us call it H$_1$), but of the subject matter of the historian's scientific concern (let us call it H$_2$).

Although the idea of historicality (*Geschichtlichkeit*) goes back to Hegel, in its present usage, it is derived from Heidegger and Jaspers. For Heidegger, the historicity of *Dasein* does not mean being in a social world, but rather the very ontological mode of being; *Dasein's* historicity is not an ontic feature. Ontologically, *Dasein* is always ahead of itself and exists in the sense of *eksistenz*, to be stretched outside of itself, it is being-toward-death; and consequently, finite, which makes both its temporality and historicity possible. In his Marburg lectures of 1919–20, Heidegger distinguished between several senses of "history": history as science (what I have earlier called H$_1$), history as a domain of enquiry (H$_2$), history as the merely past, history as tradition, and history as a unique decisive event. Of these, he regards the first, second, and third as being inauthentic, derivative, and not *ursprünglich* in relation to concrete existence. The fourth can be either authentic or inauthentic. The fifth is the most *ursprünglich* for concrete human existence.

Without agreeing with Heidegger's analysis, let me, however, single out the two *authentic* conceptions of history: that of tradition and a unique decisive event in one's life. (For the latter, Heidegger cites the locution "This person had a sad history.") Tradition, in the authentic sense, is not simply a past accumulation of accomplishments (that would be close to the first and the second senses of "history") but having this accumulation as a component of one's self-consciousness in the present. In this sense, historical consciousness is not the knowledge of history (of the books), nor simply knowledge of the objective past, but is rather awareness of the way the past, as sedimented structure of meanings, is present as constitutive of my self-understanding. Historical consciousness requires consciousness of the past as constituting the present and as heading toward the future. This would not be possible if all were in flux (unless we give a different meaning to "flux" than the word would normally be taken to mean). Consciousness must have the ability to gather together what is past and what is present. It must be able to retrieve and reactivate the traces of what is past. The past must have, in Whitehead's words, "objective immortality," which historical consciousness can capture in an act of subjective appropriation.

It can, as a matter of fact, be claimed that without some thematic identity, one cannot speak of "history of. . . ." We need not decide right now whether this identity is pregiven or "constructed." Even if the identity is constituted, it is constituted along with its history. "History of x" as an item is constituted *along with* the constitution of x. There is no history that is not a history of. . . . It is in the light of this remark that we will be able to reflect on the meaningfulness of the locution "All things are historical." "All things" is a formal concept, and cannot fill in the empty place in "history of. . . ." There is no history of all things. Nor can there be a history of one unique thing, of a this-there, *tode ti*. The this-there comes to be. There is change, production, creation, but not history. History must be history of an essence. Nominalism has no place for a concept of history.

V

It is well known that the theme of history comes to the center of Husserl's thinking in the late work *Crisis* (although the theme of time was there ever since 1905). It is to be noted that Husserl uses "history" in the *Crisis* mostly within quotation marks—which suggests that he was not using it in the standard sense (of either H_1 or H_2), but rather in an unusual sense. Elisabeth Ströker has identified this sense as "intentional history." Intentional history is the history of constitution of meaning and explores its genetic constitution—as Husserl does in the case of Galilean mathematization of nature (and as Foucault does in the case of "madness"). It is, therefore, in the nature of things that for Husserl the ideality of meanings and essences not only is compatible with their historicity, but historicity precisely requires ideality. Only ideal entities are historical. Nominalistically conceived real, particular events only *perish*.

If H_2 is history of meanings and H_1 as science requires ideal meanings as well as facticity (the historian, *writing à la* Derrida, for example), we can assert the equivalence of (3) and (3*) with (4) history is history of meanings.

Sedimented meanings constitute a tradition. In this sense, a tradition is both the result of history and makes history possible. History is history within a tradition, even when it takes us beyond the given tradition and opens up new possibilities.

But is anything whatsoever possible? Can history take any direction in the next moment? Logically, yes. Really, no. Real possibility is motivated possibility, possibility motivated by the course of experience up until now. Mere logical possibility is free possibility, for which nothing in the course of experience up until now counts. The idea of motivated possibility is narrower than free, merely logical, possibility, but is wider than real possibility construed as what is compatible with the known laws (of nature or of society). In this sense, the future of history is unpredictable, but not everything is possible.

VI

What I have argued for, in classical metaphysical terms, is the thesis that change, time, and history all involve something invariant, abiding—if not everlasting. This classical thesis seems to be opposed to what seems to be Margolis's fundamental thesis about flux and radical history. Sometimes, the best you can do to pay homage to a philosopher friend is set up for him an opposition that he can then set out to demolish. I am sure, Margolis would love doing that.

Notes on the Ontology
of the Disciplines

Peter Caws

The following essay addresses the metaphysical problem of the mode of existence of cultural objects, in particular of those objects we call academic disciplines, in which we certify one another as competent by the mediation of other cultural objects: artifacts that we call books and papers and reviews, events that we call lectures and courses and conferences, and institutional mechanisms that we call programs and degrees and associations.

I use for exemplary purposes a discipline from the natural sciences, the one in which I grew up, and speak of "science" and "the sciences" throughout. But the argument applies to disciplines in the social sciences and humanities as well. Because it seems to me useful, even desirable, to refer to these other disciplines collectively as the "human sciences," partly to rescue the sense of "science" from its comparatively recent appropriation for merely quantitative ends, I have not found it necessary to modify the language of the paper to include them.[1]

At the end, I will consider briefly the application of the model developed in the paper to the discipline of philosophy. In doing so, I shall not try to settle the question as to whether philosophy belongs among the human sciences or whether it undergirds the sciences, natural and human. It is not inconsistent to think of philosophy as undergirding itself. The question of its own ontology belongs, at any rate, to no other discipline.

I shall also point, in closing, to an exemplary practitioner of the discipline of philosophy in the person of Joseph Margolis. But I should say now that I did not undertake the inquiry whose results I sketch here with Margolis in mind; these preliminary remarks post-date the body of the paper, whose appropriateness to the present purpose became apparent to me only after I had finished reworking it.

Science, whether regarded as a human activity or as a body of propositions, is nothing (I maintain) apart from the human beings who carry on the activity or who enunciate or understand the propositions. This makes heads ontologically more fundamental than books, because heads without books would still constitute a locus for science but books without heads would not. (I use books as metonymic for texts and discursive practices in general.) Books are essential to science as it has developed, because any given head is incapable of holding it all, but in the books it exists only potentially. It is true that a book of physics is likely to contain very little that is not physics, whereas a physicist's head will almost certainly contain a great deal that is not physics—in fact, the head will function as that of a physicist only for a small proportion of its waking life. Still it is in that limited time that any contribution to the being of physics will be made.

How are we to distinguish the times of active involvement in physics from the times when, like the book, the head embodies physics only dispositionally? (Clearly there must be something in common between what is in the head and what is in the book, which is similarly activated when it is a question of solving a problem; for the purpose at hand, it is a matter of indifference whether the formula is remembered or looked up. Also what is in the book can always be got into a head, assuming the head to have appropriate training, while what is in a head can always in principle be put into a book.)

We might ask the physicist to identify the physics for us, to point to those utterances and inscriptions, among all the other things he or she may say or write, that belong to the discipline. This is an obvious way of beginning the inquiry, but it poses some problems of its own. First of all, how do we recognize a physicist as such? It would be rash to assume, from the fact that a book was labeled

Physics, that it contained a reliable account of physics, and it would be equally rash to assume that someone who claimed to be a physicist knew the subject authoritatively. (Furthermore, even a bona fide physicist will not pretend to know *all* of physics.)

Still physicists have had scientific training, and presumably they knew which science they were being trained for. But they knew it by purely external indications, such as the titles of courses, professors, books, degrees, and the like. Astronomy, physics, psychology, zoology are in fact self-perpetuating disciplines, so that a student is admitted to the professional circle by people who at earlier stages of their career were similarly admitted by other people, and so on. Most of the sciences as they exist today are comparatively recent: at some stage in the last couple of hundred years, the learned society and the university curriculum became formalized, and this was done by a group of people who already recognized one another as colleagues; since then, the patterns of admission and exclusion have followed familiar and predictable lines. The usual criteria are getting a degree or publishing a bit of recognized research, and the authorities who award the degree and publish the research are just those who have been agreed upon by other workers in the field as fit to discharge these functions. Or at any rate, their fitness to do so has not yet been successfully challenged.

The fact that ontological inquiry thus finds itself involved with sociological issues is not, in this context, surprising, because knowledge at any level above that of immediate nonlinguistic acquaintance has an irreducible element of the social. The heads that contain a given science will belong to members of an academic or other intellectual community, who know one another or can recognize persons who claim membership in the group from their behavior, in particular from their language.

The linguistic clues involved in this process of recognition are two-fold: the ability of the interlocutor to use correctly a certain number of technical terms, which I will call the *lexicon,* and his or her tendency to assert or to agree with a certain number of propositions, which I will call the *corpus.* The corpus is multilayered; it not only contains propositions about things in the domain of the science in question, but propositions about those propositions—how they should be formed, how they may be validated. Each science has its lexicon and its corpus, although, of course, different sciences may overlap. We might add to these a number of techniques, of inference or of experimentation, collectively called the praxis, but the judgment that somebody does or does not belong to the group will ordinarily be made according to verbal rather than practical criteria.

The lexicon at any given time will include not only the names of objects or concepts but also the names of scientists. It is quite characteristic of a first meeting between two people in any intellectual discipline for them to try one another out, as it were, by allusions to problems or discoveries or publications or colleagues, which will be understood and responded to if the new acquaintance really does qualify as a member of the group in question. And it is in just such discursive ways that the group achieves its intellectual and professional cohesion. In fact, this kind of dialogue is only a specialized form of the universal method of mutual recognition, whether between speakers of the same language or residents of the same locality or even rational beings.

The reality of a given science is to be sought in the community of people who submit to and satisfy mutual inquiries, formal or informal, in which a specific lexicon and corpus are invoked. And the science itself, of which we are in search, will presumably lie either in what is common to the lexicons and corpuses of the members of a group so constituted, or in the superlexicon or supercorpus formed by the conjunction of the individual examples. Each of these alternatives, however, leads to insuperable difficulties. For the intersection of the individual sets of terms or propositions will turn out to be almost empty, while their sum will certainly be inconsistent.

Before dealing with these problems, however, a prior difficulty has to be faced. For the method employed so far has systematically begged the question: There must be people who think they know physics, and therefore a conception of physics as what they think they know, before the sum or the intersection of the terms and propositions understood and agreed to by them can be arrived at in the first place, so looking to such a sum or intersection as constitutive of the ontological reality of physics is circular. However, there is a way around this snag, which, although completely impossible in practice, shows how one might in principle arrive at the individual sciences without presupposing their existence.

I imagine, then, a vast research program along the following lines: Everybody in the world is asked to write down all the lexical items he or she recognizes and can use, and all the propositional items of whose truth he or she is convinced (or, better, all the propositional items whose truth or falsity he or she thinks worth trying to establish, because people who take opposing views on an issue belong to the same community of inquiry). No categorization is required, and the items can be written down in any order. This information is coded by an army of computer operators, so that two enormous reservoirs of data are created, one consisting of lexical items each tagged with an individual name, and the other consisting of propositional items similarly tagged. These data are analyzed and tabulated in such a way that it can be seen what lexical and propositional items are recognized and agreed to by which people.

Each person will be found to belong to a series of clusters of people who use roughly the same vocabulary and know roughly the same things (or consider the same things important), and each term or proposition will similarly belong to a cluster of terms or propositions considered significant by roughly the same people. One cluster of people (among millions of such clusters, large and small) will be members of the same family who know the same names and the same bits of family history; another will be people living in the same locality who know the same local politicians and the same items of news or gossip or folklore; yet another will be people who have read the same books, seen the same plays or movies, and so forth.

There will be some lexical and propositional items shared by almost everybody, others that are anomalous or idiosyncratic. Most clusters of intermediate size will represent genuine, if not always interesting, communities of knowledge, although there will no doubt be cases in which an apparently shared item conceals an ambiguity of meaning. But among the most definite and sharply defined clusters, either of shared items on the one hand, or of the people who share them on the other, will be the lexicon and the corpus of astronomy, psychology, zoology, and so on and the community of professional workers in those fields.

Some surprising or perhaps half-suspected results will no doubt emerge from such an enterprise. Some disciplines—psychology is a good candidate—will be found to show a bimodal distribution of items and people, reflecting an internal debate about the proper object or method of the science. Some people belonging by training and institutional affiliation to one science will find themselves naturally clustering with the specialists in another; this phenomenon can be expected, for example, in borderline areas such as molecular biology or nuclear chemistry. It may be found that some of the newer interdisciplinary sciences show stronger cohesion than the older disciplines from which they have branched off and so on.

All this, however, is incidental to my purpose, which is simply to show that we do not have to assume that there are such things as the various sciences but can in principle arrive at them from an examination of the language people use and the things they think they know. The question that still remains is what, in the end, the being of these sciences consists in and how they may be defined. I revert, therefore, to the problem of forming either the sum or the intersection of the lexicons and corpuses of a group of scientists who have enough of these things in common to form a cluster in my thought-experiment.

The experimental production of scientific disciplines will not work at all if complete identity of the lexicon or the corpus is insisted upon. No two people, even those with the most closely similar upbringing and training, know and use just the same terms and propositions. So the analysis will have to indicate *sufficiently similar* repertories, and this will mean more or less vague boundaries to the clusters, because close similarities, like just noticeable differences, are not transitive. This means that there can be no such thing as *the* lexicon or *the* corpus of any science. There is no body of propositions that everybody can be counted on to know, and there is nobody who can be counted on to know every proposition.

Also people at different stages and in different areas, even within the same science, will claim to know contradictory propositions. Colleagues on the same research team, students in the same class, can be expected to have very closely similar partial lexicons and corpuses, but even those will vary as the inquiry moves into areas remote from their common interest. What admits to the group, then, is an acceptable minimum repertory of terms and propositions held in common with the members of one of its subgroups. (Some terms, like "DNA," and some propositions, like "$E = mc^2$," will show up quite widely in the population at large, but that will not admit everybody to the community of molecular biologists or relativity theorists.) And what is acceptable will depend on who is making the decision.

A student who passes an oral examination brilliantly with one professor may fail the same examination with another. But there is no objective standard of arbitration that will justify or invalidate the result in either case. A third judge may be called in, or a fourth, and, of course, as a matter of practice, some consensus will eventually be arrived at. But the nearest we will ever get to physics, for example, is just this overlapping of the separate judgments of a number of physicists. Even the textbook writer will at best succeed in getting down the major items of agreement characteristic of the discipline over a brief period, generally past by the time the book is published.

The conclusion, then, is that there is no such thing as physics, understood as a complete and consistent body of knowledge. The reality of physics is the inconsistent aggregate of theoretical structures, one in the head of each physicist, which have the property that when any pair of physicists meets and discusses physics, the overlap of lexicon and corpus is sufficient for intelligibility and conviction. A few items in the lexicon and corpus will be known and correctly used, perhaps, by 99 per cent of all physicists, but the bulk of the items will be shared by some intermediate proportion, and a few items will be known only to a handful of specialists.

The sciences, in other words, have the structure of families in Wittgenstein's sense, in that these structures, each representing the whole science for the scientist in whose head it is, bear to one another a series of more or less striking family resemblances. Formalize as we may, the reality will always remain personal and variable; the most elegant axiomatization of the foundations of physics will count as physics only for the scholar who achieves it and those who follow the argument. But surely it counts as a *better* rendering of physics? The answer is only if one has already defined a science as an axiomatic system; all such a definition does is to raise the question of the ontological status of axiomatic systems. They, too, will turn out to be in heads, or in intentional domains, those of mathematicians and logicians.

Admittedly mathematics and logic, in comparatively tight communities, over limited ranges, and during brief periods, achieve a uniformity of lexicon and corpus unknown in the empirical sciences. But to impose this uniformity on the other sciences would be misguided even if it were not impossible. And besides, who would impose it? Disciplinary communities are self-defining, and they set and maintain their own standards; there can be no reforming or redeeming of them from without. At the same time representatives and critics of the disciplines form their own (second-order) community, which practices its own inclusions and exclusions. This accounts for the absence of astrology departments in major universities.

To return to the argument about the distributive embodiment of the sciences in individuals: It is a general truth that the possibility of our communication with others depends on our having enough experience and hence enough language in common. It is also true that if the common element is sufficiently extensive, we hardly need to use language at all. So scientists at an advanced stage of their research may be quite taciturn and yet communicate extremely complex propositions with a monosyllable or a gesture. What enables them to do so is the homology of the relevant structures that have been built up, element by element, over a long period of time, in their respective heads.

Although we cannot at this stage specify exactly the physiological nature of these structures, there is no reason to doubt that they are really inscribed in brains and therefore as material as any other inscription, in a book for example. (The modes of inscription characteristic of books on the one hand and brains on the other are radically different; at this point, we have no formal mechanism for translating one into the other.) The way in which mental structures are built up, or "instructed" (to give an obvious neologistic use to a familiar term), is a proper object of psychological and epistemological inquiry, but it is also relevant to the question of scientific development.

I cannot go here into the details of the emergence of significance and subjectivity out of merely physical complexity, which would require a full-fledged philosophy of mind, but an essential feature of this emergence as I have come to conceptualize it involves the *prior* existence of *two* matching structures (embodied in two interacting physical systems) as a condition for the realization

of consciousness or meaning.[2] Perception involves a sensory structure and a conceptual structure, embodied respectively in the sense
organs and the brain; language involves a conceptual structure and
a phonic structure. (The products of these matchings will differ
accordingly as the structures in question are temporal, spatial,
causal, and so on; it seems likely that for conscious awareness at
least one temporal component would be necessary.)

In the case of scientific understanding, a theoretical structure and
a phenomenological structure are required in the first instance,
although, thanks to the power of language, the theoretical structure
can soon go off on its own. (By a "phenomenological structure," I
mean a set of learned relations—of relevance, of expectation, of
habitual association—between elements of the domain of appearances.) But one implication of the theory of structural matching is
that the theoretical structure is never *derived* from the phenomenological one; it is always provided independently and then matched,
even though, in simple cases, it may look like a copy of the observed
state of affairs. And this means that discovery is never merely the
uncovering of something in the world, but is also (and often only)
the "instruction" of a new component of theoretical structure.

It happens that making new theoretical structures is an incurable
habit of the human mind—fortunately, because in that habit lies its
power of adaptation to its environment. And discovery is just the
selection, under observational constraints, of structural novelty appropriate to the physical structure under investigation. How a particular bit of novelty gets generated will depend on the mental structure
on to which it is grafted and the success of the discoverer in chan-
neling the natural tendency to structural innovation, but although the
process is complex, there is nothing mysterious about it.

The kind of ontological reality science has can perhaps be made
clear by recourse to a new version of an old analogy, the analogy of
scientific theories and maps. We are all familiar with the notion that
theories map various features of the world, but the analogy usually
treats the map itself on the abstract level. I wish to draw attention to
the distributive reality of maps, the fact that there can be one in
every glove compartment. If someone were to ask, Where is the
map of the state? the best that could be done would be to produce
all the available copies of all the various versions of maps of the

state. In one sense, any one of them will do—every pair of them will have something in common, although there may be nothing except perhaps the name of the state that they all have in common, because they will serve different purposes and exhibit different degrees of simplification and schematism.

But in another sense there is no map, not even the one in the state surveyor's office, that is *the* map of the state. So I would wish to compare the sciences, not so much to the abstract map as to the real maps, the bits of folded paper that we can actually pick up and carry with us. If our maps are sufficiently similar, we can get to the same place, and if our theories are sufficiently similar, we can come to the same conclusions. Theories have their place in the world, in the heads of theoreticians, ready to be activated when a scientific problem is to be solved, just as maps have their place, ready to be unfolded and consulted. And just as, if all the maps were destroyed, there would be no map, so without the heads, there would be no theories.

The *concept* of a scientific theory belongs to another domain altogether; the structure of which this concept forms a part is reproduced in the heads of philosophers of science rather than in those of scientists. Also the fact that a bit of theory exists in a scientist's head does not in itself say anything about its adequacy to the world. The question whether a proposition belongs to physics is quite independent of the question whether it is physically true—logically independent, that is (historically, it is to be hoped, there has been and will be a progressively closer relation between the two). This does not mean that the sciences are untrustworthy; it only means that trusting propositions is something people do and not an intrinsic feature of the propositions.

We may hope that by now, considering how many people have been involved in the scientific enterprise and the generally high standards of empirical adequacy they have insisted upon, the errors in accepted theories are at a minimum. But the theories themselves are not in the first instance true or false, they are just there. And they are there just as fully and concretely as their objects, and can in turn serve as objects of theoretical interest in their own right: objects, we might say, of the human sciences rather than the natural sciences, but giving rise to disciplines nonetheless deserving of the name of science as I have been construing it here.

*   *   *

What now of the discipline of philosophy and its embodiment in its practitioners? "Philosophy" is one of the lexical items that will show up quite generally in the fantastic global inquiry sketched above: People have philosophies of this or that (how to play the stock market, how to cure the common cold), and even technocrats without a trace of philosophical appetite as the rest of us conceive of it will often provide what they are pleased to call a philosophical background for their technocratic excursions. As a discipline, though, with its departments and meetings and books and journals (Festschriften even), philosophy is constituted in just the same way as its sister disciplines: by a process of continual exchange and mutual recognition among individuals instructed and socialized into a family of texts and practices.

Like many disciplines, philosophy undergoes periodic crises of coherence and identity. Sometimes these are mainly political, as, for example (to be historically specific), when the movement known at the time as "pluralism" fought in the 1970s to open up the offices and programs of the American Philosophical Association. Sometimes they arise from theoretical reflection about the nature of the enterprise, as when (at about the same time) Richard Rorty, in a meditation about the future of American philosophy, floated his concept of cultural conversation: "No one," he said of a conjectured intellectual polity of the future, "will be asking which ones are the Americans, nor even, perhaps, which ones are the philosophers."[3]

As will have been clear from the preceding argument, however, disciplines have, as it were, lives of their own; philosophy will continue to exist as long as there are writers and talkers who recognize one another as philosophers (they don't have to ask which they are), who share terminologies and points of reference and a commitment to their common enterprise. How strong the center is and how well defined the boundaries (and this applies to any discipline, not just philosophy) will depend on the intensity of the activity in the field, and on the overlapping and the degree of internal connectedness of its networks of exchange. It will also depend crucially on the presence of figures who command, not only the techniques and the literature of the domain, but the respect of the other workers in it, and who are able to articulate on a metadisciplinary level the shape of the field and its history.

Such figures are at once the conscience and the self-consciousness of their discipline. There will not be too many of them at any given juncture. They have to be passionately attentive to the whole sweep of the field, an exhausting project in a discipline like philosophy, and willing to concede prima facie at least the possible worth of the most diverse contributions to it. One way to earn respect is to show it, and failure to do this has limited the effectiveness of many brilliant but curmudgeonous minds—the analytic philosophers who knew without looking that Continental philosophy had to be feeble, the Continentals who knew without looking that analytic philosophy had to be soulless. The other way to earn respect is to be worthy of it: to demonstrate in one's own discourse, philosophical and metaphilosophical, the care and resourcefulness in argument that has been the compelling mark of good work since philosophy began.

The ideas presented above were not, as I remarked at the beginning of this essay, worked out with Joseph Margolis in mind; they arose from a disinterested inquiry in a quite different context (see note 1). But it occurs to me as I conclude that I have been sketching on the one hand a picture of the discipline of philosophy that has deep affinities with Margolis's position, and on the other a picture of the key players in the philosophical enterprise that fits him to the life. Knowledge for him is necessarily partial and necessarily social—I have simply suggested some ways in which these features are interconnected. And his own mastery of the discipline, the scope of his reading and the generosity of his exposition, his concern to bring diverse strands of philosophy together into mutual intelligibility, make him one of those invaluable points of intersection in the network that help to hold philosophy together.

Margolis's most recent book, *Historied Thought, Constructed World: A Conceptual Primer for the Turn of the Millennium,*[4] maps, in his own words, "a possible—a plausible—view of how the philosophical work of the close of the twentieth century *will* flourish in the twenty-first" (emphasis in the original).[5] In the course of it, he canvasses nearly all the major players in the recent history of the subject: Austin, Chomsky, Churchland, Danto, Davidson, Dennett, Derrida, and so on through the alphabet. One of his favorite verbs is "collect," which is what he does to themes and arguments, lexical and propositional items that help to ballast and to right the philosophical vessel he aims to pilot through these millennial waters. This is a work of preservation and stabilization, carried out not in the service of some prior conception of what the discipline of philosophy should be but from a deep and deeply understood sense of what it is.

But of course in the process he is helping to make it what it is. That is what it means for a discipline to be alive. The heads, as I said at the beginning, are fundamental to the ontology. To say that Margolis is among the chief exemplars of this truth is only to put the same point in another language.

NOTES

1. This paper had its origin in a lecture intended for an audience of natural scientists, as part of a program of talks given during a stint as national lecturer for Sigma Xi, the scientific honor society. The wider relevance of the point it made was brought home to me after a presentation at the Westinghouse Research Center in Pittsburgh (in 1976), when I was challenged during the discussion: "If we took your lecture and, wherever you say 'physics,' we put 'music,' would it still be the same lecture?"—to which I could only answer yes, the point about the mind-dependent nature of the discipline of physics (though not of the physical world to which we take it to refer) would apply equally well to music.

2. This is a generalization of Saussure's insight that meaningful speech depends on the matching of two differential systems, one of ideas and one of sounds. See Ferdinand de Saussure, trans. Wade Baskin, *Course in General Linguistics* (New York: Philosophical Library, 1966), p. 112.

3. Richard Rorty, "Genteel Syntheses, Professional Analyses, Transcendentalist Culture," in Peter Caws, ed., *Two Centuries of Philosophy in America* (Oxford: Basil Blackwell, 1980), p. 239.

4. Joseph Margolis, *Historied Thought, Constructed World: A Conceptual Primer for the Turn of the Millennium* (Berkeley, Los Angeles, and London: University of California Press, 1995).

5. Ibid., p. 299.

Practically Ontology:
A Writerly Reading of Margolis

Joanne Waugh

I

Contemporary philosophers have many reasons to be grateful to Joseph Margolis, as this volume of essays and their authors make clear. For my part, I am grateful that he has questioned the tenets of contemporary philosophy that have constrained discussion of philosophical issues about the arts, literature, and history, areas, which, Margolis points out, are the "natural site for interpretation."[1] It is not "usual for American or Anglo-American philosophers, writing on mainstream topics, to write on either interpretation or history" (*IRU,* ix). This neglect of the world of human culture *is* puzzling, because most contemporary philosophers accept that the world-as-experienced is "always already" an interaction between "brute reality" and some beliefs, habitual behaviors, and technologies that are generated in and through the world of human culture—a position Margolis calls "the cognitive intransparency of the world" (*IRU,* 3). A belief in cognitive intransparency is hard to square with the disposition to believe that we confront the world more or less directly and, consequently, do not need, except during temporary periods of ignorance and lack of evidence, "to construe our cognitive interventions as interpretatively freighted" (*IRU,* ix). Margolis contends, however, that analytic philosophers' neglect of interpretation stems from just this disposition.[2] No doubt dispositions are harder to get rid of than they are to acquire, as is any ontological baggage that comes with them. Certainly Michael Dummett sounds as if he has a disposition to believe that we confront the world directly, albeit, perhaps, a disposition of which he may not be conscious. To quote Dummett:

> Interpretation, in the strict sense, is of necessity an exceptional occurrence. . . . In the normal case, the speaker simply says what he means . . . knowing the language, he simply speaks. In the normal case, likewise, the hearer simply understands . . . knowing the language, he hears and thereby understands; given that he knows the language, there is nothing that his understanding the words consists in save his hearing them. There are . . . many exceptional cases. . . . They are, however, in the nature of things, atypical cases: if taken as prototypes for linguistic communication, they prompt the formulation of an incoherent theory.[3]

For Dummett, interpretation is "exceptional" and "atypical in the nature of things," because it only comes in when a linguistic confrontation does not go smoothly, for example, when one speaker has a problem understanding what another speaker is trying to say. If one takes the "nature of things" to include the world of human culture, surely interpretation is neither exceptional nor atypical. Dummett's "prototype for human communication" resembles a direct confrontation with a physical object more than it does an interaction within a language or culture. Dummett does invoke the cultural world, of course, in his claim that meaning is derived from language as a social practice:

> Words have meanings in themselves, independently of speakers . . , they do not have them intrinsically, and hence independently of anything human beings do. They have them in virtue of belonging to the language, and hence in virtue of the existence of a social practice. But they have them independently of any particular speakers. No speaker needs to form any express intention, or to hold any particular theory about his audience, or, indeed, about the language: he has only to know the language and to utter

the words in an appropriate context, such as that of a sentence. (*TI*, 473)

Dummett makes this statement in response to Donald David-son's assumption that all acts of communication involve interpreta-tion. Davidson would seem an obvious exception to the generaliza-tion about analytic philosophers' neglect of interpretation though he is usually taken as the example *par excellence* of one who believes that we confront the world directly. Certainly Davidson's concept of radical interpretation is usually seen as having little to do with the world of human culture.[4] In his more recent writings, such as "A Nice Derangement of Epitaphs" and "The Third Man," Davidson argues that an account of successful communication need not assume that two parties share some language "governed by rules and conventions known to the speaker and interpreter in advance" or that what speaker and interpreter know in advance is necessarily shared, for example, "a language governed by shared rules or con-ventions" (*TI*, 445).[5] For Davidson, convergence on what he calls a passing theory between speaker and hearer is sufficient to account for successful communication. A passing theory is, apropos of the speaker, the "theory" the speaker *intends* the hearer to use; of the hearer, the theory that he or she *does use* in interpreting the speaker. The ability to converge on a passing theory is nothing like the stan-dard conceptions of language mastery; it requires neither "a learn-able common core of consistent behaviour" nor "shared grammar or rules" (*TI*, 445).[6] The appropriate model for linguistic ability is thus not a "portable interpreting machine set to grind out the meaning of an arbitrary utterance" (*TI*, 445). Moreover, the ability of language users to converge on a passing theory from time to time results not only in abandoning the ordinary notion of a language, but in erasing

the boundary between knowing a language and knowing our way around in the world generally. For there are no rules for arriving at passing theories, no rules in any strict sense, as opposed to rough maxims and methodological generalities. A passing theory really is like a theory in this, that it is derived by wit, luck, and wisdom from a private vocabulary and grammar, knowledge of the ways people get their point across, and rules of thumb for fig-

uring out what deviations from the dictionary are most likely. (*TI*,
445–46)

Davidson's dramatic conclusion is that "there is no such thing
as a language, not if a language is anything like what many philosophers and linguists have supposed. There is, therefore, no such
thing to be learned, mastered or born with. We must give up the idea
of a clearly defined shared structure which language users acquire
and then apply to cases" (*TI*, 446).

The piece in which one finds these statements, Davidson's "A
Nice Derangement of Epitaphs," is itself a fine example of issues
surrounding interpretation. Ian Hacking's initial reaction is that
Davidson's conclusion raises doubts about the point of all his earlier work, noting that "we do not expect Davidson's philosophy to
be the one challenged by his conclusions" (*TI*, 447). Assuming that
Davidson is "not intending philosophical suicide," Hacking settles
on the claim "that there is an element of retraction in his [David-
son's] paper" (*TI*, 448). Certainly, Davidson's dismissal of philosophers' and linguists' traditional concept of language is more than
Hacking and Dummett expect, even from one who professes radical
interpretation. Davidson *au contraire* proclaims astonishment at his
having been interpreted in ways that suggest that he has moved to a
position that is inconsistent with his earlier conceptions of philosophy, or, indeed, with philosophy itself.[7] Margolis's take on the
theses enunciated in "A Nice Derangement of Epitaphs" is that
Davidson has to make "concessions to the profound intentionality,
contextedness, historicity, and cultural divergence of human language and behavior," concessions that Margolis would certainly
find congenial.[8]

Even if I had a clue of how to reconcile Davidson's "Derangement" with his earlier work (well, perhaps, I have just *a* clue), this
is not the place to undertake a project that has struck so many of his
readers as an enormous puzzle, readers that include the likes of
Hacking, Dummett, and Margolis. I do think, however, that
Davidson's minimalist account of successful communication by
speech does suggest some interesting avenues to pursue, and I am
particularly interested in an application it might have to a problem
I have found in Margolis's account of interpretation, viz., his use of

the concept of social practices in accounting for the stability of cultural entities throughout their careers, careers that include alterations in these entities themselves as a result of ongoing acts of interpretation.

What follows, then, is a "a writerly reading" of Margolis's *Interpretation, Radical But Not Unruly* (and, no doubt, of "A Nice Derangement of Epitaphs" and "The Third Man" as well). In any case, a writerly reading of Margolis seems fitting, because the notion of writerly reading that Margolis borrows from Roland Barthes plays a prominent role in Margolis's account of interpretation. Moreover, "writerly reading," I hope to show, is just another way of describing the kind of activity in which philosophy—as well many other forms of cultural communication—consists. The notion of a writerly reading, it turns out, will be a way of correcting mistakes in our view of language that have resulted from studying language that is written and read, or to be more precise, from assuming that it makes no difference whether language takes the form of speech or writing. Were we to take spoken language rather than written language as our prototype for communication, we might not need for the concept of writerly reading to explain how a text can sustain more than one "correct" interpretation.[9]

II

A writerly reading is some reader's interpretation of a work, where "work" refers to something "concrete, occupying a portion of bookspace in a library, for example."[10] This writerly reading or interpretation constitutes a Text, in Barthes's sense, which, as Margolis describes it, is the product "yielded *by* interpretatively addressing 'something else' that, in the ongoing (serial) process of reading and rereading, *is uniquely affected by that very process*" (*IRU*, 36; emphasis added). Writerly readings are possible because the "galaxy of signifiers" (i.e., the sentences "found in" the work) do not constitute only one literary text, but a plurality of Texts depending on the meanings assigned these sentences by the writerly reader.[11] Writerly reading stands, then, as a corrective to the more traditional view that there is a specific way in which the writer intends the reader to read the text, a specific message that the text conveys, what Margolis following Barthes calls a "readerly reading." A "canonical reading" is a readerly reading, although before it attained this status, it may well have been a writerly reading.[12] In any case, we do identify, individuate, and refer to the work, text, or "galaxy of signifiers" of which a reading, whether writerly or readerly, is a reading. For some literary or cultural theorists, it is a problem to explain how a text can be a stable referent and at the same time be subject to change *as a consequence of interpretation* although it is not clear, as Margolis points out, why we should think that fulfilling a grammatical requirement like reference will of necessity have "metaphysical import" or convey "metaphysical intent" (*IRU,* 33).[13]

Margolis thus distinguishes "strong interpretation," the kind of interpretation typically practiced in history and the arts which yields writerly readings, from Interpretation, that is, the activities which constitute the relatively stable referents that are part of the physical, natural world, as well as the referents of the cultural world on which interpretation of the first [strong] sort is practiced (*IRU,* 21, 25). We can, of course, constitute stable referents as things that are not in the normal course of events subject to change as a result of strong interpretation; this is how physical objects have typically been constituted in modern thought. The physical world as constituted by Interpretation is sometimes misunderstood (one suspects willfully) as the claim that we can make the world any way we want, as though the world was a fiction in the same way that *Alice in Wonderland* is fiction. Such a claim is thought to be easily refuted by pointing out the "brute" character of what exists besides us, say, by kicking a stone and thereby demonstrating how the world "objects" to certain interpretations, how it is "real." From the claim that something is "real" it does not follow, however, that it is not subject to Interpretation or not a product of interaction embodied speakers of a language and "brute reality." Developing theories about whatever exists besides us requires that we experience it through and in these interactions as belonging to the kinds of things recognized by our community of language users.[14] Because such theories require that we experience brute reality not as brute but as belonging to kinds or being instances of the concepts recognized by our language(s), we must grant that whatever exists besides us is not "cognitively transparent," and that such cognitive intransparency applies even to theories we have about ourselves, because these theories will also consist of concepts and judgments from and in our language. The same will apply to our theories about the artifacts we make in our interactions. Because we cannot always, if ever, separate in our experience the "contributions" made by brute reality and those made by us and by our technologies, we may speak, as Margolis does, of the "symbiosis" of brute reality and human reality (*IRU*, 3).

Philosophers may prefer to reserve the epithet "real" for the physical objects and events out of which cultural phenomena or artifacts emerge in distinction to the cultural phenomena and artifacts themselves, but this preference cannot be justified on the ground that like brute reality, physical objects are not constituted by Interpretation. "Brute reality" refers to whatever exists besides us *prior* to our interaction with it; physical things are a way we have of characterizing things with which we interact. The identification of physical objects with brute reality may have made sense when a thing's ontological possibilities were restricted to either *matter,* which was thought to be cognitively transparent (most of the time, anyway), or *mind,* which "apprehended" matter. Acknowledging the interactive character of our theories about the world thus denies neither its reality nor its resistance to us. That "Interpretation" refers to the constitution of relatively stable referents in our interactions with the physical world is not equivalent to saying that we can constitute the world any way we want. "We open our eyes and see a world we cannot ignore; still, what we see is due to what we are; and what we are we are as a result of our continuous self-formation and transformation within a larger history and the larger processes of nature. So the 'resistance' of the encountered world is not at all incompatible with its being 'constituted' " (*IRU*, 91).[15]

Cultural artifacts are also constituted as stable referents; the difference is that they are constituted in such a way that they can undergo change as a result of strong interpretation. It is not clear why a thing's being subject to change as a consequence of strong interpretation should require the concession that it is not a real thing. If we deny the reality of culture, we also deny, as Margolis points out, the reality of ourselves *qua* selves (*IRU,* 141), as well as a source for our concepts and judgments. It is peculiar, to say the least, that the goal of "naturalizing" epistemology through the project of physicalism denies a source for the goal and for the project. The doctrines of physicalism are always raised *after* the fact of our being culturally endowed inquirers (*IRU,* 54);[16] physicalism requires linguistically endowed and culturally endowed inquirers who can "recognize, individuate, identify, and reidentify spontaneous events and phenomena . . . of the relevant sort—regarding which, thereupon the supervenience thesis and its physicalist analogues are first pertinently broached" (*IRU,* 54). We take our "selves" to be these culturally endowed inquirers. "*We* cannot attribute Intentional properties to ourselves *extrinsically*"; we experience these properties as intrinsic (*IRU,* 135).

If we concede "that the epithet 'real' is meant univocally as between nature and culture," and that the distinction of what belongs to the natural, physical world and the cultural world is drawn by means "belonging to the cultural, and not the natural, physical world" (*IRU,* 128), then it is no longer obvious why we should continue to draw the distinction. Speaking of the natural in opposition to the cultural seems to imply that our being culturally endowed inquirers is not a part of natural history, that human culture is not "natural," though the evidence suggests that cultural resources such as language played a central role in the evolution and survival of human societies and their members.

Abandoning the distinction between the natural and the cultural does not, of course, resolve how we are to explain the relationship of the cultural to the physical. That cultural artifacts and events may alter as a result of (strong) interpretation precludes their being supervenient on the physical, because, as Margolis notes, there does not appear to be any way of maintaining any "modal or necessary invariance (*de re*) between what 'supervenes' and that from which it does so" (*IRU,* 53).[17] Rejecting physicalism and rejecting supervenience amount to the same thing: as Margolis points out, there is

> no known procedure (rule, criterion, algorithm, law or the like) by which, *from,* a description of any physical events, we could infer in a reliable way any culturally significant events we sponta-

neously (normally) recognize; nor, *for* any culturally significant events, could we infer any reasonably detailed and pertinent physical events in which they would be embodied and by reference to which they could then be indexed. (*IRU,* 52)[18]

Margolis suggests that the cultural be seen as "incarnate" or embodied in the physical. As embodied in physical objects or events, cultural entities, including humans, can undergo changes as a consequence of strong interpretation without having these changes adversely affect their numerical fixity as referents or necessarily alter their physical properties (*IRU,* 47). But it is not clear whether and how their being real and their numerical fixity are related to their being "in" the physical. If we return to example of a written literary text, we can, of course, point to the inscribed marks in an enduring substance as the physical thing, but the text is not incarnate in these marks, but in the performance of reading them. Such performances presumably constitute what Margolis describes as a narrative history of the description and interpretation of Texts "that preserves the public identity of 'what' is affected and the sense in which its 'nature' may be altered from step to step" (*IRU,* 55). This narrative history is found, Margolis suggests, in the consensual memory of an encultured society (*IRU,* 41). Indeed, Margolis suggests that the solution to the problem of providing and preserving stable referents for ongoing interpretation is not symbolic or linguistic, but *lebensformlich* (*IRU,* 118). Thus Margolis introduces a term with broader scope—the Intentional—to refer to all cultural practices that are "about" something, whether linguistic or not.[19] The Intentional "belongs primarily to the collective life of historical societies" and appears as an ingredient in the properties of its cultural artifacts, where "cultural artifact" is understood broadly enough to refer to artworks and texts, institutions and personal careers, utterances and actions, and histories and theories, among other things (*IRU,* 14). As such, it is incarnate in physical or biological properties and is an "indissolubly complex property" of such properties (*IRU,* 15). The Intentional is thus descriptive of "the collective features of encultured life as they are instantiated in art and artifacts" (*IRU,* 108). All these things are then considered Texts, because they must be Interpreted to be recognized as what they are, and they are also open to strong interpretation that may alter their properties (*IRU,* 45, 172). Margolis's concept of the Intentional as collective more or less corresponds, he says, to Wittgenstein's "forms of life," Bourdieu's "*habitus,*" Marx's "praxis" or "modes of production," Hegel's "*sitten,*" Gadamer's "*wirkungsgeschichtliches Bewusstein,*" or Foucault's *epistemes* (*IRU,* 41).[20]

III

Pace Dummett, we interpret each other and the world in all cases in which our responses are not habitual, that is, in cases where communication is viewed not on analogy with a physical object but as an interaction with a cultural artifact that is constituted as subject to further interpretation. The appeal to *Lebensformen* or cultural practices is a familiar move in recent philosophy, not only for the major figures of nineteenth- and twentieth-century continental philosophy whom Margolis cites, but also for leading analytic philosophers such as Dummett.[21] Yet these social conceptions of practice seem to be based on an analogy to either a physical object or to linguistic communication, or as Margolis would have it, linguistic communication inscribed in a physical object—a Text. In any case, they are conceived, as Dummett conceived of them, as that in virtue of which meanings are fixed independently of speakers, or as Margolis conceives of them, as that which preserves the stable referents for ongoing interpretation. On the social theory of practices, practices are real, something that is already there.

Indeed the notion of practices arose, Stephen Turner observes, as a substitute for first principles once philosophers recognized that there were no unproblematic first principles; practices seemed even better than first principles because practices seem to be more 'first' than principles (*STP,* 9). The first principles of traditional philosophy were just an attempt "to substitute something explicit and universal" and to "justify and explain something we already do"; to accept that "these practices are the 'ground' is to accept something that's already there."[22]

Individual behavior can then be explained as resulting from the acquisition of the practices that replace first principles in causing—

and/or justifying—this behavior. Practices are thought to accomplish this, because they persist in and beyond the performances in which an individual is said to acquire them; they are *not* just the individual's "overt" behavior or a habitual performance of some kind. This "outer, substantive" character makes them a better "explanatory backstop," as Turner says, because they are considered "real" and not merely theoretical or "fictive" entities.[23] But this "outer substantive" character of practices is most peculiar, for they are not visible, despite the obvious analogy with physical objects or Texts. Consequently, practices and their means of transmission are epistemologically elusive. The "outer substantive" character of a practice implies that it somehow exists independently of the individual, but it is not clear how nor where it exists, nor how its capacity to effect causal consequences is related to where it is and where it goes. Traditional explanations of practices as the consequence of some Durkheimian-like collective object with causal powers—a collective mind, group *Wille,* or *Zeitgeist*—illustrate their major flaw: subsequent changes in scientific metaphors result in the realization that "the mechanisms by which . . . [these explanations] are supposed to operate are inconsistent with everything we know about causal processes in other domains" (*STP,* 53). We have scarce reason to hope that our versions of such solutions will not subsequently seem as "ludicrous as the talk of 'currents' in Durkheim" (*STP,* 54). More recent versions of the collective object hypothesis that conceive of practices on analogy with *public* collective objects, for example, explicitly agreed to conventions or rules, avoid the problems of location and transmission through their choice of an analogy which assumes that the rules are somehow "inscribed" in the practices themselves. Theories allowing that individuals can acquire the same practice without having it transmitted through the same means or on the same occasion have to account for the alleged sameness of the practice among these individuals. The Kripkean solution that practices be viewed as "rules" and that command assent will not do, Turner points out, because there are many practices that do not exhibit the level of agreement that rules of this sort should compel, and the suggestion that the community "tests" its members to see whether they have understood these rules is simply not descriptive of most of the practices in which this level of agreement is supposedly present.[24]

As inquirers, we come to the notion of practices through the indirect route of inferring their existence from what we observe, but this behavior could, of course, be explained as resulting from different causes. Repetitive behavior in individuals, for example, is taken as evidence of a certain habit caused by the practice, but repetitive behavior is not enough, Turner notes, to guarantee that those behaving in this way are doing so from habit, and not because of biological causes, impulses, reasons, or instincts (*STP*, 15–16). Moreover, we cannot simply assume that the "manifestations of mind that are most visible, and that we can make reasonable inferences about the existence and content of, constitute all of someone's habits" (*STP*, 17).

Because habit involves some mental component acting as a cause for repetitive behavior, some theorists construe practices as "collective presuppositions." These explanations also suffer from underdetermination and causal opacity, trading as they do on the assumption that a person can be described as holding certain presuppositions if it can be shown that, if one or more of that person's beliefs were the conclusion of a logical argument, the argument would require additional premises to those she avows to be valid (*STP*, 29). This assumption, in turn, leads to the inference that the person somehow "possesses" the tacit premises that *caused* her to believe the conclusion. But the same conclusions may be drawn from arguments with different premises, so there is no reason to believe that the alleged presupposition is "the only one possible or the one that corresponds uniquely to the psychological reality of the person to whom the presupposition is attributed" (*STP*, 30). Moreover, we cannot assume that the "psychologically or historically effective presuppositions"—if the same assumptions were to be equally effective in all individuals which is unlikely—would necessarily be the ones that philosophers find preferable or logically persuasive (*STP*, 31). Different people "often have different reasons for assenting to something in public; there is no reason to suppose that they do not have different 'presuppositions' as well" (*STP*, 31). Theories that practices are collective presuppositions "may establish that phenomena of order may be produced by people acting *as if* they were acting in accordance with certain shared procedures or rules, but this is not the same as showing that these (or any) shared procedures are the causes of the 'order' " (*STP,* 43; emphasis added).

The claim that repetitive behavior in a society is a manifestation of *social* habits of mind presupposes that although practices or traditions are like "natural objects" with "natural powers," our acquisition of them and access to them is cultural, as if they were a Text inscribed somewhere in our common space. Distinguishing social from "natural" behavior requires cross-cultural or historical comparisons that things have been done differently in some other society, or in one's own society at some earlier period. "We need a starting point *within* culture or practice to recognize something else *as* practice" (*STP,* 103). We also need a starting point from within culture to recognize something as natural, and this concept of what is "natural" changes over time within a culture.[25] Yet as *recipients* or practitioners of a practice, we need not know how nor that we have acquired it, and from this it follows that we do not know how, when, and from whom we acquired it, or, indeed, what it is that we acquired (*STP,* 47).[26] That the constitution and identification of practices is so opaque and so contingent undermines their claim to reality as substantial facts.

What we know, that is, directly observe or experience, is that a number of people, including ourselves, engage in the same public performances, though what counts as "sameness" is none too clear.[27] We assume that this sameness of performance is due to habit, and that the acquisition of such habits indicates that their possessors have acquired a social practice. But sameness of habitual *performance,* or even the disposition to produce the same performance under the same conditions, does not entail "sameness of the causal history by which the habitual action is produced"; one may relearn a skill after an injury, say, and in so doing one "presumably replaces the causal structure that previously produced the performance" (*STP,* 59–60). Whatever causal mechanisms of feedback and correction that effected the relearning of some skills "may be given as means of accounting for external sameness" (*STP,* 59–60).

At bottom, then, external sameness—sameness of public performances—is all that we have to go on. Social practices were inferred as the causes of these public performances because there seemed to be no other way to account for the fact that individuals from social groups and subgroups behave in quite similar ways, that this behavior appears to be learned, and that similarity of behavior persists through generations of individuals who are members of, or are descended from, these groups. There also seemed to be no alternative to the supposition that some collective thing causes this behavior, although this collective thing is not publicly observable though it is somehow inscribed in what we do observe: *"Practices appear to come along as baggage with the formal teaching of, for example canonical texts"* (*STP*, 45; emphasis added).

Turner concludes that explaining the persistence of a practice or tradition does not require the notion of a collective object, but instead can be said to consist in an individual's emulating performances of public observances, rituals, and performances.

> If acting in accordance with a tradition is acting in accordance with the ways of life in a community, and if the way of life in a community includes certain observances, performances, and activities, and individual habits and mental habits arise from engaging in the relevant performances, nothing need follow with respect to the causal role or status of practice understood as a kind of collective fact. All that need follow is this: by performing in certain ways, people acquire habits which lead them to continue to perform, more or less, in the same ways. The observances . . . cause *individual* habits, not some sort of collectively shared single habit called a practice or a way of life, which one may possess or fail to possess. (*STP*, 99–100)

IV

The motivation for the social theory of practices was to provide an explanation or justification of individual behavior and not to reduce the notion of practice to individual performances. For Dummett, language as a social practice accounted for the fact that meanings are fixed independently of speakers and hearers; for Margolis, the Intentional as a social practice provided the stability necessary to preserve the public identity of cultural referents, despite the fact that their "nature" could be altered from step to step. In both cases, the practice accounts for the sameness of individual performance rather than the performances accounting for the practices. The social theory of practices seems to assume that were tradition to be nothing more than habitual individual performances, there would be no way to account for the claim that meanings can be fixed independently of speakers, or to explain how the Intentional belong to the collective life of historical societies.

Davidson's account of communication as an interaction in which speakers and hearers adapt their "passing theories" in response to each other's behavior suggests a way to account for linguistic interactions and other cultural artifacts without invoking the idea of as a collective object. Davidson does not deny that successful communication *by speech* entails that something is shared; what he disputes is that the explanation of linguistic communication entails a rule-governed social practice in which the meanings of words is *fixed* independently of any particular speaker (or hearer) such that a speaker (or hearer) need not form any express intention or hold any particular theory about his or her audience (or interlocutor). Margolis claims in a similar vein that although interpretation proceeds in accordance with past habits of reference, explanation, and the like, the "consensual memory" in which these past habits persist, is not the same thing as acquiring and applying rules: "there are no rules that can replace such memory and such memory functions without rules itself" (*IRU*, 86). The consensus in terms of which Margolis construes the objectivity of interpretation is therefore not the consequence of applying criteria, but of remembering past successful performances, and of developing the habits that enable one to carry out such performances proficiently. Without these performances, there would be no rules, for the latter are *models* which some community or subgroup may formulate to explain the former. The important point, I would argue, is that the performances do not depend on the transmission of these rules, conceptual frameworks, interpretative schemes, theories, or paradigms *as such*; rather, it is the ability to carry out some performance proficiently that is subsequently described by the rules or theories. Not only could one carry out these performances without having formulated the rules; these performances are also subject to alternative descriptions.

Davidson's account of how "thought itself is essentially social" (*TM*, 608) provides a sense of how the cultural, though not itself a collective object, may serve as the means by which we come to the concept of an object or an objective world. For Davidson to say that thought is essentially social means that we come to "the concept of an objective world, a world independent of our sensations or experiences" with the acquisition of concepts and judgments, and these, in turn, require "the corroboration of others who are tuned to the same basic events and objects we are, and who are tuned to our responses to those events and objects" (*TM*, 608). Interaction with another person allows us to correlate our responses with his or hers: "For the first time it makes sense to speak of responses being 'the same,' that is relevantly similar" (*TM*, 608–609). It is also at this point that it makes sense, Davidson says, "to speak of responses as responses to external objects rather than to immediate sensations; when two (or of course, more) creatures can correlate their responses, those responses *triangulate* the object. It is the common cause of the responses, a cause that must have a location in a shared interpersonal space" (*TM*, 609). Thus, Davidson can deny that what we share is *known in advance; it is* the *sharing of this interpersonal space that makes knowledge possible.*

Davidson's triangle of two observant observers in a shared space is not yet a prototype of linguistic communication; such a triangle could exist, he suggests, without language, although this triangle is the necessary condition for language, which "fills in and enriches the base of the triangle" and "reaches far beyond what can be immediately and jointly experienced" (*TM*, 610). Linguistic communication would seem to occur when these interactions are correlated in constitutive acts of Interpretation, that is, in the recognition of something in this shared space as an object or stable referent. Doing so requires "erasing the boundary between knowing a language and knowing our way around in the world generally," because correlating responses in this shared space *is* getting to know one's way around in the world. This would seem to accord with Margolis's claim that "language is not an isolated or autonomous aptitude among humans" and that "the linguistic is, everywhere, an abstraction from ampler forms of intelligent action and intervention in the real world" (*IRU*, 172).

That a passing theory is "derived by wit, luck, and wisdom from a private vocabulary and grammar, knowledge of the ways people get their point across, and rules of thumb for figuring out what deviations from established meaning are most likely" seems to me another way of saying that as speakers and hearers the only thing we have to draw on is those past correlations which resulted in constitutive acts of Interpretation, that is, in the recognition of something in this shared space as an object or stable referent. Thus may a society's "consensual memory" of its own successful practices be preserved both in our and others' successful past performances.[28] Given these past successes, it seems not to matter much that there is no more "chance of regularizing or teaching this process" than there is "of regularizing or teaching the process of creating new theories to cope with new data in any field." That we successfully engage in strong interpretation at the same time that we recognize a shared context of stable referents does not account for how the collective persists in individual performances; it simply demonstrates it. The Intentional is *already there,* and it is incarnate; we are able to perform the activities of speaking, writing, and making gestures, movements, sounds, and objects that are "about" something—we are able to negotiate meaning—because we are embodied, not despite it. That we do these things is as undeniable as any claim we might make about physical objects.

But Davidson thinks that his minimalist account of how thought is social and what is necessary for successful communication by speech will not do for artworks—those things which have been "created with the idea of being read or seen or heard by others (or perhaps by its creator at a time subsequent to its creation)" (*TM,* 610) Artworks enter "the conceptual scene at a more advanced stage. Artist, writer, and audience are equipped from the start with a vast overlapping set of common assumptions. . . . Writing deviates startlingly from the original triangle" (*TM,* 610). What is "directly observed by both reader and writer is the text" and the interaction between perceiving creatures that is the foundation of communication is lost, which, as Davidson notes, Plato pointed out in the *Phaedrus.*[29] While the text," unlike most objects, has meaning," Davidson takes its meaning to be produced by the interaction between "the intentions of the writer to be understood in a certain way and the interpretation put on the writer's words by the reader." Davidson, unexpectedly echoing Dummett, remarks that "for the most part this interplay is, and is meant to be routine, in the sense that the writer knows pretty well how he or she is apt to be understood, and the typical reader knows pretty well how the writer intended to be understood" though Davidson acknowledges that this is not always the true of literary works (*TM,* 610).

> Writers like Shakespeare, Dante, Joyce and Beckett strain our interpretative powers and thus force us into *retrospective dialogue with the text,* and through the text with the author. Authors may choose from many devices to rouse the reader to wrestle with the text. . . . But however it is done, and to whatever extent the reader's connivance is won, authors have contrived or commandeered an arena of ideas and assumptions large enough to contain both themselves and their audience, a common conceptual space. (*TM,* 610, emphasis added)

The prototype for a communication is thus not direct confrontation with an object, but the triangulation between speaker, hearer, and an object. Davidson's account of communication and his conclusions are startling precisely because meaning is not fixed but negotiated by speakers in a shared context. It is peculiar that although speech is his prototype for linguistic communication and interpretation, in discussing literature he emphasizes the fixity of written texts in contrast to their ambiguity, and extends this fixity to the meaning of these texts.[30] It is true, as Thomas Cole observes, that a written text is less subject to distortion through a series of transmissions, but as an act of communication, writing involves ambiguities not present in oral communication. Speech occurs in a situational context in which aspects of the embodied speaker's delivery—phrasing, gesture, and so on—convey his or her intentions and where he or she is physically present to explain, repeat, and rephrase to negotiate, as it were, a passing theory with the hearer, in which the boundary between knowing a language and knowing one's way around in the world is erased.[31] Written texts are no less communicative acts for being written; it is not just the literary texts of Joyce, Shakespeare, or Beckett that require writerly reading or strong interpretation. And if we take Davidson's minimal speech situation rather than Dummett's habitual linguistic behavior as the prototype for communication, then even "writerly reading" insofar as it is a metaphor based on inscription misleads us. Literary texts should not be perceived as written artifacts with fixed meanings; rather they are, to paraphrase Stephen Greenblatt, ways we communicate with the dead. Or perhaps we should say, in light of Davidson's observation that writers such as Shakespeare, Dante, Joyce, and Beckett force us into retrospective dialogue with the text and through the text with the author, that literary texts are the way that the dead communicate with us.

Of course, written texts are not necessary to preserve and transmit narrative history; this can be done by the performance of oral, traditional narratives on culturally significant occasions. There is triangulation in this oral situation just as there is in Davidson's elementary speech situation, consisting of the performer, audience, and the shared memory or tradition of successful performances.[32]

Although it is a mistake to conceive of written texts as having "fixed" meanings and thus as more real than oral performances or the performances of those who read them,[33] it is also a mistake to ignore that inasmuch as written texts themselves are fixed in some enduring substance, and thus can be preserved, transmitted, and consulted, that they serve the purposes of recording a society's consensual memory and fixing meanings in a way that makes *them independent* of speakers of the language. Indeed, written artifacts and the repositories in which they are kept—libraries, archives, museums, universities, computer banks—constitute a tremendous cultural resource, because they *are* collective resources or *Lebensformen* which both *constitute* part of a society's narrative history of interpretation and reinterpretation, and *preserve* and *transmit* this history. If, as Margolis says, the processes by which culturally endowed inquirers become so endowed are themselves subject to change in accordance with historical and cultural contingencies, then it seems important to point out that written artifacts and the institutions of literate societies in preserving and transmitting culturally significant communication constitute the kind of *collective, public objects* that *can effect* changes in individual behavior and in a society's "habits of living."[34] This is especially significant in light of Margolis's claim that thinking itself has a history, and "the reality of our cognitive powers is inseparable from the effective reality of the enculturing society in which they are first formed and exercised" (*IRU,* 127).

From the fact that the practices of meaning and reference are collected or "fixed" in lexicons, dictionaries, and grammars, as well as in habitual performances of standard usage or "the right thing to say" in the circumstances, it does not follow that a speaker and hearer need not form any intentions about each other, nor that one can write or read a text without taking into account the author and audience. The incarnation of the cultural in the physical, like its poetic original—"the Word has been made flesh and has pitched its tent among us"—means among other things, that the meanings of utterances and inscriptions are partly a function of how they are embodied or performed, and before whom.

Habitual or conventionalized linguistic behavior thus is not, *pace* Dummett, a very good prototype for linguistic communication, whether spoken or written. Assumptions that communication involves such conventional behavior tend to undermine communication; conventional or consciously planned responses to anticipated remarks or situations indicate that one is not listening or noticing things that are particular to the context or person on whom she inflicts her conventional behavior, that she is not part of a *Lebensformen.* Communication may *not* be occurring precisely because the speaker, believing that the meaning of words is independent from the occasion of the utterance, recognizes only her own intentions and not those of her audience or interlocutor.

Analytic philosophy's theories of communication and interpretation have not adequately taken in account the historicity of our cognitive powers, their inseparability from an enculturing society, and the role that writing and reading might play in this process. Analytic theories seem to rest on the metaphor of language inscribed in some collective object that, in turn, provides for the fixity of meaning. Thus, we find the notion that truths are inscribed in the soul because of its previous experience with the Forms; or they are innately in the Mind lying in wait for the natural light of reason to discover them; or they are written in the book of Nature (in mathematics), or they are guaranteed by *a priori* categories, syntactic or semantic structures; or they are grounded in social practices, or they are preserved in the written artifact of an author. Texts,

I would suggest, are better understood as embodiments of performances and as records of acts of communication, which can, in turn, give rise to further acts of communication or interpretation.

In the analytic tradition, philosophical writing is not supposed to lend itself to writerly readings and philosophers are not supposed to be very interested in such readings; such readings are the province of imaginative literature, the arts, and history.[35] The arguments of philosophy are what is supposed to matter, and presumably philosophical texts should be read in a readerly way; it is not clear that analytic philosophers think that they can be read in any other way. But if the arguments of philosophy are construed as texts with fixed meanings rather than as interactions between speaker and interlocutor or writer and reader, why does there continue to be disagreement, discussion, indeed, *interpretation and writerly readings* of philosophical texts? What are we to make of the fact that philosophers, especially the great, dead ones, have offered writerly readings of their own earlier texts, as well as the texts of their predecessors? It cannot be that difficult simply to grasp an argument. They must be telling us, as I think that Margolis and Davidson are telling us in their respective ways, that despite traditional philosophy's claims to some eternal privilege and cognitive transparency, it is a form of writing, and as such is not fixed but instead subject to "writerly readings," that is, acts of strong interpretation in which meaning is negotiated. At least that is how I read them.

NOTES

1. Joseph Margolis, *Interpretation, Radical But Not Unruly: The New Puzzle of the Arts and History* (Berkeley: University of California Press, 1994), p. ix. Additional references to this work will be indicated by the abbreviation *IRU* accompanied by the page number in parentheses following the material cited.

2. Michael Dummett notes there has been a divergence in the analytic tradition as practiced in the United States and in the United Kingdom, although by the middle seventies, British philosophy was becoming aligned with the American school. Michael Dummett, "Can Analytical Philosophy be Systematic, and Ought It to Be?" in *Truth and Other Enigmas* (Cambridge, Mass.: Harvard University Press, 1978), p. 441. The question posed in Dummett's title, as he observes, would be a ridiculous question to pose to Carnap, or to those American philosophers who tend to regard philosophy as "at least cognate with the natural sciences" (437–38).

3. These are, as Dummett observes, just the cases that aroused Davidson's interest. Michael Dummett, " 'A Nice Derangement of Epitaphs': Some Comments on Davidson and Hacking," in *Truth and Interpretation: Perspectives on the Philosophy of Donald Davidson,* ed. Ernest LePore (Oxford: Basil Blackwell, 1986), pp. 471–72. Davidson's "A Nice Derangement of Epitaphs," also appears in the LePore volume. Further references to Dummett's and Davidson's essays will be indicated in the text by the page number and the abbreviation *TI.* Dummett observes that one's orientation in the philosophy of language is a function of whether she takes the primary function of language to be an instrument of communication or a vehicle for thought. Dummett takes the communicative function of language to be primary: "Language is a vehicle of thought because it is an instrument of communication, and not conversely," *TI,* p. 470.

4. For radical interpretation, see Donald Davidson, *Inquiries into Truth and Interpretation* (Oxford: Clarendon Press, 1984). For criticisms of Davidson's denial that there are interpretative *tertia,* see Joseph Margolis, "Donald Davidson's Philosophical Strategies," in *Artifacts, Representations, and Social Practice: Essays for Marx Wartofsky,* ed. Carol C. Could and Robert S. Cohen (Boston: Kluwer Academic Publishers, 1994), pp. 291–322.

5. Donald Davidson, "The Third Man," *Critical Inquiry* 19, no. 4 (Summer 1993): 607–15, 607. Subsequent references to this article will be noted by the abbreviation *TM* in parentheses following the passage cited.

6. David Gorman observes that Davidson's disallowal of things such as conventions from "the theoretical apparatus of a properly explanatory account of human linguistic behavior" is not the same as denying that there are conventions of language or even languages; instead, his point is that "at best, such things are matters of practical simplification for language users and that *in principle,* linguistic communication can occur in their absence." Gorman understands Davidson's project as accounting for the abstract situation; once this is done, he has done justice to whatever is openly observable in linguistic activity.

> . . . Conventions and the like are secondary phenomena, of little philo-
> sophical interest (it is implied) in comparison with the basic dichotomy
> of truth conditions and interpretative strategies.

In *Literary Theory After Davidson,* ed. Reed Way Dasenbrock (University Park: Penn State, 1993), p. 211.

7. In "The Third Man," Davidson writes that "nothing has surprised me more than to discover myself anthologized in books with titles such as *Post-Analytic Philosophy* or *After Philosophy.* That *after* haunts me again from an about-to-be published book with the title *Literary Theory After Davidson.* Is there something sinister, or at least *fin de siècle,* in my views that I have failed to recognize, something that portends the dissolution not only of the sort of philosophy I do but of philosophy itself? Why else would I find my name linked with Heidegger and Derrida?"

8. "Donald Davidson's Philosophical Strategies," p. 317. Of course, these

are just the themes, Margolis notes, that have typically been take to mark the different between Anglo-American and continental philosophy.

9. This is, of course, one of the central themes of Jacques Derrida. See Jacques Derrida, *Dissemination*, trans. Barbara Johnson (Chicago: University of Chicago Press, 1981); and *On Grammatology*, trans. Gayatri Chakravorty Spivak (Baltimore: Johns Hopkins, 1974).

10. The quotation is from Roland Barthes, "From Work to Text" (trans. Josue V. Harari) in *Textual Strategies: Perspectives in Post-Structuralist Criticism*, ed. Josue V. Harari (Ithaca: Cornell University Press, 1979), p. 74; the passage from the work in which the quotation occurs is cited by Margolis in *IRU*, pp. 35–36.

11. Roland Barthes, *S/Z*, trans. Richard Miller (New York: Hill and Wang, 1974), p. 4; cited by Margolis in *IRU*, p. 36.

12. It is important to note that a classic work is both classic and fixed because it has been written down. The oral tradition that was public and collective became the *Iliad* and *Odyssey* of Homer, although interestingly enough, we are not really sure when, just as we are not really sure that there was a Homer or who he was. What was oral performance—epic, lyric, even tragedy—became a "fixed" work in the sense that it was agreed which sentences made up the work. Even the earliest Greek inscriptions represent the objects on which they appear as speaking: "Mantiklos dedicated me to Apollo the far darter"; "To he who of all the dancers sports most playfully." These inscribed objects are better seen as embodying the act of speaking than of bearing inscriptions for reading. See, for example, L. H. Jeffery, *The Local Scripts of Archaic Greece* (Oxford: Clarendon Press, 1961); and Kevin Robb, "The Dipylon Prize Graffito," *Coranto*, pp. 7, 11–19; and *Literacy and Paideia in Ancient Greece* (New York: Oxford University Press, 1994).

13. Thus Margolis concludes that postmodernists such as Rosalind Krauss err in supposing that the need for reference commits one to a modernist ontology regarding the cultural—the view that the nature, essence, or boundaries of artworks or other cultural Texts cannot be altered by interpretative interventions. See Rosalind Krauss, *The Originality of the Avant-Garde and Other Modernist Myths* (Cambridge: MIT Press, 1983).

14. Cf. Davidson, *TM*, p. 608. Even if one grants that there may be nonlinguistic awareness or nonlinguistic experiences of "brute reality," it remains true that inasmuch as such experiences are "theorized"—thought and spoken about—they are subject to interpretation.

15. Margolis points out that a "temperate" realism requires that the world with which we interact be both "constituted" and resistant. "Put in the simplest terms: the apparent invariances of physical phenomena are just invariances noted under the changing, formative conditions of human history. We posit them, from within that history, as realities independent of that history" (*IRU*, 91). See also p. 82.

16. I take the very apt expression "culturally endowed inquirers" from Michael Krausz, "The Metaphysics of Culture: Four Questions for Margolis," in this volume.

17. Rejecting the physicalist claim that "cultural phenomena have properties that can be suitably expressed as purely physical properties" (*IRU*, 138) need not be construed as a commitment to mind-body dualism. One may remain a materialist in the sense of taking "the real world to be composed in some sense of some fundamental stuff," as long as she acknowledges that "whatever is so composed cannot also exhibit intrinsic properties that are not physical or material or not merely physical or material" (*IRU*, p. 138).

18. The suggestion that the mental is supervenient on the physical was, of course, introduced by Davidson; see "Mental Events" reprinted in *Essays on Actions and Events* (Oxford: Clarendon Press, 1980). It is no longer clear that Davidson holds this thesis; see, for example, Simon Evnine, *Donald Davidson* (Stanford: Stanford University Press, 1991), esp. pp. 67–71.

19. Cultural practices that are not linguistic would presumably include things such as music, dance, or reading a map.

20. The resources provided by a natural-language community's habits of life are necessary, Margolis argues, to ensure the success of discourse whether or not one attributes a fixed nature to what is interpreted and/or to the cognitive and interpretative powers of those doing the interpreting. These *Lebensformen* "are as much needed by the partisans of invariance as by the partisans of the flux," and this is true, he suggests, independently of what we take the supposed structure of these habits of life to be (*IRU*, p. 75).

21. All the variants Margolis cites come from continental philosophy, though this is not usually recognized in the case of Wittgenstein's forms of life. Stephen Turner points out that Wittgenstein borrowed the concept of *Lebensformen* from the philosopher-sociologist Eduard Spranger, for whom *Lebensformen* was a technical usage. Stephen Turner, *The Social Theory of Practices: Tradition, Tacit Knowledge, and Presuppositions* (Chicago: University of Chicago Press, 1994), p. 1, 130 n. 26. Further references to the Turner volume will be noted by the abbreviation *STP* and the page number in parentheses following the material cited.

On Dummett's view, ordinary linguistic behavior does not require interpretation in Margolis's strong sense (the type of interpretation characteristic of history and the arts), because of the larger social practice of which ordinary linguistic behavior is a part, the larger social practice that Margolis calls Interpretation. For both Dummett and Margolis, language is defined in terms of a social practice of which it is itself the prototype, although it is not clear they both mean the same thing by "social practice."

22. *STP*, pp. 9–10. As Turner observes, *this* practice—substituting social practices for first principles—began with Hume, for whom habit becomes the "ultimate principle," because habit provided for an explanation in causal terms: "The habit of inferring causes is itself a cause of belief, and it is a cause like other habits and customs" (p. 7). Turner's criticisms may apply to many of the concepts used synonymously with practice. He raises questions about the notions of tradition, tacit knowledge, *Weltanschauung*, paradigm, ideology, framework, presupposition, inherited background, Ryle's "knowing that" and "knowing how,"

Quine's "theory of the world" (as held by a particular person), David Lewis's "conventions without conveners," Elster's "culture-specific norms," and Unger's "reasonless routines," as well as other variant forms of the notion of social practices, including the continental variants that Margolis cites.

23. In response to the possible objection that his argument is just part of the "usual struggle against fictiveness, an attempt to privilege a form of description as 'matching reality,' " Turner observes that "either the process of 'making' is real, or the process is a fiction. If 'worlds' are not 'made', there is no basis for calling them fictive. If the 'making' is real, the practices that are part of the making must be real as well. Explanations end someplace: these explanations end at practices" (*STP*, p. 45).

24. Again, language is the most obvious example: "The community of language-users is one in which there are many slightly 'deviant' persons, and perhaps even a good number of fairly serious deviant ones and perhaps no perfect speakers" (*STP*, p. 74). The solution attributed to Kripke comes from Saul Kripke, *Wittgenstein: On Rules and Private Language* (Cambridge, Mass.: Harvard University Press, 1982).

25. See *STP*, p. 20. Racial and gender differences, for example, that were once considered natural, are now seen as cultural artifacts the origins of which are no longer seen as benign, despite any claim that those who originally formulated these views were doing "science." Opponents of race, sex, and religious discrimination, and of xenophobia and class privilege, note that the same natural characteristics (or inferiorities) are frequently assigned to the various victims of discrimination—women, non-Europeans, the proletariat, Catholics, Jews, Muslims—when all that their groups have in common is *not* being Northern European Protestant white men of property. The fact that those who advocate discrimination against homosexuals deny that their "differences" are natural constitutes an important exception to this practice. Of course, the charge that homosexuality is unnatural cannot have any force if one accepts that what is natural is, at bottom, a cultural concept, and consequently, it is not surprising that this is the charge leveled frequently by those who link the doctrine of natural kinds with a commitment to a religious concept of God as the creator of Nature.

The claim that a practice is biologically rather than culturally based depends on the theories of biology that are current in one's culture, and thus does not ensure an "objective" account in the sense of being "culture-free." Even if one limited his or her attempt at objectivity to matching or replacing "exterior, cultural descriptions and interior biological descriptions," the idea, as Turner says, "that the whole of 'cultural' variation, or even a large part, could be matched up to biological variation would require a scientific miracle." He acknowledges that the project of matching up biological descriptions with cultural descriptions may succeed in some cases, that it is probably true that there are biological influences on culture, that culture cannot be understood with references to the causal facts of biologically, and that there are some biologically based commonalities that are part of the causal background to particular practices (*STP*, p. 23). His point is that as far as we can tell, we are not going to have correspondences between biological and cultural descriptions that are going to help in the identification of practices.

26. "We can recall . . . [at least some of us can] the minute when we heard that Kennedy was assassinated, but we cannot recall our acquisition of the capacity to speak a foreign language or do proofs in elementary logic. In the latter cases we seem instead to discover that we have learned to do these things . . . or conclude that have done so on the basis of our observations (and the observations of others) of our performances" (*STP,* pp. 46–47).

27. See *STP,* pp. 62–77.

28. Turner points out that Spranger, from whom Wittgenstein took *Lebensformen*, understood this concept in the sense of a background to understanding, or "preunderstanding." "Although Spranger insists that 'Society is an overindividual context of effects' that 'determines from the beginning every individual's whole mental structure', and sees this context as the result of historical development, his point is that every individual's experience of this context is only partial. . . . So for Spranger the individual's experience of the historico-cultural background that is shared with others is distinctive. There is no internalized common object. . . . The inherited background of which Wittgenstein wrote is open to a similar interpretation: a background is a common thing . . . but a thing experienced differently by different people, with different effects, enabling them to understand different things. Two points need to be made about this account. One is that it is not 'the rules model of culture'; because the historico-mental world which is the cultural world is not composed of rules. The other is that our acquisition of culture differentiates or individualizes us" (*STP,* p. 69). Turner's account of inherited background in Wittgenstein is similar to what I am suggesting that *Lebensformen* mean for Margolis.

29. Davidson's point that "in the case of literature, the text is alienated from its creator by the lapse in time between when it is made and when it is read" applies, of course, only to written literature and not to the performance of oral, traditional literature.

30. Davidson does mention that in constructing a passing theory we need to consider what deviations from the dictionary are most like, but that is the only reference to written artifacts in this discussion of oral communication.

31. Thomas Cole, *The Origins of Rhetoric in Ancient Greece* (Baltimore, Md.: Johns Hopkins University Press, 1991), 44.

32. I am indebted to Butler Waugh for this point.

33. Reading, then, should be seen as a kind of transaction or production in which we are more or less active participants depending on the context in which this transaction or production takes place, on what we know about the context in which the work was written, and on its interpretative history. For a thorough formulation of a transactional account of reading, see Louise Rosenblatt, "The Transactional Theory of Reading and Writing," *Theoretical Models and Processes of Reading,* ed. R. B. Ruddell and M. R. Ruddell (Newark, Del.: International Reading Association, 1994).

34. Because Margolis cites as important Barthes's recognition that modernist theorists and literary commentators neglect "the changing context and history of *reading*—hence of the continually and historically changes codes of reading accessible to a living society" (*IRU,* 39), it presumably would be equally as important to consider the change that the very activities of reading and writing might effect in our communicative and interpretive activities.

Margolis does cite J. C. Nyiri's discussion of oral traditions in *Tradition and Individuality* (Dordrecht: Kluwer, 1992), as well as Walter Ong's *The Presence of the Word* (New Haven: Yale University Press, 1967), although Margolis insists that "in *whatever* sense tradition is 'oral', grounded in consensual habits and practices, a literate society is *qua* literate, intrinsically also 'oral': there is no disjunction, in literate societies, between the oral and the written" (*IRU,* 267, n. 4). That there is no disjunction between the oral and the written *in a literate society* does not preclude that the inscription of language has effected how the members of that society view communication, both oral and written. Indeed, they might claim to privilege speech and in so doing, disguise how their conception of speech rests on the notion of inscription. I take this to be Derrida's point, a point with which Margolis expresses sympathy. Derrida would not be sympathetic, as Margolis is not, to the notion that taking the oral situation as primary might allow us to escape our particular version of logocentrism.

Changes in how language is viewed when a society moves from being non-literate to literate has received a great deal of attention from students of epic and folklore since Milman Parry's demonstration that the *Iliad* and the *Odyssey* are composed in a style typical of oral traditional composition. See, for example, Parry's collected papers, *The Making of Homeric Verse,* ed. Adam Parry (Oxford: Clarendon Press, 1971); Eric Havelock, *Preface to Plato* (Cambridge, Mass.: Harvard University Press, 1963); *The Muse Learns to Write* (New Haven, Conn.: Yale University Press, 1986); Robb, "The Dipylon Prize Graffito," and Cole, *The Origins of Rhetoric in Ancient Greece.*

35. It is a less than precious irony that this notion of philosophical writing is supported, if not derived, from a reading of Plato that fails to see his dialogues as *dialogues* or philosophical dramas which invite writerly readings, just as Socrates invites his interlocutors repeatedly to reformulate their views. I have argued against this view in "Neither Published Nor Perished: The Dialogues as Speech, Not Text," in *The Third Way: New Directions in Platonic Studies,* ed. Francisco A. Gonzalez (Lanham, Md.: Rowman and Littlefield, 1995), pp. 61–77.

Look, This Is Zeus!

Eddy M. Zemach

This is an essay on Seeing, Ontology, and Representation, especially representation of nonexistents. I assume two metaphysical theses for which I do not argue: Scientific Realism and Nominalism.[1] Margolis subscribes to neither thesis, so it is interesting that these theses led me to a view similar to his theory of representation as expounded in his essay "Puzzles of Pictorial Representation."[2] Margolis claims that representation is basically monadic. I think so, too.

I

In a museum, a guide points to a picture and says: "Look, this is Zeus!" I have two questions: Q1: Does she refer to Zeus? Q2: When you do as she says, do you see Zeus?

Most philosophers answer Q1 in the negative. Searle, for instance, would say that the guide referred to nothing and expressed no proposition.[3] According to Walton, the guide only played a make-believe game in which the guide pretended to refer to Zeus.[4] I think that is wrong, but will not argue it here.[5] Let me just say that the entire attempt to deny that fictional names genuinely refer, common to Fregeans and Millians alike, trades a fundamental semantic insight for a dubious, pseudosociological story on the meaning (Searle) or on the provenance (Kripke) of names. The fundamental semantic insight I think we ought to retain is the Disquotational Axiom of Reference, of which the following is an axiom-schema:

I: 'a' denotes *a*.

Substituends of " 'a" ' in (I) are provided by the linguistic category of proper names (hence "'Zeus' refers to Zeus" is an axiom). (I) holds for all names. If it turns out that *a* does not exist then, well, 'a' denotes a nonexistent. Language supplies legitimate substituends for " 'all' " in (I) just as it provides legitimate substituends for " 'p' " in

II: 'p' is true iff p.

(II) holds for all declarative sentences. We need no pseudohistorical account on how 'p' came to be connected with the proposition that p, nor is the validity of (H) conditional upon a search of Plato's (or Katz's) heaven to verify that 'p' expresses that p. If 'p' is a declarative sentence, it is true iff p. That's all. The same goes for (I): if 'a' is a name, it denotes *a*.

Philosophers think that we cannot refer to Zeus, for he does not exist. Walton also holds that, when the museum guide says (pointing to a painting): "Look, this is Cézanne's woodstove!" the guide does not refer to Cézanne's woodstove; although that woodstove did exist, it is not in the museum, so in that case, too, the guide does not refer. Given that reply to Q1, the answer to Q2 is that what you see when you look where the guide tells you to look is paint on canvas, not Zeus (nor a woodstove). You just pretend, make-believe, that a spot of paint is Zeus (or a woodstove).

That answer is reminiscent of the line taken some time ago by sensedata epistemologists. The following problem was then popular. A flier points down and remarks: "See that round red spot? It is my house." Surely the flier cannot reside in a red spot? The explanation given was that the object directly perceived by the flier is a phenomenal object, a spot. That spot, however, is caused by a physical object, a house, and represents that house. The flier does not claim to reside in the phenomenal object the flies sees, but, rather, in the object it represents. The flier's words are to be taken as short for "I reside in the cause of what I see, that is, in the object that this spot represents."

That answer went, rightly, out of favor. The dyadic view of seeing (you directly see *a, b* causes *a, a* represents *b,* you indirectly see *b*) is too cumbersome. It is better to say that the flier sees his or her house, which, under these conditions, from high above, appears round and red. A gray house seen under such conditions appears round and red. The flier directly sees his square gray house; red and round is how such a house *will* look under these conditions. Those who do not know how houses appear under observation conditions C, report seeing a round red spot, but the flier knows better. You need training for Round and Red to serve you as cues for Square and Gray; given that training, however, a square gray house can be seen as such by looking round and red.

A passenger unfamiliar with that way of seeing will say that he or she sees a red round spot. Since what the passenger sees is gray and square, what is red and round? Nothing. The passenger is so affected that he or she senses as if there is something red and round there. It is a modification of the passenger's sensing, not a feature of the object he or she sees. The passenger has no idea what he or she sees, but, because grammar requires an object for 'I see . . .', the passenger reifies the way the house appears and treats it as an object in its own right: a phenomenal object. It does not imply that, among the houses in the neighborhood, there also sit some phenomenal entities, spots, or that spots hover in midair between the airplane and the house. The spot does not exist: it is how the house looks, how one's senses are modified by the house. Yet that trait of the perceiver may be reified, that is, posited as an object.

Looking at a tree through binoculars I see the tree, but when I adjust the glasses, it grows sharper or fuzzier, bigger or smaller. What is the thing that changes? Not the tree—*it* does not change when I tune my binoculars—but the way it appears to me does. I change. An appearance reified, treated as an object, is a phenomenon. Phenomena do not stand between the observer and the observed: They are features of the perceiver, that is, they do not exist.

Years ago I claimed[6] that objects can be directly seen through various artifacts (binoculars, periscope, television, etc.) and natural conditions (*fata morgana,*[7] after-images, dreams, etc.). Against

Ryle,[8] I argued that after-images and dreams are ways of seeing physical objects, but seen in these ways the objects we see do not appear as they appear when we use more standard ways of observing them. An incandescent filament can be seen even after you close your eyes, in an after image. A red bottle looks green and not in its proper place (it looks pasted on the white wall and not where it is, on the table) when you observe it in a nonstandard way, for example, through a complementary after-image. Yet the object you see in that way is a physical object, a red bottle, which, under nonstandard conditions, does not look as it usually does. There are no two things that you see at once, one phenomenal and one physical, but one thing only. If you know enough about your observation conditions, you see it as a (physical) red bottle on the table; if you do not, you see it as a (phenomenal) green bottle-image on the wall.

You see your mother-in-law in a dream; seen under these nonstandard conditions, she does not look as she would when seen in broad daylight. In your dream, she looks as a cobra, but that look of her, like any other, is due to the nature of the perceptual device used, which in the dream case is your subconscious mind. If you are familiar with these mechanisms you may use that visual observation (for dreaming is a visual observation) to learn about her, and about yourself, too, for observation always informs the observer about the observing device as well as about the observed item. Then, you see your mother-in-law and she looks cobralike. If you are not familiar with the said way of seeing, you will be aware of a cobralike appearance only. Not knowing which public object you see, you will reify the way your mother-in-law looks, treating it as an object in its own right, a cobra image.

In sum, perceiving a in condition C requires training in seeing a under C. Otherwise, you treat b, the look a presents in condition C, as a thing you see. So,

III: a is a visual representation of $b \equiv a$ is a reified look of b.

I now extend that account to pictorial representation, that is, to objects we see in paintings, be they real (e.g., Cézanne's woodstove) or imaginary (e.g., Zeus). I think that what the museum guide says is literally true: With his or her guidance, you can directly see Cézanne's woodstove, and you can also see the God Zeus.

II

Let me start with the less controversial case of Cézanne's wood-stove. A direct-perception epistemologist need not be hostile to my view that a painting may be treated as a tool that facilitates seeing that very stove. The causal route from the stove to our eyes is in that case circuitous indeed, not the one taken in standard cases of perception, but that is no reason to deny that we see Cézanne's wood-stove. There is a growing number of ways to see things by means other than a straight-line propagation of seen light from an object to the retina (e.g., seeing by means of X-rays, or magnetic resonance, or electromagnetic waves) which no one wishes to disqualify as seeing.

We see through devices that divert light: spectacles, binoculars, telescopes; we also use electron-microscopes, telescopes, television, and videocameras, where photons are replaced by electrons that take yet other routes to the eye. Yet it is the president himself that you see on TV, even though the route particles took from him to your eyes is not standard. It is the star itself that you see when you look up at night, even though it perished millions of years ago.

All that we see took place prior to our seeing it; no event exists at the time we see it: we see nothing in "real time." Surely, that does not imply that we see nothing? You can see one football match many times, using various seeing-strategies: in the field, in "live" transmission on TV, and in slow-motion replay. The way the game looks depends on the way of seeing it, but it is the same match every time. Those who were born after Kennedy's assassination can yet see it. You see your late father in a home movie, in a still photograph, and also in a portrait painted by an artist friend, just as you could see him when he was alive through your eyeglasses or you hear *him* on the telephone.

Walton, who holds that by looking at a photograph one sees the photographed object, denies that the same can be achieved by a painting.[9] Like Scruton,[10] Walton stresses the mechanical nature of the photographic process; that mechanical character, he says, makes photography what painting cannot be, a way to see a thing out there. Yet how is photography, given the wide choice of digital and optic photographic devices one can choose from, mechanical?

In another sense, mechanical processes link all objects in nature, yet Walton would not say that by looking at any object at all you can see every other object in the world! What is special to the process that does allow us to see an object *o* through a device *x* is that by looking at *x* we can see *o* as we think it is, but that is true of realistic paintings no less than it is true of realistic photographs. By using irrealistic (if you wish, perverse) techniques, a photographer may generate pictures no one would regard as pictures of *o*. Processes that do produce realistic photographs, hence ways of seeing *o*, are therefore special not because of their unique causal link to *o*, but because they are carefully selected to make us see *o* as it would look to us in standard conditions.

Causal theorists of perception hold that some causal route, CR, is so privileged that we can see *o* through *x* only when *o* and *x* are linked by CR. But why is CR superior to other causal routes? The inventor of photography did not philosophically deduce the identity of the route CR and then proceed to make a machine to instantiate it. No: Mr. Daguerre, who made us see *o* through a silver plate, adjusted the mechanism he invented for producing the latter, so that it resembles the former as it appears to us in standard conditions, and it is counterfactually dependent on it. These features, however, are possessed by realistic paintings as well. When we wish to see *o*, we do not look for the causal chain CR to lead us to it. Rather, we find ourselves visually encountering *o* while looking through *x*, even though we have no idea what is the causal route between *o* and *x*. The causal theory of seeing is false: seeing involves a variety of causal routes, or (as I shall later show) no causal route at all, but mere counterfactual covariance.

Makers of photographic equipment, like painters, take pains adjusting *x* to *o*. What makes us see *o* in *x* is not the causal route between *o* and *x* but the fact that, with proper training, we can, by looking at *x*, see *o* as we are wont to see it. Like the photographer, a painter selects a process that makes *x* diaphanous, a mere tool for seeing *o*. Pictorial representation is successful when it goes unnoticed, when we see through it rather than see it, and that can be achieved by painted and photographic representation alike.

Having said all that I now turn around and say that a picture need not be used as a tool for seeing. It can also be used as a repository of images, the looks of things. We *can* see phenomena, namely, images, the (nonexistent) ways things appear to us. We may see physical objects *through* a picture, but we can also see an image, a phenomenon, a look captured in a picture. One may, but need not, reify appearances. When you see the president on TV, you are not usually aware of the image on the screen; you see the president directly. Suppose, however, that your television set is one of those which can manipulate the image: you magnify it, tilt it, freeze it, twist it, impose a stored image on it, or print it. Now it is quite natural to say, as I just did, that you see an image of the president, not the president himself, on the screen. So, what you see depends, to a high degree, on you: if the president interests you more than his image, he is your intentional object. If you are interested in the image (as your manipulation of it indicates) more than in the person it represents, you perceive a phenomenon, an image that does not exist.

Interest also explains why we regard looking at a photograph as looking at the object photographed much more often than we regard looking at a painting as looking at the object painted. Looking at Cézanne's painting of his woodstove, you are normally not interested in that woodstove; the way Cézanne saw it is of much greater interest to you, so you think of yourself as seeing the image he saw, that look of the woodstove. On the other hand, a photograph of your son costs only pennies to produce, while he is what you cherish most in the whole world, so, naturally, you take yourself to be seeing him and not his photographic likeness (image).

Seeing an image is not epistemically prior to seeing the pictured object: an image is not an epistemic "simple" that we see with a "naked eye"; no concepts are involved. The Myth of the Given is, indeed, a myth: Images, like the things whose images they are, require a conceptual framework to be seen as such. Whether it is the president or his electronic image that you see depends on your interest and perceptual ability, but it takes training to become aware of either one of them. We teach our children how to see things by means of pictures, but we also teach them to see images as such. You can see, be visually aware, of either object, but if you reify one you cannot reify the other.[11]

A painting *may*, then, have a phenomenal object. Instead of seeing Cézanne's stove through the painting, you may see it as a representation of Cézanne's stove, as holding an image of that stove. But you do not *have* to do this: You need not see a woodstove image in the painting. You need not reify images as you need not reify sights or sounds. You may see Cézanne's stove just as you see yours: directly. Goodman is right that a person ignorant of the conventions of western painting may see the painting yet fail to see the stove, but the opposite is also true: a person lacking the notion of painting may see the stove by means of the painting but not see the painting as holding an image of it (a perfect *trompe l'oeil*). Neither of these objects is epistemically primitive, needing no concepts to be seen. Images as well as stoves require concepts to be seen as such; seeing either one is a complex task that those who lack the relevant concepts will fail. The dyad, *a* Represents *b*, is, therefore, not a relation at all. Representation is a monadic property of a perceptual state P. It is not the causal relation between *a* and *b* that explains representation. Rather, the alternative of positing *a* or else positing *b* shows what representation is.

A perceptual state P is caused by ambient nature, but physics does not say what item in P's past (in the lightcone defined by its spatiotemporal location) is the one perceived; that depends on our interests. When I look at a puddle, do I see water, the light it reflects, or the sun? It all depends on what I treat intentionally. If the puddle is oil, that is, crushed wood, do I see wood as crushed, or the things that crushed it? Oil represents wood, or the sun, or whatever, but that dyadic relation is parasitic on a (monadic) seeing some visual object as disclosed by the oil, that is, on what is intentionally posited. A painting, too, can be taken to represent anything of its causal past; what we do see via it (or, see it as representing) is determined, however, by our cognitive habits: our way of seeing-as.

One need not, therefore, be an idealist to hold that "what is represented is represented only on the sufferance of the larger 'aboutness' or Intentionality of the painting itself."[12] To regard *a* as a representation of *b* is to reify *a,* instead of using it as a tool for seeing *b* directly. But an image need not be reified, and no object need be designated as the one that we see by means of *a.* Instead of *a* representing, or being a tool for observing, one specific object, the whole world it opens up may be the object we posit in interpreting what it shows.

III

Now, the big question: Can you see Zeus? I argued that the museum guide can help us see Cézanne's woodstove, though it ceased to exist many years ago. I now add that this is true of Zeus, as well: We can also see Zeus, though Zeus has never existed. If you find that hard to believe, it is perhaps because you think that observation requires causal connections between the observer and the thing observed. Perhaps you believe that we see Cézanne's woodstove only because we are causally connected to it: a causal chain that started with photons reflected off of it, reached us. Zeus, on the other hand, never existed, and no chain of causes and effects links us to him, so we cannot see him. Seeing is believing, but we do not believe in Zeus.

All these beliefs, however, are false. We see things that never existed, hence are not causally connected to us; in fact, we see no other things. My argument for that thesis is based on scientific realism; it will not convince those who think that physics has nothing to say about reality. However, addressing those who maintain that the success of science justifies a tentative acceptance of its ontology, I ask: May we believe that the objects ordinary perception presents us with—the blue sky, the green grass, that woodstove, this table—things that populate the world Wilfrid Sellars called 'The Manifest Image' (as distinguished from The Scientific Image)[13] also exist? I think not.

Here is a simple proof that no scene we see could exist in reality, based on the fact that propagation of light takes time. In every scene you see, some part is further away from you than other parts, so the light from it comes to you from a time earlier than their time. Therefore, the segments of every scene you see belong in different times and have never coexisted. Thus no scene we see can be real, for its parts come from different times; when some of them existed others did not. Thus no seen scene is real; everything we see is a collage, a chimera concocted out of noncontemporary bits.

But each bit of the scene is real! Is it? Some scientific realists think that the ontology of physics can live with the ontology of common sense. Atoms exist, and so do tables and stoves. How are they related? The answer usually given is that atoms are the building blocks out of which molar things are constructed. Like Sellars, I think this is impossible. Sellars asks how can a thoroughly pink cube have only colorless constituents? Whence its color? Here the Building-Block metaphor breaks down: molar things have color, so you can not build them out of building blocks that have no color. I think that Sellars's objection is decisive, but let us ignore it for a while, for weightier ones are coming.

Locke tries to convince you that this table is shorn of color and of all other secondary properties. I think that is conceptually impossible, but let us ignore that objection, too. Let us consider primary properties only. Take, for example, shape: this table has no color, says Locke, but it is truly square; that is, all its sides are of equal length. Can there be anything such as that in reality? No. Relativity says that the question, whether a spatial interval x is larger than, smaller than, or equal to a spatial interval y has no sense in our world: for all spatial distances x and y, both "$x > y$" and "$y > x$" are true, depending on choice of framework. There are equal and unequal spatiotemporal intervals in reality, but no spatial ones. just as nothing in space is above or below another, so nothing in reality is the same length as another; thus the predicate "square" can have no compliants in the real world. Perhaps you can (I cannot!) conceive a table that has no color, but you cannot conceive of a table that has no shape.

Now, if there is anything I know, I know that this table is square, and that this disk is round. Foregoing such rock-bottom beliefs is tantamount to a loss of sanity. If I lose faith in simple truisms, I can believe nothing. Our applying "square" to this table is a paradigm of applying descriptive predicates, and if it is discredited, no empirical predicate can be applied to anything. I therefore maintain that "this table is square" is true. But I have just shown that nothing in the real world is square. Therefore, this table is not in the real world. The sentence "this table is square" is true because it is meant to be evaluated, not in reality, but in an unreal possible world, the world of Common Sense, the world of human phenomena, and in that world the said sentence is, indeed, true.[14]

A world is a mereological whole of compatible states of affairs (those whose descriptions do not contradict each other) and objects that constitute those states. This view is captured in the following axiom-schemata:

IV: True('Fa', w) ≡ ($Fa \in w$).

In words: the sentence 'Fa' is true in a world w iff the state of affairs Fa occurs in w. (Epsilon signifies overlapping, not set membership; italics signify thinghood.)

V: ~($Fa \rightarrow$ ~Gb) ≡ [($Fa \in w$) & ($Gb \in w$)].

In words: if two sentences do not contradict each other, their corresponding states of affairs occur in the same world.

VI: ($Fa \in w$) → ($a \in w$).

In words: if a state of affairs Fa occurs in a world, the object a occurs in that world, too.

I claimed that the sentence "this table is square" is true. It is true iff it is satisfied at the world where it is intended to be evaluated. What world is that? Not the real one, where spatial distances are neither equal nor unequal. It must therefore be meant to be satisfied in some other world, a world where it can be true. By (IV), if "this table is square" is true, the state of affairs which is its truthmaker occurs in some world, and by (VI) this table occurs in it, too. That world is the commonsense world, the world of phenomena, our *Lebenswelt*, the world we know and which we usually take to be real. That world, however, is not real; reality is not a familiar landscape.

The strongest arguments against the reality of this table come from quantum mechanics. For instance, in QM elementary particles are also describable as waves; that has far-reaching implications for the thesis that molar objects are "built out of" molecular ones. For example, this table is right here in this room, nowhere else. It is neither in India nor in Africa and certainly not in the Andromeda galaxy; it is, all of it, located in one clearly demarcated area in 3-space, and it stays put in there even when no one checks up on it. Is there in reality anything that has that trait? The answer is, again, No. No elementary particle is, when its location is unchecked, in any one place in spacetime. When not in a location eigenstate, it is in *all* places; it is represented by a wave function that has a nonzero value throughout the world. Now a congregation of ubiquitous things is still ubiquitous, so if the table consists of elementary particles, it is in a superposition of places all over the world, in China as well as in the Andromeda galaxy. Yet the table is not ubiquitous, it is in this place only and nowhere else, so it is not a congregation of elementary particles.

This table has both location and velocity: We can know where it is and where (and how fast) it goes at any time. None of its alleged building bricks, the elementary particles, have that feature; observed, they acquire one property and are in a superposition of all the others. Were tables made of particles, the particles would have both location and velocity at a time, for if at T the table is in L and moves at speed V so do all its parts. Thus, elementary particles are not parts of things; a thing cannot be in an eigenstate of one property only. In the sense in which a brick wall is made of bricks, a table cannot be made of elementary particles: they belong in different worlds. Now since (by science) elementary particles do exist and make up all material reality, this table does not exist; it is an appearance, a phenomenon.

This table has its properties regardless of what happens outside its light cone's past section. It has nothing to do with events that cannot causally influence it. Is that true of anything in reality? No. Bell's inequalities show that nothing in reality is what it is independently of what is elsewhere observed, even in regions too far to have a causal impact on it. This table is a commonsense object, an Aristotelian substance, but Bell proved that no Aristotelian substances exist. Therefore, this table does not exist.

IV

If the molar world does not exist, if it is a phenomenon only, how can its events serve as evidence for science, which purports to describe the real world? And *vice versa*: science explains and predicts events in the molar world; if the molar world is phenomenal, hence nonexistent, how can a theory about reality explain it?

My answer to the first question is that although traits of the molar world are cited as evidence for and against a scientific theory, they are not so used because they are traits of the commonsense world; statements about the molar world, too, must be supported by evidence. A mere set of statements about the molar world is just a story; like any other story or fairy tale, it is unworthy of belief and does not require scientific explanation. The unique feature of those statements about the molar world which serve as evidence for science is that they are *empirical*. They are statements about experience. For example, the statement "the dial moved," if accepted without evidence, or if its evidence is nonempirical (say, it is a dogma of some religion), is no evidence for science, because it is itself unbeliefworthy. It is used as evidence for science only if it is based on experience, that is, if the reason for believing it is that some observer saw, heard, or otherwise sensed as if the dial moved. The ultimate evidence for science is, then, beliefs about mental events: experiences. These beliefs are not about phenomena but about events in the real world, for experiences (although not their content) are real events. Thus, evidence for science comes from beliefs about the real world.

My answer to the second question is that science explains the phenomena because the molar *supervenes on* the molecular. Moreover, statements about molar things are true *because* some statements about elementary particles are true. That does not imply that tables are "made of" particles. Rather, that descriptions of tables are irreducible to descriptions of particles despite the supervenience of the former on the latter indicates that tables do not exist.

To explain this point, I must first clarify what kind of supervenience is involved here. Usually, a set of properties A is said to supervene on a set of properties B with respect to a domain D. Thus, we say that A properties supervene on B properties if objects in D cannot have the same B properties unless they have the same A properties. That is, however, not the kind of supervenience we have here, for molar objects do not have quantum properties and elementary particles have no phenomenal properties. We need supervenience for multiple domains of one of the kinds discussed by Kim,[15] that is, when distribution of B properties in domain D uniquely determines the distribution of A properties in domain D*.

What explains that supervenience? It can be explained by identity: If A properties are reducible to B properties, then it is clear why As supervene on Bs. That is not the case here, however, for phenomenal properties are not reducible to properties mentioned by physics. Another possible reason is causal connection: If x's in D having a certain B property causes y in D* to have a certain A property, then again it is clear why As supervene on Bs. But that is not the case here either: quarks, leptons, and gluons do not causally interact with chairs and tables. The only other plausible explanation for the supervenience in question is that D*, the domain of the A properties, is unreal. The objects in D* do not exist, and A properties are attributed to them *because* certain B properties are attributed to certain objects in D.

Here are some examples. It is correct to attribute the property of being a prince to Hamlet *because* Shakespeare wrote certain words; all properties of fictional entities supervene on features of words. Yet Hamlet is not made of Shakespeare's words, nor does he causally interact with them. What explains that supervenience of his properties on real properties of words is the nonexistence of domain of the supervenients. For another example, suppose that the tribe T has a false, but successful, medical theory. If they say that Abu and Babu are possessed by the same demon, we find that they have the same illness, and so forth. Thus, the T theory dovetails medicine, that is, demon-properties in the tribe's belief-world supervene on virus-properties in the real world. Now, demons are not made of viruses nor do they causally interact with viruses; rather, the truth of statements about demons covaries with the truth of statements about viruses because there are no demons.

Finally, consider antirealism in ethics. All ethical properties supervene on nonethical properties, yet are not reducible to them. Antirealists explain that by saying that there are no ethical properties. The attribution of ethical predicates is determined by sociological properties, and so we can tell which ethical statement is true although we cannot check things for ethical properties (there are none).

The case of this table is similar. It is a commonsense thing, a physical substance, but the real world has no place for it. Real entities cannot be parts of substances. A part of a physical thing is a physical thing, too, but no physical thing can obey the quantized equations of motion, where each physical state is an addition or subtraction of other physical states (represented by added or subtracted vectors). In the sense in which a brick wall is made of bricks, this table is not made of elementary particles. Because elementary particles make up all the matter in the real world, this table has no place in it; it never existed. It is a denizen of a different world.

I summarize. The various ways in which the world appears to us may be reified, that is, considered as objects, although they do not exist. Nonexistents can be observed; seeing aids help us observe them. For example, we can see Zeus by using a painting as our seeing aid, and we can see tables by using binoculars, though neither Zeus, nor tables, exist. Why Zeus has the properties we observe him to have is explained by investigating Greek culture, not the gods. Similarly, why tables have the properties we observe them to have is explained by investigating elementary particles, not molar objects.

V

We now have a proof that the causal theory of perception, that is, the view that to perceive an object, x, one needs causally to interact with x, is false.

1. I (the experiencer) exist.	(Truism)
2. I am in the real world.	(1)
3. I see this table.	(Truism)
4. This table is square.	(Truism)
5. Nothing in the real world is square.	(Relativity, QM)
6. This table is not in the real world.	(4,5)
7. Items in distinct worlds cannot causally interact.	(V)
8. I do not causally interact with this table.	(2,6,7)
9. Seeing requires no causal interaction.	(3,8)

One way of countering this proof is to deny (4): Say that though the table appears square, it is not square. A crypto-Lockean (or, a Kripko-Lockean) may try this gambit: "I refer to this table by ostension, so 'this table' denotes the real thing I point to now, whether it is square or not."

Can "this table" be defined by ostension, regardless of the properties we wrongly attribute to it? Certainly not. Wittgenstein has shown that one cannot single out an object by sticking a finger at it; that is no definition. Outside the context of a discourse, with no description in mind, purported ostensive definitions cannot nail down anything in particular. For an ostensive definition to work, we need to know at least the following: Is the indicated object to be found inside the space indicated or is it just identified by means of it? Where in relation to the finger and how far from it is the indicated object supposed to be? How big is it (a city or a pea)? How cohesive is it (a compact or a scattered object)? With no rules and concepts to specify the kind of thing defined by ostension, a stuck out finger indicates all and nothing.

For ostensive definitions to work, the world must be a 3-D space of fixed distances and directions, inhabited by stable, sharply demarcated molar objects that have colors and other perceptible salient traits. But these features belong in the Manifest Image; they are in the commonsense world and not in the real world as portrayed by modern science. Donnellan[16] is right that a true description is not necessary for successful reference; we can successfully indicate a certain thing even though our description of it is inadequate. But the items that science talks about are not Aristotelian things, they are not in the same category as the molar objects that satisfy our descriptions. Thus, the pious hope that my term "this table" picks out one specific thing in reality, a thing that roughly corresponds to my commonsense table as I know it, is bogus. Apparently, there are no individual self-identical things in reality: The question "is this the same boson we met before or a new one?" has no sense; bosons (e.g., photons) are more like a level of energy than like a thing whose energy is measured, a disturbance rather than an object. To a lesser extent that is true of fermions (e.g., electrons); they, too, are not things, because the question whether the electron emitted by the atom is the same as or different from the electron previously swallowed by it, makes no sense. Ostensive definitions cannot pick out such entities.

A Causal Theorist may reply: "The term 'this table' denotes not a phenomenon but the real thing that is its cause. The real thing causes us to see it as colored, in 3-space, as square, etc. A phenomenon *represents* a real thing. The represented object is what causes observers to represent it through such-and-such phenomena." That is a bold move, but it, too, fails, for the notion of *the cause* it uses is not science's, but a commonsense, interest-relative, notion. What is "the" cause of this traffic accident—the driver's drinking, his driving, the invention of automobiles, or the big bang? These and infinitely many other events are necessary for the accident to have happened. *The* cause of x in physics is *all* the events in the past—section of x's light-cone. That cause is not a nice solid table-sized object but a vast chunk of spacetime. Coloring-book metaphysics such as Plato's and Eddington's, holding that there is a noumenal table that is not very much unlike our phenomenal, garden-variety table, pathetically fails to grasp how different is reality from our phenomenal world.

Perhaps one may reject (3), saying that "I see the table" is not true but truthvalueless, because like all thing—terms "this table" denotes nothing; when we speak of molar objects we say nothing. That view, however, is self-defeating, for if ordinary discourse fails to refer to anything at all then it is just babble, and has no meaning, for no one can learn what our terms mean. Even the statement that thing-terms do not refer does not refer to thing-terms, for "thing-term" is a thing term. The only way is, then, to admit that thing-terms do denote what they purport to denote (e.g., tables), but the things they denote are not real: they occur in possible worlds other than the real one. We can visually project such worlds, and one of them, the world of common sense, is such that human beings who believe in its reality are more likely to survive than those who do not. That world, however, does not exist; it is, as Kant said, a phenomenon. But phenomena can be seen: visibility does not require existence.

Margolis, who says that representation is monadic, for the world that a painting opens up may have entities that are unique to it, is thus on the right track: Looking for the real object that the table represents may be conceptually confused, for a culture need not structure its cultural worlds so as to adumbrate the ways of the real world. The table is an object we intentionally posit and observe in one commonsense world; the lady that Vermeer lets us observe by his *Lady Reading a Letter at an Open Window* is in another world; and Zeus, another nonexistent who, thanks to Greek art and culture, we can literally see, inhabits yet another kind of possible world.

Having started from scientific realism, we arrive, with respect to the commonsense world, to a view similar to Margolis's: *that* world (albeit not the real one) results from a symbiosis of reality with human concepts and categories. The Manifest Image is culture-constituted, it is a world based on the world-building conceptual strategies of a society. Because those strategies and systems change in the course of history (culture is in flux), we can say of the Manifest Image what Margolis says about the real world: that it is in flux, or (which is the same thing) that there are many common-sense worlds, constituted by the various cultural practices of human beings, that is, by their various ways of life.

VI

To reject the Causal Theory of Perception is not to deny that reality influences perceptual states. Perceiving this table, or Zeus, are real events; they take place in the real world and hence are causally connected to whatever else takes place in it. What is false is only that causal influence is exerted by the intentional objects of perception. My intentional object is this table, but it is a phenomenon, it does not exist, hence it did not cause my experience. As Margolis says, the objects we are conscious of are suffused with cultural categories, they are based on the human range of sensitivities, hence (I add) they do not exist. I see this square table, the blue sky, the green grass, Cézanne's woodstove and the God Zeus, yet none of them exists.

Watching *Gone with the Wind,* my visual experience of Scarlett O'Hara is real, but Scarlett is not, so she is not the cause of my experience that posits her as its intentional object. Materialists hold that my awareness of Scarlett is an event in my brain, dualists deny that, but both should agree that it is not an event of the commonsense world. The manifest world, the world as I find it (to quote Wittgenstein in the *Tractatus*) cannot contain its own representing. Because consciousness, be it material or spiritual, is real, it cannot causally interact with the mere possibilia that it represents, its phenomena.

Because neither Zeus nor this table exist, how do they ontologically differ? Not in reality, perceptibility, or causal impact on the observer. In these respects, Zeus and this table are alike: They inhabit not the real world but mere possible worlds that we project and envisage. But they do differ. Zeus inhabits a different kind of possible world than the commonsense worlds that host this table. Merely possible worlds do not exist, but they differ in other ways. Common sense successfully manipulates reality; it works for us:

Thinking it is real facilitates human action and is highly conducive to our survival. It is good for us to hold that time passes, that things are located in absolute space, that things have color and shape, that each event has a cause, although all these beliefs are false of reality. Evolution adapted us to accept the commonsense world as an operator is trained to think in terms of the tools he uses, never worrying about what makes them work. Molar things are our guide for action, and belief in their reality makes us thrive. That is the "animal belief" Santayana spoke of: We need the illusion of molar things. The *Lebenswelt* is a necessity of life and is thus more important to us than worlds that play no such role, worlds cast by creative imagination. We envisage worlds that satisfy Greek mythology, those where Zeus has pride of place, but they are poor aids to survival. Such worlds are valuable for other reasons; we enjoy them and are instructed by them, too. We visualize things in these worlds through art and culture; art and culture make us see entities in mythological worlds, and so we get to see Zeus.

I said that we can see the actor himself on television rather than a mere electronic image that represents him. But an actor, too, functions as an image-bearing television screen with respect to the object he represents. In a production of *Hamlet* you may see, not an actor who duly represents Hamlet, but Hamlet himself as he is in the target worlds of *Hamlet,* those worlds that Shakespeare, in his play *Hamlet,* has opened up for us.[17] Just as when you look at Vermeer's painting you need not see an image that represents a Letter Reader, for you can see the Letter Reader herself, you can see in a theater more than actors strutting on a stage. Like a painted canvas, an actor can make you directly see things in other possible worlds. Once we relinquish the superstition that a causal interaction with an object is a necessary condition for seeing it (as I argued, that condition is *never* satisfied), there is no reason to deny that we can see Hamlet himself in a target world of *Hamlet,* a world that complies with the constitutive vision of the author, the director, and the actors.

Margolis argues:

> *no* painting is primarily a representation, in that it does not substitute or stand in or is imagined to stand in for another thing but discloses—uniquely, to those rightly trained in the pertinent cul-

tural skills and practices—a visible "world" not otherwise thus accessible.[18]

My argument was meant to establish the same claim. The tenet that "aboutness is not exclusively representational,"[19] far from contradicting scientific realism, is, I think, a natural development of it.

VII

What is the value of nonrepresentational and nonfigurative art? Is it not a counterexample to the view that art constitutes of possible worlds? Margolis, I think, concedes too much to the opposition when he says that

> There *are* "objects" represented in the Vermeer, then; there are none in the Kandinsky. But both are "expressive" in the generous sense conceded, the (grammatical) sense of being intransitively "about" the artifactual visible "world", the one made accessible only through the two-dimensional painted surface of each of those canvases.[20]

How can a Kandinsky express a world unless it represents some of it? It cannot be about a world if it is about nothing in it. If a Kandinsky must be seen as representing nothing, what is there to distinguish its expressing *w* from an essay about *w*? If some art is nonrepresentational, if a Rothko or a Kandinsky are about no object, then the theory of art as monadically representative is untenable, and we are back in Goodman's yard, looking for a language that is Art. I thus think that, via a Kandinsky or a Rothko, we can see individual things.

Most Rothkos are about despair, death, and depression; Kandinskys are often about hope and happiness. Are these individuals? Yes. In my nominalistic logic,[21] terms like "on," "blue," and "cat" are construed as names of material things that, like all other material things, recur at many indices. *On* is found wherever one thing is on another, and *there* it consists of these things so arranged; *cat* is found wherever matter is so-and-thus-ly shaped, and *there* it consists of that thus-shaped matter. We learn the word "sad" when sad people are pointed out to us. This *is* sadness: it is the thing that recurs at all and only those items to which we rightly apply the predicate, "sad."

Man is a material thing that recurs at all and only those indices where there is a man, that is, at all the items to which we may correctly apply the term "man." So Man and Sad may overlap: at the index I, these two things are identical: ($M =_I S$). To say that all men are sad is to say that wherever Man is, Sad is also to be found ($M =_M S$), and to say that none but men are sad is to say that Man and Sad are identical (not at Man, but) at Sad: $M =_s S$. "Plato is sad" is thus expressed in my Logic by "$P =_P S$."

Sad is, then, an individual thing that recurs at many indices, including many worlds, and at each index it is identical with some other things. Rothko's work is about that individual thing: Sad. The Rothko target-worlds are worlds in which what these works say is *true*; these are worlds dominated by sadness, horror worlds in which no hope can be found. Sad, Stalin, and Zeus are individuals that artworks may represent, allowing us to see them. Sad and Stalin have occurrences in the real world (as well as in others) whereas Zeus does not; He only occurs in unreal worlds. In some of those worlds Zeus is just as the Greeks described him; these are the target-worlds of Greek Mythology.

I conclude with a test case for the present theory of pictorial representation. Rembrandt used Hendrickje, his wife, as a model for his picture of the biblical Bathsheba. If the picture is a device for observing an object in a world that the picture opens up for inspection, who is it that we see there by means of the picture, Hendrickje or Bathsheba? It cannot be both, for Hendrickje and Bathsheba are different persons. Causal theories must say that the painting is about Hendrickje, for Rembrandt had no immediate causal commerce with Bathsheba. Furthermore, if Bathsheba never existed, that answer becomes mandatory for the causal theorist. But that is the wrong answer.[22] Rembrandt intended to picture Bathsheba and merely used his wife to enhance his imagination, just as he had used a new, wide brush, or a drink, or the biblical text, to inspire and help him in his portrayal of Bathsheba.

But how can the person we see in the painting be the Lady

Bathsheba herself, if Bathsheba, supposedly a tenth-century B.C.E. Israelite, did not look anything like the seventeenth-century Dutch-looking women we see in the picture? The answer is that although Bathsheba did not look like that in reality, she *could* have looked that way. Logically, she could have looked like Hendrickje and dressed like Hendrickje. That is tantamount to saying that in some world *w* Bathsheba *does* look like that, and that world *w* is the one in which we see her thanks to Rembrandt's constitutive intention. If Bathsheba is a literary figure, then the world *w* where we see her (*via* Rembrandt's picture) is not one of the bible's target-worlds, for in *w* Bathsheba does not comply with the description and historical background implied by the biblical text. Yet *w* is a world where Bathsheba does occur, and in which she has other features (not represented in Rembrandt's painting) that the Bible imputes to her. Why did Rembrandt open up *w* for us to see Bathsheba in it? Because *w* is an interesting and edifying world, and one beautiful scene in it, a scene that involves Bathsheba, is very much worth our while to observe.

A last remark. During the last thirty years, starting with Goodman's *Languages of Art,* there has been a steady drift in the philosophy of art toward conceiving plastic arts on the model of language. Paintings were regarded as texts to be interpreted, that is, as constituted by stipulation of values. I think that entire trend is wrong-headed, neglecting the visual foundation of visual art. You may read *Anna Karenina* from cover to cover and never see Anna, but you cannot watch the movie for a minute without seeing Anna herself. Painting and sculpture are like that, too: they do not denote things but show them to us. Of course, like all conceptual boundaries, the line between denoting and seeing, between description and depiction, is fuzzy, but that does not mean that there is no major distinction there.[23] Those who erase that line and reduce seeing to reading do great injustice to visual art.

NOTES

1. For my version of nominalism, see chaps. 1–3 of my *Types: Essays in Metaphysics* (Leiden: Brill, 1992).

2. J. Margolis, ed., *Philosophy Looks at the Arts,* 3d ed. (Philadelphia: Temple University Press, 1987), chap. 18 (hereafter, "Version I"); J. Margolis, *Interpretation Radical But Not Unruly* (Berkeley: University of California Press, 1995), chap. 4 (hereafter, "Version 11").

3. J. R. Searle, *Expression and Meaning* (Cambridge: Cambridge University Press, 1979), pp. 58–75.

4. K. L. Walton, *Mimesis as Make-Believe* (Cambridge, Mass.: Harvard University Press, 1990), pp. 217–20, 385–419.

5. I did so in "Existence and Nonexistents," *Erkenntnis* 39 (1993): 145–66 and in "Emotion and Fictional Beings," *Journal of Aesthetics and Art Criticism* 54 (1996): 41–48.

6. "Seeing, 'Seeing', and Feeling," *Review of Metaphysics* 23 (1969): 3–24.

7. In *fata morgana* cold air trapped between two layers of hot air functions as a long tube, allowing you to observe an oasis many miles away. An inexperienced traveler thinks the oasis is just ahead; rushing forward and finding nothing, he concludes that the whole scene was an illusion. That, I said, is a mistake.

8. G. Ryle, *The Concept of Mind* (London: Hutchinson, 1949), chap. 8.

9. K. L. Walton, "Transparent Pictures," *Critical Inquiry* 11 (1984): 246–77.

10. R. Scruton, *The Aesthetic Understanding* (London: Methuen, 1983), pp. 102–36.

11. For a discussion of that point, see P. Maynard, "Seeing Double," *Journal of Aesthetics and Art Criticism* 52 (1994): 155–67.

12. Version II.

13. See his *Science, Perception and Reality* (London: Routledge and Kegan Paul, 1963); and *Science and Metaphysics, Variations on Kantian Themes* (London: Routledge and Kegan Paul, 1967).

14. I hold that things *occur* in many words, but in only one world, the real world, do they have the property Existence (reality is the world where everything has that property). This table does not exist, that is, it does not occur in the real world, but it occurs in some other possible worlds, and in one of them, the Human-Common-Sense-World, it is square. For details cf. 5 above.

15. J. Kim, *Supervenience and the Mind* (Cambridge: Cambridge University Press, 1993), pp. 109–30.

16. K. Donnellan, "Reference and Definite Descriptions," *Philosophical Review* 75 (1966): 281–304.

17. The target worlds of Hamlet satisfy all that is said or implied in Hamlet, but they differ in facts not mentioned or implied in the play. See "Existence and Nonexistents."

18. Version I, 341–42.

19. Version II.

20. Version II.

21. See note 1.

22. Nicholas Wolterstorff discusses that question at length in *Works and*

Worlds of Art (Oxford: Oxford University Press, 1980) and concludes that the painting represents Bathsheba and not Hendrickje. I think that is correct, but for Wolterstorff (who follows Goodman), all that means is that a part of the picture is a *label* that stands for Bathsheba (see pp. 18–30, 262 ff.).

23. As explained, abstract art is a visual representation, hence a tool for seeing individual things such as hope and despair, though not people or tables. In Picasso's painting of Dora Maar, we can still see Ms. Maar, but in his *Ma Jolie,* which is supposed to depict Eva Gouel, she cannot be seen. Does that mean that *Ma Jolie* is a description and not a picture? No, for other physical things can be directly seen by means of it: joy and tenderness, for instance.

PART IV

Reply

Replies in Search of Self-Discovery

Joseph Margolis

I

I begin at an arbitrary beginning, but not arbitrarily. I may as well say at the start that I cannot imagine honoring any philosophical claims or charges if they are walled off too quickly from the salient questions of any sizable sector of professional inquiries, no matter how alien or exhausted they may seem. Philosophy is not a solitary exercise, though it has its stunning athletes, of course. Furthermore, I am convinced that now, at the end of the century, we are at the edge of a very large transformation of philosophical vision, one that may continue to be postponed for some time but cannot long be resisted. I think it will sweep out the principal doctrines of the canon that has dominated English-language philosophy for the better part of our century. We are bound to give up at least the following, I daresay: (1) that we can in principle occupy a neutral stance epistemically; (2) that there are *de re* necessities; (3) that, transhistorically, reason, whether theoretical or practical, has a normatively invariant structure; (4) that the seemingly complex structures of human existence and human culture are either not real or are reducible in physicalist terms; and (5) that an adequate theory of mind can be construed solipsistically, merely biologically, or subjectively, or in any way disjoined from our cognizing and legitimative powers. My own way of anticipating these changes is to postulate that the world is a flux, that thinking is historicized, and that selves are socially constructed and are or have histories rather than natures. Believing all this, I cannot agree with Laurent Stern, therefore, when he says, in the opening essay, opposing my own convictions, that "not much is lost if they [that is, Anglo-American analytic philosophers and continental European philosophers] ignore each other or are contemptuous of each other" (37). I don't see how that can be decided if the verdict has not been explicitly confirmed, and I think the evidence shows, on several counts, that it cannot be convincingly confirmed. All of my own efforts, as Stern knows, have acknowledged the *need* to achieve a certain rapprochement between the "two" traditions: on the analytic side—let me confine myself to that—at least in terms of the full role of history in the analysis of knowledge, our own natures, the nature of the real world, as well as in terms of the contingency and artifactual constitution of our rational and cognitive powers and our inability to fathom completely how that condition affects our claims to truth, objectivity, a grasp of what is real, any necessary constraints on reason and knowledge, and the like.

I take my resistance to Stern's judgment to be at least in accord with Aristotle's *Protepticus*: Even if we demur, we will have taken a philosophical stand—but we will not have earned it. Analytic philosophy (which I am unwilling to abandon) has been preposterous in its self-congratulation in dismissing the best work of continental philosophy, which (I am bound to say) has rightly called its own philosophical strategies in doubt. I am sorry to part company with Stern so quickly, because we agree, as he rightly says, on so much. But a great deal of analytic philosophy is unnecessarily self-crippling and deliberately illiterate about continental philosophy (hence, about its own resources). I remember, for instance, addressing the Philosophy Department at Syracuse University on the relationship between analytic and continental philosophy. The invitation had been tendered by the graduate students, but the first question out of the gate was Jonathan Bennett's. Bennett wanted to be given an "example" of a continental philosopher's argument that would pass muster on any criteria of analytic rigor. When I obliged, he thought for a moment and said with perfect candor: "Well, I guess there is at least one case."

Stern opposes my linking the theory of interpretation with the need to answer certain questions and with certain views of mine regarding the relevance of metaphysics and epistemology. He does not agree with me because he does not believe there is a connection, and he does not believe there is a connection because he does not share my views on "First Philosophy" (36–37). In fact, he believes "the philosophical study of the history of philosophy is an ahistorical study" (33). (I do not.) In any case, I think this means that he *does* have views on First Philosophy (he believes in First Philosophy: I do not); what he says commits him to addressing the same metaphysical and epistemological issues I favor and, if I may say so, commits him to investigating the bearing of continental views on history—which he eschews. He is caught by the *Protepticus,* as is Quine (I might add) whom he is surely glossing. He has other things to say about interpretation proper, to which I shall return. But I take advantage of his having opened the discussion in this way, because what he says ramifies unexepectedly through a number of the other papers of the collection. I shall come back to these as well. But I'd rather not appear—if possible—to be merely an argumentative fool.

Let me, therefore, come to what I have barely broached (in mentioning Stern's views) by way of a more constructive, perhaps a less familiar, strategy. I can be brief about it, because there is a full and accurate summary of what I have in mind in Michael Krausz's contribution. I suppose my central intuition is that the world is a flux. I don't mean that I have the evidence that it *is* a flux, although I concede that there may be logically inconclusive (but plausible) arguments to show that I am mistaken. I don't believe there can be strict confirmatory evidence on either side. I insist on the symmetry of this asymmetry. I insist that I may be mistaken, but that I cannot *show* that I am right! (The matter bears on the logic of relativism, but I shall postpone examining it.) On my usage, the "doctrine" of the flux is a *myth*—not capable of being true, not (I trust) false as such, yet it *is* indirectly falsifiable by the indirection of falsifying (if we can falsify) what may otherwise be affirmed (and therefore found false) that would have to be reconciled with the flux itself. What would remain might no longer be congenial to its vision.

The "doctrine" of the flux is a philosophical *bet*—a bit like the work of negative theology (or deconstruction, for that matter)—that recommends itself in the way of a *faute de mieux* vision, one that rises parasitically on the defeat of *all* truth-claims congenial to the opposite vision: The doctrine that reality necessarily possesses an invariant structure and that human understanding consists essentially in grasping that structure. The strongest version of this thesis known to me is Aristotle's, in *Metaphysics* Gamma (where Aristotle claims to expose the fatal error in Protagoras). I claim that there are no known arguments that successfully show that reality *does* necessarily (or "modally") possess an invariant structure. I cannot pretend to have canvassed all the relevant arguments, and I cannot (in showing merely that I know of no successful arguments) *show that it is necessarily true that there are none!*

Most critics suppose that I have been drawn to commit a blunder here. I deny it; but it is the point of my opposing Stern's judgment. The clearest version of the charge occurs in Carl Page's extremely interesting new book, *Philosophical Historicism and the Betrayal of First Philosophy.*[1] (I find a related argument in Gail Soffer's contribution to this collection, and another implicit in Jitendra Mohanty's contribution. I shall touch on them later.) Page addresses my views on historicism and the flux and (if I'm not mistaken) consigns my view to self-defeating paradox. (He writes, I believe, as a former student of Stanley Rosen's and a champion of First Philosophy.) He treats me more kindly than he does Richard Rorty, but the objection remains very much the same. I can hardly imagine a slimmer and more transparent specimen of the view that I heartily oppose. Here, then, is what Page says (he draws the exemplifying passages from my *Pragmatism without Foundations* [48] and from *Texts without Referents* [371]:

> Historicism [is committed] to what I shall call the *idiom of universality.* It is committed on two main counts. First, philosophical historicism is consistent with and embraces universality as a cognitive ideal. . . . Second, universality appears not only in the domain to which philosophical historicism applies, but also in the statement of the doctrine itself. Historicism asserts that all forms of human judgment will always be situated within and deter-

mined by an essentially contingent framework and that no form
of human judgment can in principle transcend that contingent sit-
uatedness in any final way.

Page finds that Hans-Georg Gadamer explicitly embraces the
paradox. About me, he says: "Margolis is a little more indirect: *The
human condition* [according to Margolis] is such that *all* claims of
universal invariances are problematic in a sense in which general
claims are not."[2]

Page has missed the essential point. I am not being "a little
more indirect"; *I am not making any universal claims about the flux
at all!* That is precisely what I mean by a "philosophical bet." I have
traced the issue in Stanley Rosen's view of First Philosophy (Page's
mentor) and in Aristotle's *Metaphysics,* where the thesis receives its
classic form.[3] My point is that we are (I am) entitled to a *faute de
mieux* stand on the basis of having demonstrated (if I have) that the
claims of modal necessity fail in all known particular cases. My
stand, then, is only logically—not philosophically—weak. Obviously, it would produce a self-defeating paradox if it were construed
as a universally binding principle. I should add (against the real
meaning of Stern's remark) that Quine and Donald Davidson are
also committed to a form of First Philosophy, though they rather
cleverly hide the fact. (I should also add—very lightly—that Stern
suggests that I have been unfair to Davidson. This is not the place
to pursue the matter, but I have given a fuller account of the relevance of the passage Stern cites in the *Interpretation* volume. I ask
you only to have a look at that.[4] There's no question that Davidson's
views and mine are diametrically opposed. More than that, I take
Davidson to be mistaken on nearly every philosophical issue he has
ever touched, and I believe I have shown that that is so—in the
longer paper I mention and in several other accounts. In fact, I know
of no other similarly sustained account, although Ian Hacking and
others have drawn attention to Davidson's more than curious philosophical lapses. Even more than that, I am persuaded that *Stern*
would not be able to square the thesis he says he shares with me—
namely, that "interpretation is constitutive of history" (1)—with
Davidson's theory of "radical translation." My view, you see, is that
even if one eschews historicism (with Stern), ahistorical philoso-

phies require intervening interpretive *tertia* (Rorty's term), unless one opts for one or another form of cognitive privilege. It's for that reason that I believe Stern's argument is a non sequitur.

I exclude Rorty's postmodernism here, because, in my opinion, Rorty is a self-selected victim of a self-defeating paradox. Rorty believes (wrongly, I believe) that all second-order legitimative arguments are (if viable at all) transcendental arguments, that all transcendental arguments illicitly invoke some form or other of cognitive privilege, and that (as a consequence) first-order inquiries can (and should) be detached from second-order considerations.[5] Which is to say: philosophy is *kaput*. I say that that is incoherent— the very mark of Rortyan "postmodernism." My own claim is that first-order inquiries are blind without second-order inquiries, that second-order inquiries are empty without first-order inquiries, and that the distinction between the two is itself a second-order distinction.[6] It is not possible, on my view, that either first- or second-order inquiries make sense when separated from the other. If you construe this judgment in terms of a historicized and constructivist account of the self—as I do—then the need for a rapprochement between analytic and continental philosophy becomes patent.

I note in passing, therefore, that Richard Shusterman, who shares with me (as he remarks in his contribution to this collection) some themes of pragmatism, wishes to distance himself from the need for "metaphysical" inquiry (which he finds inordinately pursued in my own work). I think he cannot succeed in this and does not quite see why; also, *he* inadvertently concedes the point (against his own resistance and Rorty's) by admitting "considerable seepage and flexibility between [first- and second-order levels]" (199). (I take this to be tantamount to admitting the relevance of metaphysics—tacitly reversing himself. In any case, I see no formulable difference.) He agrees with me in discounting "the questionable motives and sources of invariance" (198). I take this to be (in his own work) a dabbling with metaphysics, but I shall not press the point. In any case, Shusterman says (mistakenly) that Margolis "confines his new locutions [e.g., "unicity," "intentional," "lingual"] to what he calls second-order discourse, criticizing pragmatists like Rorty and Stanley Fish for rejecting this distinction and thus denying [a] role for second-order projects" (199).

Let me simply say (1) that "metaphysical" analysis is continuous with and inseparable from "scientific" analysis, hence present in both "first-" and "second-order" discourse; (2) that first- and second-order discourse are never more than "functionally" distinct - (as Shusterman also says), hence second-order discourse is not cognitively privileged and not addressed to any "higher grounding or justificational levels of inquiry" (199); (3) that metaphysics and second-order discourse are not ineluctably committed to modal necessity or invariance, hence are entirely compatible with endorsing the flux; and (4) that *any* "reconstruction" or philosophical invention—"advocating linguistic reforms . . . new ways of talking" (199)—cannot fail to be colored by constraints (1) and (2), hence implicate the distinction between first- and second-order discourse and the relevance of metaphysics. I cannot see how any of this can be can be denied without falling back to Rorty's incoherence, and, of course, my own work has been absorbed with "advocating . . . new ways of talking." I have no wish to discount any of Shusterman's own inventions, but I don't believe he can make out a viable difference here. To attempt to do so is, as I suggest, to fail in Rorty's way. (Fish's line of reasoning is slighter and, I think, more guarded.)

I agree in a general way with Rorty's attack on cognitive privilege (Kant's transcendentalism, for instance), though I am bound to say that Rorty is a *rapporteur* here. Nevertheless, in defeating certain second-order arguments, Rorty enlists an obvious non sequitur in disjoining first- and second-order discourse and then dismissing second-order discourse. Frankly, I think that that amounts to a return to First Philosophy under masked conditions. This is also how I understand Quine's and Davidson's "naturalisms." I fear Shusterman has fallen too far under Rorty's spell: he misses its illogic when, for instance, "speaking as a reconstructive pragmatist" (rather than a "descriptive-metaphysical" pragmatist—myself, apparently), Shusterman confesses: "I just don't see here [Margolis's] ontological constructions of the flux, which explicitly rest on discursive practice, provide any more robust grounding than those discursive practices themselves" (200). But that is the supposed point of Rorty's failed strategy: the insistence that ontology must be privileged *if admitted* and that the analysis *of* "discursive practices" *never implicates metaphysics.* Where is the argument?

I claim to be offering a fresh way of understanding our "discursive practices"—exhibiting (and defending) its *promise* (ontically, epistemically, logically, practically, normatively) against all the alternatives that I know. I say that Shusterman offers no responsible alternative here: He falls back to Rorty when he says the enterprise "seem[s] relatively pointless" (200). What, I ask, makes "reconstructive pragmatism" *reconstructive* if it is not engaged dialectically in something like the way I recommend? I see no plausible answer. "Metaphysics" need not be invariantist or privileged: There is no convincing disjunction between semantics and metaphysics (*contra* Carnap and Dummett) or between science and metaphysics (*contra* Popper). You may place Quine, Davidson, Putnam, Rorty— and Dewey—wherever you please in all this: It won't affect the bottom line in the least.

Here, I find Shusterman and Stern diametrically opposed to one another: Rorty himself, of course, is a devilishly equivocal figure drawn at one and the same time to Davidson's First Philosophy (Stern's option) and to rejecting canonical philosophy, apparently on the strength of interpreting Davidson (Shusterman's option). Otherwise, Shusterman owes us an explanation of *what* remains of philosophical work that does *not* fall under Rorty's knife.[7]

Shusterman goes on to say:

> Reconstructive pragmatism, as I construe and practice it, can recognize a functional distinction between these levels of discourse but it insists on considerable seepage and flexibility between them. It also insists that philosophy's poetic efforts of innovative discourse should be directed at first-order discourse, not simply at higher grounding or justificational levels of inquiry. (199)

For my part, though not for the sake of protest alone, the vocabulary I have been preparing—for instance in literary and art criticism, in the resolution of moral and political matters, in the interpretation of history and personal life, and even in the sciences—is intended to affect our *first-order* practices. I contend that the "seepage" of legitimative matters cannot fail to color what we find reasonable and unreasonable to recommend in *first-order inquiry*. The idea of the flux centers our attention in a powerful way, but there are actually subtler issues to explore. For the moment, I can say that I am *not* speaking of *any* "higher grounding or justificational levels." (That is "Rorty-speak.")

I see a clear connection between the doctrine of the flux and all my other themes: for instance, why First Philosophy fails, why relativism is unavoidable, why the puzzles of reference and predication undermine modal invariance, why rationality and objectivity are artifacts of human history, why the logic of interpretation depends on the metaphysics of culture, why first- and second-order questions are inseparable, and so on. The doctrine of the flux is, as I say, a *faute de mieux* conception (a "myth") of the entire universe generated—in a way that cannot be directly confirmed as a determinate truth-claim (or confirmed by approximative means)—from the failure of all known efforts to confirm one or another form of modal invariance (First Philosophy).

The argument is remarkably straightforward. Consider only this. Every truth-claim has meaning and is open to confirmation within some context or other of relevant evidence, and all such confirmatory evidence is itself evidentially secured in some further context. Let the *universe* be the "context of all contexts," and let a *world* be any relatively large, well-ordered context within which a range of truth-claims are regularly serviced (the physical world, for instance). Every "world," then, is contexted within the "universe." To say that the universe is the context of all contexts is merely to say that nothing we assert can be excluded from having a bearing on whatever else we assert. (It makes no sense to assign boundaries to the "universe.")

Call truth-claims a *discursive* use of language, or (simply) discursive acts; acknowledge, also, that discursive acts are *contexted,* meaning by that that they obtain within some "world" or, at the limit, within the inclusive "universe." Two theorems fall out at once: one, that there can be no discursive claims about the universe as such, though there can be about particular "worlds"; second, that discursive acts implicate a mythic use of language, meaning by that that not all the contexts of discursive acts can be themselves addressed discursively in turn. *If,* then, on a reasonable philosophical "bet," the universe is (mythically) pictured as a flux, then the contextedness of discourse precludes our supposing that *any world is a closed system,* because, on the hypothesis, (1) there are no modally necessary structures to affirm, and (2) the contexts in which truth-claims can be affirmed and confirmed cannot themselves be discursively exhausted.

On the argument, then, truth-claims cannot be reduced extensionally and cannot be confirmed in contextless ways; or, let us say, to whatever extent we treat discourse as extensional and context-free, our procedures and the "worlds" they subtend are already viewed as artifacts of our intentionally irreducible interests—whether in science or in literary criticism. Hence, at a stroke, such analytic models of language (or First Philosophy) as are offered in Quine's *Word and Object* and in Davidson's attempt to apply Tarski's semantic conception of truth to natural language (against Tarski's own conviction) are seen to be entirely without defense. But if that is so, then it is a foregone conclusion: (1) that the pursuit of first-order inquiries makes no sense without second-order direction, however subject the latter may be to the same contingencies, and (2) that there can be no way of justifying any methodology (in science or criticism) without theorizing about the metaphysics of its "objects." I take that to go completely against the philosophical advice of Davidson and Rorty and, for cognate reasons, against the views of Stern and Shusterman (and, as I have hinted in passing, against the views of Soffer and Mohanty).[8]

One way of collecting the notion I have in mind may be put as follows: *objectivity* is itself a provisional artifact of the reflexive critique of inquiry; it answers to the stablest parts of a society's experience and interests, but it can never validly claim to have reached that unique point—beyond constructions, beyond all limiting contexts, beyond history—at which the universe stands before us as the inclusive system that it is apart from human inquiry. *There is no such neutral stance.* (Here, I have sought to recover Thomas Kuhn's important claim—in section X of *The Structure of Scientific Revolutions*—against his principal detractors, and, I may as well say, against "final" Kuhn himself.) It may help to say that, in my view, *modernism* is the commitment to some sort of neutral stance, whether in science, in morality, in interpretation, or what have you. However different they may be, therefore, Quine and Davidson and Putnam (and now Stern) are modernists. So was Husserl (hence, also, Mohanty and Soffer). On this reading, postmodernists, are those who affirm, paradoxically, that there cannot be a neutral stance but that that doesn't matter because we are (after all) quite capable of knowing what we know and believe and understand and take to be factually the case. Lyotard and Rorty are, in different ways, the postmodernists of our day (hence, also, Shusterman, on the testimony of what he says). *Postmodernists, therefore, are modernists manqués.* The *poststructuralists,* I may add—preeminently, Derrida and Foucault and Barthes—are (at least initially) those French philosophers who, against the structuralists and, by courtesy, against Husserl and Hegel, reject the idea of a neutral stance but *not* objectivity as a social or historical artifact. (I am happy to admit that I have learned a great deal from their labors in this regard, though I am more impatient than they about the reconstructive work that's needed.)

I should also add, lest I be misunderstood, that I take it to follow from my argument that *realism* must be of a constructivist sort if it is viable at all; but that *that* does not entail that *reality* must also be a construction of the human mind. I have already acknowledged that human selves and human nature *are* social artifacts but physical nature need not be metaphysically "constructed" in the idealist's way—as a result of these admissions. For, although what is real may not be constructed, no truth-claim about the independent world can escape the constructivist constraints of our *realism.* Here, though I do not agree entirely with Nicholas Rescher's "pragmatic idealism," I think we converge at least on this.

II

I was aware, in beginning with the flux and in yielding to the deflections Stern's and Shusterman's remarks encourage, that the papers of this collection belong to an invisible conceptual unity drawn from the dialectical scatter of very different reflections—my own and those of others. Jitendra Mohanty's challenge confirms the impression of that unintended conspiracy: First, because Mohanty's questions give point to Stern's and Shusterman's opposed demurrers and help to determine just how serious their demurrers are, and because my own remarks about the flux anticipate part of the answer to Mohanty's questions. Mohanty queries historicism in general and my version of it in particular. But his doubts about historicism are really doubts about subaltern matters. His primary question is explicitly about the flux itself: "On what ground [he asks] is the premise 'everything is a flux' to be justified?" He says he knows of two arguments only: "one advanced by the Buddhists"; another that makes "use of elementary particle physics." Neither, he thinks, "can *prove* that things—all things—are in a flux" (263). Of course, I agree! I nowhere speak of *proof* of the flux. (*I oppose the idea.*) But, in agreeing, I do not accept the point of Mohanty's challenge. For, of course, Mohanty, too, is worried about any retreat from First Philosophy. It's a little uncanny to note the thread of argument that runs from Aristotle and Rosen (through Page) to Quine and Davidson (through Rorty and Stern and Shusterman) to Husserl (through Mohanty and Soffer).

I'm not certain that I understand Mohanty's reference to physics, unless he means that, on something like the Big Bang theory, none of the evolving structures of the known physical world are invariant—also, that there are no invariant laws governing the original Big Bang itself that would account in a necessary way for all the transformations that have evolved from it. This is what, as I understand matters, is meant by calling the Big Bang a "singularity." The Buddhist thesis is even more explicit (if I understand that much of it), for it construes all determinate structures as utterly provisional within the encompassing "space" of *sunyatta*. (I have, as Mohanty knows, been explicit in my admiration of Nāgārjuna.) But the answer, surely, is that the flux is a "bet" about the universe—on the failure of all First Philosophy—the unsecured presumption that there are "things" that are modally necessary.

There is a natural way to meet Mohanty's question. First, to establish whether the flux is affirmed as true or as a *faute de mieux* bet. (I have answered that.) Second, to determine whether the conception is internally coherent or paradoxical on its face. (I think Mohanty himself supposes it is coherent in the forms he mentions; I imagine he would extend the compliment to my own version.) Third, to show that no determinate claims about the "things" of our world commit us to any form of necessary invariance that would falsify the flux. (This is obviously what Mohanty thinks won't work.)

Mohanty's puzzles are formulated in terms of time and history, but they are not confined to either. For instance, he mentions "the Pythagorean theorem" and "the number 0." He says they are "objects" that "are not in time . . . in the sense that ascribing temporal predicates [to] them does not make sense" (263). I agree that "they" are not in time, but I cannot see how that affects either the doctrine of the flux or historicism. On my view, "they" are not things at all—except in the grammatical sense: They are nominalizations of what may be abstracted from our thought (the Pythagorean theorem) or what may be predicated of things (number). I see no reason to resist the invariance imputed to either *on the basis of* the definitions we make of each but I also see no necessity in adhering to Euclidean geometry (*pace* Kant and the Marburg Kantians) or to the function of "0" among the "natural" numbers. (I don't think theorems and numbers are "things" or "objects," in any case.)

I agree that flux, change, time, and history are not the same—and that there are variant views of each. I am content to treat time, with Aristotle, as the "measure of change," *if*, against Aristotle, it is possible to say so without supposing that whatever does change must also possess an invariant structure *in order to* change or to be intelligible as changing. (That is what I take Protagoras to have anticipated and Aristotle to have *misconstrued*.) Time itself is not a "thing" but an adverbial qualification of the predicables of change ascribed to things. It is another nominalization. I suspect Mohanty would find this too lax, but I don't see the basis for a demurrer. My remarks about time are meant to take the ontological bite out of his own theorems (1) and (2).

Theorem (1)—that "everything is in time"—now means what theorem (2) means—that "everything is [in] a process of change" (1). That is, I claim that nominalization accounts for any supposed distinction between (1) and (2)—as also with his use of the Pythagorean theorem, the number "0," and time itself. I agree I have not "proved (2), but I say it can't be done and it does not need to be done. Theorem (2), I should say, is no more than the "mythic" projection—with regard to the "universe"—of having shown that, in all determinate cases, no necessary invariance has been or can be proved.

So far, Mohanty's countercases do not succeed. I claim the shoe is on the other foot. Anyone who subscribes to First Philosophy or to necessary (real) invariances must *prove* that they are ineluctable. That is, it would hardly do to show that there were certain "necessary" or "universal" invariances, only to find that, when all is said and done, those invariances were not really necessary *if* we but introduce a change of "conceptual scheme." The point is very well stated in Tom Rockmore's contribution. It captures my view precisely (on that particular). On my reading, it is the nerve of Foucault's "archaeologies"—which, in *The Order of Things* and *The Archaeology of Knowledge,* is named the "historical *a priori.*" I am entirely comfortable with the idea, which goes some distance to explaining what I mean by "flux." Certainly, flux is not chaos, the total absence of order or intelligible order. It is also not anything like the transience of Hume's *official* philosophy of sense impressions, because Hume's official philosophy is utterly incapable of tracking any "ideas" or "impressions" at all—*any* intelligible order whatsoever. (That is why Hume abandons his official theory at every drop of his philosophical hat.) Flux, as I say, is the absence in the universe of any modal necessity—not the absence of any stable or intelligible structure in any "world." I cannot prove *that.* I don't need to. But I am prepared to prove that no determinate claim to the contrary works. (Hence, it holds against Frege's and Husserl's antipsychologism.)

It's when you come to Mohanty's theorem (3) that the challenge makes itself felt. Mohanty introduces, before he comes to (3), theorem (1*)—that "all experience is temporal" (2). But that was meant to be a deflection in the manner of theorem (1), because, of course, "the object of [any] experience may not be" temporal (in the sense already explored). As I say, nominalization takes care (it seems) of all the counterinstances (thus far). Theorem (3) holds that "all things are historical" (266). This mutates into theorem (3*)—that "all things of human significance are historical" (266)—on the strength of the thesis, theorem (4), that "history is history of meanings" (10). These adjustments are not troublesome in the least. Although I have my own way of wording Mohanty's point. I would not say that "all things are historical": stones are not. But *realism is* (on my argument) *historicized* and whatever we *posit* of independent reality is (accordingly) historicized. But *reality,* part or whole, may not be. (Remember: the world of culture is both real *and* historicized.)

Perhaps the most important adjustment to make, given Mohanty's penchant, is that there are no "meanings": meanings are not things but, once again, nominalizations of what may be abstracted from what is structured in certain ways. I shall come back to the issue, but let me simply say that, in my own ontology, cultural entities and phenomena have "Intentional" properties, which are "complex," indissolubly "incarnate" in physical or natural properties, and such as to range over linguistic, symbolic, semiotic, and related properties; correspondingly, the "objects" in question are "complex," indissolubly "embodied" in physical or natural "objects." This bears on the "emergence" of the cultural world with respect to the natural world—a complicated issue that requires separate attention. I mention these distinctions solely to make clear *why* I admit, as structures of predicables (Intentional structures, as I call them), such structures as permit us to abstract (but not to isolate) "meanings" in the manner of the nominalizations mentioned. For instance, Michelangelo's *Pietà* possesses (as a sculpture, *not* as a block of marble) certain representational properties: Those properties are incarnate in the properties of the marble, and the sculpture "emerges" ("embodied" in the marble) in a cultural space or world—in a sui generis way that reductive physicalism cannot account for. (Here, I am happy to share Marx Wartofsky's and Dale Jacquette's judgment that analytic reductionism is preposterous, even philosophically irresponsible, in not explaining how it avoids what I call "cultural realism"—the realism of Intentionally qualified phenomena.

The details are not yet needed here, only the sense that nothing so far mentioned leads to Mohanty's essential charge, namely, "that change, time and history all involve something invariant, abiding—if not everlasting." "This classical thesis," Mohanty adds, "seems to be opposed to what seems to be Margolis's fundamental thesis about flux and radical history" (269).

I don't see that Mohanty has established his point. I agree with his sense of my views but not with his assessment. I cannot see that his own idiom and claim are justified (in effect, the generic doctrine of which antipsychologism is a specific variant). I cannot see that Husserl or Frege have succeeded where Aristotle has failed.

Mohanty has other cards to play, of course. He gives us only an inkling of his argument. I must say a word about that, although what I can say leads only to a stalemate. (Here, I count stalemate a victory over First Philosophy *pro tem.*) Mohanty distinguishes a number of different notions of time and comes eventually to his option "(d) the inner, phenomenologically lived time in which the internal stream of consciousness flows" (264). It is only (d), he thinks, that leads us to an invariant structure—one that "promises to present a monistic framework, not for all things but for all experiences." He draws this out a little, characterizing "a stream of experience [as] constituting the mental life of a transcendental ego" (265). This is a complicated matter. I'm not sure how persuasive I can be to a skilled phenomenologist like Mohanty, but I must make the effort.

First of all, I cannot see that admitting (1*) entails as such the invariance of any "subject" of experience (a self or ego or mind or what not). I agree that it makes no sense to speak of experience without admitting a "subject" of experience. Strawson was surely right about the "no ownership" theory of experience. To that extent, I agree with Husserl as I do with Kant. Second, I confess I don't recognize the need for a "transcendental ego." In any case, I cannot see how a phenomenologically attentive "ego" can be different from or separated from a "natural" (or "naturalistic") ego or can have cognitive resources that are different or separable from the resources attributable to "naturalistic" egos (conceptually or metaphysically or epistemically). At the very least, the theory that would disjoin the two (in terms of cognitive resources) depends on a presumption of privilege that I believe Husserl never managed to secure and that those around him eventually realized he had not managed to secure.

I venture to say that Husserl never succeeded in explaining (unless circularly): (1) the need for a transcendental ego, (2) what the relationship was supposed to be between a "natural" ego and a transcendental ego, or (3) the necessity for supposing that we may count on a "transcendental intersubjectivity" drawn from our experience of our "fellow humans." These difficulties are noted in various ways by Heidegger and Merleau-Ponty and, preeminently, by

Eugen Fink. I content myself with noting only that Mohanty's for-mulation of (d) is quite close to the language Fink uses in posing the essential incompleteness of Husserl's account of the transcendental ego.[9] Mohanty assumes the success of Husserl's argument, in *Cartesian Meditations* for instance; but he does not complete the argument. I see no reason to think it can be successfully com-pleted—which is not to say, of course, that it is incoherent.

The stalemate I offer, then, is this: The alleged invariances of "meanings" as "objects" (or "essences") depend on Husserl's (or Mohanty's) demonstrating the necessity of there being already in place (with respect to experience) any of the supposedly changeless structures of the transcendental ego. Without that demonstration, the doctrine of the flux is home free—as far as phenomenology is concerned. I see no prospect of its being strengthened. The argu-ment (in Husserl) seems to me to be a non sequitur. Let me make this quite clear: Husserl nowhere (as far as I know) "proves" (to use Mohanty's term) (1) that there must be a transcendental ego pos-sessing conceptual resources separable from those of a "natural," psychologically qualified human subject; (2) that such an ego (any "subject") possesses, *a priori,* whatever powers are needed to make natural (social) communication "possible"; or (3) that the exercise of that ego's cognizing powers are capable of discerning, or of approximating to discerning, what is universally or neutrally neces-sary for all forms of rational understanding. (I think that that is what Fink was on to. It is certainly part of what *I* mean by the flux.)

Phenomenology cannot be invoked to defeat the doctrine of the flux if it cannot ensure the universal or invariant structure of the tran-scendental ego; for, the putative invariances of thought and experi-ence that Mohanty invokes are what they are *only for* the transcen-dental ego: they have no independent standing. I subscribe to another theory of the self or subject altogether—one that, if admitted, would preclude the phenomenologist's counterthesis, namely, that the human self is an artifact of a contingent cultural history. (It would not preclude a more moderate phenomenology.) I shall postpone saying more about what I mean by a "self" or "subject" or a "history." For the moment, I am only interested in the philosophical strategies avail-able to me and to the opposing phenomenologist.

I admit three principal countermoves. One I have stalemated:

the claim that the analysis of experience leads us to recognize the necessity of admitting the transcendental ego and certain invariant structures involved in experience. A second I have only barely touched on, namely, that of the fixity of the "objects" of thought and experience. I shall return to that in terms of reference and predication. The third is simply a variant of the argument I drew from Page: I find it, as I have already said, in Gail Stoffer's account—which is an analogue also of Mohanty's argument. After reviewing my treatment of relativism (to which I shall return), Soffer offers a final challenge. She notes my "denial of universal lifeworld structures" but goes on to affirm: "If his own philosophical analysis is supposed to fall under the same multivalent logic as cultural/intentional interpretive phenomena in general, then he would have to concede that 'opposing' views may also be true. If, on the other hand, he is claiming a bivalent, univocal validity for his own theory, one wonders on what basis a philosophical theory . . . could be thought to escape the consequence of the flux" (73).

Soffer's challenge introduces certain complications due to relativism. I shall take advantage of the opening to mention some useful distinctions. But, on the issue Soffer raises, which links her argument to Page's and Mohanty's, I think I may claim that, first of all, I never invoke the flux in a criterial or evidentiary way. I treat the flux holistically and only with "reference" to the universe (which is to say, only "mythically"—*not* in any referential way at all). The "universe" is "one," remember, in the vacuous sense (which Husserl himself urges) in which it makes no sense to speak of its partition or of its boundaries or of a multiplicity of universes. Second, I hold that bivalent logic (that is, a purely formal policy about truth values) is compatible with a relativistic logic, if only the ranges of their application be segregated and relevance constraints imposed. Third, the use of a bivalent logic does not entail the admission of any modal invariance (unless bivalence itself be construed as exceptionless), but the doctrine of invariance presupposes our adherence to a bivalent logic. On the argument, I find myself entirely free to appeal, where flexibility is wanted, either to bivalent or relativistic (that is, the counterpart alethic) considerations or (as with the flux) to considerations that do not invite truth-values at all. That's not to say that there is no rigor in advocating the flux, but whatever rigor the doctrine commands comes from assessing the fruitfulness and congruity of its picture (of the universe) and the endlessly many determinate claims we may confirm or disconfirm. (We may assess its "fit with regard to what is true, but *not* anything like "correspondence" between truth and flux!) In any case, because I do not subscribe to bivalence unconditionally, and because I subscribe to the flux as a "bet," I do not (as Soffer seems to think necessary) admit incompatibles as *true*.

I may say I concede a benign equivocation on "real"—which is not of my own making. Whatever we treat as *epistemically* internal to our "realism" is "constructed." We remain entirely free, nevertheless, to posit *some* subset of what is thus "internal" *as* "independent reality," as independent of such conjectures. Here, contrary to what Soffer suggests, I do not favor (or converge with) Husserl's constructivism (his phenomenology, in effect). In fact, I am not entirely sure what Husserl intends, because Husserl never satisfactorily explains (as I have already remarked) what relationship holds between our "naturalistic" and our "phenomenological" powers and between the independent world and the world phenomenologically "constituted." I am reasonably clear about my own view but not about Husserl's. If Eugen Fink is right in the way he questions Husserl, then I think Soffer's finding is decidedly premature.

In any case, contrary to Soffer's reading of my own argument: (1) the alethic policy on relativism does *not* depend on such grounds as "the essential undecidability of conflicting interpretations in many instances of literary and historical interpretation" (72), but (rather) on the cognizable structure of what we can discern in particular domains of inquiry; and (2) the policy of favoring many valued truth-values (*not* a mere three-valued logic, conceding "indeterminacy"—which, on Soffer's account, Husserl allows) is meant to service (alethically) certain deeper ontological commitments (for instance, regarding the "Intentional" structure of cultural phenomena and entities) that would favor relativism over bivalence. I am unwilling, therefore, to speak of mere "*epistemic* 'relativism' " (72), as Soffer does, as if epistemic and ontic considerations could be disjoined. On my own view, as I say, there are excellent reasons for favoring (What Soffer calls) "an *ontological* relativism" (72), which, of course, has both epistemic and alethic implications. You must bear in mind that *if,* as

I hold, relativism can be legitimated in epistemic and ontic terms (in opposition to a strict bivalence), then it cannot be due to mere "*evidential* indeterminacy," as Soffer hints (71). The upshot is that Husserlian phenomenology cannot but be thrown into considerable doubt—without disallowing phenomenology itself.

Having come this far, I can now return effectively to a deeper question of Stern's that I had to leave unmentioned earlier. Stern asks, regarding interpretation, if "there is no convergence to the best interpretation [in testing competing interpretations] . . . why do we argue against our opponent? And, if we don't succeed in convincing our opponents, why do we charge them so easily with violence in interpreting? Why do we charge them with dishonesty? After all, once we have admitted that there is no convergence to the best interpretation, we also admit that at least some interpretations are impervious to our arguments?" (16).

I cannot hide the fact that I regard this as seriously mistaken—a complete non sequitur. *If* we were restricted to a bivalent logic, *if* relativism (a relativistic logic) were utterly unavailable or irrelevant, then Stern *might* be right in what he says. (He would still need something like First Philosophy to make his case: something akin to Davidson's doctrine about truth and knowledge or something like Stanley Rosen's or Carl Page's view.) But once you concede the relevance of relativism—and relativism *is* central to my own theory—then the answer to Stern's question stares you in the face: on my view, interpretations *may be shown to be false,* in their denying or in their being incompatible with certain features of what is interpreted, without its ever being the case that we can confirm any uniquely valid or "best" interpretation (as true). The negation of a false claim need not be construed as an independently true claim: bivalence need not hold (say, in disallowing excluded middle). So, there *is* a basis for "argu[ing] against our opponent" (whether in interpreting literature or painting or in assessing the burdens of philosophy). I infer, therefore, that Stern has neglected to show a sufficient reason for adopting his own view of "misinterpretation" (20) or scuttling my relativistic view. (In particular I see no reason to accept his view of "interpretive authority" [22–23]. I see no reason—certainly, no reason is given—to think that any form of "authority" is "constitutive of interpretation.") It goes against historicity. Here, Stern betrays his own allegiance and, I may add, an allegiance that (as I say) is incompatible with his own reading of interpretation as "constitutive" of history. The issue depends on the fortunes of relativism. In any case, against Shusterman (and Rorty), this also shows the need for a sustained metaphysics and epistemology of interpretation. (I'm afraid Stern's annoyance at my own style of argument shows through his own words, for instance when he mentions J. L. Austin's remarks. But I hope I have somewhere in my books and papers provided an argument for every charge I've made against a named colleague. I dare say no more about that.)

Let me say, by way of summary, that all the puzzles I've collected involving Stern, Page, Rorty, Shusterman, Mohanty, and Soffer bear on the intricacies of a confusion Rorty is responsible for. All of Rorty's work, I find, is focused on the contest between postmodernism and transcendentalism, but Rorty himself invariably construes it in terms of a contrived but utterly pointless contest between modernism and postmodernism. The first relies on a principle of division; the second does not. To grasp the point is to realize that Rorty's verdict (that "philosophy is over") is both a non sequitur and an incoherence, *and* that the defeat of transcendentalism is *not* tantamount to incoherence or postmodernism. By modernism, I mean the presumption that there is a form of epistemic neutrality that we can occupy in principle. Objectivity and neutrality are, however, second-order posits that we make, reflexively, within the horizonal limits of our form of life. By transcendentalism, I mean that supposed second-order competence by which, neutrally and objectively, we discern the universal or necessary or apodictic conditions under which first-order objectivity is possible. I agree with Rorty that transcendental objectivity is indemonstrable, but *that* is not equivalent to what postmodernism claims. By postmodernism, I understand the second-order claim that legitimation is either transcendental or impossible. So I reject postmodernism on the grounds that it is a non sequitur; it is also incoherent, because postmodernists (Rorty, preeminently) plainly mean (as in supporting Davidson) to concede first-order objectivity in science and ordinary communication. Rorty never addresses the charge that first- and second-order objectivity cannot be disjoined. Shusterman, therefore, risks Rorty's incoherence by dismissing "metaphysics"; and Mohanty and Soffer insist too much on retreating to transcendentalism.

III

Relativism is a much-maligned but most important thesis. It does not depend on subscribing to the doctrine of the flux, but, given the flux, one cannot avoid relativism. Historically, the two notions are linked because Plato (in *Theaetetus*) and Aristotle (in *Metaphysics*) link them. I link them also because the combination is so extraordinarily powerful and because I am able to draw attention, by doing that, to the fact that the issue has been with us since the beginning of Western philosophy. Protagoras obviously had a grasp of it, but we cannot say for certain what his views were. Still, the literal reading of the *Theaetetus* and the explicit argument of *Metaphysics* Gamma make Protagoras out to be a fool, in a way his reputation does not support at all. I am immodest enough to regard my resolution of relativism's *aporia* and its connection with the doctrine of the flux a reasonable reading of what Protagoras may have originally intended. My own account is contemporary in that I introduce historicism as a particularly strategic application of the union of relativism and the doctrine of the flux. But neither of these presupposes or entails historicism. (Also, it would be a mistake, of course, to confuse the ontic claim about the historicity of human existence with relativism's treatment of the logic of truth-claims.)

The *aporia* that needs to be resolved centers on how to account for the apparent contradiction of validity affirming two incompatible propositions. As I see the issue, the formal solution is easy enough; the serious question concerns *why* we should adopt it. Many critics pretend that the puzzle cannot be solved even formally; or else, if they think it requires something more than a formal solution, they attribute to the relativist a form of stupidity they would never think of assigning any other doctrine of the sort—for instance, solipsism or skepticism. There can be no doubt that Hilary Putnam, who is certainly one of the most dogged critics of relativism, repeats himself again and again along these lines.[10] I am prepared to admit—indeed, insist—that alethic, epistemic, and ontic questions cannot really be disjoined from one another, although our shorthand treatment of logical, cognitive, and metaphysical matters wrongly suggests that each can be treated independently. Michael Dummett, for instance, explicitly disjoins "semantic" and "metaphysical" issues and assigns priority to the first over the second.[11] I take that to be indemonstrable and more than implausible. But, admitting these caveats, the resolution of the relativist's *aporia* is "entirely" managed by a choice of truth-value policy. All that is needed is this: Admit a many-valued (not a mere three-valued) logic in place of bivalence (at least in some domain); admit its compatibility with a bivalent logic (where suitably segregated and provided with relevance constraints); and admit that claims or propositions or judgments that on a bivalent logic but not now would be or would yield contradictories may be confirmed as jointly valid.

The policy is entirely self-consistent. If, for example, two expert interpretations of *Hamlet* are incompatible (bivalently), and if we wish to regard them as jointly valid, then we must, in the context in question, disallow bivalence and opt for a many-valued logic. In my idiom, the judgments in question will be "incongruent," not contradictory or incompatible in the way of truth-value (although, of course, they remain incompatible in the sense of not being able to be united, unless trivially—as by disjunction—in a single unified interpretation). The solution is an alethic one, in the sense that it depends entirely on the choice of a logic regarding the ascription of truth-values. (But a full-blooded relativism will need more than this.) Soffer does not see this possibility.

What is needed in the alethic sense is this: Truth and falsity are treated nonsymmetrically; truth is abandoned (in context, though that can be reconciled with the use of "true" in the bivalent sense) and replaced by many-valued truth-values, which may themselves be graded (for instance, "reasonable," "apt," "plausible," and the like). It is certainly possible that substantive objections from epistemic and ontic sources may be raised. But there would be no point to doing so if there were no coherent alethic policy to propose.[12] (I take the values mentioned *to be truth-values, not* epistemic appraisals of what may be supposed to be true!) Furthermore, not every many-valued logic is a relativistic logic; a relativistic logic is not a three-valued logic (formulated by adding "indeterminate," say, to the bivalent pair, as in Soffer and, of course, Peirce). It is also not a probabilistic logic (as Rescher suggests). And, finally, the relevant truth-values are *not* construed relationally, as they are, for instance, in Myles Burnyeat's interpretation of the *Theaetetus* and as they are in Putnam.[13]

No one to my knowledge seriously denies that, epistemically, the ascription of truth-values is "relativized" to evidence, point of view, conceptual scheme, or the like, although many believe that "in the limit" there is a uniquely correct ("neutral") way in which to ascribe truth-values. The paradoxical view attributed to the relativist requires him to construe "true" as meaning "true-in-*L*," where (1) the *meaning* of the truth-value conjoins alethic and epistemic considerations, and (2) the relativistic truth-value is construed relationally and variably from language to language, from world to world, from epistemic subject to epistemic subject, or the like.

Tom Rockmore, who offers a very clear account of my own view, attempts at the last moment to claim that "relationalism" (as I dub the latter doctrine, in contrast to my own "robust relativism") *is self-consistent,* entailed in my view, and well-nigh ineluctable in any case. But to agree with Rockmore that "claims to know are never neutral or free of context . . . [are] always relative to one or another conceptual framework in respect to which they are intelligible" (180) is *not* tantamount to saying that "Margolis is unsuccessful in avoiding relationalism" (182). Rockmore has simply conflated (1) the alethic policy regarding relativistic *truth-values,* (2) the (trivial) "relativity of epistemic or evidentiary matters *in applying* truth-values, (3) the alethic policy of *"relationalist"* truth-values, which (to be sure) incorporates into the definition *of* such values, and (4) reasons for disallowing strict epistemic neutrality; in a sense that favors neither relativism ism or antirelativism. The doctrine of the flux is *not* a form of relativism, though relativism is congruent with it, of course. Furthermore, both a strict bivalence and a relativistic logic are compatible with the flux. Flux, on my view, is a way of modeling the universe (a "myth," as I say): one in which *de re* necessities are disallowed. Relationalism is a (failed) theory of truth or truth-value ascription applied to determinate claims and judgments within the terms of whatever model of the universe we favor. There's where Rockmore goes wrong. On my view, it's not possible to make truth-claims about the universe; *a fortiori,* it's not possible to make "relational" claims about the universe.

I take this to be what is seriously misleading (and therefore wrong) with Rockmore's concluding that "if not in theory at least in practice *claims* for knowledge cannot be separated from the historical framework in which they are embedded" (183). The statement itself is perfectly reasonable, but it is *not* a form of relativism as such, and it is certainly *not* equivalent to the relationalist's position. What has happened is that Rockmore has conflated the conditions of knowledge with the bare meaning of certain truth-values (possibly, with what he takes to be an ingredient in the meaning of any and all truth-values). If I understand him correctly, then, on Rockmore's theory, *any* epistemic policy entails a relativistic logic—or worse, a relationalist logic! I think that cannot be right. But then, the good sense of what he means (and plainly says) entails a change of sense in what *he* calls "deep relativism" or "relationalism" (or "sickly relativism") (181).

I agree with Rockmore entirely about "folk epistemology," but I think that that is a distinct issue. With this resolution in hand, it is easy enough to dissolve Soffer's paradox about "true," as when she says (she repeats the point) that "in some domains two judgments may be 'true' which would be contradictory on the standard bivalent model, or may be neither true nor false but some third value, for example, 'undecided,' 'undecidable,' 'possible,' 'plausible' " (62). As I have already said, "true" and "false" are, on my view, treated asymmetrically in a relativistic logic: "True" is bracketed or abandoned and "false" obtains, and values like "plausible" are *not* "third" values in the way of undecidability or the like. No, the judgment that a claim is "plausible" is, on my view, an entirely determinate assessment *of* would-be evidence or grounds *in a domain in which a bivalent logic (engaging both excluded middle and tertium non datur) is inadequate but not necessarily irrelevant.* I emphatically do not, as Soffer claims I do, suggest that "the interpretation that Hamlet is a self-seeking scoundrel [and] the interpretation that he is a just avenger . . . may nevertheless be 'true,' in the sense of multivalent 'interpretive' truth" (66). (They cannot both be true, but they may be plausible as "incongruent" claims.) I am also not here contesting Aristotle's view on noncontradiction or Husserl's adherence to Aristotle's principle. I say, rather, that noncontradiction is vacuous (pretty well in Wittgenstein's sense) until interpreted *and* that *no* substantive interpretation of any sector of the world—in accord with noncontradiction—*yields a necessary truth.* But I agree with Husserl (and Soffer) that "reality itself is constituted by 'interpretive' (or sense-bestowing) activity" (64), *if* one is speaking of what is (intentionally) internal to epistemic conjecture (say, the world-as-it-appears). It's at this point that I say that, on the one hand, Husserl has not met the objections of Merleau-Ponty and Heidegger and Fink and, on the other, has not explained the relationship between reality and phenomenological "constitution." That is why Soffer's (and Mohanty's) claims of a threatening paradox confronting my view of the flux may be turned aside.

Soffer, I may add, mentions the issue about noncontradiction in connection with contrasting my adherence to the flux and the difference between my view and Husserl's, despite certain convergences. I am grateful for the comparison. I take Husserl to have been an immense intelligence—which is not gainsaid by also insisting that he failed, fundamentally, in ever establishing that there was a modal invariance inherent in the "sense-bestowing" work of human thought or the "constitution" of reality. Here, I may say, I agree with Karl Popper's perspicuous reading of Charles Sanders Peirce's essential theme, when Popper says: "I believe that Peirce was right in holding that all clocks are clouds, to some considerable degree —even the most precise of clocks. This [he adds] is a most important inversion of the mistaken determinist view that all clouds are clocks."[14] I don't happen to subscribe to Popper's philosophy, and, although Peirce is one of my "best" teachers, I depart from Peirce in my own version of pragmatism (particularly regarding fallibilism).

I mention the point because Soffer herself mentions two versions of a deep problem on which, as she correctly notes, I diverge from Husserl. I do diverge from Husserl—by way of the flux, which I associate with Peirce and (Popper), though *they* would not agree with me.

I take the liberty of mentioning Soffer's formulations here—but will save the discussion for a later moment. My detour will be seen to bear on explaining the flux and explaining how it ramifies through my entire theory. (It bears particularly on my account of predication.) First, Soffer says that (on my view) "*nothing* remains constant throughout interpretation/intentional activity, that cultural phenomena possess no properties which endure through variations in interpreters and interpretations" (66–67); second, speaking of "the problem of universal structures of the cultural- or life-world," she says that "in the end [Margolis] seems to be quite comfortable with the admission of 'pragmatic' universals, universals which are not necessary or unexceptionless" (72). She puts her finger here on a decisive issue: I want to do it justice—but not quite yet. In any case, she finds the matter problematic.

In this regard, I should add that I agree largely with Rockmore's summary of certain developments of modern Western philosophy—in particular, the following, which provides the clue (though not the argument) for offsetting Soffer's preference for Husserl's stand (and for offsetting other "Cartesian" options, which Rockmore correctly traces to Davidson at least). "It is . . . one thing," Rockmore says, "to claim that we have genuine invariances and another thing altogether to claim that such invariances as we have are relative to a given framework that is itself not necessarily invariant but subject to historical change" (164). This is precisely what I had in mind in citing Foucault's notion of the "historical *a priori*" (and in opposing Stern's and Mohanty's views). I may add that I take this theme in Foucault to be ultimately Hegelian. For the moment, I claim only that Rockmore's thesis, which I heartily share, is neither incoherent nor unreasonable. (I recommend comparison here, with Krausz's summary of my published views.) Rockmore's thesis is, I think, the opening wedge to the defeat of all "First Philosophy" and the presumption of modal invariance (as in Aristotle's *Metaphysics* Gamma), simply because the denial of all these versions of invariance are not themselves demonstrably self-contradictory, self-defeating, paradoxical, or anything of the sort. (I do not quite agree with Rockmore about the compatibility of holism and relativism; I do believe Quine's view of the relationship between holism and existential claims is either incompatible with relativism or meant to preclude relativism. In fact, Quine's argument does not succeed.[15])

IV

I need to take one step backward to take two steps forward. I remind you that in trying to defend relativism I conceded (or insisted) that alethic, epistemic, and ontic considerations could not be rightly separated from one another. Nevertheless, I have tried to formulate a purely alethic account of relativistic truth-values. I drew particular attention to the fact that Soffer persists in speaking of incompatible "truths" in relativistic discourse and (favoring Husserl) of many-valued logics in three-valued terms and that Rockmore conflates alethic and epistemic questions and (as a consequence) evidentiary relations and the logic of relationalism. Both policies lead to unwanted paradox. Soffer is right to recognize that we want to be able to hold, as properly valid, claims that on a bivalent logic would be formally incompatible or contradictory, but she is wrong to think that this signifies that incompatibles can be jointly *true*. Rockmore is right to recognize that the epistemic processing of truth-claims is "relativized" to evidence, point of view, and the like, but he is wrong to think that that sort of relativity had anything, as such, to do with the choice of appropriate truth-values. It's an understandable slip but it is terribly widespread and seems to be difficult to shake off. (It certainly appears in Putnam, for instance.) What is at stake but so deeply buried that it fails to be perceived is the troubling matter of whether the (seemingly) benign—relativized "frameworks (or "contexts") of evidentiary testing are themselves incapable of being sorted within a single, neutral, encompassing "universe" of discourse ("context of all contexts"), with the result that *the benign "relativizing" of epistemic testing comes to implicate a relativistic—possibly even a relationalist—account of truth-values.* That is simply too quick. A nonrelativistic account of the relativity of epistemic testing has been lost without a skirmish!

Here, I remind you of Davidson's profoundly failed attack on incommensurable conceptual schemes. (Davidson's argument appears in the influential paper, "The Very Idea of a Conceptual Scheme."[16]) Two points are all that are needed: for one, mention of "one universe" is logically vacuous (though unavoidable) and has no bearing whatsoever on the prospects of incommensurable or alternative conceptual schemes; for a second, just as the individuation and reidentifiability of different things does not *entail* our *ever* sharing neutral criteria of meaning, truth, individuation, reidentifiability, or the like, so, similarly, neither do the individuation and reidentifiability of different conceptual schemes. What, rightly amplified, this shows is the nonparadoxical possibility of *relativizing epistemology.* Davidson, who is regularly cited as having demonstrated the elementary incoherence of the "very idea" has both utterly failed to make good his charge and (if the truth be known) has himself undermined the supposed force of his own claim.

Nevertheless, we need to bear in mind that the mere "relativizing" of epistemic contexts is *not* tantamount to a relativistic reading of same. I find a confusion similar to (but different from) Davidson's confusion in Putnam's accounts. I cannot see *how* Putnam can disallow the prospect of a relativistic epistemology if, as is plain he favors (did until recently favor) (1) an "internal realism," (2) the absence of any principled demarcation between the "subjective" and the "objective," (3) the benign "relativizing" of epistemic considerations, (4) the historicizing of scientific inquiry, (5) the denial of any invariant rule for fixing reference, and (6) the denial of any uniquely correct account of what "there is." Yet, of course, he does oppose relativism (also, incommensurabilism *à la* Feyerabend and Kuhn) and clings (did recently cling) to the (now arbitrary) idea of truth as a *Grenzbegriff* or regulative principle.[17] (Putnam, of course, has now definitively abandoned his "internal realism.")

There are two distinct issues here. One is that the relativizing of epistemic contexts is not tantamount to relativism. Rescher, as we shall see, construes "objectivity" as necessarily internal to "our" epistemic practices, without presuming privilege, hence, as precluding relativism. The other is that admitting the relativizing of epistemic contexts and denying any principled disjunction between the "subjective" and the "objective" implicate the viability of relativism *if* it can be shown to be internally coherent. Putnam, at least up to the appearance of *The Many Faces of Realism,* took (the important part of) both of the positions just mentioned and yet precluded relativism. He would have been within his rights if relativism were demonstrably paradoxical or self-contradictory. I take Putnam to be mistaken in his argument, but my point for the moment is merely that such a position (Putnam's charge) need not be formally self-defeating: It happens to be indefensible, because relativism *is* alethically self-consistent.

There is no satisfactory demonstration to the effect that a relativistic epistemology is (cannot but be) incoherent! Still, *that* is not tantamount to the benign "relativity" of epistemic testing. I am bound to say, therefore, that Peter McCormick's interesting speculation on the interpretation of Yannis Ritsos's poems goes too far—in fact, in just the same way Rockmore's argument does. Actually, McCormick conflates two separate and entirely different conflatings when he says (imagining a "second-order" dispute about interpreting Ritsos):

> Whereas I want to espouse here some kind of relativism such that talk about objectivity must remain relative to a particular culture, or conceptual scheme, or language, or family of language uses, or whatever, you [McCormick's imagined opponent] want to hold out for there being at least in some important cases certain ways the world is independent of our particular cultures, conceptual schemes, and so on. (80)

McCormick believes he can win the argument by drawing attention to the fact that "there is no determinate fact of the matter to be discovered" (11). He means this in a way that is friendly to my own theory, and I am glad to have his company. But I don't think the argument works. First of all, it *is* possible to speak coherently of "the world . . . independent of our particular cultures"; the thing is it is possible only on the condition that "objectivity" and "independence" are themselves *second-order posits* within the scope of our critical reflections on our science, interpretive practices, and the like. *There is no neutral fact of the matter confirming our neutrality or our neutrally discovering how the independent world independently is.* That is the point of exposing Davidson's and Putnam's failed arguments. Second, admitting their failure and admitting the benign form of "relativizing" evidentiary testing are (as I have said) *not* the equivalent of endorsing a relativistic epistemology. I cannot see that McCormick escapes these strictures. (I may, perhaps, remind you of Stern's insistence on the "best" interpretation and his favoring authorial intent and "interpretive authority." That Stern is committed to something like Quine's unacknowledged neutralism is fairly explicit in his assertion—which I cannot accept—that "the philosophical study of the history of philosophy is an ahistorical study" [33].) I do not claim that I can *demonstrate* that the notion of a neutral (hence, privileged) cognitive stance is impossible. (No one can demonstrate that.) I claim only (on pain of paradox) that there is no known compelling argument that there is or must be such a stance. My own view (once again recalling Page), is a philosophical *bet,* namely, that neutrality cannot be recovered in the way Descartes, Kant, Husserl, and (now) Davidson and Putnam suppose. But saying that is *not* tantamount to endorsing epistemic relativism! It is also not tantamount to precluding it.

Now, I want to endorse much of McCormick's summary of my objections to Putnam's running attack on relativism, particularly his attention to Putnam's "Kantianism." He is quite right about what I say. My interest in Putnam's theory is, precisely, that, for all its unresolved difficulties, it is Putnam—rather than Quine or Goodman or Davidson or Rorty—who has had the best grasp of the family of questions that a viable relativism would have to accommodate. I do not say that Putnam *has* a sufficiently generous or resilient reading of relativism itself. His own discussion of referential fixity and the demarcation between the subjective and objective makes one doubt that he does. No, I think Putnam's account of relativism is a disaster, which, if I'm right, explains why he is not himself a relativist! I expect that he will concede—somewhere in his career—as he has conceded so many times before in his philosophical *passage* on other matters, that finally he is a relativist "of sorts"! But I won't hold my breath.

It is true that I regard Putnam's notion of "cultural relativity" as trivially true: It is altogether neutral to the dispute between epistemic relativism and nonrelativism. Deny cognitive privilege, and epistemic "relativity" follows. But it looks as if McCormick equates this with "relationalism," which he then attributes to me (90). I do not regard relationalism as trivially true but rather (in agreement with Putnam) as paradoxical and self-defeating, and, in any case, it is not a position I "affirm" anywhere. What puzzles me is that McCormick has warned that my own account of Putnam's "cri-

tiques of relativism" is "importantly incomplete" (82). To be
honest, I've read McCormick's discussion with considerable profit
but have not found a single place where he claims or shows that
Putnam has produced a different or more interesting attack on relativism than the various maneuvers I report him as holding. I find
that McCormick makes no new move in Putnam's favor, though he
seems to believe he has. I can't find it. What I find rather is that he
returns to the "no fact of the matter" thesis; by contrast, my own
claim is that it is entirely coherent to admit first-order disputes
under relativistic constraints!

If, however, what I have said about objectivity being an artifact
internal to our reflexive ("second-order") conjectures regarding
what we believe (is true and believe we know), then I cannot see
how McCormick *can* consistently claim that "our most basic disagreement about interpretation"—that is, the "second-order"
quarrel about what to regard as "objective" and as "independent" in
the world, and the like, rather than the mere "first-order" interpretive disagreement about (say) Ritsos's poems—can rightly be said
to involve "not any objectivity but [only] subjective constructions"
(102). *If* McCormick agrees (as I think he does) with Putnam at
least (if not also with me) that there is no (epistemically) principled
demarcation line between the subjective and the objective, then,
certainly, (1) it cannot be true that "there is no fact of the matter"
(for, what "the fact of the matter" is is, epistemically, a construction), and (2) McCormick is no longer entitled (on his own argument) to introduce a fresh disjunction between the subjective and
the objective that somehow takes precedence over (1) (neutrally, I
suppose).

This would have been all that I could have reasonably said on
reading the original draft of his paper, but McCormick has revised
it some. Without wishing to quarrel about the issues now developed,
I take the occasion to make a few additional remarks that may be
helpful responding to what I see is now featured in the final draft.
For one thing, it is not quite true that I regard relativism as an
"alethic" rather than an "epistemic claim" (89). It's rather that most
critics of relativism (certainly, Putnam) believe that relativism is
self-contradictory or paradoxical on formal grounds alone. That led
me to attempt to demonstrate that relativism could be formulated

coherently as far as alethic and purely formal considerations were concerned. But, I have always maintained that there is no principled disjunction between alethic, epistemic, and ontic matters; furthermore, the denial of any principled disjunction between the "subjective" and the "objective" leads to the same conclusion. (I have now, I may say, drafted a fuller account of how relativism plays out in epistemic and ontic terms.)

This leads me to a complex second point. McCormick's nice example regarding Ritsos's poem strikes me as obscuring certain crucial distinctions. Thus, in addressing the interpretation of a *poem* as opposed to judging whether "the sky is blue" (see the epigraph drawn from Putnam), "objectivity" in the sense of independence of "our particular cultures, conceptual schemes, and so on" makes no sense at all, because poems just are cultural artifacts even if we suppose the sky's being blue is not. Furthermore, the question of whether the sky's being blue *is* "independent" regularly confuses and conflates the distinction between (physical) "reality" (what, as Peirce held, was independent of the opinions of you and me) and "realism" (what, as Putnam would concede, concerns what, on *our* evidentiary grounds, we judge to be real or independent). My own thought is there's no paradox involved in holding that what falls within "reality" (ontically) is *not* independent of what (epistemically) provides the evidentiary grounds for so judging.

If you hold, as I do, that there is no principled disjunction between the ontic and the epistemic (the denial of which leads to Cartesian doubt and skepticism), then there is no reason why relativism and realism should not be reconcilable. The only trouble is that the "objectivity" (the evidentiary grounds for objectivity) cannot be the same in dealing with physical nature and with the artifacts of human culture. (That is due to intentionality at least.) Notice, also, that, on any view that denies a principled disjunction between the ontic and the epistemic, *that* what is real in epistemic terms (realism) is "constructed," is *not* tantamount to saying that *what* is independently real in ontic terms (reality) is, as such, constructed as well. (Certainly, one does not want to say that the universe immediately following the Big Bang is a fiction or an artifact of late human science.)

Now, if you have these distinctions in mind, then, I suggest, you will be hospitable to the following as well, namely, that the admission of an "independent" physical world is *not* tantamount to what is meant by "objectivity" relative to truth-claims. For, for one thing, we must distinguish between the ontic and the epistemic, and, for a second, there is no argument to show that what may be "objectively" validated must be conformable with a bivalent logic. Putnam, I say, ignores this and therefore fails to see the compatibility of realism and relativism. (In particular, he misreads James's *Pragmatism,* which he professes to follow.) There is another distinction that I must press, this time against McCormick: In interpreting poems (as opposed to judging whether the sky is blue), we may not be able to preclude what can only be (interpretively) "imputed" to a poem as opposed to what can be "discerned" in it, and we may not be able to draw a principled distinction between the two. If you grant that, then McCormick's speaking of there being "no fact of the matter" is equivocal: as between holding that no truth(like) values at all may be invoked and holding (merely) that no bivalent truth-values will do. My own thought is if you admit the worry about the "impute"/"discern" distinction and its epistemic importance, then, admitting relativism (and "incongruent" judgments), you need never admit that there is no fact of the matter—regarding interpretive objectivity—in retiring or restricting bivalence. McCormick fails us here, when, in the interpretive quarrel he describes, he says, "No empirical strategy can be adequate" (100) to its resolution. Obviously, he is thinking that the relevant "facts" would favor bivalence, but that has to be shown; or he is thinking that there cannot be a fact of the matter involving our electing a bivalent or relativistic picture of the quarrel, but *that, too,* has to be shown! I shall have to leave the matter there.

Noël Carroll picks up the relationship between interpretation and relativism as well, but from an entirely different point of view. I must confess that Carroll has sent me back to my earliest publications to find out what I did say about "myths." I am a little unsure about how to answer him—for a reason I think is perfectly understandable but awkward. Carroll mentions my new book, *Interpretation Radical But Not Unruly*; but as far as I can see, he makes no use of it. I'm not surprised, because I may not actually use the term "myth" in any important sense in that book. (Carroll cites the introduction, but I haven't been able to find the reference to "myth" in the actual text! It may be a form of hysterical blindness on my part.) The trouble, quite frankly, is that the idiom of cultural "myths" that I introduce in chapter 7 of my *Art and Philosophy*[18] represents my earliest and most fledgling efforts to understand the logic of interpretation and its relationship to relativism. Most of what I say there I have now found a more perspicuous way of presenting, and, in the meantime, I have reserved the term "myth" for a new technical use of a quite different (but not altogether unrelated) sort, namely, in connection with the epistemic standing of truth-claims. (That usage is quite explicit in *Historied Thought, Constructed World,*[19] although I have made use of it in print already. I've mentioned the point earlier in this essay.) Suffice it to say that it would not be of much interest here to labor over a merely autobiographical paraphrase of everything I said in chapter 7 of *Art and Philosophy* (which Carroll relies on) and everything I've written in the fifteen years since that book appeared.

I think I am right in claiming that the book and the articles on which the notion of interpretive "myths" was based introduced the problematic nature of the logic of interpretation and the possibility of defending relativism in a careful way—a way that had not been noticed before. (I take Carroll's attention to the matter to confirm the fact.) But, I now see many things more clearly than I did then: about the relationship between bivalence and many-valued logics, the informality of reference and predication, historicity and the constructed nature of the world, intentionality and Intentional (or cultural) attributes, the nature of truth and reality and fact, the puzzles of individuation and numerical identity, disputes regarding realism and idealism, the difference between nature and culture, the artifactual nature of human selves, the problematic standing of epistemic neutrality, and the nature of philosophy itself!

There is another reason for embarrassment. I don't believe I ever offered what Carroll calls "the myth argument"—about which he says: "I am skeptical about the success of this argument" (41)— *an argument meant to demonstrate the validity of relativism with respect to "artistic interpretation"* (41). I certainly did try to show the reasonableness of invoking relativism in interpretive contexts, and I certainly did try to show that the interpretation of art and literature generates puzzles that the usual way of treating the logic of factual judgments simply can't manage. But I think I am right (I hope I am not misrepresenting things) in claiming (chiefly against Monroe Beardsley and E. D. Hirsch Jr.) that my reasons had to do with three considerations: (1) that works of art (I would now say all Intentionally qualified "things") lack determinate boundaries or assignable natures, in virtue of which we cannot say what is "in" a work and what is merely "imputed" to it;[20] (2) that, insofar as "things" (artworks, in the present instance—I would now say all "cultural entities") possess "meanings" or other significative properties ("Intentional" properties, in the idiom I offer in *Interpretation Radical But Not Unruly*—I use the term already in *The Flux of History and the Flux of Science*[21] and in earlier publications) are intrinsically interpretable; and (3) that the range of meanings to be ascribed to a work is a function of the salient cultural "myths" that may change for various reasons (I would now put this in terms of the historicity of thought—historicism—and my own stand on "cultural realism," which has affinities with the views of Hegel, Gadamer, Barthes, and Foucault at least).

In short, what, in *Art and Philosophy,* I offer as specimen "myths" (the Freudian, the Marxist, the Catholic, for instance) are part of the *data* that *both* relativistic *and* nonrelativistic theories of interpretation would have to accommodate, *not* an actual *argument* for relativism itself. (Carroll does not make room for this possibility.) Many philosophers, in fact, have since tried to show that the considerations I bring forward need not entail relativism—might support *pluralism* for instance.[22] (I take it that that is what Carroll would himself favor.) Pluralism and relativism are utterly unlike, however, in logical terms, although (of course) I hold both to be coherent. (I shall come to the distinction shortly.)

In the *Art and Philosophy* book, I hardly went further than to show the viability of preferring relativism, given the failure (particularly in analytic philosophy) of coming to terms with (1)–(3). In any case, I certainly think I have strengthened the argument since the appearance of chapter 7, and I should have supposed Carroll would have addressed the matter in the context of chapter 1 of the *Interpretation* book. He does not. I am at a loss to know why.

In *Art and Philosophy,* I say very plainly (I had forgotten!):

"The question here [distancing Wittgenstein's notion of "seeing-as"] is rather: 'Could you defend this way of seeing it [interpreting a given object]?' . . . For Wittgenstein, you may be *doing* something wrong if you are not able to see what is required; here, your *account* of a particular work may be inadmissible. For him, it is basically a perceptual question; here, it is a question of evidence and justification—applying as much to literature as to the visual arts."[23] I don't think I have relinquished the puzzle, but I think I now understand it in a better way. I suppose people just don't remember (possibly this is also true of Carroll) how dependent (in the United States) the theory of interpretation was (as late as the seventies and early eighties) on the model of knowledge in the unity of science theory. (Certainly, Beardsley was in a general way committed to that model.) I think I had a small hand in breaking out of that false vision in Anglo-American aesthetics—and perhaps in other parts of English-language philosophy as well.

On the substantive side, I see (on rereading my essay) that I had already introduced historicity and a certain respect for Barthes's interpretive strategy (which is central to my account in the *Interpretation* volume), and the all-important concept, of "incongruent" interpretations and the notion that a relativistic logic could not rightly be captured by a three-valued logic. So my intuitions were already in place but (I fully admit) they were inadequately developed. I also had not fully grasped the import of distinguishing between description and interpretation—ontically as well as epistemically. (I admit all that.) On the specific issue of "myths," I shall venture one further remark. I say (in chapter 7): "We know a myth to be objective for criticism, though it may not be so for science, when the habits of thought, perception, and imagination of a society or substantial subpopulation—including of course productive artists —are educable in its terms, and when their responses to appropriate stimuli are generally predictable or congruent with such myths. Systematic traditions of belief may serve as our paradigms here."[24] This conception is *not* (yet) relativistic. It could easily support pluralism.

It may be made to support relativism on two conditions, both of which I mention: First, that "incongruent" judgments may be validated in accord with some salient "myth" or other; and, second, that there be no neutral conceptual scheme (recall my objections to

Davidson and Putnam) that may be shown to replace any run of viable "myths" of the sort mentioned. Put another way, *if* objectivity and neutrality are themselves *no more than* artifacts of our competing "myths" (which is not how I would put things now), then there would be no way to preclude a relativistic conception of interpretation. Since writing *Art and Philosophy,* I have come to advocate what I call *symbiosis* (in the *Interpretation* book and elsewhere) by which I mean not merely a Kantian constructivism but a constructivism in which the disjoint "contributions" of the "brute world" and the "sense-bestowing" functions of human subjects (to fall back to Husserl's idiom) cannot be reliably assigned, except as artifacts of that same symbiosis. Historicism, hermeneutics, poststructuralist liberties all contribute to a plausible reading of such a constructivism. (Remember: I treat constructivism primarily as a form of realism but not as an out-and-out idealism.) *That* was not in place in the *Art and Philosophy* book: The notion of "myths," I concede, was a primitive notion favored along these lines. But the earlier use of "myth" *was* compatible with both pluralism and relativism. Pluralism, but not relativism, entails a neutral stance.

I make these concessions to do justice to Carroll's criticism, as well as to collect in a fair way the further pertinent remarks offered by Nicholas Rescher and Michael Krausz. Carroll argues that "the myth argument" fails and that, contrary to my "theory" (to the effect that it is a "matter of logical necessity" that relativism wins out), it is true "in *practice* (rather than in theory) [that] plausible claims are quite often the best we have before us" (59). I think I am right in claiming that, both in *Art and Philosophy* and in all of my recent work (including, preeminently, the *History* and the *Interpretation* volumes—and the *Relativism* volume), I nowhere claim that interpretation must be relativistic as a matter of "logical necessity." It is, in fact, central to my advocacy of the flux that there are no *de re* (modal) necessities at all (and that *that*, too, is not a modal necessity!). Against Carroll, I claim only that relativism is coherent and viable (despite charges to the contrary) *and* that, in interpretative contexts (where Intentional properties are involved)—particularly where historicity and constructivism and symbiosis are conceded (in the way I propose)—it is a foregone conclusion that no other conceptual strategy is dialectically as apt as a relativistic methodology. (I think that can be shown.) Furthermore, relativism is a *faute de mieux* argument regarding legitimative issues—not a matter regarding contingently deficient evidence (as Carroll suggests).

I acknowledge Carroll's complaint and I have tried to meet it. But I don't see any argument on Carroll's part to support the view that interpretation is best construed in nonrelativistic terms. At the very least, such a counterargument would require a theory of Intentional properties. I shall touch on that in a bit, but I think that recognizing the conceptual connection is the decisive thing (Carroll does not see that). I know of no satisfactory argument about general predicables, or Intentional predicables in particular, that weakens rather than strengthens the case for relativism. In fact, I know of *no* contemporary critic of relativism who has even advanced a full-blooded theory of general predicables—that is, one that is at once ontologically and epistemologically explicit.

Krausz offers the most detailed and accurate overview of my entire effort among the papers of this collection. I'm very grateful to him for this careful labor. We have exchanged on this many times, and I have benefited from trying to answer all his questions. On nearly all the essential issues—on flux, symbiosis, social construction, "myth," the realism/idealism matter, the culture/nature distinction, legitimation, relativism, individuation and identity, ontic indeterminacy, intentionality, *de re* necessity, consensus and criteria, and predication—Krausz has, on the whole, a very accurate command of my views. (I am fussy enough to make some adjustments, but that is not the essential thing.) Krausz is also aware of my views on history and cultural realism, that is, my treatment of "embodiment," "incarnation," "tokens-of-types," "Intentionality," and "historicity," though he does not summarize these notions in the essay here included. (Others address these other topics.)

I draw attention to two adjustments that seem to me important and that may go some way toward nipping possible misunderstandings before they arise. Krausz correctly notes that the doctrine of symbiosis is itself part of the organizing "myth" of my view of the flux, consequently, that "the thought that subject and object are symbiotically related cannot itself be a particular truth-claim, because particular truth-claims are posited within the space such a myth provides." But then, I think he slips when he goes on to conclude that "there cannot be plural myths from any one context" (110). What I say (here is the point of the change of language Carroll does not consider) is that a "myth" is a picture of the "universe," the "context of all contexts." The universe is all-inclusive in a sense in which (as Husserl remarks) "it" has no number. But I don't see why the universe cannot, at any point in discourse, be pictured in plural ways. On the contrary, I insist that "it" can *and* that, though there is "no fact of the matter" (for technical reasons that McCormick does not consider, namely, that there can be no further context in which the context of all contexts is itself contexted), we can assess the "fit" (not the "truth") of proposed myths in terms of their fruitfulness and amplitude with respect to ordinary truthclaims. (I may say that, in speaking of "myths" in this improved way, I have in mind recovering what I think Plato was after.)

Krausz certainly sees the point I'm making (as his comparison between Collingwood and me shows), but he falters here. (If what he says is what Collingswood believed, then there is an important difference between us.) The offending view (which Krausz also notes) I associate with Heraclitus, who admits the flux and then (apparently) insists that there is an invariant *logos* that rules the flux. Heraclitus's myth, I say, cannot be made to fit the flux perspicuously, because it appears to endorse *de re* necessities at the level of discursive truthclaims. Krausz rightly sees all this as a way of articulating my own version of pragmatism. In general, I may say, I am closer to Dewey's "Hegelian" vision than to Peirce's "Kantian" form of evolutionism; but, philosophically, Peirce is incomparably more interesting than Dewey; and Dewey himself was a very limited sort of Hegelian since he was not a historicist. In any case, Krausz sees how these views bear on the dismissal of "First Philosophy" (1–2), which I say is a "philosophical bet"; why the real = the constructed (9), which is an articulation of the myth of the flux; why "the indeterminacy of cultural entities" is congenial (115), despite being both a determinate and debatable claim; and why the defense of relativism is closely linked to the "indeterminacy of cultural entities" (115), which, once again, is dialectically accessible.

The second adjustment is trickier. I offer an encompassing "myth," the myth of the flux, but I never argue for it in the way of confirmation: First, because, it is a picture of the inclusive universe, about which there cannot be truth-claims if (as I say) truth-claims are contexted; and second, because, in spite of that we can assess the "fit" (not the "truth") of competing myths by considering whether and how particular doctrines (which can be disputed) can be perspicuously reconciled with it and it with them. Now, some important "philosophical" doctrines are *only* articulations of our executive myths, for instance, the symbiosis of subject and object. But there is no point in pursuing the details of such a myth unless there are also strategic truth-claims of a philosophical sort that are already in place. For instance, I *claim* that relativism *is* conceptually viable (against familiar objections), genuinely debatable, and particularly well suited to interpretive contexts. I cannot, therefore, quite accept Krausz's formulation, viz.:

> Denying the globalism of the theory of the flux would be tantamount to affirming that the cognizing self and the cognized world are not symbiotized in some universe of discourse, and that such universes are not artifactually posited. On Margolis's view one gives up the idea of *de re* necessities: there are no necessary structures in the world. Yet this allows apparent necessities, seen as such from within the perspective of one's historical place. (119–20)

The "globalism" of the flux is itself a benign equivocation: *qua* myth, *it* is not disputed in the way of truth-claims. (If you say it is "disputed" in the way of a "fit" between the discursive and the mythic, I should not object. The same is true of symbiosis.) *For each element in the myth,* there will be, subtended, *some* important set of determinate philosophical claims on the resolution of which the felicity of the myth we favor may be decided. It is, as Krausz rightly remarks, never more than a holistic picture, never criterial with respect to truth, a picture such that all substantive questions are construed as arising within the inclusive "space" of the universe (120–21). But, if so, then, in a strict sense, I do not *affirm* symbiosis (as Krausz puts it), and I do not merely "give up the idea of *de re* necessities" (as Krausz also indicates). That is, I do not draw the *truth* of symbiosis from the flux, and I do not *treat* the *denial* of *de re* necessities (which the flux "subtends") as *entailed* by the myth of the flux. Rather I *demonstrate* that there are no compelling arguments in favor of *de re* necessities (contrary to what Aristotle thought); that there is no necessity in subscribing to Kant's view of transcendental necessity and synthetic *a priori* truths; and so on. Because I cannot regard my own demonstration as yielding an affirmative *de re* necessity of its own, I treat it as a philosophical *bet* (about what *can* be demonstrated) and raise that up into my "myth." Hence, also, what I say regarding the logic of interpretation (relativism) is both argumentatively supported and mythically reconciled! That *de re* necessities will seem compelling from this "horizon" or that or from this *episteme* or that is precisely what I take Foucault to have had in mind in speaking of the "historical *a priori*"; it is part of his "genealogical" outlook on his archaeologies, which I find entirely congenial.

Perhaps the single most important application of these rather fussy distinctions rests with the following. "Mythically," symbiosis is a picture of the universe oriented to epistemic matters—in which, that is, there is no principled disjunction between the subjective and the objective; "discursively," I claim to be able to demonstrate that general predicables ("real generals," in Peirce's idiom) cannot be accounted for except in terms of the consensual tolerance of the collective practices of historical societies. I treat the problem of universals, or of nominalism and realism regarding the use of general predicates, as a philosophical *claim*. I have an answer! But the answer, which entails a "discursive" symbiosis between the subjective and the objective (a most strategic notion) is then itself subtended by, or reconciled with, my ("mythic") picture of the entire universe (the rejection of *de re* necessities of any kind). What that helps me to make clear is that our picture of *reality independent of inquiry* cannot fail to be an inference or a projection from *a constructivist (or symbiotized) realism*. That is not an idealism in the standard sense, but the augmented argument would show that a realism that insists on the independence of physical reality is always a subaltern, easily accommodated thesis. If any one thinks such a realism can be made stronger, then I say he must be able to demonstrate at least the cognate independence of general predicables. I say that that cannot be done—in the sense in which I "bet" it can't be done—given that all known efforts fail in the way they do!

Straight off, therefore, I am bound to disagree with Nicholas

Rescher: "Claims to the truth of statements at the level of our scientific concerns [he says: that is, he said in the original draft of his essay] involve an element of idealization. No doubt 'the real truth' is one, but in this real and imperfect world of ours we have to accept the limitations of imperfection and face the fact that different inquirers living at different times and in different circumstances do have—and are bound to have—different ideas about the truth of things." (I take the liberty of citing a line that I have not been able to find in the final version. I think it is still Rescher's view; it is also particularly helpful in pinpointing the essential *aporia* of his thesis. The rest of the essay bears this out.) With due respect, I confess I cannot see how what Rescher claims *can* be demonstrated or how it can be shown that its denial produces self-contradiction or self-defeating paradox or is epistemically impoverished in any way. Truth is not demonstrably "one" in any epistemically objective sense!

There you have the link between Rescher's master claim and Aristotle's *Metaphysics* Gamma—and what I have already said about Davidson and Putnam and Rosen and Page and Stern. I simply insist that Rescher's inability to demonstrate his *Grenzbegriff* (it is the inability of all of us) opens the way to the defense of relativism. I cannot see how Rescher can deny the point. He himself betrays its tone when he says (by way of an argumentative ellipsis he cannot overcome): "Relativism is the doctrine that people make their judgments by standards and criteria that have no inherent validity or cogency because their standing and status lies solely and wholly in their acceptance by the group" (1). I take this to be true, although mere "acceptance" is *not* criterial (as Wittgenstein makes clear); but I don't see what it is supposed to rule out in the way of normative or critical or objective (or "realist") rigor or comparative appraisals or the like. On the contrary, *if* (with Rescher) one insists that there must be some "larger, group-transcending 'position of impersonal rationality'" (1), then I must respectfully ask for the relevant epistemic clues for supporting *that* "position." I'm afraid there are no superior rules that could be supplied, unless we are already in a privileged position—which Rescher would deny. I do not think the puzzle can be resolved by favoring "us" over the Azande or the Nuer! There is no real difference between intra- and inter-societal exchange where there are bilinguals and no privileged rules for individuating societies and languages (see 130–34, Rescher).

I offer two objections: First, the condition from which we putatively begin we cannot escape; second, consensus "by the group" is initially holistic, not criterial at all, but *whatever* are posited as epistemic criteria are no more than artifacts of *that* consensus. So I deny Rescher's claims about "rationality": First, because (*pace* Aristotle) rationality cannot be discerned in any way that is not subject to the constraints Rescher has already admitted; second, because the relativist is not obliged to subscribe to what Rescher calls "egalitarianism" or "egalitarian relativism." (*I* certainly *do* not subscribe to that doctrine.) Relativism is entirely compatible with making comparative (normative) judgments of truth, validity, goodness, reasonableness, and the like. All that is needed is the admission that the grounds for such judgments are artifacts of our own critical reflection and that we cannot guarantee that we occupy a neutral niche. Hence, when Rescher says that judgments of truth or goodness or rightness "are always made relative to a potentially variable basis" (127), he invokes the deep equivocation I have already discussed, namely, that between the meaning of "true" (and the like) and the testing of supposed truths. On pain of contradiction or paradox, we must reject the relationalist reading of "true"; and, admitting its epistemic vacuity, we may (easily) concede the benign "relativity" of the (epistemic) testing of would-be truthclaims. This is common ground for relativists and nonrelativists alike. (This was the double point I had pressed against Rockmore earlier.) I cannot agree, therefore, that "relativism opposes *reason* rather than *truth*" (the wording is a little altered in the final version). Rescher needs to show how reason or truth or both can be secured by *some* "group-transcending 'position of impersonal rationality' " (128). To be perfectly blunt: he cannot do it.

Let me be as clear as I can be. I agree that epistemic grounds are consensual, artifactually specified within the practices of one society or another. But, for one thing, "consensual" is not—is never—criterial in the sense at stake. (Consensual criteria are possible of course, but only and always in a sense subaltern to the sense here intended.) For a second, such grounds are never "final," as Rescher claims relativists maintain. (Their being final would produce self-referential paradox.) And, for a third, "cultural relativity" *is not* a form of relativism at all. (It is logically trivial *and* compatible with our being "bilingual" regarding epistemic matters ranging over different societies.) The fact is fixing epistemic differences, evidence, norms, truths, rationality; and the like is itself an artifact that presupposes the consensual sharing of a language and practice that we can never fix independently (and never need to). The heart of my argument is *not* that we must accommodate relativism because other societies (say, Winch's Azande) judge differently from us, or even use a "different logic" (as Lévy-Bruhl suggests), but rather that *we ourselves* cannot convincingly force an "our" epistemic concerns within the boundaries of a non-relativistic "logic." Rescher does not come to terms with this possibility *at all*.

Rescher says very little about my own version of relativism—which is fine. I cannot say for certain that he regards me as an advocate of "indifferentist relativism" (141). But I have tried to argue that I am not a skeptic about truth. On the contrary, it is part of my argument that idealists (like Rescher) and realists (like Davidson and Putnam, in their different ways) *are* skeptics, whether they admit the fact or not: Rescher, because truth is an ideal he admits he cannot discern or legitimately approximate; Davidson, because he believes every effort to legitimate truth is itself a form of skepticism;[25] Putnam (at least up to *The Many Faces of Realism*), because truth is a regulative ideal that, within the terms of internal realism, cannot ensure "a Dedekind cut" between the subjective and the objective. The robust relativist simply draws the consequence of what idealists and realists everywhere admit. That may explain why I posit a symbiosis of subject and object as an element of my executive "myth."

I venture one further consideration. Rescher holds that it "is literally nonsense" to admit, as anthropologists sometimes do, that primitive societies may have "a conception of rationality different from ours." The reason he gives is a vigorous one: "If they are to conceive of [iron or elephants, say] at all, then their conceptions must substantially accord with ours. Iron objects are *by definition* what we take them to be; 'elephant' is our word and *elephant* our conception. If you are not talking about *that*, then you are not talking about *elephants* at all" (131). Yes, of course. But *what we mean* by "iron" or "elephant" *in our society* is, in principle, no less disputable than what *"they"* mean by what *we* call iron and elephant! There is no principled difference between inter- and intrasocietal disputes about meaning, truth, and rationality. That is the upshot of Quine's famous argument about the "indeterminacy of translation," although I must be frank to say that Quine's version of the argument is undoubtedly incoherent and self-defeating because it privileges a neutral range of "stimulus meanings" or of what "holophrastic sentences" convey.[26] Quine's lapse is, at bottom, not very different from Rescher's idealizing of truth or Putnam's treating truth as a regulative ideal. (I don't deny that they look very different.) As is usual with Quine, Quine champions both sides of the impossible divide.

It's at this point that I claim that we cannot avoid "interpretive *tertia*" at every step in our theorizing about truth and reality and rationality. (The term is Rorty's, though Rorty and Davidson oppose the need for invoking *tertia*.[27]) The need for *tertia* is a *bet* based on a *demonstration* that no known idealism or realism can secure the one "real truth" that Rescher pursues, which itself provides part of the argumentative grounds for *positing* the myth of the flux along symbiotized lines. I cannot see any fundamental difference between Rescher's thesis and the failed thesis of Davidson's "The Very Idea of a Conceptual Scheme"—except, of course, that Davidson is not an idealist of any sort, and Rescher is an avowed pluralist confident about the asymptotic drift of rational idealization.

I need not, therefore, oppose Rescher's proposal of a *"perspectival rationalism* (or *contextualism)"* (143), but I cannot see that Rescher provides, *anywhere*, an epistemic basis (rather than an attractive hope) to support the belief that all our would-be self-corrective efforts will in the limit yield approximations to the unique truth. (Here, Rescher means to be a pluralist, whereas I am a relativist. Still, Rescher cannot secure the epistemic grounds he needs.) Here, I suggest, one may catch a glimpse of Charles Sanders Peirce as the *éminence grise* behind all the current forms of inductivism, falsificationism, liberalism, progressivism, and the like—collecting not only Rescher but Popper and Lakatos and Habermas and Putnam as well. I'm afraid Rescher has forgotten that his regulative ideal is nowhere secured—epistemically. There are three themes that must be kept in mind: One, the failure of a "regulative" idea, if there is nothing "constitutive" to back it up (see 150); second, the fact that the admission "that other people hold views different from ours" does not entail "indifferentism" but also does not overcome it (see 147); and, third, the fact that, although the pursuit of truth (goodness, rationality) is normative, it does not follow that there is a norm of truth (goodness, rationality) that we pursue. My comment on the third theme is akin to Wittgenstein's profound conception of "following a rule": to act in accord with a social practice is (in a sense) "to follow a rule"; but, on Wittgenstein's view, there is no rule that we follow in so acting.[28] Precisely.

To favor our cognitive position over *others* (143–44) is, as far as I can see, completely vacuous. Because what *we* affirm as "ours" will be an artifact of our so affirming, and what "we" affirm as our criterion of affirmation will be no less an artifact of the same sort. (There you have the clue to McCormick's and Carroll's concerns about first- and second-order questions.) Hence, Rescher is faced with a dilemma. His contextualism leads either to something like Rockmore's relationalism (which I believe is self-defeating) or to something like my own robust relativism (which he would wish to avoid). I see no other option for him. Furthermore, I take the lacuna in Rescher's argument to be precisely the same one that I detect in Quine and Davidson and Rorty. Rorty, for instance—to take Rorty as a stand—in for the others—falls back to "ethnocentric" consensus; but he does not face the fact that *that* implicates an appeal to an interpretive *tertium* that reinstates the conceptual connection between first- and second-order queries. That was the reason for my objection to Shusterman's Rortyanized version of Deweyan pragmatism. But if you admit interpretive *tertia* in all our epistemic dealings, then, of course, both Rescher's and Putnam's idealization of truth fails utterly. Interestingly, neither can secure the pluralistic realism each would champion.

I venture another distinction, because Rescher has made some adjustments in his original paper. It is no part of my argument that we do not understand one another or that we do not share criteria of truth and objectivity and neutrality and the like. I concede all that, and believe no relativist need resist such concessions. What I hold, however, is that there is no would-be absolute, self-evident, uniquely specifiable, ultimate or ultimately neutral conception or criterion of truth and the rest that is not hostage, consensually, in terms that are never more than tacit, not themselves criterially accessible in any way that might escape the same constraint. There is no argument, I claim, that permits us to move from the admitted fact that we understand one another to the modal truth that there must therefore be—and we must be able to discern—some determinate universal mark or criterion of objective meaning and understanding. Shared meanings and understanding are themselves reflexive artifacts of the encompassing consensus of sharing a language and a culture. As far as I can see, nothing that Rescher says gainsays that. In this sense, "our own standpoint" is not a "higher standpoint," a higher "mode of rationality," from which to judge the behavior of alien societies. Because what is to count as *our* standpoint will also have to be constructed within our own society! And yet, of course, we do succeed in communicative ways; that is, we quite reasonably construe what we do *as* succeeding, according to this or that epistemic interpretation. There is no final resting place and there need be none.

I don't deny, therefore, what Rescher terms "the primacy of our own position." It's only that I don't infer from that that "there is a position" that is "ours" that we can fix as having "primacy" in the sense wanted! I treat all that in the same way (already mentioned) in which, in Wittgenstein, following a rule does not entail that there is a determinate rule that one follows. That's all! I see no reason to think that Rescher has secured more ground than that. I must add that, *if* Rescher concedes this much, then the defense of relativism need not depend at all on the alleged paradoxes of communication: grasping one another's meaning, we may conclude that some judgments simply cannot exceed relativistic constraints, cannot reach to strict bivalence. Rescher misses this possibility.

Rescher has now applied his argument to my own version of relativism. But it looks as if he assumes that *I* treat a relativistic "logic" as either equivalent to, or analogous with, a probabilistic logic. I do not, of course: First, because probabilistic logics are usually tethered to bivalent logics (as Hempel has made clear); second, because I hold that a relativistic logic is a many-valued logic that replaces bivalence (in certain sectors of inquiry at least), treats the bivalent values "true" and "false" asymmetrically, and countenances "incongruent" judgments (judgments that on a bivalent logic but not now would yield contradictories). Here, against Rescher, I must say, there *is* no argument to show that *semantic* matters as opposed to *cognitive* matters must be treated bivalently. (Cognitive disagreements, Rescher concedes, may be treated probabilistically.) But, of course, if there is no principled disjunction between epistemic and ontic considerations or (against Dummett and the tradition that runs from Frege through the positivists to Quine) between semantic and metaphysical considerations, then Rescher's assumption that semantic matters must be treated bivalently remains to be secured. Certainly he has not shown that "we cannot or should not with Margolis speak of 'the space of relativistic truthvalues' as somehow not bipolar" (154). I cannot find the argument in what he offers. I think the important difference between us is this: Rescher is an idealist, who therefore believes there is a sense in which the norms of rationality can be *effectively idealized*; I am not an idealist. I deny that there is any principled disjunction between "subjects" and "objects"; hence, rationality, objectivity, knowledge, and the like are all historicized artifacts—not for that reason arbitrary in the least. (But, also, not capable of disallowing relativism!)

Before closing this matter and turning to other topics, let me add a brief word about the differences between relativism and pluralism. (I hope this will catch up the reason for resisting the rather different arguments offered by Stern, Rockmore, McCormick, Carroll, Krausz, and Rescher.) Bear in mind that the *only* way to avoid the benign "relativity" of epistemic testing is to subscribe to some form of cognitive privilege, foundationalism, self-evidence, indubitability, or the like. If you admit that, then you must admit that epistemic relativity is (as such) conceptually neutral (and trivial) as between relativistic and nonrelativistic theories of knowledge. The idea that *all* epistemologies that abandon privilege are (if viable) relativistic (Rockmore's thesis) seems to me to be completely unsupported and not in any obvious way *entailed* by evidentiary "relativity." (It needs an argument of its own—and, as I say, *that* argument cannot be an argument in favor of "relationalism," which is, in any case, initially an alethic rather than an epistemic distinction, one, of course, that is intrinsically paradoxical.)

On my view, pluralism is the thesis that, in pertinent interpretive contexts, we are prepared to favor (politically or appreciatively, say) how things "may be construed" from the vantage of this interpretive *tertium* or that—where "may be construed" is the logical counterpart of how things "may appear" in perceptual terms when viewed from this perspective or that. The important point is that pluralism, thus defined, employs an idiom that is the counterpart of the "is"/"appears" idiom in perceptual contexts: hence, that all valid appearings (plural interpretations or the like) are compatible and reconcilable with the way things (the "things" in question) actually *are*. Pluralism, therefore, construed epistemically—not in terms of social or political tolerance alone—is (1) entirely compatible with a bivalent logic and (2) does not challenge the canonical view that we can determine how things actually are.

Relativism is entirely different, because (1) it replaces, in context, a bivalent logic with a many-valued logic, (2) it countenances "incongruent" judgments (which pluralism does not and cannot), and (3) it disallows, in context, the option of determining how things *are* (in the sense analogous to the "is"/"appears" idiom). Remember: relativism and bivalence are themselves compatible if rightly segregated in accord with relevance constraints. (If you reread the *Theaetetus,* you will see that Socrates "defeats" the Protagorean argument by overriding item (3) of the tally just given. That is the point of the immense failure of the whole history of philosophy to rehabilitate Protagoras. It is, I claim, the inevitable consequence of the failure of First Philosophy.) My point is that, wherever *tertia* are required, it is possible (not yet more than possible) that relativism cannot be avoided. Rockmore, I believe, holds that this is the case everywhere. I happen to agree—in accord with the doctrine of the flux—but the argument needs to be made with care, and, in any case, saying *that* is *not* tantamount to affirming relationalism.

V

The remaining five papers take up puzzles in the ontology of culture.

Dale Jacquette and I have debated (in various ways) a number of the issues he raises in his interesting challenge. His general summary of the various lines of my "metaphysics of culture" is on the whole accurate. If I take exception to certain details (chiefly about types and kinds and predicables), it is primarily in the interest of answering his intended (his well-intentioned) metaphysical economies. He finds my metaphysics "three-tiered": centered (1) on "the material embodiment of culturally emergent entities," (2) on the "type-token distinction" (applied in resolving certain puzzles involving artworks in particular), and (3) on "historicism or contextualism" (in terms of which the puzzles involving the first two distinctions are rightly situated) (3). I find this entirely fair. Jacquette proceeds from there to offer a number of objections, particularly to the formulation of "embodiment" that I originally offered in *Persons and Minds.*

I find myself in a position not entirely unlike the one I was obliged to occupy in countering Carroll's objections. Let me say, therefore, that I believe that my account in *Persons and Minds*—or, in *Persons and Minds and in Culture and Cultural Entities*—can meet Jacquette's counterproposals; but, I have, since then, discovered stronger and more perspicuous formulations.

The main changes are these. In *Persons and Minds,* I was somewhat careless about functionalism (in the sense in which that notion has been developed in the philosophy of mind); in *Culture and Cultural Entities,* I explicitly strengthen the sense of embodiment and incarnation, so that a purely formal functionalism is avoided and replaced. I think this was always my view (but I won't protest too strenuously); in any case, I came to see the inadequacy of functionalism is grasping the inherent inadequacy of Putnam's functionalism well before Putnam conceded its failure.[29] Second, I came to see that Brentano's and Husserl's versions of intentionality were inadequate: both because they were confined to the mental or psychological (hence, were solipsistic) and because they did not recognize the complexity of certain analogous or more inclusive structures in societal practices and cultural artifacts (not reducible or analyzable in terms of the mental). These themes were already implicit in *Art and Philosophy* (chapter 3) and explicit in *Culture and Cultural Entities* (chapter 1). I distinguish my own notion of intentionality by a typographical device ("Intentionality" written with a capital "I"), which most of my more recent work has explored (notably, the *History* and *Interpretation* volumes and *Historied Thought, Constructed World*). Jacquette is interested in Brentano's notion of intentionality but he does not address the differences between our views.

Third, there was an entire family of distinctions that were rather primitively developed at the time of writing *Persons and Minds, Culture and Cultural Entities, Art and Philosophy,* and *Philosophy of Psychology* that I now feel I have a firmer grip on and that bear on Jacquette's argument more felicitously: in particular, the analysis of predicates and predicables, individuation and numerical identity, historicity, indeterminacies of reference and "nature," the logic of relativism, and the conditions of working out a coherent philosophy of the flux. Jacquette ranges over all of my books (which is a bit daunting), but I think his main criticism centers on the formulations given in *Persons and Minds, Culture and Cultural Entities, Art and Philosophy,* and *Philosophy of Psychology.* I don't regard my mentioning all this as an argument of any kind, but it may help to locate the thrust of my rejoinder. It would not be unfair to say that my present view is that all and only cultural entities (or phenomena) are (1) embodied, (2) emergent in terms of possessing Intentional properties, (3) tokens-of-types, and (4) histories or historicized by "nature." I think this accords fairly well with what Jacquette himself suggests as my "three-tiered" metaphysics.

But if that be granted, then Jacquette's counterarguments do not succeed. For instance, Jacquette's example of a valley meeting all the conditions (which he enumerates) from *Persons and Minds* fails, because the intended countercase *never* accommodates what is distinctive in the way of *properties* that obtain exclusively among cultural phenomena—namely, what I now collect as the forms of (incarnated) Intentionality, which is what condition (2) was originally all about. The seeming effectiveness of Jacquette's counterexample depends on leaving the expression, "of a kind," completely uninterpreted. So that all Jacquette does is imagine *any* property (of *any* kind) that a valley might possess that a mountain would be precluded from possessing! But, of course, valleys and mountains are natural objects, *not* cultural or culturally emergent entities at all. (His case cannot be squared with what *he* acknowledges to be my "three-tiered" metaphysics.) So he amends the example and puts "an artwork *Valley*" in place of the physical valley—in a sense akin to that of Marcel Duchamp's *Bottlerack* (231). Mind you, in the original case, he had held that "there are particulars that satisfy Margolis' seven conditions, but that intuitively are not embodied one in the other" (299). That was a mistake, because, to be embodied, the example would have had to possess an "intentional" property of the required sort, which, even by the time of *Culture and Cultural Entities* (1984), I had already dubbed "Intentional" properties. (The thesis was already in place in *Persons and Minds*.)

If you grant that much, then, plainly, Jacquette's new counterexample (*Valley*) *is* a confirming example of *a cultural entity*, not a disconfirming one! What Jacquette misses is the very point I have already pressed against Arthur Danto, namely, that an artwork *cannot* (contrary to what Danto supposes) be numerically identical with any merely physical object. The reason is that an artwork will *possess* (Intentional) properties that a physical object does not and cannot (on the usual, and on Danto's, view) actually possess. Paradox results from failing to recognize this.[30] As far as I know, Danto has never successfully met the objection. (Also, I explicitly discuss Duchamp's *Fountain* and *Bottlerack*: nothing that is culturally emergent can be identical with what it has emerged from. Danto misses the fact that *he* cannot treat persons "rhetorically" and that what holds for persons holds reasonably well for artworks (in terms of the " 'is' of artistic identification"). Jacquette does not, I think, argue consistently here—granting that he admits emergence: mereology is not the issue at all. (Jacquette goes astray here, and Danto's entire thesis collapses.)

Perhaps I do not understand what Jacquette is claiming. He offers the example of "a stone with a charcoal drawing," and he claims that "when it is scrubbed from the stone . . . if the stone remains, then the drawing's material embodiment is not totally destroyed when the drawing is destroyed" (231). But, of course, *when* the drawing is scrubbed off, there *is* no *embodiment*! I don't see the problem, and I think Jacquette pretty well admits my point. Yet he also says he is "convinced that the counterexamples I [that is, Jacquette] had posed are lethal to Margolis' original statement of the conditions for embodiment" (232). I have done the best I can to explain why I don't think Jacquette's countercases work. His emendation (viii*) seems to me to be a part of the original sense of my own tally. I certainly never intended to suggest that an embodied entity possesses *physical* properties that *its* embodying entity did not or could not possess. That would be incompatible with my notion of cultural emergence.

I *never* actually "allow the possibility of materially embodied entities that are not also culturally emergent" (230). ("Embodiment" is a term I reserve for the space of human culture exclusively.) I do acknowledge, in *Persons and Minds* and elsewhere, the important but puzzling case of biological emergence and, within the biological, the existence of societal "entities" such as a hive of bees or a colony of termites. My present view is that these have to do with the proper explanation of so-called informational properties, which have been scandalously ignored. The essential question is whether informational properties are distinct from Intentional properties and whether they are heuristically or realistically ascribed. I now regard them as "anthropomorphized" (that is, heuristically modeled on the reflexive, reportorial process of linguistically apt selves), even if distinct from cultural properties, whether heuristic or realist, sometimes reducible physicalistically, sometimes not, but in any case such as not to disturb the general lines of my account. I know of no similarly ramified view. (The ontology of "information" is widely neglected. Dretske, for instance, wrongly reverses the conceptual relationship between the informational and the cognitive—*a fortiori,* the informational and the cultural.)

On the type/token distinction, I should now say that "types" are no more than predicables and *real* insofar as they are predicated of existent entities and true of them. *No predicable is real otherwise.* That was the original intention of the tally Jacquette cites, though not the wording. What I wanted to say (and did) was that the type/token idiom was cast in terms of *instantiating particulars* (which is novel and peculiar to cultural entities) but that *types were not themselves actual (existent) particulars.*

"Types" are nominalizations of predicables (of Intentional sorts) used for purposes of counting cultural *entities* (words, artworks). The issue in the wings concerns: (1) the rejection of existent universals as abstract individual things; and (2) the saving of realism with respect to general predicables. Here, I follow Peirce's formal account of the distinction between existence (Secondness) and reality (Thirdness), though I believe I have fashioned a theory of "real generals" (Peirce's term) that Peirce would regard as too nominalistic. I think Peirce was wrong, and I have argued the matter elsewhere.[31] Here, Jacquette clearly misunderstands me (though it may be my own fault) when he says that I admit that "sets and kinds or universals exist even if their members or instances do not, and are neither created nor destroyed" (234). That is a canonical view that I report but never endorse. On the contrary, because artworks *are* created, the language of universals won't do! (I have applied this against Wolterstorff's very curious Platonism about art, because Wolterstorff is obliged to suppose that the "content" of Gogol's *Dead Souls* must be eternally in God's mind—certainly well before the history of nineteenth-century Russia!)

Jacquette seems to think that when I speak of "kinds" I am speaking of "universals" (236, also 238), but that is precisely what I oppose. Kinds *are* predicables (if real) and merely predicates (if the question of reality is not at stake). So I want to hold a realism of properties but deny the existence of universals. (That *is* Peirce's view. I think Peirce defends it brilliantly, and I am happy to follow him in this. But I also think Peirce goes wrong in his analysis of what "real generals" are. I am also quite willing to admit that not all predicables are *properties*.) My own solution is that real generals obtain only in the "sense-bestowing" constructions of what we take to be the real world (which, I say, are subtended, dialectically, by the myth of symbiosis).[32] (Here, I avoid the presumption and para-doxicality of Kant's and Husserl's doctrines.)

I think this shows that Jacquette has seriously misunderstood me. He asks: "Is it necessary to suppose with Margolis that there are particular abstract types in addition to concrete particulars and uni-versal kinds?" (237). This is the key to the second of Jacquette's intended economies. Jacquette takes it that I *have* admitted existent universals, whereas all that I admit are "real generals." Hence, Jacquette attempts to show that, *if* there are universals, then there is no need for *types*. He's right, but then I reject both existent univer-sals and existent types: types (you remember) are nominalizations of Intentional predicables.

I believe all Jacquette's would-be counterinstances—for instance, "the art type 'pyramid' " (239)—trade on this mistaken reading. I'll make one last stab at this and let the matter drop. Jacquette says, "The type-token distinction is also less competent than the traditional Platonic theory of universals" (241). But, on my view, the "Platonic" theory (as Plato must have realized) is *utterly* "incompetent," because the *only* question the theory of predicables serves is the epistemic question of how to ascribe properties to this and that: No one has the least idea how to *use* universals epistemically (as distinct from using predicates) in making true predications or ascriptions! That's why I reject universals. I know of no better argument (although I have now fashioned—and published—a further theory of predicables).

Jacquette closes his account with a rather nice perception of my historicizing all the pertinent questions. For example, he correctly notes that it falls out as a consequence that "there can be no adequate conception of transcendent *a priori* modalities" (246). But then, I think he never quite lets up on the (mistaken) idea that types *are* (meant, by me, to be) existent abstract individuals. All his discussion of the baroque, for instance—where he considers that "the type has been annihilated" (247)—loses its bite as soon as the correction is made. Predicables, after all, are inherently general, even if uniquely attributed (truly) to this or that; wherever predicates are not instantiated at all, I drop the language of realism: any attempt to revive it is Platonism. For real predicables are so denominated only in our constructed world and only in epistemic terms. There is no other recourse. (That's what Peirce had been unwilling to concede.)

All Jacquette's discussion of the "destruction" of *types* and their regeneration at some later time confuses the fact, I'm afraid, that (1) there are (there exist) no types (a fortiori, no kinds (see 250); (2) particular cultural entities are tokens-of-types (not tokens and not types); (3) types, treated as particulars, are heuristic nominalizations of predicables; and (4) predicables are real (generals) only in a world of existent things. I don't know if it is true, but Jacquette may have been influenced by Wolterstorff and Richard Wollheim, who (on my argument) have made a muddle of the type/token distinction. (They are Platonists.) Jacquette himself eschews Platonic kinds (250–51). I hope Jacquette won't find my resistance to his improvements too stingy. He himself recommends "substituting for Margolis's historicism an ontically neutral semantics for reference to and true predication of properties to kinds" (252). The fate of this, I suggest, depends on reconsidering the proper treatment of the type/token distinction. Of course, as Jacquette also rightly observes (he says he is "uncomfortable" about it (254), *if* my historicized ontology is admitted, then there can be "no neutral semantics," Of course!

I shall say very little about Marx Wartofsky's paper. The reason is in reflecting on my work, Wartofsky turns very naturally to his own; and, in addressing Wartofsky's work, I must, similarly, turn to my own. Wartofsky and I are (as I have often thought) not quite identical intellectual twins sprung from the same fertilized *praxis*. (In fact, we were, as Wartofsky mentions, graduate students at Columbia at the same time.) I'm hardly surprised to find that (as I already knew) Wartofsky is both a "historical epistemologist" and a "historical or constructivist ontologist"—which Aristotle is not (209). I find myself in the happy role of egging him on to publish his own full account (long promised). I am, I admit, a little shy in the neighborhood of Wartofsky's nice but less than innocent compliments. He knows me in a way he obviously knows himself—and I, him.

What he particularly points to is the important question, whether a "historicized ontology" applies "to precultural, prehuman 'nature', to the physical or material world itself " as it does to the world of human culture? (210). I treat this as an antinomy (in *Historied Thought, Constructed World,* which had not yet appeared at the time of Wartofsky's writing). I say that physical nature is (ontically) "prior" to the emergence of human culture, but also that the intelligible world is an artifact of a historicized human culture (which is also therefore "prior," epistemically prior) and that that is not an insoluble paradox. (The "priorities" are of different sorts, you see—and reconciled in the notion of symbiosis.) Wartofsky offers two observations, which confirm for me our common ontological fascination: First, if we admit the "two" ontologies of nature and culture, then (as he says) "one precedes or is the ontological precondition for the other" (214); second, admitting only *that* is not yet to provide for an ontologically pertinent account of either or of the relation between the two (214, 218). Precisely.

I have always thought that the "world-knot" (I think the expression is Schopenhauer's) was not the mind/body problem but the culture/nature problem, within the terms of which (though not in any simple way), the first is rightly located and then resolved. For, the phenomena we call "mind" are sometimes confined within the biological world and sometimes incarnate (as in humans) in the biological world but culturally emergent with respect to it. I see the first as "anthropomorphized" in terms of the second, and I see the second as *not* confined to the limits of the neurophysiological (though incarnated). The clue I pursue is premised on there being a strong similarity between the ontological structure of persons (or selves) and that of artworks. The human mind, I think, is a culturally formed competence that operates in cultural space but is biologically incarnate. If so, then, of course, physicalism is defeated at a stroke—merely by acknowledging the work of science!

Here, I am recalling Jacquette's and Krausz's and Rockmore's summaries of my metaphysics. Culturally emergent entities are (I say) indissolubly "embodied" in natural (physical, biological, electronic) entities; their properties are indissolubly "incarnate" in the properties of the other. For me, this adumbrates a way of escaping both dualism and reductionism. I associate the solution (thus far) with certain more or less logical problems (reference and predication, numerical identity and individuation) and also with our sense of the experienced world (existence and reality, the presence and absence of Intentionality, and, especially, the conceptual link between realism and reality). But these matters are never entirely disjoint. (That is important and neglected.)

I should say that (for me) the most interesting American philosopher is Peirce. I believe Peirce's most important intuition (which I don't think he always pursued in the most fruitful way) was centered on his distinction between Secondness and Thirdness. To put things in a nutshell: I resolve the antinomy Wartofsky and I share by a use of Peirce's categories and by construing the solution as *ontologically historicized* within the terms of symbiosis. Peirce was an evolutionist, not a historicist. I am a historicist as well as an evolutionist of sorts, but I give up all of Peirce's purple notions of evolutionary love and objective mind or thought in nature apart from humans and the like. That is why I find Dewey so attractive (but dull), Wittgenstein so natural (but halfbaked), Foucault so daring (but careless). The anticipation of the best features of all three (but not more) I find in Marx's notion of *praxis*.[33] Rockmore says I am a Hegelian. I am happy to concede the point: Hegel pruned of Hegel is the master of Marx, Peirce, Dewey, Wittgenstein, and Foucault—and, I may as well say, of Nietzsche, Husserl, Heidegger, and Derrida as well.

The resolution I offer runs as follows: Nature is prior to culture, in the way of Secondness; culture is prior to nature, in the way of Thirdness; but "seconds" (existing things) are "seconds" *in* the space of Thirdness, and "thirds" (intelligible structures) are "thirds" *in* application to the space of Secondness; and neither can be reduced to the other. The very distinction between cognizing subjects and cognized objects is an artifact drawn from the symbiotized world—and is open to revision along historicized lines. (Think of this as a solution to Kuhn's problem.) I may as well add that, since the drafting of my replies to the papers collected here, American metaphysics-*cum*-epistemology has taken a somewhat new turn—with the publication of John McDowell's *Mind and World* and Putnam's Dewey Lectures (influenced by McDowell).[34] This is not the place to explore their work, but, in my opinion, they have, *via* (what I call) symbiosis, hit on a reasonable way to recover a viable realism without risking the usual forms of skepticism. The trouble is, granting that, they do not (yet) address the *epistemic* relationship between subjects and objects, which (admitting the artifactual nature of our conceptual resources) *cannot* be ignored *if* skepticism is to be genuinely avoided. That is precisely why I regard the analysis of reference and predication as so strategic. (William James seems to me to have come very close to the theses I am advocating here. Putnam, who professes to follow James to a large extent—and who indeed does—misconstrues the treatment of epistemic *and* ontic matters in James and thus neglects them in his own new view. I myself am not taking James's lead here, though I admit its charm. Have a look, for instance, at "Pragmatism and Humanism," which is the best clue I know for reading Putnam!)

Physical nature is *not* Intentionally structured (we say), but *its* not being Intentionally structured is an Intentional imputation. Human culture *is* intrinsically Intentional (we say), but its existence (as intentional) *presupposes* the non-Intentional powers of actual physical nature. At any time t, what we suppose to be the structure of nature and culture is, at t' later than t, altered by our changed conceptual horizon at t'. The change is epistemic, in terms of our discursive claims; but it is also ontic, in terms of a symbiotized constructivism. (The later concession is *not* a form of traditional idealism.) So its historicity has both an epistemic and an ontic face. To say that actual things are really thus and so is to say (1) that they are thus constituted epistemically; and to say that they are thus constituted is to say (2) that we find them to be independently thus and so; and to say that these are two ways of saying the same thing is (3) to say that, within the myth of symbiosis, our accounts of what exists and is real vary genealogically. Reality's independence of inquiry—independence *tout court*—cannot be anything but holistic; once made determinate, it cannot violate the symbiotized constraints of the epistemic.

The clue Wartofsky and I share (I am very glad of it) is that *knowledge cannot be naturalized but is real.* I take that to be the theme pragmatism shares with Hegel and Marx. Grant that, I say, and the plausibility of the antinomy and its resolution will seem genuine. Deny it and you will dismiss the whole structure as a house of cards. That is why I believe Quine's "Epistemology Naturalized" is such an unsatisfactory essay: It promises what it never delivers; also, of course, Quine's slyer progeny suppose they need never give an accounting.[35] (They never do.) So I accept Wartofsky's good-natured chiding about the promissory note of my "praxism." (I have already abandoned the term: It has hurt the ears of several good philosophers.) I claim only that in my (most recent) *History* and *Interpretation* volumes, I have tried to give a fair sense of how *praxis* genuinely enters into my thinking about science, history, and interpretive criticism. I think my best shot here is not so much in the close interpretation of the history of science and history and criticism, as in the theory of reference and predication. Wartofsky never mentions that. It is a neglected topic but a strategic one: It is one, in fact, in which a *praxis*-centered account of language must make its way. I have given a brief sense of my views on the matter in answering Jacquette, and I return to it briefly in responding to Joanne Waugh.

I shall insert here, only for the record, a word to the effect that

I have very little to say in response to Peter Caws's essay. What I had thought worth pressing in its first draft now seems much less so to me although there are important questions that Caws takes up. I find myself rather adroitly co-opted by Caws's reference to my own work. I simply agree with him about the open standing of any discipline like physics or philosophy and am happy to join him in saying so. I thought I saw some points on which we disagreed, but I now think I must have been reading in an unnecessarily fussy way. I trust he will not take my flat agreement now—hence, also, my having nothing to add—as a mark of a deeper disagreement that I am unwilling to let surface. His essay has no need of any quibbles on my part.

VI

In turning to Joanne Waugh's analysis of the main themes of my *Interpretation Radical But Not Unruly,* I must say that I am more than pleased to see this latest book examined with such thoroughness and a little puzzled by Waugh's mention of a "problem" she finds in it. The reason is simply that she *seems* to find nothing terribly problematic in it.

The "problem," however, is worth considering. I think the right locus of it is in these lines, which follow a few remarks of Waugh's on Davidson's "A Nice Derangement of Epitaphs" and "The Third Man":

> Davidson's minimalist account of successful communication by speech does suggest some interesting avenues to pursue, and I am particularly interested in an application it might have to a problem I have found in Margolis's account of interpretation, viz., his use of the concept of social practices in accounting for the stability of cultural entities throughout their careers, careers that include alterations in these entities themselves as a result of ongoing acts of interpretation. (286–87)

I find a certain weakness in Waugh's formulation, if she won't mind my putting the point so frontally. On my view, by analogy with the problem of universals (responding to Jacquette), I should say that "social practices"—in the sense Waugh favors here—does *not* signify "public collective objects" existing "independently of the individual" (293) but a nominalization of a run of (collective) predicables. (Collective entities—corporations—are fictions.) Furthermore, when I invoke Wittgenstein's notion of a *Lebensform* or plural *Lebensformen* (although Newton Garver has made an interesting case for insisting on the singular[36]), I never mean to speak of "social practices" (*qua Lebensformen*) as explaining or "accounting for" *any* behavior at all. There is a deep equivocation in most readings of Wittgenstein (and of what the Wittgensteinian texts allude to). "*Lebensformen*" ("social practices") signifies, to me, the holist, consensual, Intentional "space" within which the life of individual humans takes form and is exercised. My point is reference to a *Lebensform* is never explanatory or criterial for Wittgenstein—or for me. But when Wittgenstein speaks of "language games" (which are also nominalizations of collective predicables), he speaks of *what* ("social practices"), *within* an encompassing *Lebensform, do* have explanatory power. Waugh is clear about this (in my own work), because she sees that I do not invoke Lebensformen in explanatory ways. The explanations of social life are themselves constructed within a *Lebensform,* as are the phenomena to be explained.

I emphasize the point because it is easily obscured if one reflects (as Waugh does) on Stephen Turner's observation that Wittgenstein took the term "*Lebensform*" from Eduard Spranger (note 21) *and* that the notion of "social practices" arose "as a substitute for first principles once philosophers recognized that there were no unproblematic first principles" (292). Here, too many complications arise: for one, the disastrous Durkheimian idea of a "collective mind" (which slips too easily into a "collective public object"); second, the conflating of the holist, noncriterial, and nonexplanatory notion of a *Lebensform* and the relatively determinate nominalization that *can* play an explanatory role, namely, a "language game," which obtains within the holist "space" of the other; and third, the collective "nature" of individual human selves and what that attribution means.

Turner appears to conflate Wittgenstein's use of "form of life" and "language game": First principles, after all, are *always* explanatory. Waugh sometimes follows Turner in this *and* perhaps, as a consequence, notes a "problem" in my account, which she pursues. Davidson *never* admits anything like a collective *Lebensform* within the space of which we, as linguistically apt individuals, *first* acquire our cultural skills (including language). Davidson is (in the "Derangement" paper) a methodological solipsist who believes that *social* (a fortiori, collective) practices can be accounted for by communicative *relations between* autonomous speakers. If you look carefully at Davidson's notion of a "passing theory" (which Waugh seems to believe is close to my own thesis), you will see that it is fundamentally solipsistic. My own view is that *we* emerge as culturally formed selves by internalizing the *collectively* articulated aptitudes that (reflexively) we nominalize as "language games," "rules," and the like. Davidson cannot admit anything of the sort, because (1) it would entail interpretive *tertia,* and (2) it would entail a *sui generis* form of (cultural) emergence incompatible with supervenience.

I must add an additional point (which picks up on the issue of predication I touched on in responding to Jacquette and Wartofsky). All general predicables, on my view, are *consensually* (collectively) entrenched—within our *Lebensform.* It makes no difference whether we are speaking of physical nature or human culture. (This is the point I had originally meant to press against Caws's first draft. It has proved unnecessary.) But, among our predicables, there are some— the Intentional ones—that are intrinsically collective in their *sense.* (They are all collective in terms of their mode of functioning and their being successfully applied to the world.) I say there is no way to understand physical nature, therefore, except as an *abstraction* made within the symbiotized space in which the physical world cannot be assigned ontic standing *prior* to some "sense-bestowing" cultural world. That explains the strategic linkage between "reality" and "realism." Furthermore, whatever fixity predicables may be assigned, they can be assigned only consensually, in terms of the ongoing collective *tolerance* of a viable society regarding any and all continually improvised extensions of its predicates. There are no rules that we follow in "following a rule" (as Wittgenstein very clearly intends). I agree with this profound discovery of Wittgenstein's, but I also hold (returning to Waugh) that *that* is neutral as between "readerly" and "writerly" reading! The trick is to see that all predicates/predicables are Intentionally formed and effective and that, among them, there are special predicates/predicables that are intrinsically Intentional. The preference for readerly or writerly reading (in Barthes's idiom) *does not affect the practices of reference or predication at all*; it has to do only with conforming to or departing from *further* canonical constraints on the interpretation of intrinsically interpretable (because Intentional) texts. That's all. I hope this dispels Waugh's sense of a "problem."

About Eddy Zemach's essay, what can I say? Apart from my uneasiness about how Zemach imagines you see your mother-in-law in a dream ("like a cobra" [313]), what he says is, as usual, delicious. In general, I agree with him about how we see actual things under rather special conditions, although I am not persuaded that, in *all* dreams (setting aside, say, the dreams Freud reports about shell-shocked soldiers, which may be more than dreams), we are (while dreaming) seeing actual objects. This is not because I deny we dream about actual objects, but rather that I deny that, in dreaming, our visualizations are usually, or ever, "seeings" of actual objects. I think it is an empirical matter; hence, that Zemach's conjecture cannot be ruled out a priori. I see no reason for thinking it preposterous that *some* "dreams" are rather like after-images or actual perceivings. It's a pretty idea. Of course, there may also be an equivocation here. For, I may "see" my mother-in-law in a dream, where I do not *see* her in any way that could be counted a fair extension of actual visual perception: I may merely "see-my-mother-in-law" in my dream, where what I specify is no more than the usual "intentional" or internal accusative of my dreaming. In the first, we might say that "seeing" was dyadic and in the second, monadic. If that were conceded, I should say that where we invoke the monadic idiom, we mean to say we are not seeing in the sensory and perceptual sense at all.

Zemach is a bit of an embarrassment—because he agrees with me and I confess I agree with him. He finds my notion—that pictorial representation is "basically monadic" (310)—congenial. I agree with him that Searle's and Kripke's and Walton's views, which he mentions, are "dubious" and "half-baked." In particular, I agree with him when he says that "a representation . . . is a reified look"

(313). That's pretty well what I mean by a nominalization of a predicable (as applied to the way things look). But I demur at a point. I am not unused to finding that Zemach and I agree on very precise claims though we come at them from utterly different premises. (That's what I find delicious about his eccentricities, I suppose it conforms with his being "surprised" at how I arrive at views that converge with his.)

In any case, where we *begin* with actual objects and wonder whether we are seeing *them,* I am inclined to think there is no need for intervening *representations*—certainly not always and not usually. (Zemach concurs.) The empiricists were dead wrong, I should say, and so was Kant. But when we begin with *representations,* as in paintings, then, I say (with Zemach), that they are monadic in their representational capacity. I don't deny that they may also be construed dyadically, as in supposing that a representation-of-Washington is a portrait of Washington (that is, that a Washington-representation is, of Washington, a portrait). But I draw your attention to the fact that the dyadic reading of a *representation* interprets a monadic representation dyadically.

If I'm right in this, then, without disagreeing with Zemach (at least not yet), when I see a Cézanne painting of a woodstove, I see a (monadic) woodstove-representation. (I do not or may not see the woodstove.) I *may* judge, on whatever evidence I have, *that* the monadic representation is, in fact, a (dyadic) *representation* of Cézanne's woodstove. I have no trouble with that. But, although it is an open possibility, I don't see what the grounds are as yet for saying (as Zemach does) that I *see* Cézanne's woodstove *when I see a representation of it.* I really doubt that I *am* seeing his woodstove.

I think Zemach must agree with me, though he seems not to. For he says (correctly): "*We* see through devices that divert light: spectacles, binoculars, telescopes . . . television and video cameras, where photons replaced by electrons take [different] routes to the eye" (314). I frankly don't see that the route light (from the woodstove) took to Cézanne's eye is assuredly connected in the "right way" with the route light from Cézanne's painting of his woodstove takes to my eyes—so that that connection justifies my saying that I now *see* Cézanne's woodstove (in the dyadic sense). (I find myself falling into line with G. E. Moore's relentless prose in pursuing similar matters.) I don't think the link with representation is sufficiently like the link in the photograph and the television image and the like. But I agree that Zemach's conjecture cannot be ruled out a priori. I'd go that far.

I agree with Zemach (if I understand him rightly) that "we see *nothing* in 'real time'" (314), although I would not say that "*we see nothing* or that *we see nothing in real time.*" But I still think there is a deep equivocation lurking in Zemach's remark: "You can see your late father in a home movie, in a still photograph, and also in a portrait painted by an artist friend" (314). It's true but it's not the same—*qua* "seeing"—as *seeing him* in a home movie. Seeing one's father in a portrait is seeing a representation-of-a-man (a monadic representation) as a representation of one's father (dyadically); whereas, in a home movie, one sees one's father by means of the movie. Roughly, in the first, one sees a representation and *interprets what is represented* as one's father; in the second, one *sees one's father by means of a certain technical device* (that happens to produce dyadic representations). To see one's father in a photograph implies a certain *causal* connection (I should say) linking normal seeing and the production of the photo's image; to see one's father *in* a painting implies a certain *intentional* or *interpretive* connection between what might have been seen in the normal way and what one now can see (which is no more than a monadic representation). (I can even imagine a blind Cézanne painting a representation of his woodstove, *which* I now see and rightly interpret dyadically; or a blind painter's painting a "portrait" of my father guided by certain verbal instructions.)

Zemach presses harder. For he says: "What makes '*s* sees *o*' true is not the causal connection between *s* and *o* but the fact that, with proper training, by looking at *x, s* can see *o* as *o*" (266). (Here, I favor the wording of the original draft. There's a typo in the final version that affects its sense.) I am not convinced, but I won't rule it out. If I understand him rightly, Zemach would have us believe that a right interpretation of the (represented) *o* might count as seeing (the actual) *o*. Possibly, but I can't see it yet. It seems to me that the causal linkage cannot be entirely discounted. I am drawn to all of Zemach's illustrations (in section II of his paper), but I wonder whether he wouldn't be satisfied with the equivocation I suggest. In any case, I don't yet see that what hangs on it *can* be anything like the supposed solution to the Sallarsian question of the relationship between the "manifest-image" world of common sense and the "scientific-realist" world of subatomic physics. *I don't know the final answer to that.* I don't think anyone does. But whatever the answer is, it can't be disjunctive in the way Zemach has it. It *can't* be that the commonsense world is one of a number of possible worlds other than the real one—possible worlds we visually project, for instance, "the commonsense world, the world of phenomena, our *Lebenswelt,* the world we know and usually take to be real" (320)—but isn't real. *That can't be right.* The reason is elementary—and Zemach traps himself in its puzzle, just as Sellars had when he first formulated the well-known puzzle Zemach refers to. For, if you read what Zemach says with care, you cannot fail to notice that *"we"* figure in both the commonsense world and the quantum world. But that's not possible on Zemach's scenario.

My own conjecture is that we occupy the real world, that (in a deep sense) that probably is tautological; but that it is also very likely true that we are frequently (profoundly) mistaken about *some* range of the properties of ourselves and our world. The Bell inequalities, for instance, have baffled *everyone*! We don't know what the quantum world is like (ontologically) and we don't know how "it" is related to our "real" world. We certainly don't know how to replace our standard descriptions of "the" world with quantum-mechanical descriptions. But we never need to. We begin and end every discourse involving quanta with the "commonsense" world. We tolerate the intervening paradoxes that we say arise, because we have no idea (as yet) about how to domesticate the one or to replace the other. But I don't see how *that* affects the sense in which *we live in the real world.* (Now, I must be frank to say that some of what Zemach says here belongs, it seems, to the final draft of his paper. I hope I have understood him rightly. I cannot recover the first draft or check completely on where the two drafts diverge. Frankly, the same difficulty has arisen with other papers. I do hope I have done justice to all the discussants, though I'm not entirely sure.)

Zemach has given me some excellent homework to complete. I see the point of his agreeing with me that "representation is monadic." He says it very nicely—if extravagantly: "The table is an object we intentionally posit and observe in one commonsense world; the lady that Vermeer lets us observe by his *Lady Reading a Letter at an Open Window* is in another world; Zeus, another nonexistent who, thanks to Greek art and culture, we can literally see, inhabits yet another kind of possible world" (326). I freely admit many disjoint "worlds" within the "one universe" (as I have already suggested). But *they cannot be disjoint in the way of reality, if we are in them* (in any or some or all). The world of Vermeer's painting is Intentionally controlled or projected by Vermeer and by us (in different ways), but *we and Vermeer are in the same real world*; the commonsense table is in the same real world we are in; the lady of Vermeer's painting is *not*; neither is Zeus. Hence, nothing bearing on this extraordinary problem bears on whether I *see* Cézanne's woodstove when I see a representation of Cézanne's woodstove! I don't think Zemach can gain any mileage there. But I agree (if I understand him rightly): *The real world is monadically Intended by our conceptual scheme(s)*—epistemically constituted and symbiotized, as I say. It's up to us to say what, in addition, dyadically, reading *that,* we construe as real (as independent of our conceptual schemes). (Here, I find myself guided by Peirce's notion of Secondness.) So I agree that we are puzzled about *part* of what *is* real (in being puzzled by quantum physics). But *we cannot deny that we exist, that we are real.* (Descartes was right but drew the wrong conclusion. We need not, anymore than Descartes, be clear about our own nature.)

I'm afraid Zemach has confounded an important equivocation. He raises the question of the *reality* of our commonsense world: He says that *that* world is not real, but he does not say what *we* are doing "*in it*"! More pertinently, he conflates the first question with a second—which bears *on what we see in our commonsense world,* taken as real—namely, whether we *see* Zeus in the same sense we see my father in a home movie. The first question is an "external" question: Whether we see anything, because our commonsense world is (on Zemach's view) as unreal as the possible world in which Zeus may be found. (I cannot agree with that; but, more to the point, I cannot see how Zemach can hold his position without contradiction. *In what world* are he and I and Vermeer to be found?) The second question is an "internal" question: Whether, admitting the relevance (to "seeing") of certain causal connections, we can say we see Cézanne's woodstove or Zeus in a way in which we see Cézanne's representation of his woodstove.

What I find in Zemach's skillful play of possibilities is a very strong reason for cleaving to a constructivist and symbiotized view of reality. That is not at all negligible. Still, I want to say, with Wittgenstein and with Zemach, that "the manifest world, the world as I find it . . . cannot contain its own representing" (327); but, against Zemach, it *can* contain its own "representations." Kant could already admit (or insist on) that much; the trouble is, Kant did not quite grasp the implications of admitting "representations." I am vain enough to think I have escaped the conundrum. But, if I have, then I cannot agree that "the Manifest Image is successfully used to manipulate reality; it works for us" (see 327: the phrasing seems to have dropped out of the final version). For, I cannot imagine what, in Zemach's picture, we should understand *our* "manipulative" role with respect to ourselves to be. Explain that, please.

Ultimately, Zemach and I disagree—for the reasons I've given, but also, more locally, regarding representation. I *think* we agree about Intentionality, though Zemach really speaks of intentionality in the sense of Brentano's "aboutness." On my view, Intentionality ≠ representationality; so that representation (which, as we both say, is monadic), expressivity, and other such phenomena are alternative modes of Intentionality. That's really all I mean in saying that there are no "objects" in Kandinsky's *Improvisations*. But, I shouldn't at all quarrel with Zemach in saying that a particular Kandinsky *represents* "hope and happiness" (329). (I say something similar about Jan Steen's *Easy Come, Easy Go.*) Zemach insists on this point, partly (I think) because he probably does not share my somewhat heterodox notion of Intentionality: Hence, expressivity is, or entails, as he says, representationality. Fine, I happen to think Brentano's and Husserl's views are inadequate, say, for capturing Vermeer's painting. But, apart from that, *I* claim that nominalism is hopelessly untenable and that "real generals" cannot (as Peirce seems to have thought they could) be entirely freed from conceptualism. That is a long story. But, on the essential issue Zemach raises, I'm happy to say our disagreement (though serious in the long run) is largely verbal (in the short run). I also say that Intentionality need not be linguistic, but it must be at least "lingual," that is, structured in the way it is, in virtue of the linguistic competence of human selves. I am entirely content to say, with Zemach, that Goodman's account is "wrong-headed" (first draft); but Zemach has yet to persuade me (1) that our common sense world is not real; (2) that we see, in the same sense of "see," Zeus and my father in a photo; and (3) that nominalism is viable. Zemach subscribes to "scientific realism" in something like Sellars's sense. I do not: I believe Sellars never solved the problem of *our reality as persons*.

I must stop here. I end with a lovely sense of having been among friends who have no pointless qualms about straight philosophical talk. And I ask their pardon if I have not responded fairly or accurately.

NOTES

1. Carl Page, *Philosophical Historicism and the Betrayal of First Philosophy* (University Park: Pennsylvania University Press, 1995).

2. Ibid., p. 92. The passage cited is from my *Pragmatism without Foundations; Reconciling Realism and Relativism* (Oxford: Basil Blackwell, 1986), p. 41; italics added.

3. See Joseph Margolis, *Interpretation Radical But Not Unruly* (Berkeley: University of California Press, 1995), chap. 2. The notion of a philosophical "bet" is developed in my *Historied Thought, Constructed World: A Conceptual Primer at the Turn of the Millennium* (Berkeley: University of California Press, 1995).

4. Further on Davidson, see Joseph Margolis, "Donald Davidson's Philosophical Strategies," in Carol C. Could and Robert S. Cohen, (eds.) *Artifacts, Representations and Social Practice* (Dordrecht: Kluwer, 1994).

5. I take this to be the essential theme of Richard Rorty, *Philosophy and the Mirror of Nature* (Princeton, N.J.: Princeton University Press, 1979).

6. See, for instance, Margolis, *Interpretation Radical But Not Unruly,* pp. 238–39.

7. See Joseph Margolis, "Situer Rorty en philosophie," *Archives de Philosophie,* forthcoming.

8. See, for instance, Donald Davidson, "A Coherence Theory of Meaning and Truth" and Richard Rorty, "Pragmatism, Davidson and Truth," both in Ernest Lepore, ed., *Truth and Interpretation: Perspectives on the Philosophy of Donald Davidson* (Oxford: Basil Blackwell, 1986).

9. See Eugen Fink, *Sixth Cartesian Meditation: The Idea of a Transcendental Theory of Method,* trans. Ronald Bruzina (Bloomington: Indiana University Press, 1995), particularly § 1.

10. See, for instance, Hilary Putnam, "Materialism and Relativism," *Renewing Philosophy* (Cambridge: Harvard University Press, 1992), for a recent version of a largely invariant complaint.

11. See Michael Dummett, *The Logical Basis of Metaphysics* (Cambridge: Harvard University Press, 1991).

12. See Joseph Margolis, *The Truth about Relativism* (Oxford: Basil Blackwell, 1991); and "Plain Talk about Interpretation on a Relativistic Model," *Journal of Aesthetics and Art Criticism* LIII (1995).

13. See M. F. Burnyeat, "Protagoras and Self-Refutation in Plato's Theaetetus," *Philosophical Review,* LXXXV (1976).

14. Karl Popper, "Of Clouds and Clocks," in *Objective Knowledge: An Evolutionary View* (Oxford: Clarendon, 1972), pp. 214–18.

15. I argue the issue in *The Truth about Relativism,* chap. 9.

16. This was the text of Davidson's presidential address before the American Philosophical Association (1973). It is reprinted in Inquiries into *Truth and Interpretation* (Oxford: Clarendon, 1984). I discuss it briefly in my "Donald Davidson's Philosophical Strategies." But Davidson himself subverts his account—as well as the rest of his best-known views—in "A Fine Derangement of Epitaphs," in Lepore, *Truth and Interpretation.*

17. See Hilary Putnam, *The Many Faces of Realism* (La Salle: Open Court, 1987). Since the original draft of these replies, Putnam has repudiated "internal realism." I have reviewed some of the changes in his treatment of realism elsewhere, but there would be no point to doing so here. In any case, my remarks are still appropriately keyed to what he says in *The Many Faces of Realism* and the replacing doctrine is still quite incomplete as a form of realism. Putnam does not seem to have changed his view about relativism. See, for instance, Hilary Putnam, "Sense, Nonsense, and the Senses: An Inquiry into the Powers of the Human Mind" (The Dewey Lectures 1994), *Journal of Philosophy* 91 (1994).

18. Margolis, *Art and Philosophy* (Atlantic Highlands, N.J.: Humanities Press, 1980).

19. Margolis, *Historied Thought, Constructed World* (Berkeley: University of California Press, 1995).

20. See, for instance, Margolis, *Art and Philosophy,* pp. 113–14.

21. Margolis, *The Flux of History and the Flux of Science* (Berkeley: University of California Press, 1993).

22. See "Plain Talk about Interpretation on a Relativistic Model."

23. Margolis, *Art and Philosophy,* p. 146.

24. Ibid., p. 152.

25. See Donald Davidson, "A Coherence Theory of Truth and Meaning," in Lepore, *Truth and Interpretation.*

26. See W. V. Quine, *Word and Object* (Cambridge: MIT Press, 1960); *Pursuit of Truth,* rev. ed. (Cambridge: Harvard University Press, 1992).

27. See Richard Rorty, "Pragmatism, Davidson, and Truth," in Lepore, *Truth and Interpretation.*

28. See Ludwig Wittgenstein, *Philosophical Investigations,* trans. G. E. M. Anscombe (New York: Macmillan, 1950), § 201.

29. See Hilary Putnam, *Representation and Reality* (Cambridge, Mass.: MIT Press, 1988).

30. See Margolis, *Art and Philosophy*; and *Culture and Cultural Entities* (Dordrecht: D. Reidel, 1987).

31. See Joseph Margolis, "The Passing of Peirce's Realism," *Transactions of the Charles Sanders Peirce Society* 29 (1993), which Jacquette cites.

32. See, for instance, Margolis, *Interpretation Radical But Not Unruly,* chap. 4.

33. See Joseph Margolis, "Praxis and Meaning: Marx's Species Being and Aristotle's Political Animal," in George E. McCarthy, ed., *Marx and Aristotle: Nineteenth-Century German Social Theory and Classical Antiquity* (Savage, Md.: Rowman and Littlefield, 1992).

34. See John McDowell, *Mind and World* (Cambridge: Harvard University Press, 1994–1996); and Putnam, "Sense, Nonsense, and the Senses."

35. See Joseph Margolis, "A Biopsy of Recent Analytic Philosophy," *Philosophical Forum* 26 (1995).

36. See Newton Garver, "Naturalism and Transcendentality: The Case of 'Form of Life,' " in Souren Teghrarian, ed., *Wittgenstein and Contemporary Philosophy* (Bristol: Thoemmes Press, 1994).

Contributors

NOËL CARROLL is the Monroe C. Beardsley Professor of the Philosophy of Art at the University of Wisconsin at Madison. His books include: *Philosophical Problems of Classical Film Theory, Mystifying Movies, Theorizing the Moving Image, The Philosophy of Horror,* and *The Philosophy of Mass Art.*

PETER CAWS has been University Professor of Philosophy at the George Washington University since 1982; previously he taught at Hunter College (City University of New York) and before that at the University of Kansas. His undergraduate work was in physics at the University of London, and he has a Ph.D. in philosophy from Yale. Among his seven books are Sartre in the series "The Arguments of the Philosophers" (Routledge, 1978); *Structuralism: The Art of the Intelligible* (Humanities Press, 1988); *Yorick's World: Science and the Knowing Subject* (University of California Press, 1993); and *Ethics from Experience* (Jones and Bartlett, 1996).

DALE JACQUETTE is Professor of Philosophy at The Pennsylvania State University. He has received research fellowships from the National Endowment for the Humanities and Alexander von Humboldt-Stiftung, and in spring 1996 held the J. William Fulbright Distinguished Lecture Chair in Contemporary Philosophy of Language at the University of Venice. His recent publications include *Philosophy of Mind* (1994) in the Prentice Hall Foundations of Philosophy series; *Meinongian Logic: The Semantics of Existence and Nonexistence* (Walter de Gruyter, 1996); *Wittgenstein's Thought in Transition* (Purdue University Press, 1997); and an edited collection of contemporary scholarship on *Schopenhauer, Philosophy, and the Arts* (Cambridge University Press, 1996). His articles, primarily on philosophical logic, metaphysics, and philosophy of mind, have appeared in *Synthese, Philosophy and Phenomenological Research, Philosophy, Philosophical Studies, History and Philosophy of Logic, The Philosophical Quarterly, American Philosophical Quarterly, Minds and Machines, The Journal of Aesthetics and Art Criticism, The Monist,* and *Kant-Studien.*

MICHAEL KRAUSZ is the Milton C. Nahm Professor and Chairman of the Department of Philosophy at Bryn Mawr College. Trained at the Universities of Toronto (Ph.D., 1969) and Oxford, he has been visiting professor at Georgetown University, University of Oxford, Hebrew University of Jerusalem, American University in Cairo, University of Nairobi, the Indian Institute of Advanced Study, and the University of Ulm, among others. Krausz is the cofounder and former Chairman of the Greater Philadelphia Philosophy Consortium. His publications include *Rightness and Reasons: Interpretation in Cultural Practices* (Cornell University Press, 1993) and *Varieties of Relativism,* with Rom Harré (Blackwell Publishers, 1995). As well, Krausz is editor and contributor to seven volumes on such topics as relativism, rationality; interpretation, cultural identity, creativity, interpretation of music, and the philosophy of R. G. Collingwood.

PETER McCORMICK is Professor of Philosophy at the University of Ottowa, Canada. He is the author of *Heidegger and the Language of the World* (Ottowa University Press, 1976); *Fictions, Philosophies, and the Problems of Poetics* (Cornell University Press, 1988); *Modernity, Aesthetics, and the Bounds of Art* (Cornell University Press, 1990); and *Rationality and Interpretation.*

JOSEPH MARGOLIS has authored more than thirty books, including, most recently, four volumes under the title *The Persistence of Reality* (1986, 1987, 1989, 1996); *The Flux of History and the Flux of Science* (1993); *Interpretation Radical But Not Unruly* (1995); *Historied Thought, Constructed World* (1995); and *The Truth about Relativism* (1991). He is currently at work on a number of projects, including an account of competing forms of realism. He has taught and lectured widely and is currently Laura H. Carnell Professor of Philosophy at Temple University. He is best known for his work on historicity, interpretation, and relativism, which, in the spirit of pragmatism, he has applied systematically in nearly all areas of philosophical inquiry, ranging over Anglo-American and continental European thought.

J. N. MOHANTY received his Ph.D. from Göttigen University and is currently a Professor of Philosophy at Temple University. He is a member of the Institut Internationale de Philosophie, Paris, and in 1992 was appointed Humbolt Forschungs—*piristräger* for 1992. Mohanty is the author of *Essays on Indian Thought: Traditional and Modern* (Oxford University Press, 1993); and *Phenomenology between Essentialism and Transcendental Philosophy* (Northwestern University Press, 1999).

NICHOLAS RESCHER is University Professor of Philosophy at the University of Pittsburgh where he served for many years as Director of the Center for Philosophy of Science. A former president of the American Philosophical Association, he is a member of Academia Europaea and several other learned academies, as well as an honorary member of Corpus Christi College, Oxford. In 1984, he was awarded the Alexander von Humboldt Prize for Humanistic Scholarship. A visiting scholar at Oxford, Constance, and Salamanca, Professor Rescher has received four honorary degrees from universities in the United States and abroad. Author of more than seventy works ranging over many areas of philosophy, he is currently writing a book on the role of complexity in science and in everyday life.

TOM ROCKMORE is Professor of Philosophy at Duquesne University. His many books include *Fichte, Marx and German Philosophy* (1980); *Hegel's Circular Epistemology* (1986); *Lukács Today,* ed., with an introduction (1988); *Habermas on Historical Materialism* (1989); *The Heidetgger Case: On Philosophy and Politics,* edited with Joseph Margolis (1992); *Irrationalism: Lukács and the Marxist View of Reason* (1992); *On Heidegger's Nazism and Philosophy* (1992, 1997); *Antifoundationalism Old and New,* edited with Beth Singer (1992); *Hegel: Avant et après* (1992); *Before and After Hegel: A Historical Introduction* (1993); *Hegel et la tradition philosophique allemande* (1994); *Fichte: Historical Context and Contemporary Controversies,* edited with Daniel Breazeale (1994); *Heidegger and French Philosophy: Humanism, Anti-Humanism and Being* (1995); *On Hegel's Epistemology and Contemporary Philosophy* (1996); *New Perspectives on Fichte,* edited with Daniel Breazeale (1996); *Georg Wilhelm Friedrich Hegel, Prima/Dopo,* trans. Ignazio Volpicelli (1996); *Hegel's Lectures on the History of Philosophy,* edited (1996); *Cognition: An Introduction to Hegel's Phenomenology of Spirit* (1997); *Transcendental Philosophy and Everyday Life,* edited with Vladimir Zeman (1997).

RICHARD SHUSTERMAN, a graduate of Jerusalem and Oxford, is Professor of Philosophy at Temple University and Directeur de Programme at the Collège International de Philosophie, Paris. A former NEH Research Fellow and Fulbright Professor in Berlin, Shusterman's books include *The Object of Literary Criticism*; *T. S. Eliot and the Philosophy of Criticism*; *Analytic Aesthetics*; *Sous l'interpretation*; *Pragmatist Aesthetics* (Blackwell, 1992) which has been translated into seven languages; and *Practicing Philosophy: Pragmatism and the Philosophical Life* (Routledge, 1997).

GAIL SOFFER is Associate Professor of Philosophy at the Graduate Faculty of Political and Social Science, New School for Social Research. Her publications include *Husserl and the Question of Relativism* (Kluwer, 1991), and numerous articles in the areas of Husserl studies, hermeneutics, and the history of philosophy.

LAURENT STERN is Professor of Philosophy at Rutgers University. He has published articles on interpreting and translating, and he is working on a book on these topics.

MARX W. WARTOFSKY was a CUNY Distinguished Professor of Philosophy at Baruch College and at the Graduate Center. He taught for many years at Boston University. He was the author of *Conceptual Foundations of Scientific Thought* (1968); *Feuerbach* (1977); and *Models: Representation and the Scientific Understanding* (1979); and of many articles. He was a founding coeditor of the series, *Boston Studies in the Philosophy of Science*. He edited *The Philosophical Forum,* a quarterly journal and, at the time of his death in 1997, was working on a book on historical epistemology and on the relations between pictorial representation and visual cognition.

JOANNE WAUGH is Associate Professor of Philosophy at the University of South Florida in Tampa, where she also teaches in the University Honors Program. She has published articles on aesthetics, early Greek philosophy, and Plato. She is the editor, along with Linda Lopez McAlister and Cheryl A. Hall, of *Hypatia: A Journal of Feminist Philosophy.*

EDDY M. ZEMACH is the Ahad-Haarn Professor of Philosophy at the Hebrew University of Jerusalem and taught at many universities in the United States and Australia. Published extensively in philosophy (about 120 articles) and literary criticism (six books). His recent books are *The Reality of Meaning and the Meaning of "Reality"* (Brown University Press, 1992); *Types: Essays in Metaphysics* (Brill, 1992); and *Real Beauty,* advocating ontological realism about aesthetic properties (Penn State University Press, 1997).

Index

415